THE EUROPEAN CONVENTION ON HUMAN RIGHTS AND PRIVATE LAW

In this book a team of expert contributors address challenging issues concerning the relationship between private law and the rule of law and human rights, with specific focus on case studies from South-Eastern Europe.

The book examines the broadening application of human rights to the private law fields and the resulting effects. Contributors offer a truly interdisciplinary perspective drawn from comparative law, civil law, procedural law and public law. By so doing, for the first time, they offer insights into the fascinating questions the region poses for private law and human rights.

Volume 127 in the Series Modern Studies in European Law

Modern Studies in European Law

Recent titles in this series:

The Changing European Union: A Critical View on the Role of Law and the Courts
Edited by Tamara Capeta, Iris Goldner Lang and Tamara Perisin

The Structural Transformation of European Private Law:
A Critique of Juridical Hermeneutic
Leone Niglia

The Future of EU Constitutionalism
Edited by Matej Avbelj

The Changing Role of Citizens in EU Democratic Governance
Edited by Davor Jancic

The EU and the Baltic Sea Area
Edited by Allan Rosas and Henrik Ringbom

The Evolving Governance of EU Competition Law in a Time of Disruptions:
A Constitutional Perspective
Edited by Carlo Maria Colombo, Kathryn Wright and Mariolina Eliantonio

The European Integrated Border Management: Frontex, Human Rights,
and International Responsibility
Giulia Raimondo

Private Autonomy in EU Internal Market Law: Parameters of its
Protection and Limitation
Rufat Babayev

Free Movement and Welfare Access in the European Union:
Re-Balancing Conflicting Interests in Citizenship Jurisprudence
Victoria Hooton

EU Trade and Investment Treaty-Making Post-Lisbon: Moving Beyond Mixity
Gesa Kübek

The Normative Foundations for EU Criminal Justice:
Powers, Limits and Justifications
Jacob Öberg

EU Neighbourhood Law: Wider Europe and the Extended EU's Legal Space
Alessandro Petti

The Dynamics of Powers in the European Union
Edited by Christina Eckes, Päivi Leino-Sandberg and Anna W Ghavanin

The European Convention on Human Rights and Private Law:
Comparative Perspectives from South-Eastern Europe
Edited by Mateja Durovic and Cristina Poncibò

For the complete list of titles in this series
see www.bloomsbury.com/uk/series/modern-studies-in-european-law/

The European Convention on Human Rights and Private Law

Comparative Perspectives from South-Eastern Europe

Edited by
Mateja Durovic
and
Cristina Poncibò

• HART •
OXFORD • LONDON • NEW YORK • NEW DELHI • SYDNEY

HART PUBLISHING

Bloomsbury Publishing Plc

Kemp House, Chawley Park, Cumnor Hill, Oxford, OX2 9PH, UK

1385 Broadway, New York, NY 10018, USA

29 Earlsfort Terrace, Dublin 2, Ireland

HART PUBLISHING, the Hart/Stag logo, BLOOMSBURY and the Diana logo are trademarks of Bloomsbury Publishing Plc

First published in Great Britain 2024

A catalogue record for this book is available from the British Library.

A catalogue record for this book is available from the Library of Congress.

Library of Congress Control Number: 2024940204

ISBN: HB: 978-1-50995-808-5
ePDF: 978-1-50995-810-8
ePub: 978-1-50995-809-2

Typeset by Compuscript Ltd, Shannon

CONTENTS

LIST OF CONTRIBUTORS

Gianmaria Ajani, University of Turin

Branka Babovic Vuksanovic, University of Belgrade

Raluca Bercea, West University of Timişoara

Julija Brsakoska Bazerkoska, 'Ss. Cyril and Methodius' University, Skopje

Fjoralba Caka, University of Tirana

Giovanni Cimbalo, Università di Bologna

Nada Dollani, University of Tirana

Mateja Durovic, King's College London

Mitja Kovac, University of Ljubljana

Emilia Mišćenić, University of Rijeka

Cristina Poncibò, University of Turin

Sabrina Praduroux, University of Turin

Darko Spasevski, University 'Ss. Cyril and Methodius', Skopje

Aleksandar Spasov, Ss. Cyril and Methodius University, Skopje

Federica Torta, École Pratique des Hautes Études, Paris

Svitlana Zadorozhna, University of Turin

PART 1

General Discussions

1

Private Law, Rule of Law and the European Court of Human Rights: Comparative Perspectives from South-Eastern Europe: An Introduction

CRISTINA PONCIBÒ AND MATEJA DUROVIC

Introduction

Our edited book, titled *Private Law, Rule of Law, and the European Court of Human Rights: Comparative Perspectives from South-Eastern Europe*, is a comprehensive and innovative exploration of the intersection between private law and the jurisprudence of the European Court of Human Rights (ECtHR), with a particular focus on one, rather under-researched part of Europe, the South-East. This scholarly work, emerging from an international workshop held in Turin, Italy, in September 2022, brings together a distinguished array of both international scholars and the leading academics from the region who have contributed with their chapters to this edited collection.

Our book sets up a comprehensive comparative analysis of various South-Eastern European countries, each presenting unique challenges and developments in the realm of private law as influenced by the fruitful case law of the ECtHR. This book is not merely a collection of legal analyses; it is a rich exploration of the dynamic and continuous interplay between private law and human rights jurisprudence. By adopting an interdisciplinary approach and combining insights from public law, EU law, comparative law, and private law, it offers a unique lens through which the role of the ECtHR in shaping private law in South-Eastern Europe can be understood. This work is an essential read for scholars, legal practitioners, policy makers, judges, and anyone interested in the evolving landscape of private law under the auspices of human rights and the rule of law. It challenges traditional perspectives, broadens the understanding of the rule of law in private relationships, and provides a comprehensive view of the ECtHR's case law impact on the national legal systems of the South-Eastern European countries.

The Intersection of Private Law, Rule of Law, and the ECHR Jurisprudence

The European Convention on Human Rights (ECHR) is, globally, the most complete and advanced contemporary codex of human rights, with far reaching effects and implications, that go beyond the European continent. It was drafted just after the end of the Second World War, agreed in 1950, and entered into force in 1953. During the last seven decades, the Convention has had an incredible impact on practice, affecting all spheres of life, society, and state. The European Convention on Human Rights enshrines fundamental rights such as, for example, the right to life, the prohibition of torture, the right to liberty and security, the right to a fair trial, the right to respect for private and family life, the right to effective legal remedy, freedom of expression, and the prohibition of any kind of discrimination. The Convention is not a static document, but a living document and its scope is continuously being expanded, in particular through its Protocols, securing that it provides a framework for protection of the widest set of human rights. Almost all the countries that geographically belong to the European continent are signatories to it with the European Court of Human Rights in Strasbourg as the principal guardian of the rights that are enshrined in this Convention. The European Court of Human Rights in Strasbourg (ECtHR) is in charge of supervising the implementation of the European Convention on Human Rights in the member states, including all of the jurisdictions of South-Eastern Europe. Any individual can bring complaints of human rights violations to the Strasbourg Court once all possibilities of appeal have been exhausted in the Member State concerned.

This Court has developed a very fruitful case law on the ground of the provisions of the European Convention, proving that the Convention is a living instrument, enabling, for example, the protection of citizens from the challenges that new technologies and the ongoing process of digitalisation have brought, or global climate change and its implications.

There is always a very tight connection between human rights, on the one side, and private law, on the other.[1] Private law, encompassing traditional areas such as contract law, tort law, family law, succession law, and property law, traditionally governs private relationships between individuals and/or entities. The rule of law, a foundational principle in democratic societies, demands that laws be clear, publicised, stable, and applied evenly. It requires that legal processes uphold individual rights and allow for equitable access to justice. In the context of private law, the rule of law manifests through the predictability of legal outcomes, fairness in legal processes, and the accountability of private powers. Legal philosopher

[1] C Mak, Human Rights in Private Law M Bartl, L Burgers and C Mak (eds), *Uncovering European Private Law. European Private Law Handbook.*, Amsterdam Law School Research Paper No. 2022-51, Amsterdam Centre for Transformative Private Law Working Paper No. 2022-10 Available at SSRN: https://ssrn.com/abstract=4304817.

Ronald Dworkin's theory of law as integrity emphasises the role of fairness and moral reasoning in judicial decision-making, linking private law adjudication with broader principles of justice and equality under the rule of law.[2]

The European Court of Human Rights has played a crucial role in this framework. As a supranational court, the ECtHR interprets the European Convention on Human Rights, impacting national legal systems of the countries who are signatories of this major international treaty. Its decisions often influence how private law is understood and applied within Member States, ensuring that private law disputes and resolutions adhere to the fundamental rights and freedoms enshrined in the Convention. For instance, in cases such as *López Ostra v Spain* (1994), the ECtHR has expanded the scope of private law, especially in case of tort law, by incorporating aspects of human rights, such as the right to a healthy environment.[3] Similarly, in*Bărbulescu v Romania* (2017), the Court's ruling influenced employment law, balancing employers' rights with employees' right to privacy, confirming that the Member States also have positive obligations to secure that Article 8 rights are always respected even as between private parties.[4] In addition, the ECtHR's judgment in *Pla and Puncernau v Andorra*,[5] published in 2004, is very important as it has specifically affirmed the inheritance rights of a grandchild by adoption where the grandparent had died in 1949, having very far reaching effect on the law of succession.

The relationship between human rights, on the one side, and private law, on the other, is a very complex one and the strict borderline between the two has been blurring in the last few decades.[6] In this period, the ECHR has had material effects also on private law.[7] On a European level, the impact of the ECHR on private law has become rather obvious after the judgment of the ECHR in *Marckx v Belgium* (1979),[8] which was a landmark private law case decided in 1979. In this case, the ECtHR has asserted that adopted or illegitimate children must always be treated in the same way as natural and legitimate issue.

Still, the real effects of the ECHR on private law are not fully clear and there is an urge for more coherence.[9] The integration of human rights into private law

[2] R Dworkin, *Law's Empire* (Harvard, Belknap Press, 1986).

[3] *López Ostra v Spain*, Application No 16798/90, European Court of Human Rights, Judgment of 9 December 1994.

[4] *Bărbulescu v Romania*, Application No 61496/08, European Court of Human Rights, Grand Chamber Judgment of 5 September 2017.

[5] *Pla and Puncernau v Andorra*, Application No 69498/01, European Court of Human Rights, Judgment of 13 July 2004 (Final 15 December 2004).

[6] See OO Cherednychenko, 'Fundamental Rights and Private Law: A Relationship of Subordination or Complementarity?' (2007) 3(2) *Utrecht Law Review*, 1–25, Available at SSRN: https://ssrn.com/abstract=1083653.

[7] M Fornasier and MG Stanzione, *The European Convention on Human Rights and its Impact on National Private Law: A Comparative Perspective* (Cambridge, Intersentia, 2023).

[8] *Marckx v Belgium*, Application No 6833/74, European Court of Human Rights, Judgment of 13 June 1979. Available at: https://hudoc.echr.coe.int/fre#%7B%22itemid%22:%5B%22001-57534%22%5D%7D.

[9] J Zglinski, 'Doing Too Little or Too Much? Private Law Before the European Court of Human Rights' (2018) 37 *Yearbook of European Law*, 98. Available at SSRN: https://ssrn.com/abstract=3723231.

through the ECtHR's jurisprudence presents both challenges and opportunities. On the one hand, it enhances the protection of individual rights in private legal relationships. On the other hand, it raises questions about the boundaries between public law and private law and the extent to which human rights should influence private law doctrines.

The Region of South-Eastern Europe

The region of South-Eastern Europe is one of the least legally explored corners of the continent. The jurisdictions of this part of Europe have gone through a long and complex process of social, cultural, economic, and, most importantly, political changes that have substantially affected the legal systems of these countries. One must not forget that the region was the place where several wars also took place in the last decade of the twentieth century and the very beginning of the twenty-first century, with severe human rights consequences. That same period witnessed the establishment of several new independent countries and the construction of new national identities. All of these have had substantial impacts on human rights. The ECHR has played an essential role in constructing these new narratives.[10] In the last three decades, many of these countries have become member states of the European Union, while the rest, who also want to join and have started the accession process, are developing at a very different pace and pathway.

With regards to the rule of law, one must not forget that the European Union imposes very strict and compulsory requirements on its candidate states. Rule of law is one of the common values of all EU Member States, enshrined in Article 2 of the Treaty of the European Union. Still, despite such a requirement, many of the countries have not secured an adequate level of rule of law, which has diverse human rights implications as also identified by the ECtHR. This is why the Council of Europe has also played an important role in strengthening the rule of law through the development of judiciary, training judges, investing in expanding courts capacities, etc. In tandem, for example, the Council of Europe has been running a diverse array of activities targeted to regulators, journalists, and public service media in order to secure freedom of expression and general media freedom. Some other cases deal with extremely sensitive issues, such as missing babies, who were proclaimed dead at the time of birth, and whom their parents have claimed were stolen as in *Zorica Jovanović v Serbia* (2013).[11]

The lack of legal research is especially marked when it comes to the ECHR perspective despite the fact that there is a very fruitful case law of the ECtHR that

[10] L Hammer and F Emmert (eds), *The European Convention on the Human Rights and Fundamental Freedoms in Central and Eastern Europe* (The Hague, Eleven International Publishing, 2011).

[11] *Zorica Jovanović v Serbia*, Application No 21794/08, European Court of Human Rights, Judgment of 26 March 2013.

addresses the issues coming from this region. In the region, among the provisions of the Convention, the right to fair trial and access to justice has traditionally been two of the major legal issues, but many others have arisen for example in relation to the right to property, prohibition of any form of discrimination, and the freedom of religion. The judgments of the ECtHR have substantially shaped national law of these jurisdictions, but some of them remain unenforceable for years. An excellent example is the ECtHR judgment in *Sejdic and Finci v Bosnia Herzegovina* (2009)[12] that was adopted more than 15 years ago, but which has not yet been implemented into the legal system of Bosnia and Herzegovina.[13] The reason behind this judgment is that the existing rules in Bosnia and Herzegovina still do not allow the election of someone who is not an ethnic Bosniac, Serb, or Croat to be a Member of Presidency of Bosnia and Herzegovina which has been seen as problematic by the ECtHR.[14] However, the stakeholders in Bosnia and Herzegovina have struggled all these years to reach a consensus on how to remedy this problem. The failure to implement this ECtHR judgment has been continuously identified as one of the major obstacles for Bosnia and Herzegovina to integrate further into the EU. In addition, in 2024 the relevant stakeholders in Bosnia and Herzegovina cannot still agree on their nominations of the judge for the Strasbourg Court although the mandate of the previous judge ended in 2022.

In case of some other powerful judgements, such as *Orthodox Ohrid Archdiocese (Greek-Orthodox Ohrid Archdiocese of the Peć Patriarchy) v the former Yugoslav Republic of Macedonia* (2017),[15] the internal developments in the country concerned led to the resolution of the problem that was put before the ECtHR. In this case, the cause was the presence of two Orthodox Churches in contemporary North Macedonia. The Orthodox Ohrid Archdiocese was the canonical church, i.e. recognised by all other Orthodox Churches but the issue was not that it was recognised by the majority of the Macedonian population and the Macedonian Government, but that the Macedonian Government continuously refused to recognise it as a religious community. The other was the Macedonian Orthodox Church which was not canonically recognised by any sister Orthodox Churches, but was still massively supported by the people and the Government. Eventually, these two structures united into one and, in that way, the problem has disappeared. This case has been thoroughly examined in this book, as an excellent case study. Likewise, in Montenegro, a similar ecclesiastical issue, primarily connected with the Church property, that seemed likely to end up before the Strasbourg Court was resolved through the repealing of a problematic piece of legislation and

[12] *Sejdic and Finci v Bosnia Herzegovina*, Application No 27996/06 and 34836/06, European Court of Human Rights, Judgment of 22 December 2009.

[13] D Pavlovic, C Ribicic, and Z Begic, *Bosnia and Herzegovina after Sejdić Finci case* Entwicklungen im Europäischen Recht, Vol. 10 (Regensburg, Universitätsverlag Regensburg 2016).

[14] https://hudoc.echr.coe.int/fre#%7B%22itemid%22:[%22001-96491%22]%7D.

[15] *Orthodox Ohrid Archdiocese (Greek-Orthodox Ohrid Archdiocese of the Peć Patriarchy) v The Former Yugoslav Republic of Macedonia*, Application No 3532/07, European Court of Human Rights, Judgment of 16 November 2017.

was concluded with an agreement between the Republic of Montenegro and the Serbian Orthodox Church.

In case of South-Eastern European countries, ECHR and private law, one article seems to be of particular importance. That is Article 1 of Protocol 1 to the ECHR that secures protection of the right to the peaceful enjoyment of property. In its case law the ECtHR has developed a very clear approach on how the right to property is to be understood, what it should consist of, and what remedies should be available to secure the protection of this right. However, what remains challenging is that the autonomous meaning of the notion of 'possession' under the ECHR mechanism is not always identical to the one that exists under the national laws. The presence of this discrepancy causes problems in applying the relevant rules in a consistent and coherent manner.

The ECtHR cases in relation to this important Article of the ECHR include cases that tackled issues with the restitution of nationalised property, or old savings in banks that were established in the federal units of the former Socialist Federal Republic of Yugoslavia. All these cases are also situated in the post-conflict and post-transition perspective that adds another layer of complexity to cases that were already complex. These kinds of cases are very particular to the Western Balkans. However, some common cases in the region are similar to those that exist in the rest of Europe, in particular those related to non-enforcement of the court decisions or with the failure to pay pensions.

In that sense, one of the most important cases that has affected several countries in the region is the judgment of the ECtHR in *Ališić et al v Successor States of SFRY* (2011).[16] The importance of this decision is heightened as it was decided by the Grand Chamber of the ECtHR which confirmed what the ECtHR had already found: that the Republic of Serbia and the Republic of Slovenia are to be held liable for the debt in foreign currency owed to the applicants. The *Alisic* case dealt with three bank customers with savings who, in 2005, filed their application against all of the successor states of the SFRY. The reason behind this was that they were not allowed to withdraw their savings, in foreign currency, which were deposited in the ex Tuzla branch of Serbia based Investbanka ex Sarajevo branch of Ljubljanska banka. Eventually, the Grand Chamber of the Court decided Serbia and Slovenia violated the applicants' right to the protection of property, guaranteed by Article 1, Protocol 1, and the right to an effective legal remedy secured by Article 13 ECHR. In this case, the ECtHR was examining whether the authorities had struck a fair balance between the general interest of the community and the protection of the applicants' property rights.

Eventually, in this judgment, the ECtHR required that Serbia and Slovenia adopt all measures necessary to remedy this issue, within the period of one year, and under the supervision of the Committee of Ministers of the Council of

[16] *Ališić et al v Successor States of SFRY*, Application No 60642/08, European Court of Human Rights, Judgment of 17 October 2011.

Europe, including legislative amendments. The aim was that the applicants and all the others in the same situations get paid their old foreign-currency deposits in the same manner as the ones who had such deposits in domestic branches of these banks. The ECtHR has also concluded that there had been no good reason for the applicants to have been kept waiting for so many years for repayment of their savings as they had in this the case.

In recent years, the Council of Europe has been helping the Western Balkan countries with the development of legislation aligned with the ECHR. That is the case, for example, with the law on the finalisation of the transitional processes of the property in Albania; the amicus curiae brief on the question of the appellate review in the Court of Bosnia and Herzegovina; the law on life partnership of same-sex persons in Montenegro; the law on the state of emergency in North Macedonia, and the law on gender equality in Serbia.

The Intersection of Private Law and Rule of Law: Comparative and Interdisciplinary Perspectives

This book starts with the preliminary sections which establish the theoretical frameworks underpinning the relationship between private law, the rule of law, and the ECtHR's influence. The authors delve deeper into some of the nuanced topics these sections address, particularly focusing on the intriguing evolution of ECtHR jurisprudence in the context of South-Eastern Europe.

It opens with a general, introductory chapter by Gianmaria Ajani, which focuses on the general European approach towards rule of law: the defence of common values and the rule of law within the EU, the impact of the COVID-19 pandemic on the EU financial aid policies, the introduction of conditionality in fund disbursement based on adherence to the rule of law, and the challenges of defining and enforcing this principle among diverse national legal cultures. The first section delves into the EU's response to the health crisis, particularly the wide-ranging package of financial aid adopted to mitigate the pandemic's impact. Central to this discussion is the emerging hypothesis that the disbursement of these funds should be contingent upon Member States' adherence to the rule of law. Ajani's analysis points out the inherent vagueness and complexity in defining the rule of law as a normative standard within international institutions. This part of the chapter examines these challenges, particularly how the rule of law's content and normativity vary among EU Member States, affecting the Union's legal order based on legal interdependence and mutual trust.

The chapter then discusses the adoption of a conditionality regulation on the EU budget, which enables the EU Commission and the EU Court of Justice to assess the rule of law as an enforceable normative standard in budget implementation. This section evaluates the effectiveness of this regulation and its role in upholding the rule of law within the Union. Reflecting on Ajani's insights, it emphasises the need for more action at both scholarly and political levels. It argues for the necessity of a better connection between the principle of the rule of law and national legal cultures, and to emancipate it from purely economic considerations. This section explores potential pathways and strategies to achieve these goals. The chapter concludes by illustrating the author's findings, reflecting on the importance of maintaining the rule of law as a cornerstone of the EU's functioning. It underscores the need for continued vigilance and innovative approaches to ensure that the rule of law remains a dynamic and effective principle guiding the Union's policies and practices, especially in times of crisis.

The book continues with Sabrina Praduroux's chapter, which examines the complex and evolving nature of property rights under the European Convention for the Protection of Human Rights and Fundamental Freedoms, particularly focusing on Article 1 of Protocol 1. This chapter provides an in-depth analysis of how the right to property, initially a controversial inclusion, has developed into a cornerstone of the ECtHR's case law over the past 70 years. The chapter traces the dynamic interpretation of Article 1 of Protocol 1 of the European Convention by the ECtHR, highlighting how the Court has expanded the scope of property rights to address emerging legal, political, and societal issues in Europe. This rich body of case law illustrates the Court's role in navigating property regulation challenges, both in established and newer democracies.

Further, the chapter delves into how the ECHR has adapted its interpretation of property rights to the changing European landscape. This includes exploring cases that have arisen due to political shifts, societal changes, and legal developments. The analysis shows the Court's commitment to ensuring that the protection of property rights remains relevant and robust in the face of evolving circumstances. This detailed exploration of property rights under the ECHR is particularly relevant in the context of South-Eastern Europe. Our book's comparative approach sheds light on how different countries in the region have integrated the ECtHR's jurisprudence into their national legal systems, especially concerning property rights. This provides a unique perspective on the interplay between international human rights standards and domestic legal traditions in these transitioning democracies.

The next chapter, by Svitlana Zadorozhna, explores the multifaceted concept of the rule of law, especially in the context of the EU enlargement strategy for Western Balkan countries. It delves into the varying definitions and understandings of the rule of law, stretching from narrow legalistic interpretations to broader ones encompassing human rights and democracy. It particularly focuses on the aspects of judicial reform and access to justice as integral components of the rule of law within the EU enlargement package. The author discusses the complexity and varied interpretations of the rule of law in contemporary political and international discourse. The chapter also examines how this concept has evolved and is utilised by different international institutions, highlighting the disparity in its definitions from narrow legal frameworks to broader conceptions that include human rights and democratic principles. This part of the chapter shifts focus to the specific context of the Western Balkans and their path towards EU integration. Finally, the author analyses how the EU enlargement package interprets and applies the rule of law, emphasising the significance of this principle in the accession process.

The author also examines the EU's approach to fostering democracy and protecting human rights in these countries. Central to her discussion is the EU's emphasis on judicial reform and improving access to justice in Western Balkan countries. The chapter explores the challenges and progress in these areas, discussing how judicial reforms are instrumental in strengthening the rule of law and ensuring effective legal protection for citizens. This contribution delves deeper into the interconnection between the rule of law, human rights, and democratic values within the EU enlargement context. It discusses how these elements are interdependent and crucial for the overall stability and integration of Western Balkan countries into the European Union. Indeed, Zadorozhna's chapter reflects on the pivotal role of the rule of law in shaping the political and legal landscapes of Western Balkan countries. It underscores the importance of judicial reforms and accessible justice systems in aligning these countries with EU standards, thereby facilitating their path towards EU membership. The conclusion also touches upon the broader implications of these reforms for regional stability and integration.

This general part of the book subsequently delves into the intricate dynamics of consumer contracts and protection, guided by Darko Spasevski's comprehensive analysis. The foundational premise of consumer protection lies in the perceived imbalance between consumers and businesses, a concept deeply embedded in modern legal frameworks. The essay explores the mechanisms devised to protect the consumer, the weaker party in contractual agreements, and engages in the broader discourse on the nuances of these mechanisms. The first section of the chapter discusses the inherent imbalance between consumers and businesses, which forms the basis for consumer protection regimes. It examines the special mechanisms established across various legal systems aimed at safeguarding consumer interests and rights. A pivotal aspect of Spasevski's work is the exploration of the relationship between consumer rights and human rights. This section analyses how these two realms intersect and diverge, drawing on legislative examples from Southeast Europe. The essay seeks to elucidate the degree of closeness, similarities, and differences between these two types of rights within this geographical context.

The core of the chapter involves a detailed analysis of the legislation regulating consumer protection in Southeast Europe. This investigation aims to provide a clear understanding of how consumer rights are framed, protected, and potentially limited within this region, and how they align with or differ from the broader human rights framework. It contains the insights from Spasevski's analysis, offering a nuanced perspective on the complexities of consumer protection laws in Southeast Europe. It reflects on the implications of these findings for both the legal community and the broader societal understanding of consumer rights as they relate to human rights.

South-Eastern European Countries and the European Court of Human Rights

The fifth chapter, authored by Darko Spasevski, delves into the intricate relationship between consumer protection systems and human rights protection within the context of Southeast Europe. In this pivotal fifth chapter, Spasevski explores how consumer rights, often seen as an extension of fundamental human rights, are upheld through various legal and institutional frameworks in the region. He provides a detailed analysis of the existing consumer protection mechanisms, evaluating their effectiveness and identifying potential areas for enhancement. Additionally, the chapter underscores the broader implications of these protections for the overall human rights landscape, advocating for a comprehensive approach to safeguard the well-being and rights of consumers in Southeast Europe.

The sixth chapter of the book explores specificities and characteristics of one particular jurisdiction of the region, Albania. In their chapter, Fjoralba Caka and Nada Dollani also provide a comprehensive analysis of the intricate relationship between fundamental human rights and private law, while considering the case of Albania, with a particular focus on the right to property. Drawing from the chapter's insights, the essay explores how the right to property, entrenched as a human right in international instruments like the European Convention on Human Rights is reflected and enforced in the Albanian legal system through the jurisprudence of the ECtHR and the Albanian Constitutional and Supreme Courts.

The first section delves into the historical context of property rights as human rights, a concept affirmed in the drafting history of the ECHR and the adoption of its First Protocol. The chapter examines the unique challenges Albania faced in transitioning from a communist regime that severely restricted human rights, to a democratic system embracing Western ideals of human and fundamental rights, culminating in the ratification of the ECHR in 1996 and the adoption of a new constitution in 1998. This part of the chapter focuses on how the principles of the ECHR have been integrated into the Albanian legal framework, especially in cases regarding property rights. It discusses the significant role of the ECHR in shaping Albanian legal precedents, including the landmark pilot judgment in 2012 which addressed compensation for property rights violations during the communist era. The core of the authors' views involves an analysis of the three main methods identified by Spielmann for incorporating fundamental rights into private law relations: the state positive obligations doctrine, the constitutionally confirmed interpretation of legal provisions, and the balancing technique between fundamental rights and public interests in court decisions. The chapter evaluates how these methods have been applied by the Albanian Constitutional and Supreme Courts, with a particular focus on property rights. It also reflects on the evolution of property rights in Albania from a human rights perspective. It highlights the critical role of both national and international jurisprudence in shaping these rights within the private law domain and emphasises the ongoing challenges and progress in the Albanian legal system regarding the implementation and protection of fundamental human rights.

This is then followed by Emilia Mišćenić's chapter on the example of Croatia. Mišćenić provides an insightful examination of the rule of law's impact on private law relationships, with a specific focus on the legal framework and case law in the Republic of Croatia. By analysing the fields of anti-discrimination and consumer protection, the essay highlights how the rule of law is recognised and protected in private legal relationships, offering a broader perspective on the interplay between rule of law principles and private law. The first section discusses the shift in legal scholarship, highlighting the growing attention private law scholars have given to the rule of law. Traditionally dominated by public law considerations, the rule of law is now increasingly seen as a guiding principle in private law relationships. This part sets the stage for understanding the importance of this shift. Focusing on the Republic of Croatia, this section explores how the rule of law manifests in various areas of private law.

The essay examines the normative legal framework in Croatia, providing context for how private law is structured and governed by rule of law principles. Central to Dr Mišćenić's analysis are case studies in the areas of anti-discrimination and consumer protection. This part of the chapter delves into specific Croatian cases, illustrating how the rule of law is enforced and upheld in these fields. It assesses how these areas contribute to the broader achievement of the rule of law in private relationships. The chapter concludes by reflecting on the broader implications of Mišćenić's work. It emphasises how her analysis of the Croatian context provides valuable insights into the general values and applications of the rule of law in private law. The conclusion highlights the importance of this perspective in understanding the complex interplay between legal principles and private legal relationships on a broader scale.

The eighth chapter examines the example of North Macedonia. Specifically, Julija Brsakoska Bazerkoska and Aleksandar Spasov discuss the nuanced application of Article 15 of the European Convention of Human Rights in the Republic of North Macedonia during and in the aftermath of the COVID-19 pandemic. The focus is on the conditions under which a state can derogate from its obligations under the ECHR during emergencies, and how this was implemented in North Macedonia. They discuss the legal framework of Article 15, providing the background necessary to understand its use in times of emergency. It explains the criteria for derogation, including the necessity of a public emergency, and outlines the supervisory role of the ECtHR in ensuring that any derogations are limited and appropriate. This part of the chapter delves into the specifics of how North Macedonia applied Article 15 of the European Convention of Human Rights during the pandemic. It explores the government's decisions to limit certain rights and freedoms, the extent of these limitations, and the process of providing formal and public notice of derogation, as required by the Convention.

A critical aspect of the chapter involves analysing the existing case law of the ECtHR in the area of derogations under Article 15. This analysis helps in understanding how the Court interprets the conditions and limits of derogations during emergencies, providing a comparative backdrop to the Macedonian case. An important element of the chapter, and consequently the essay, is the examination of how different vulnerable groups were affected by the derogations in North Macedonia. This section assesses whether the needs and rights of these groups were adequately considered and protected during the crisis. It reflects on the balance between state responsibilities to protect public health and the need to uphold human rights during emergencies, using the Macedonian case as a focal point. The conclusion also offers insights into the broader implications of this case for future applications of Article 15 in similar circumstances.

The ninth chapter is also on North Macedonia. In her chapter, Federica Torta examines property rights and religious dynamics in North Macedonia and discusses the role of the ECHR Jurisprudence and religious entities. The religious landscape of North Macedonia has undergone significant changes since its independence in 1991. This essay delves into the complexities faced by two religious communities, one major one and one smaller one: the Archbishopric of Ohrid and the Bektashi community. It examines their legal challenges, the impact of national and ECtHR jurisprudence, and the consequences on private property rights. The essay also explores the recent development within the Orthodox community, notably the granting of autocephaly to the Macedonian Orthodox Church. During the last three decades, North Macedonia has navigated the delicate balance between secular governance and religious freedom. The constitution guarantees freedom of religion, but the implementation in cases like the Archbishopric of Ohrid and the Bektashi community reveals complexities.

It outlines the legislative environment governing religious institutions in North Macedonia. The Archbishopric of Ohrid has faced significant legal challenges. The chapter will discuss the impact of national legislation and ECtHR rulings on this religious entity, focusing on issues related to its recognition, autonomy, and property. Contrasting with the Orthodox community, the Bektashi, a Sufi order, has its unique struggles in North Macedonia. Despite international efforts, their situation remains unresolved. This section will explore the legal battles and the broader implications for religious minorities in the country.

The tenth chapter is on Serbia, in which Branka Babovic Vuksanovic analyses the significant effects of legislative changes in the area of consumer collective redress in the Republic of Serbia, particularly focusing on the right to a fair trial for consumers. It begins by discussing the landmark decision of the Serbian Constitutional Court, which repealed certain provisions as unconstitutional, and delves into the traditional aspects of procedural law in Serbia that do not traditionally incorporate collective redress. A key focus of the chapter is the decision of the Constitutional Court regarding the organisational claim and its alignment with Serbia's procedural law tradition. The essay examines whether this 'blast from the past' approach was suitably interpreted and argues that it was not, leading to various procedural inadequacies.

The legislative changes have led to a substantial influx of mass claims in Serbian courts, signalling procedural inadequacies. This essay explores how these changes have affected consumers' access to justice and the overall effectiveness of consumer protection laws in Serbia. The consequences of these legislative changes extend to the relationship between consumers and traders. The author discusses how these changes have disproportionately affected consumers, making the weaker party even more vulnerable. It also analyses the lack of effective procedural mechanisms to deter traders from collectively infringing consumer rights and interests. The chapter clearly highlights the challenges and inadequacies in the current consumer collective redress system in Serbia. It emphasises the need for reform to ensure fair trials for consumers and a balanced relationship between consumers and traders.

The eleventh chapter by Mitja Kovac focuses on Slovenia. Kovac offers in his chapter an in-depth analysis of the rule of law in Slovenia, especially within the domain of private law. Kovac meticulously examines the interplay between Slovenian legal practices and the European Court of Human Rights judgments, focusing on property rights and access to justice. His work critically evaluates how the rule of law is materialised in property law and influences the horizontal relationships among citizens. The book explores the manifestations and challenges of the rule of law in Slovenia's private law sector. It discusses specific ECtHR judgments pertinent to Slovenian cases, offering insights into the state of property rights and judicial accessibility in the country.

A significant aspect of Professor Kovac's analysis is the concern over the potential shift from the rule of law to rule by law, and further into rule by judges. The essay addresses this critical perspective, highlighting systemic issues in the Slovenian judiciary, such as prolonged trial durations and inefficiencies in the administration of justice. Kovac identifies the lengthy legal proceedings and property law issues as significant triggers for the need to improve the principle of rule of law in Slovenia. This chapter will delve into these systemic problems and conclude with a discussion of this economically informed policy suggestions to enhance the rule of law in the country's private law domain.

The twelfth chapter contains Raluca Bercea's insightful analysis of the rule of law in Romania, particularly in the context of private law and the recognition of same-sex relationships. It explores the intricate relationship between societal perceptions, legal formalisations, and fundamental human rights, offering a novel perspective on private and family life in contemporary Romania. It begins by examining how same-sex relationships have been perceived in Romanian society and the corresponding legal regime. This section explores the tension between societal attitudes and the gradual legal acknowledgment of same-sex couples, highlighting the unique Romanian experience in this regard. A significant focus of the author's work is the judicial dialogue emerging over the topic of same-sex relationships. The essay discusses the notable 2018 referendum on redefining the family and the Romanian Constitutional Court's engagement with this issue. It analyses the Court's decision to refer to the CJEU under Article 267 TFEU, marking a pivotal moment in Romania's legal history. Part of the chapter delves into the involvement of the ECHR and CJEU in shaping the legal landscape surrounding same-sex relationships in Romania.

This chapter discusses the landmark 2019 ruling by the Grand Chamber of the CJEU and the recent developments under Article life of the ECHR, particularly in light of the ECtHR Fedotova standards. An essential aspect of Professor Bercea's chapter is the exploration of the synergies resulting from the multi-layered societal and judicial approach to same-sex relationships. The Chapter evaluates how these interactions have influenced the rule of law in Romania, particularly concerning private and family life. It emphasises how this work opens up new perspectives on the intersection of private law, fundamental rights, and family life in Romania. It highlights the importance of understanding the complex interplay between societal attitudes, legal frameworks, and judicial decisions in shaping the legal recognition and protection of same-sex relationships in the context of evolving European standards. We believe this chapter underscores a contribution to the broader discourse on the rule of law and fundamental rights in the context of changing societal norms and legal landscapes.

The book concludes with a more general chapter by Giovanni Cimbalo, who examines the growing influence of Orthodox Christianity in the European Union, especially in light of the accession of new states and the potential entry of Ukraine and Moldova. With over 110 million people in the EU belonging to states with an Orthodox majority, and a burgeoning Orthodox diaspora in Western Europe, Cimbalo investigates the potential impact on rights. The Chapter also draws connections to Federica Torta's analysis of religious communities in North Macedonia, offering an interdisciplinary view of the evolving religious landscape in the book.

2

Rule of Law and the Next Generation EU Recovery Plan: A Bumpy Road from Vagueness to Conditionality

GIANMARIA AJANI

1. The Rule of Law as a Vague Notion

In contrast to what was common practice until the middle of the last century, when the progression of legal reforms via legal transplants occurred mainly at a slow pace, and generally through the vehicle of legal scholars, an important share in the promotion of legal reforms has been entrusted, in the last three decades, to supranational institutions, such as the International Monetary Fund, the World Bank, and the European Bank for Reconstruction and Development.[1]

Unlike the theories produced by the 'Law and Development' movement in the 1960s and 1970s,[2] the doctrine for economic development endorsed by the World Bank, under the direction of its General Counsel Ibrahim Shihata[3] (1983–1998) identified the Market, as opposed to the State, as a catalyst for change and institutional reforms. The rationale was essentially the following: as more private actors began to influence the direction of national economies, their competition would not be limited to the marketplace, but also felt in the courts, and whenever the courts seemed not to be up to the task (for numerous reasons, like obsolete procedural laws, judicial corruption, or lack of modern case management), sweeping legal reforms were needed. Accordingly, by the mid-1990s, the World Bank and other UN agencies started targeting 'poor governance' and corruption as factors undermining both development and the implementation of solid economic policy reforms.[4]

[1] G Ajani, 'The Transplant of Vague Notions' in IH Szilàgyi and M Paksy (eds), *Ius Unum. Lex Multiplex. Festschrift in Honour of Zoltàn Péteri* (Budapest, Istvan Tarsulat, 2005) 17.

[2] A Santos, 'The World Bank's Uses of the Rule of Law Promise', in D Trubek and A Santos (eds), *The New Law and Development: a Critical Appraisal* (Cambridge, Cambridge University Press, 2006) 253.

[3] I Shihata, *Complementary Reform: Essays on Legal, Judicial and Other Institutional Reforms Supported by the World Bank* (The Hague, London, Boston, Kluwer Law International, 1997).

[4] LK Sarwar, *Evolution of the World Bank's Thinking on Governance. World Development Report Background Paper* (Washington, World Bank, 2016).

These institutions did, and still do, promote legal change through a matrix made of soft laws, proposals, and recommendations for legal reforms. In doing this, the same institutions have refreshed a notion that had remained silent for decades in the vocabulary of international law: the rule of law.[5]

In the past a new statute, a Code, or a Constitution, was adopted or emended on the assumption that the 'prestige' of the imported set of rules was sufficient to legitimise the change.[6] Later, in the age of progressing globalisation, the process of legitimising a legal reform could not be built upon a simple and circular argument such as the reputation of a foreign normative model. Within this new situation, we notice that the process of legal transplantation has been strengthened by the recourse to vague formulas, such as due process, governance (and good governance), reasonableness, rule of law, transparency, accountability.[7] Those formulas have been used as 'global standards' in the process of validating the compatibility of national legal reforms with the global values enshrined in fundamental Treaties and Charters.

At the same time, linking the contents of national legal reforms to universal values and indexes of good quality of the laws was intended to ease local adaptation of new rules brought within local orders by the same reforms. In other words, a process of substitution has occurred whenever large new reforms have been solicited by external actors: while in the past legal change had to consider the system of national (local) taxonomies and had to be consistent with local scholarly opinions, the acceleration of legal harmonisation initiatives all over the world pushed national legislators to cut short their dependence on local contexts, and to pay stronger consideration to universal values enshrined in international Treaties and Charters.

Let us consider the case of the European Union: if we examine the style of EU laws, we cannot fail to notice that, while drafting directives and regulations, the EU institutions do not feel the compulsion to adhere to the system of concepts and doctrines practiced at state level by local jurists.[8] This approach led, in the last 25 years, to a proliferation of vague notions and to their inclusion within the rhetoric of 'good governance for the market'. Furthermore, because broad formulas expressed in ordinary language are more palatable to the media, a bundle of concepts, whose juridical/technical content is far from certain, has become the paradigm for assessing the modernisation of a legal system.

The process of transplanting new laws has been piloted by following two steps:

- bringing the rule of law and other related and vague notions to the attention of reformers;
- conveying operational rules as necessary consequences, that follow the adoption of rule of law as a major 'constitutional standard'.

[5] The founding documents establishing the European Communities in the 1950s made no reference to the rule of law, but to the principle of legality.

[6] G Ajani, 'By Chance and Prestige: Legal Transplants in Russia and Eastern Europe' (1995) 43 *American Journal of Comparative Law* 93.

[7] G Ajani, 'Ruling by Indicators: How the Use of Vague Notions and Quantitative Indicators Facilitates Legal Change' (2017) *Cardozo Bulletin Law Journal* 1.

[8] R Schulze *New Features in Contract Law* (Berlin, New York, Otto Schmidt/De Gruyter, 2007).

This process is manifest in the strategies adopted by major financial institutions, as well as by other institutions, such as the European Union, or the World Trade Organization.[9]

Its recognition, however, should not lead us to the immediate identification of that two-step process as a sort of an abstract scheme; using vague notions has been conducive for an intense homogenisation of the 'rules for economic development' conceived by the International Financial Institutions as beneficial to liberalisation of trade.

The 'rule of law' concept has not only become a substitute for discussion on the effects of development policies, but also an instrument to circumvent, at least during the initial stages of dialogue between donors and recipient countries, an embarrassing confrontation on the inner meaning of widely debatable political notions such as democracy, pluripartitism, and judicial independence. Such an opportunity proved to be useful not only for the international financial organisations, like the World Bank or the IMF, seeking to sidestep problems with their mandate, but also for the European Union institutions, involved in the extremely delicate issue of outlining the conditions for the Union enlargement towards East.

Vague notions were perceived as valuable as they responded to some persistent problems of globalisation: scarcity of time and deficit of consensus. Within this context the rule of law

> an immature legal term, made its triumphant journey. It soon became fertilised in use by politicians and political scientists; it was transferred to international diplomacy; integrated into the language of the United Nations; and finally, into that of the World Bank and International Monetary Fund.[10]

Absent a theoretically developed background, the rule of law formula was meant to convey a necessary link between legal reform programmes aimed to the achievement

[9] The Hungarian legal philosopher Csaba Varga reminds us that 'the creation of the United Nations (1945) was an ordeal for the parties drifting towards the Cold War, and the adoption of the Universal Declaration of Human Rights (1949) implied straightforward multiplayer factional struggle over what and how to name it. Back then, it seemed sufficient to edify a law + rule/state conglomerate as the broadest framework for their safeguard so that they would be implemented and not forced out by popular rebellion. For this reason, the Declaration had to state that "human rights should be protected by the rule of law" (where the term may have stood for some rule(s) of the law, not the classical rule of law)'; C Varga 'Rule of Law, Contesting and Contested' (2021) 2 *Central European Journal of Comparative Law* 245.

[10] Varga has rightly noted that, at the turn of millennium, the General Secretary of the UN, Kofi Annan, launched a campaign to honour the rule of law, with a definition attached to it: 'In his statement, venerable but devoid of legal force, he crammed into his notion everything he could bring from the various aspects of law and the state. The rule of law, he orated, refers to a principle of governance in which all persons, institutions and entities, public and private, including the State itself, are accountable to laws that are publicly promulgated, equally enforced, and independently adjudicated, and which are consistent with international human rights norms and standards. Measures to ensure adherence to the principles of supremacy of law, equality before the law, accountability to the law, fairness in the application of the law, separation of powers, participation in decision-making, legal certainty, avoidance of arbitrariness, and procedural and legal transparency', C Varga, Rule of Law, 250.

of democracy and other 'public goods'. In the case of the European Union, to achieve goals listed by Article 3 of the Treaty of the European Union (TEU).[11]

What is particularly noticeable in this context is the fact that major part of the scholarly debate on the rule of law was rooted in the English\Common Law-based narrative of the idea. Yet, unlike real objects of the world, like mountains, tables, or houses, legal concepts do not exist per se; in fact, their existence is the result of agreed definitions among human beings, and consequent behaviours. Unlike the real objects of the world, legal objects exist in time, but not in the space we live in. We can call them 'social objects' (such as, e.g. contracts, promises). The very nature and the meaning of these social objects derive from a set of variables, such as the language and the taxonomies organised by expert communities. This applies also to vague formulas with a legal significance, like the rule of law, good faith, transparency, and due process. Their meaning is highly dependent on the scholarly discourse that originates around them.

The story of the rule of law idea is no exception. As a concept, in its continental version it achieved fame thanks to the German *Begriffsjurisprudenz* (literally 'conceptual jurisprudence'), as in the second half of the nineteenth century German legal scholars like Otto Mayer and Carl Friedrich von Gerber managed to relate a sophisticated structure to a situation as convoluted as the state-citizen relationship. The *Rechtsstaat* idea was intimately connected to a pattern whereby citizens were holders of subjective public rights (*subjektive öffentliche Rechte*) in their relations with the state. Through the works of Mayer, the newly established 'science of administrative law' elaborated in juridical terms the Hegelian idea of the state as a 'living organism' whose life, aims, and means are superior to those of the individuals who form it. Thus, the state became the public entity *par excellence.* No body superseded it; it was the primary source of juridical rules, and its acts were all authoritative.

[11] Vagueness is not the only instrument that has been used to promote legal change. Global goals, rankings and indicators have been increasingly designed and adopted by international organisations and NGOs to facilitate the transplant of legal norms in transitional countries. In the last two decades, the number of these quantitative tools has been growing significantly both at a national and transnational level. Indicators are the representation of a certain performance in classificatory terms. They are characterised by specific features: a name that has the power of defining a specific phenomenon; an ordinal structure that facilitates comparison and ranking, thus, exerting pressure for enhancing the measured performances; a numerical representation that simplifies complex social phenomena; a scientific justification founded on a methodology adopted by global experts; the possibility of being used for evaluative purposes. The production and use of these quantitative instruments have both a knowledge and a governance effect. As form of knowledge, indicators rely on the magic aura that numbers convey and on the appearance of impartiality and certainty that they communicate. A key aspect of their power consists in the capacity to transform complexity into clear and non-ambiguous measurements. They manage to submerge particularities and local idiosyncrasies in universal categories, generating a standardised knowledge, which is comparable among different nations and regions. As a form of governance, they are extensively used by decision-makers to adopt important decisions, such as how to tackle specific gender equality issues or where to provide humanitarian aid. By replacing judgments based on politics or values with more (allegedly) rational decisions based on numbers and rankings, the use of statistical information and indicators determines a significant shift in the power dynamics of the decision-making process.

Within this design, the ends of the state were made to coincide with the 'public interest'. Such aims, however, had to be defined by statute, since the state was no longer an organisation free to act 'arbitrarily', like the absolutist regime referred to as a *Polizeistaat*. Hence, *Rechtsstaat* was a term born to counter the idea of *Polizeistaat* and conceived to design a relatively simple situation: a legal system where the public powers affecting citizens' interests had to be assigned to state institutions based on a legal rule intended to protect individuals against possible abuses of public power, or misuse of administrative capacities. Its proponents, thus, intended the *Rechtsstaat* standard to assume a constructive meaning; it was to constitute a principle superior to all those fundamental laws and constitutions attributing guarantees to individuals. The idea shared the success enjoyed at the time by German legal doctrines and spread over the lands of Central and Eastern Europe, including those under the Austrian or the Russian Imperial rule.

Following the decline of the cultural hegemony of the *Begfrisssjurisprudenz*, towards the end of the nineteenth century, German scholars started to endow the notion of *Rechtsstaat* with the most varied meanings. Throughout those years and up to the eve of World War I, we find that *Rechtsstaat* was interpreted by the various authors:

- as an equivalent of the constitutional state idea, for its formal guarantees of individuals' rights;
- as an equivalent of the establishment of administrative tribunals;
- as a synonym of rule of law;
- as a notion linking administrative action to the respect of 'supremacy of law'.

All those interpretations were not only different, one from another, but sometimes even contradictory. This confusion also derived from the fact that continental legal terminology did not possess a way to translate and precisely express the notion of rule of law. All the translations which include the term 'state' (*Rechtsstaat*, *Etat de droit*, *rządów prawa*, *stato di diritto*) are, in fact, inappropriate, as they misconstrue the essence of the rule of law. In fact, the key element of the rule of law is not the state, but rather a set of rules and principles that precede the state. Rule of law, thus, exists above all 'before' the state or, more precisely, where the state does not assume the production of law exclusively as its prerogative. The strong, but misleading, link which has bound, and continues to bind, the common law based notion of rule of law and the European continental concept of *Rechtsstaat* (or *Etat de droit*, *stato di diritto*, and so forth) may be explained by the fact that both notions embody different methods to reach the same goal: the subordination of political power to the observance of rules intended to preserve the citizens' freedom.

To bring that long story to our present days, it seems clear that the dispute on the meaning and effect of the rule of law between the EU Commission and some Member States hints to another, still ambiguous, issue: the double status, European, and national, of our citizenship. When nationally entrenched political party's leaders talk to their voters, at the best they insist on the national version of the rule of law/*Rechtsstaat* tale. More frequently, they find an easy game in representing the rule of law idea as a vague statement.[12] In doing this, they propose a new version of the immanent tension between European and national constitutional values.[13]

2. Interlude: The Rule of Law as a General Conditionality and the Mandate of International Financial Institutions

Vague notions, like rule of law, transparency, and due process, are characterised by a narrative style. Two decades of national legal reforms driven by the action of international organisations show that insistence on the reception of those vague formulas has escorted worldwide the adoption and implementation of legal reforms.

Indeterminacy of language and terminological vagueness allows the reaching of consensus within a reasonable span of time. In fact, a vague language enables the following:

- postponing the tackling of difficult issues related to implementation;
- avoiding a dive into the details of distributional nature;
- keeping the governance of macro-economic decisions under the control of 'external standards provider' (for instance, the EU Commission, during the process of enlargement towards Central and Eastern Europe).

All these facilitating factors support an uncontested transplant of laws that is considered necessary for proper market functioning and economic development. At the same time, however, they produce a false image of law as a static and neutral set of rules, good for universal implementation, under the unique condition that governments express a commitment to the rule of law.

[12] Not only political leaders: a Hungarian Constitutional Court judge has defined the rule of law 'as a normative yardstick' which 'is little more than an empty nineteenth century ideal and a political joker for all purposes'. Quoted by L Pech, 'The Rule of Law as a Well-Established and Well-Defined Principle of EU Law' (2022) 14 *Hague Journal on the Rule of Law* 107.

[13] A prologue to the tensions on rule of law came, however, not from Warsaw or Budapest, but from Karlsruhe, the seat of the German Federal Constitutional Court. On 5 May 2020, the Second Chamber of the German Federal Constitutional Court handed down a judgment in a constitutional challenge against the Public Sector Purchase Programme (PSPP) established by the European Central Bank (ECB) The Court declared the ECB decisions as well as the EUCJ judgment in *Weiss* reviewing and approving those Decisions to be *ultra vires* and thus not binding in Germany. It was then required for the European Central Bank to provide additional guarantees to Germany. By openly challenging the primacy of the EUCJ as ultimate judge over EU law, the German Court established a reference welcome to the Hungarian and the Polish governments in their attempt to challenge the EUCJ authority in stating the impact of the rule of law principle. See: A Viterbo, 'The PSPP Judgment of the German Federal Constitutional Court: Throwing Sand in the Wheels of the European Central Bank' (2020) 5 *European Papers* 671.

As evinced, there is not a commonly shared definition of the rule of law concept. Numberless international organisations, governments, NGOs, policy think tanks, financial institutions, and foundations have been truly committed in 'promoting the rule of law'. Most of them view the rule of law in different ways.[14] What is common to those entities, however, is the acknowledgement of the standard as normative.

Let us consider, as an example, some excerpts from the *Agreement Establishing the European Bank for Reconstruction and Development*, signed in the year 1991[15] (author's emphasis):

> *Preamble.*
>
> The contracting parties, **committed to the fundamental principles of multiparty democracy, the rule of law, respect for human rights and market economics**; (…) welcoming the intent of Central and Eastern European countries **to further the practical implementation of multiparty democracy, strengthening democratic institutions, the rule of law** and respect for human rights and their willingness to implement reforms in order to evolve towards market-oriented economies;
>
> (…)
>
> Have agreed to establish hereby the European Bank for Reconstruction and Development (hereinafter called "the Bank") which shall operate in accordance with the following:
>
> *Chapter I*
>
> Article 1. Purpose
>
> In contributing to economic progress and reconstruction, the purpose of the Bank shall be to foster the transition towards open market-oriented economies and to promote private and entrepreneurial initiative in the **central and eastern European countries committed to and applying the principles of multiparty democracy, pluralism** and market economics.
>
> Article 2. Functions
>
> 1. To fulfil on a long-term basis its purpose of fostering the transition of Central and Eastern European countries towards open market-oriented economies and the promotion of private and entrepreneurial initiative, the Bank shall assist the recipient member countries to implement structural and sectoral economic reforms, including demonopolization, decentralization and privatization.
>
> (…)
>
> Article 8. Recipient countries and use of resources
>
> 1. The resources and facilities of the Bank shall be used exclusively to implement the purpose and carry out the functions set forth, respectively, in Articles 1 and 2 of this Agreement.

[14] On the contingency of the rule of law idea see, among many: R McCorquodale, 'Defining the International Rule of Law: Defying Gravity?' (2016) 65 *The International and Comparative Law Quarterly* 277.

[15] www.ebrd.com.

2. The Bank may conduct its operations in countries from Central and Eastern Europe which are proceeding steadily in the transition towards market-oriented economies and the promotion of private and entrepreneurial initiative, and **which apply, by concrete steps and otherwise, the principles set forth in Article 1 of this Agreement**.
3. In cases where a member might be implementing **policies which are inconsistent with Article 1 of this Agreement**, or in exceptional circumstances, the Board of Directors shall consider whether access by a member to Bank **resources should be suspended** or otherwise modified and may make recommendations accordingly to the Board of Governors.

The founding of the European Bank for Reconstruction and Development (EBRD) represented the climax in the assertion of international institutions to establish multiparty democracy, respect of fundamental rights and the rule of law as necessary preconditions for an effective functioning of a market economy.

An assertion which sounds even more intense if we compare its phrasing to an earlier document, namely the *Articles of Agreement establishing the International Bank for Reconstruction and Development (World Bank)*(1945),[16] whose Article III.5 states as follows (emphasis added):

> III.5. *Use of Loans Guaranteed, Participated in or Made by the Bank.*
>
> The Bank shall make arrangements to ensure that the proceeds of any loan are used only for the purposes for which the loan was granted, with due attention to considerations of **economy** and **efficiency** and **without regard to political or other non-economic influences or considerations**.

Even though both the World Bank and the EBRD are international financial institutions, there is a world of difference between those two quotes. The second one is the product of a historical era when the principle of national sovereignty was still untouched. Consequently, the mandate of the Bank had to represent respect for political diversity. It's only after the end of the cold war that the General Counsel of the Bank, Ibrahim Shihata,[17] had free hand to re-explain, without changing its phrasing, Article III.5 of the Bank's Statute as compatible with legal reforms vested with political significance. The reasoning, as it is well known, was to present legal reforms as a 'necessary step' in the march towards efficient and effective market economies.

According to the justificatory legal framework that was adopted, a practice of domestic institutional reform would fall outside the sphere of (prohibited) political interference if it were grounded in an appropriate and objective economic rationale.[18] Such a radical change in the approach to conditionalities was not

[16] The IBRD Articles of Agreement were drawn up at the United Nations Monetary and Financial Conference, at Bretton Woods, New Hampshire, 1–22 July 1944. The governing document became effective on 27 December 1945: www.worldbank.org/en/about/articles-of-agreement.

[17] See *supra*, n 3.

[18] See *supra* n 3.

limited to the action of the World Bank. While enabling the Bank to treat legal reform as a technical matter, immune from suspicions of interference in a country's political affairs, it also favoured a wider and global consensus towards the recognition of the rule of law concept as pre-condition of multiparty democracy, and as a general standard, able to drive national governments in the building of economic structures based on technical consideration of economy and efficiency.

As a collateral, but not irrelevant, side effect, law (meaning rules, practices, and judicial organization) became, so, functional to economic performances compatible with the requirements of globalisation.

Following the cultural shift introduced by the World Bank in the early 1990s, times were mature for the identification of a set of explicit political and legal conditionalities. This was made possible when the Charter of a new institution, the European Bank for Reconstruction and Development was designed in 1991.

In other words, those two Charters, while establishing their institutions' mandates, have marked the route from a (supposed-to-be) neutral approach in the promotion of national legal reforms, towards a declared request for political guarantees, to ensure sustainability for long-term States' debts in a (quasi)neo-Keynesian context.[19]

This change was accompanied, in the global political discourse, by a celebratory and rhetorical assertion of the necessary interdependence between the rule of law and the good function of economies in a democratic context. Similar comments greeted the accession of the PR of China to the WTO, agreed by the contracting parties in the year 1999 (to become effective in 2001), following a constitutional amendment declaring that China 'shall practice law-based governance and build a socialist state under the rule of law'.[20] On a different case, more than some hope for improvements in the march towards the rule of law, even if not a plain enthusiasm, had welcome the admission, in the year 1996, of the Russian Federation to the Council of Europe, also based on the formal recognition of the rule of law idea within the text of the Federal Constitution dated 1993.

In a span of time lasting less than ten years, the rule of law concept has become the driving standard used by international organisations to measure, over time, the compatibility with market economy and democratic principles of States deeply entrenched, in a not distant past, in not-democratic structures like, above all, the PR of China and the Russian Federation.

In the same period of the early 1990s the process of EU enlargement eastwards had been inaugurated by the inclusion of the concept of rule of law within the

[19] UW Chohan, 'The return of Keynesianism? Exploring path dependency and ideational change in post-covid fiscal policy' (2022) 41 *Policy and Society* 68.

[20] See C Li, 'Fazhi vs/and/or Rule of Law? A Semiotic Venture into Chinese Law' (2001) 14 *International Journal for the Semiotics of Law* 223.

An official English version of the PRC Constitution can be found at: english.www.gov.cn/archive/lawsregulations/201911/20/content_WS5ed8856ec6d0b3f0e9499913.html.

Accession Preparation Agreements of the EU and Central and Eastern European States.[21] The list of requirements for membership as expressed in various European Council declarations between 1991 and 1993 included the following:

- both the Union and the applicant countries need to prepare in their own ways;
- the preparedness of the applicants is to be assessed by means of a number of political and economic criteria;
- the applicants will have to prepare more extensively than has been the case with previous enlargements because their political/legal systems will also be scrutinized by the EU;
- the preparation of the Union requires institutional, financial and policy reform.[22]

In the light of the above considerations, it seems quite evident that, at the very eve of the accession of Central and East European Countries to the EU, the rule of law standard was conceived as a mixed political\legal concept. It does not seem odd to state that, in fact, it sounded more political in nature, than legal, due to the heavy stress put on the political premises required to get the process of accession on the right track.

This provoked a short-circuit within a (vague) notion, whose function was intended to be at the same time both a narrative of a process and a fundamental norm with constitutional value.

This also explains why the principle of the rule of law was frequently viewed as not justiciable:

> the rule of law is not traditionally used as a rule of law. This is not to say, however, that the rule of law, as a legal principle, lacks normative effect and merely fulfils a descriptive function. On the contrary, the highest courts tend to rely on the rule of law both as a transversal principle that must guide the interpretation of all legal norms, and a basis from which a set of hard legal principles, formal as well as substantive, can be derived to help the judiciary in their day-to-day mission to interpret and scrutinise the validity of public authorities' measures.[23]

There are some good reasons to believe that the memory of that perception and use of the notion in the international arena, the identification of the rule of law as a

[21] D Booss and J Forma, 'Enlargement: Legal and Procedural Aspects' (1995) 32 *Common Market Law Review* 95.

[22] P Nicolaides and S Raja Boean 'The Process of Enlargement of the European Union', available at aei.pitt.edu/776/1/2.htm It is noteworthy that, during the deliberations at the European Council meeting in Copenhagen in June 1993, France proposed a more detailed list of admission criteria which, in the end, did not appear in the final report. The French list included the following: (a) an index of economic development (in terms of GDP/capita), (b) an index of market economy (in terms of privately held assets), (c) a quantifiable level of social protection, (d) control over public debt and inflation, (g) open economy, (h) modern fiscal system, and (i) administrative capacity to implement EU law.

[23] L Pech 'The Rule of Law', at 108.

principle deprived of normative nature, had an influence in the political discourse of some nationalist Central and Eastern European political parties. As such, it became a suitable argument to be spent while contrasting the assertion of the rule of law as a normative principle.[24]

Spending the rule of law notion as a conditionality did not solicit contentions so long as this happened outside the borders of the EU, even if, at first sight, when tracing the deployment of the rule of law as a key concept in the conditionality procedures laid down by the EU in many of its international agreements, we do not get a clear indication of its normative value. The first conditionality mechanisms adopted by the EU were introduced in the late 1990s, with the IV Lomé Convention.[25] Like other international documents, or national acts with external value,[26] Article 5 of the Convention considered the respect of human rights and rule of law as a fundamental element of its implementation.[27]

The EU has broadly designed conditionality mechanisms similar to the ones included in the IV Lomé Convention: that was the case, before accession, for the Baltic States and Bulgarian trade agreements, the Cotonou and ACP economic partnership agreements signed in 2000, the cooperation agreements with Pakistan, Tajikistan, Chile, Vietnam, Indonesia, Syria, Israel, Albania, Serbia, Bosnia and Herzegovina, Lebanon, Ukraine, Colombia, Japan, and more. The 'rights for trade' scheme supported the respect of democracy, human rights, and the rule of law. However, Council has activated the mechanism only rarely, as a reaction to undemocratic regime changes or human rights violations. Political difficulties in reaching an agreement within the Council led most times to prefer other measures, like the targeted sanctions.

The practice of applying measures foreseen by these conditionality mechanisms somehow confirmed the vague nature of the rule of law notion, a kind of semi-political formula, coherent with the language used by analogous international documents containing conditionalities. A formula that, when it appeared on the scene of the EU recovery funds' contention between the Commission and

[24] The same *Report on the Rule of Law*, published yearly by the Commission since the 2020 'to moni tor significant developments relating to the rule of law in all Member States', in fact, points to the rule of law as a notion in progress, needing 'continuous assessments to refer to EU law requirements, including those resulting from the case-law of the CJEU 'and, quite remarkably, '… the recommendations and opinions of the Council of Europe'. commission.europa.eu/strategy-and-policy/policies/justice-and-fundamental-rights/upholding-rule-law/rule-law/rule-law-mechanism/2022-rule-law-report_en.

[25] https://op.europa.eu/en/publication-detail/-/publication/75c76a39-a551-4908-8289-da2051b1efc2.

[26] For example, the *African Growth and Opportunity Act*, a US Congress Act signed in 2000 by President Clinton, aiming to introduce respect for the rule of law and fundamental human rights as a pre-condition to ease international trade between the US and several Sub-Saharan African States: agoa.info.

[27] As it is known, the conditionality mechanism can be applied in a positive or negative perspective: while the first involves promising benefits (such as grants, privileged loans, technical supports) when the recipient countries meet the conditions, the second determines the and suspension and\or withdrawal of the agreement if the signing countries do not.

two Member States, was burdened by a long-lasting political peruse: occasionally dressed as an ancillary formula, to reiterate the mantra 'respect of multiparty democracy and human rights', or at its best, as a norm full of values, with no bite.[28]

The rule of law has been often referred to as an 'essentially contested concept',[29] and the current dispute on its impact could be filed as another case in the kaleidoscopic global story of the rule of law notion. Addressing the historical reasons of a conceptual relativism spent by some national legal scholars in support of a pretension of superiority of local law over EU law, however, is essential, particularly if we consider 'the increasingly open conceptual challenge originating from authorities subject to special EU procedures on account of the systemic threat to the rule of law their repeated actions have caused'.[30]

3. The Rule of Law in the EU: Metamorphosis of a Vague Standard

Against this background, attention can now be paid to the recent EU attempts at circumventing the impasse affecting the enforcement of Article 7 TEU,[31] by linking the disbursement of EU budget funds to the respect for the rule of law in the Member States.

[28] Quite impudently, one of Poland's former Minister of Foreign Affairs promised 'a box of Belgian chocolates for anyone who finds the definition of the rule of law in the Treaty or any other legally binding EU document', quoted by L Pech 'The Rule of Law', at fn. 5.

[29] A point first made by Gallie in 1956: WB Gallie 'Fundamentally Contested Principles', (1955–1956) 56 *Proceedings of the Aristotelian Society-New Series* 167.

[30] L Pech 'The Rule of Law', at 108.

[31] An interesting comparison can be made between Arts 1–8 of the Charter of the EBRD, quoted above, n 15, and Arts 2 and 7 of the EU Treaty.

Art 2 TEU recites:

> The Union is founded on the values of respect for human dignity, freedom, democracy, equality, the rule of law and respect for human rights, including the rights of persons belonging to minorities. These values are common to the Member States in a society in which pluralism, non-discrimination, tolerance, justice, solidarity and equality between women and men prevail.

Art 7 TEU recites:

> 1. On a reasoned proposal by one third of the Member States, by the European Parliament or by the European Commission, the Council, acting by a majority of four fifths of its members after obtaining the consent of the European Parliament, may determine that there is a clear risk of a serious breach by a Member State of the values referred to in Article 2. Before making such a determination, the Council shall hear the Member State in question and may address recommendations to it, acting in accordance with the same procedure.
>   The Council shall regularly verify that the grounds on which such a determination was made continue to apply.
> 2. The European Council, acting by unanimity on a proposal by one third of the Member States or by the Commission and after obtaining the consent of the European Parliament, may determine the existence of a serious and persistent breach by a Member State of the values referred to in Article 2, after inviting the Member State in question to submit its observations.

The story that is told describes the attempt to change the appearance of the rule of law notion, converting it from a wide-ranging rule, a kind of depository of most principles of good governance, into a real rule, with a strong normative capacity. A conversion that someone has portrayed as the move from a thin, towards a thick concept of the rule of law.[32]

This conversion, however, had a price: after the many steps taken by the Commission and a difficult dialogue with the Council,[33] the final normative outcome is a Regulation (2020/2092),[34] allowing the EU to cut funds awarded to Member States in case of an established violation of the rule of law by those States, if the said violations endanger the EU budget. By setting a link with the EU budget, the Regulation has a limited scope: it is not expected to be able per se to enforce the observance of the rule of law by Member States. The same title of the normative document (*Regulation [...] on a general regime of conditionality for the protection of the Union budget*) different from the first proposal of the Commission, made clear that the new text was not to be seen as a 'general rule of law oversight tool, following the amendments pushed by the Council, but a true budgetary instrument'.[35]

What has been defined as 'Democratic backsliding' in Hungary and Poland has become a major concern for European Union institutions since the 2010s.[36]

3. Where a determination under paragraph 2 has been made, the Council, acting by a qualified majority, may decide to suspend certain of the rights deriving from the application of the Treaties to the Member State in question, including the voting rights of the representative of the government of that Member State in the Council. In doing so, the Council shall take into account the possible consequences of such a suspension on the rights and obligations of natural and legal persons.

   The obligations of the Member State in question under the Treaties shall in any case continue to be binding on that State.
4. The Council, acting by a qualified majority, may decide subsequently to vary or revoke measures taken under paragraph 3 in response to changes in the situation which led to their being imposed.
5. The voting arrangements applying to the European Parliament, the European Council and the Council for the purposes of this Article are laid down in Article 354 of the Treaty on the Functioning of the European Union.

[32] R Coman, *The Politics of the Rule of Law in the EU Polity* (London, Palgrave, 2022) 45.

[33] The idea of creating a new instrument, allowing for the holdup of EU funds in case of rule of law defect in a Member State, has been on the agenda for several years, and was, from the very beginning, a debated one. Germany and Italy were among the first Member States to explicitly mention the idea of linking EU funds with respect for the rule of law in their position papers on the future of cohesion policy and the Multiannual Financial Framework. In May 2017, the President of the Commission Jean-Claude Juncker, when asked to comment on the German government's proposal, stunned some observers with his initial opposition to it, calling the proposal 'a threat to the unity of the EU, poison for the continent'; see: F Eder, 'Juncker: German Plan to Link Funds and Rules Would Be 'Poison'', *Politico* (June 2017), www. politico.eu/article/juncker-german-plan-to-link-funds-and-rules-would-be-poison/

A detailed reconstruction of the tense confrontation between the Commission, the Council, and the Parliament on the matter in: A Baraggia and M Bonelli, 'Linking Money to Values: the new Rule of Law Conditionality Regulation and its constitutional challenges' (2022) 23 *German Law Journal* 131.

[34] eur-lex.europa.eu/legal-content/EN/TXT/PDF/?uri=CELEX:32020R2092&from=EN.

[35] A Baraggia and M Bonelli, 'Linking Money', at 140.

[36] To explain the ongoing illiberal backlash, Ivan Krastev and Stephen Holmes have suggested that the distinction between imitation and borrowing is of crucial importance while considering the effects

It has been widely affirmed that, while facing the first phase of the 'rule of law conflict', the EU institutions showed an inability to take action against Member States not complying with rule of law principles.[37] In fact, the crisis already arose after the 2012 national elections in Hungary. Subsequently, political power became concentrated in the hands of the right-wing Fidesz Party. A two-thirds majority sustained the ruling party in carrying out constitutional reforms aimed to destabilise the system of checks and balances in favour of the executive, including the reduction of the Constitutional Court's independence.

Instead of opening a procedure based on Article 7 TEU, the Commission chose to launch various infringement procedures under Article 258 for specific breaches of EU law.[38]

While it is true that the Commission opted, at first, to focus on bits of the problem, such as the reduction in the retirement age, instead of targeting the broader issue, namely, independence of the judiciary vis à vis the government, one should also consider that, while taking a minimal path to confrontation, the Commission meant to bypass the political impasse determined by the inaction of the Council. At the same time, an infringement procedure based on Article 258 TEU had more chance to find proper judicial enforcement, as it seemed to be more firmly rooted into a certain

of emulation. Imitation is the demand to replicate the same goals that others have. This would, they contend, have much more profound effects on collective identity than simple borrowing, which implies only the adoption of certain means, without changing goals. Borrowing may be an adaptive strategy to reinforce one's ability to resist foreign influence or pressure, without conceding much beyond the form of what is borrowed, while the drive to imitate would result in a 'loss of identity and self-esteem'. While being democratised, these countries had to enact policies and laws elaborated in Brussels, while pretending to exercise self-government. For a time, imitation was justified as 'a return to Europe' and thus, in a sense, a return to their authentic identity. Still, at some point, the suspicion grew that that the original was better than the copy, while an idealised model of the West was held up to them. When the prosperity of the West suffered the blow of the financial crisis of 2008 all of this began to unravel. The universalism of human rights and open border liberalism could, thus, be blamed as an expression of the West's indifference towards national cultures and heritage. See I Krastev and S Holmes, *The Light that Failed: A Reckoning* (New York, Pegasus, 2020).

[37] See: https://www.europarl.europa.eu/factsheets/en/sheet/146/the-protection-of-article-2-teu-values-in-the-eu, eg, K Scheppele, L Pech and S Platon, 'Compromising the Rule of Law while Compromising on the Rule of Law' *Verfblog* (2020), verfassungsblog.de/compromising-the-rule-of-law-while-compromising-on-therule-of-law/.

As is known, the Commission, precipitated by the Hungarian crisis, issued, in July 2019, a Communication based on a previous (2014) 'Framework to strengthen the Rule of Law within the Member States'. The Rule of Law Framework complemented the already existing and more general legal background, to enforce the rule of law compliance by the Member States. The Council, however, did not support the Commission's initiative. Moreover, the Council focused on questioning the Commission's legal power to adopt the Rule of Law Framework. In turn, it created its own action, named 'Rule of Law Dialogue'. This led the European Parliament to make public the opinion that 'too many mechanisms and processes at EU level to govern the values of Article 2 TEU'.

[38] The Commission launched an infringement procedure against the measure of the Hungarian government to lower the retirement age of judges, prosecutors, and notaries from the age of 70 to 62 years. The Commission argued in this case that this measure constituted an unjustified discrimination based on age which is contrary to the Equality Directive 2000/78. The Court of Justice of the European Union followed the reasoning of the Commission and proclaimed that lowering the retirement age established a prohibited difference in treatment directly based on age. Consequently, the Hungarian government failed to fulfil its obligations under Directive 2000/78.

legal principle. Later events[39] had to confirm this point of view: in December 2017, the Commission decided to start suspension proceedings against Poland. Less than a year later, in September 2018, the European Parliament opened the case against Hungary.[40] The actions, however, stalled;[41] to overcome the impasse, the Commission proposed in May 2018 to link disbursements from the European Union's budget to observance of rule of law standards by means of a Regulation.[42] Following the process, the European Parliament adopted a 'Position on the Commission's proposal' in April 2019, but the Council renewed the impasse, taking no action.

It became evident that the recourse to the 'infraction of rule of law principle' arguments was not solid enough, from the legal point of view, to overcome political resistances within the Council. Considering the many mentions to the rule of law contained in the primary and second level law, as well as in the abundant soft law documents adopted by the Commission over the years, one could maintain that the main issue has never been the absence of a definition of the rule of law, rather the multiplication of references and adoption of documents emphasising different components of the rule of law. Once again, the vague nature of the rule of law concept was weakening the might of the principle.[43]

A new political scenario was determined by the adoption of the Next Generation EU recovery package in the summer of 2020.[44] Facing the uniqueness and the financial dimension[45] of the instrument, the heads of state and government

[39] In 2017 an EU Commission document concerning the reform of EU budget already had stated that:

> Upholding EU core values when developing and implementing EU policies is key. There have been new suggestions in the public debate to link the disbursement of EU budget funds to the state of the rule of law in Member States. Respect for the rule of law is important for European citizens, but also for business initiatives, innovation and investment, which will flourish most where the legal and institutional framework adheres fully to the common values of the Union. There is hence a clear relationship between the rule of law and an efficient implementation of the private and public investments supported by the EU budget.

As from the quote, the vision endorsed by the EU Commission on the nature of the rule of law clause was still indebted with the narrative made evident in this essay under para 2: a robust proxy for a constitutional pattern based on the political status quo of the EU (European Commission, Reflection paper on the future of EU finance, 28 June 2017, p. 22, https://op.europa.eu/en/publication-detail/-/publication/5f9c0e27-6519-11e7-b2f2-01aa75ed71a1).

[40] European Parliament resolution of 12 September 2018 on a 'Proposal calling on the Council to determine, pursuant to Article 7(1) of the Treaty on European Union, the existence of a clear risk of a serious breach by Hungary of the values on which the Union is founded', www.europarl.europa.eu/doceo/document/TA-8-2018-0340_EN.html.

[41] N Kirst 'Rule of Law Conditionality: The Long-awaited Step Towards a Solution of the Rule of Law Crisis in the European Union?' (2021) 6 *European Papers* 101.

[42] And, in fact, the proposed Regulation was explicitly labeled as: 'Proposal for a Regulation of the European Parliament and of the Council on the protection of the Union's budget in case of generalised deficiencies as regards the rule of law in the Member States'. eur-lex.europa.eu/legal-content/EN/TXT/?uri=CELEX:52018PC0324.

[43] See L Pech 'The EU as a Global Rule of Law Promoter: The Consistency and Effectiveness Challenges' (2016) 14(1) *Asia Europe Journal* 7.

[44] commission.europa.eu/strategy-and-policy/recovery-plan-europe_en.

[45] The total amount of the NGEU recovery program amounts to EUR 750 billion, which is 5.5% of the EU27's GDP in 2019, seemingly to be the largest investment recovery fund in Europe since the Marshall Plan.

of the EU Member States finally agreed, at the July 2020 European Council summit, that the payment of funds should be tied to a conditionality regime regarding the rule of law.[46] The Regulation provides for the Commission to propose measures against a Member State 'breaching the principles of the rule of law' (Article 6). These measures include the suspension of payments or commitments, and a prohibition on entering new legal commitments.[47] According to the Regulation (Article 2), the rule of law is understood to refer to the values enshrined in Article 2 of the Treaty on European Union, and include:

> the principles of legality implying a transparent, accountable, democratic and pluralistic law-making process; legal certainty; prohibition of arbitrariness of the executive powers; effective judicial protection, including access to justice, by independent and impartial courts, also as regards fundamental rights; separation of powers; and non-discrimination and equality before the law.

However, Article 4 of the Regulation indicates that measures may only be taken if the violations of the rule of law: 'affect or seriously risk affecting the sound financial management of the Union budget or the protection of the financial interests of the Union in a sufficiently direct way'. At this point, the rule of law controversy moved from the 'pure rule of law' context to the practicalities of securing expenditures from the EU budget. The logic was that 'breaches of the principles of the rule of law, in particular those that affect the proper functioning of public authorities and effective judicial review, can seriously harm the financial interests of the Union'. To ensure the respect for rule of law, the Regulation provides, then, for several ways in which funding can be withheld or suspended in case of breach of fundamental rule of law principles, ranging from suspension of commitments to interruption or suspension of payments (Article 5).

Facing the radical metamorphosis of the rule of law principle into a binding norm, vested with (limited) coercivity, both Hungary and Poland challenged the Regulation before the Court of Justice of the European Union (EUCJ), seeking its invalidation on the ground that 'the rule of law would neither be defined in EU law, nor could it be defined in EU law'[48] and, consequently, that there is no binding and enforceable principle of the rule of law in EU law.

[46] Germany, holding the presidency of the Council, suggested a compromise on the Rule of Law Conditionality Regulation proposed by the Commission and European Parliament in September 2020. At the European Council summit of 10 December 2020, the impasse was resolved by adopting a series of declarations on how the Rule of Law Conditionality Regulation should be adopted, implemented, and interpreted. This led to the adoption of the Regulation by the Council on 14 December 2020 and by the European Parliament on 16 December 2020.

[47] Regulation (EU, Euratom) 2020/2092 of the European Parliament and of the Council of 16 December 2020 on a general regime of conditionality for the protection of the Union budget. eur-lex.europa.eu/legal-content/EN/ALL/?uri=CELEX%3A32020R2092.

[48] See ground (iii) of Hungary's annulment application in Case C-156/21, *Hungary v European Parliament and Council* and ground (vi) of Poland's annulment application in Case C-157/21, *Poland v European Parliament and Council*.

The Court, finally, discharged both countries' complaints and ruled the Regulation to be entirely compatible with the EU Treaty and not exceeding competences of the Union.

To better precise the budget-related conditionalities, however, the Court added that any suspension of funds must not only relate to the EU law violations but also must have 'a tangible effect on endangering the correct implementation of the EU budget'.

4. Conclusions

Like most international organisations worldwide, the European Union has included 'respect for the rule of law principle' within its essential ideals. The principle was already incorporated within the text of the 1992 Maastricht Treaty,[49] and then recognised as a fundamental value with the adoption of the Treaty on European Union (2007).

This was consistent with a global trend, whereby the rule of law has become, since the early 1990s, a major standard in conditioning adhesion of States to international communities (such as the Council of Europe, the WTO), as well as for providing conditionalities on financial aids and loans by international financial institutions.

Threatening the rule of law as a vague principle, ambiguous in nature, half normative and half political, and deprived of a precise content, as both Hungary and Poland claimed the case to be[50] when challenging the 2020/2092 Regulation before the EUCJ, was not a new issue.[51]

Peculiar in the case was the (belated) intention of the EU Commission to give normative strength and judicial enforceability to the principle, insisting on its violation as a sufficient ground for triggering sanctions provided by the TEU. Peculiar, because, on a global scale, allegations of bad implementation or violations

[49] Preamble recites: 'Confirming their attachment to the principles of liberty, democracy and respect for human rights and fundamental freedoms and of the rule of law'; a couple of mentions to the rule of law also under Art 130u (Development cooperation), and J.1 (Common foreign and security policy).

[50] Following one of the many claims set by both Poland and Hungary before the EUCJ, the concept of 'the rule of law', as it is defined in Art 2(a) of the contested Regulation, would be critical with respect to legal certainty: it could not be embraced by a universal definition *since it contains a non-exhaustive number of principles whose meaning may differ from one State to another, depending on the constitutional features or legal traditions specific to the State in question*. curia.europa.eu/juris/document/document.jsf?docid=254062&mode=req&pageIndex=1&dir=&occ=first&part=1&text=&doclang=EN&cid=961 in particular, sub 312.

[51] The PR of China is one of the more captivating cases: the rule of law principle, recognized since 1999 by the PRC Constitution (Art 5) as a pre-condition to enter the WTO, differs from rule of law as internationally understood. To mention just one example, all aspirant Chinese lawyers, according to the study material for the bar exam preparation course, must commit to the belief that law is subject to the 'leadership of the Party'.

of the rule of law principle usually led to procedures managed at the level of political relations.[52]

The 'functional method'[53] that has characterised key-moments in the evolution of EU law seems to have prevailed also in the case of contested implementation of the rule of law principle. Evidence of this is the emphasis put by the EUCJ on the fact that 'rule of law violations, like failure to maintain an independent judiciary' could be touched by the Regulation only if they directly affect the 'sound financial management' of EU funds. It follows, then, that the withholding of funds under the 2020/2092 Regulation cannot be used as a sanction for rule of law violations, but only as an instrument to keep EU funds safe from possible mismanagement. At the same time, the Court ruled that the values on which the EU is established, as listed under Article 2 of the Treaty, may be implemented in many ways, and not just by reference to Article 7;[54] as judges in Luxembourg have highlighted, judicial independence may be enforced directly through TEU Articles 47, and 19.1. While inferring that the Commission could design more regulations, centred on different aspects of the rule of law, by grounding them in other sections of the Treaties, the Court practically has proposed to overcome the vagueness of the rule of law principle, and offered an alternative, rooted on more specific, and less vague, provisions of the Treaty. At the same time, it has definitively rejected further possible claims on the rule of law principle as being merely political in nature.

It is now for the scholarly debate to further expand recognition of the rule of law principle as a normative value, common to the constitutional traditions of the EU Member States, and, what is more relevant, to emancipate it from the encumbering legacy of 'imperative imitation'[55] that has characterised, in the practice of most international financial institutions, an enslavement of the rule of law to contingent needs.

[52] EU Petersmann, 'Rule of law in international trade and investments? Between multilevel arbitration, adjudication and 'judicial overreach'', *EUI Papers* (Florence, EUI, 2020); G Marceau (ed), *A History of Law and Lawyers in The Gatt/Wto. The Development of the Rule of Law in the Multilateral Trading System* (Cambridge, Cambridge UP, 2015).

[53] By 'functionalism' I signify the instrumentality of the law for a successful economic performance, a choice that has become dominant paradigm in the practice of legal reforms, being useful to justify and legitimise the process of transfer of standards from economically mature systems to systems in transition. This led to a resumption of certain discourses already conducted in the 1960s, at the time of decolonisation and of supply, to new independent states of Africa and Asia, of legal patterns aimed to favour a 'good functioning' of societies and States. In more recent times, however, the emphasis has been on a more global pervasiveness, based on the idea of 'efficient markets', of abstract legal models, offered under the anthem of the rule of law, transparency, and good governance.

[54] curia.europa.eu/juris/document/document.jsf?docid=254062&mode=req&pageIndex=1&dir=&occ=first&part=1&text=&doclang=EN&cid=961 in particular, sub 197–200.

[55] The 'Imitation imperative' is described by Stephen Holmes and Ivan Krastev as 'a feature of liberalism's hegemony after 1989', involving 'first, the acknowledged moral superiority of the imitated over their imitators, second a political model that claims to have eliminated all viable alternatives, third, an expectation that the imitation will be unconditional rather than adapted to local conditions and, fourth, a presumption that representatives of the imitated countries could legitimately claim a right to monitor and evaluate the progress of imitating countries on an ongoing basis'; I Krastev and S Holmes, *The Light*, at 8.

3

(Un)defining the Right to Property in the Light of the Case Law of the European Court of Human Rights

SABRINA PRADUROUX

1. Introduction

World War II brought about the destruction and disrespect of property. Totalitarian regimes that came into power before the war were the perpetrators of flagrant and merciless violations of property rights affecting large groups of people.[1] It is therefore not surprising that the right of property found a place in the Universal Declaration of Human Rights (UDHR),[2] adopted to reaffirm the dignity and worth of the human person as a response to the 'barbarous acts which have outraged the conscience of mankind'.[3]

Still, the inclusion of the protection of property in the European Convention for the Protection of Human Rights and Fundamental Freedoms (hereafter, ECHR), which was meant be 'the first steps for the collective enforcement of certain of the rights stated in the Universal Declaration',[4] has proven to be more difficult.

[1] Two of the best-known examples are the transfer of Jewish-owned businesses and property to non-Jews as part of the so called 'Aryanisation' process in Nazi Germany, and the forceful seizure of the farmers' lands together with the confiscation of all the grain that led to the *Holodomor* in the Ukrainian region under Stalin's dictatorship.

[2] See, Art 17. It is worth noting that 50 of the 58 States that adopted the Declaration already had a specific provision guaranteeing the right to property in the text of their Constitutions, and among the States that declared the absence of such a provision were States that, like the United Kingdom, Canada, and Australia, did not have a written Constitution, but nevertheless had a constitutional tradition that recognised the right to property. See the drafting Committee's report, available at: documents-dds-ny.un.org/doc/UNDOC/GEN/NG9/000/26/PDF/NG900026.pdf?OpenElement, 168 ff.

[3] See, the Preamble of the Declaration.

[4] See, the Preamble of the Convention.

The preparatory works echoed the fierce political debate about the appropriate limitations of private property rights against the backdrop of a Europe divided by the iron curtain.[5]

The text on which the drafters finally agreed, and that became Article 1 of the Protocol to the ECHR (Article P1-1), defines the scope of property protection using a loose terminology, and thus leaves much room for interpretation. Indeed, despite being headed "Protection of Property", Article P1-1 recognises to every natural and legal person the right to the peaceful enjoyment of his or her possessions.

The three sentences that make up the text of Article P1-1 have been interpreted by the European Court of Human Rights (ECtHR) as:

> three distinct rules. The first rule, which is of a general nature, enounces the principle of peaceful enjoyment of property; it is set out in the first sentence of the first paragraph. The second rule covers deprivation of possessions and subjects it to certain conditions; it appears in the second sentence of the same paragraph. The third rule recognises that the States are entitled, amongst other things, to control the use of property in accordance with the general interest, by enforcing such laws as they deem necessary for the purpose; it is contained in the second paragraph.[6]

The Protocol to the ECHR, commonly referred to as Protocol No 1, was signed in 1952 by the – at that time 14 – Member States of the Council of Europe (CoE) and entered into force two years later, following the ratification by 10 of them. Today it is in force in 44 out of the 46 Members of the CoE,[7] as Monaco and Switzerland have signed the Protocol but never ratified it.[8]

Over the years, ECtHR has developed a rich case law on Article P1-1,[9] which it is not possible here to discuss in its entirety.

This chapter offers an overview of the scope of both the Article and the judicial control exercised by the ECtHR, discussing some of the most critical aspects of the Court's work.

[5] For insights of the debate concerning the inclusion of property protection in the text of the Convention, see, AWB Simpson, *Human Rights and the End of Empire: Britain and the Genesis of the European Convention* (Oxford, Oxford University Press, 2001) especially ch 15.

[6] App no 7151/75 and 7152/75, *Sporrong and Lönnroth v Sweden* (1982) ECtHR para 61.

[7] It is worth mentioning that the CoE reached 47 Members, as the Russian Federation was a Member of the CoE from February 1996 to March 2022, and it ratified both the ECHR and Protocol No 1 in 1998. The ECtHR had jurisdiction to deal with applications directed against the Russian Federation occurred until 16 September 2022.

[8] See Chart of signatures and ratifications of Treaty 009, available at www.coe.int/en/web/conventions/full-list?module=signatures-by-treaty&treatynum=009.

[9] Browsing the ECtHR's database by article, there are more than 12,000 cases where Article P1-1 is invoked, and in more than 3,700 cases the court has found a violation of it. See, statistics on violations by article and by State, available at: echr.coe.int/Documents/Stats_violation_1959_2021_ENG.pdf.

2. The Scope of Article P1-1: How Far the Notion of 'Possessions' Can Reach Out?

In the first commentary on the case law related to Article P1-1 published by the Council of Europe in 1990, Professor Laurent Sermet tackles the essential question of the scope of the Article at issue acknowledging that: 'In order to define property, "the protected possessions" must first be considered in isolation. … The justification for considering possessions in isolation is that they exist as an autonomous concept.'[10] The author went on to observe that the ECtHR departed from the meaning given to the term 'possession' in international law, where it equates with 'vested right', to include movable and immovable property (i.e. rights *in rem*), rights *in personam* and intangible property.

The explanation of the – by then – scant case law that follows shows that shares, claims, rights arising from social policies, goodwill, and economic interests related to the carrying on of a business for which a licence or authorisation is required, might all constitute possessions.[11]

Over the years, the list of possessions that fall under the scope of application of Article P1-1 has lengthened to include all kind of economic interests, such as those attached to shares, to intellectual property rights, to the right to use a registered internet domain names, and so forth.[12] Even more, the Article is interpreted by the ECtHR in such a way as to grant protection not only to established legal position under domestic law, but also to reasonable and legitimate expectations of obtaining effective enjoyment of a property right.[13]

Several authors have attempted to build a clear and precise taxonomy of possessions based on the now-rich ECtHR case law; however, their efforts cannot but be frustrated by the case-by-case approach adopted by the Court, which makes the existence of a possession dependent on the circumstances.[14]

[10] L Sermet, *The European Convention on Human Rights and Property Rights* (Strasbourg, Council of Europe, 1990) 4. The work was reprinted two years later in the Human Rights Files series.

[11] It may here be remarked that from its establishment in 1959 to 1990, the Court delivered just over 100 judgments dealing with Article P1-1. To these, however, must be added the decisions adopted by the no longer existing European Commission on Human Rights.

[12] See, Guide on Article P1-1 drafted by the Registry of the ECtHR, available at: echr.coe.int/Documents/Guide_Art_1_Protocol_1_ENG.pdf.

[13] According to a well-established case law 'the concept of "possessions" is indeed not limited to "existing possessions" but may also cover assets, including claims, in respect of which the applicant can argue that he or she has at least a reasonable and legitimate expectation of obtaining the effective enjoyment of a property right … An "expectation" is "legitimate" if there is sufficient basis for that interest in national law – for example if it is based on either a legislative provision or a legal act bearing on the property interest in question … or where there is settled case-law of the domestic courts confirming it.' See, App no 77504/13, *Radio Athina Monoprosopi Etairia Periorismenis Efthynis v Greece*, (2022) ECHR, para 59.

[14] According to a formula recurrently used by the Court, indeed, 'the concept of "possessions" referred to in the first part of Article 1 of Protocol No. 1 to the Convention has an autonomous meaning which

In line with this flexible approach to the interpretation of the notion of possessions, the ECtHR never engaged in defining it.[15] This does not mean, however, that anything and everything can become a possession within the meaning of Article P1-1. In the *Parrillo* case,[16] indeed, the Court ruled out that human embryos could be regarded as possessions and pointed out that Article P1-1 has an economic and pecuniary scope.

It can, therefore, be stated that as a rule the notion of possessions as understood by the ECtHR equates with economic values or interests.

More or less exhaustive lists of protected possessions within the ECtHR case law can be found in the various commentaries and works on Article P1-1; but, lacking, as said, any definition of the term itself, and since a given economic value or interest may, or may not, be considered as a possession depending on the specific circumstances of each individual case, it would be impossible to draft the definitive list of what amounts to a protected possession.

Finally, it is worth noting that, notwithstanding the economic nature of the right protected under Article P1-1, its scope, as stressed by Pasquale De Sena, 'has evolved not only in relation to the protection of *purely economic* interests, but also in close relation to the protection of *other interests* … Furthermore, the notion of 'property' has been extended due to the need to protect interests of *great social* importance' (author's emphasis).[17]

Non-economic values associated with the public interest, together with the rule of law principle, play an important role in shaping the case law on Article P1-1.[18] In particular, they are given consideration in the second stage of

is not limited to ownership of physical goods and is independent from the formal classification in domestic law. The issue that needs to be examined in each case is whether the *circumstances of the case, considered as a whole*, conferred on the applicant title to a substantive interest protected by Article 1 of Protocol No. 1.' See, *ex multis*, App no 49969/14, *Pintar et al v Slovenia* (2021) ECtHR, para 90 (author's emphasis).

[15] The Court merely stated what its scope is not, affirming that the concept of 'possession', by virtue of its autonomous meaning, 'is not limited to ownership of material goods and is independent from the formal classification in domestic law: certain other rights and interests constituting assets can also be regarded as "property rights", and thus as "possessions" for the purposes of this provision.' *Ex multis*, App no 53080/13, *Béláné Nagy v Hungary*, (2016) ECHR [G.C.], para 73.

[16] App no 46470/11, *Parrillo v Italy* (2015] ECHR [G.C.), para 215.

[17] P De Sena, 'Economic and Non-Economic Values in the Case Law of the European Court of Human Rights', in PM Dupuy, EU Petersmann and F Francioni (eds), *Human Rights in International Investment Law and Arbitration* (Oxford, Oxford University Press, 2010) 210. Likewise, L Mardikian, 'In-Between an Economic Freedom and a Human Right: A Hybrid Right to Private Property' (2021) 81 *Zeitschrift für ausländisches öffentliches Recht und Völkerrecht / Heidelberg Journal of International Law* 341, 346, maintains that: 'the ECtHR has advanced a conceptualisation of property which incorporates its distinct, but highly interconnected, economic and non-economic aspects.'

[18] For my thoughts on the extent to which EctHR's judicial review is value oriented and which values prevail in adjudicating property cases, see S Praduroux, *The Protection of Property Rights in Comparative Perspective. A Study on the Interaction between European Human Rights Law and Italian and French Property Law* (Groningen, Europa Law Publishing, 2013), ch 6. As a conclusion of my study, I suggest that, although the ECtHR has never expressly clarified the core values and purpose of Art P1-1, it serves mainly as 'a guarantee for the rights of individuals over assets through respect for legal certainty and fairness in respect of property entitlements.' See ibid 252.

judicial review, when the ECtHR assesses the proportionality of States' interference with protected possessions under the fair balance test.

3. Extending the Scope of Article P1-1 Through the Positive Obligations Doctrine[19]

Article P1-1 can be considered as guaranteeing the last of the so-called negative rights, because it places, first and foremost, a negative duty on the States to refrain from interfering with one's peaceful enjoyment of his possessions.

Accordingly, Article P1-1 cannot be used, for instance, to found a viable claim against the State to acquire property,[20] nor can it be interpreted as guaranteeing to every individual access to the minimum of property needed for living a life in dignity.[21]

The ECtHR nevertheless acknowledges that a violation of Article P1-1 can originate from a failure to act of the State. Indeed it has repeatedly held that:

> the genuine, effective exercise of the right protected by Article 1 of Protocol No. 1 did not depend merely on the State's duty not to interfere, but might require *positive measures of protection*, particularly where there was a direct link between the measures an applicant might legitimately expect from the authorities and his effective enjoyment of

[19] Within ECHR law, the positive obligations doctrine is grounded in Art 1, which provides that each Contracting Party shall secure to everyone within its jurisdiction the rights and freedoms proclaimed in the Convention. As remarked by M Beijer, *The Limits of Fundamental Rights Protection by the EU. The Scope for the Development of Positive Obligations* (Cambridge, Intersentia, 2017) 70, '[b]y imposing positive obligations on states parties, the ECtHR has expanded the responsibility of states for violations of fundamental rights, as this goes beyond responsibility for interferences caused directly by its agents, and even includes responsibility for violations caused by private parties or breaches caused by the particular vulnerabilities of individuals. The Court has not set out clearly how and to exactly what extent obligations to prevent violations can be imposed on the states parties. The main rationale for the recognition of positive obligations seems to be that states have an obligation to ensure effective protection of the Convention rights.' On positive obligations in general, see also, A Mowbray, *The Development of Positive Obligations under the European Convention on Human Rights by the European Court of Human Rights* (Oxford, Hart Publishing, 2004); D Xenos, *The Positive Obligations of the State Under the European Convention of Human Rights* (Abingdon, Routledge, 2012); L Lavrysen, *Human Rights in a Positive State. Rethinking the Relationship between Positive and Negative Obligations under the European Convention on Human Rights* (Cambridge, Intersentia, 2016).

[20] It is a well-established principle in the ECtHR case law that Art P1-1 'does not guarantee the right to acquire property'. *Ex multis*, App No 44912/98, *Kopecký v Slovakia*, (2004) ECHR [G.C.], para 35.

[21] That being said, I Leijten, 'The right to minimum subsistence and property protection under the ECHR: Never the twain shall meet?' (2019) 21 *European Journal of Social Security* 307, analysing the ECtHR social security case law shows that a subsistence minimum is a relevant factor both in the interpretation of the notion of possessions and in determining whether a public authority's interference with a social security benefit complies with the fair balance requirement. However, according to the author, even though there is a clear trend towards protecting claimants' means of subsistence, 'this is unlikely to result in the recognition of a self-standing right to minimum subsistence', and the ECtHR, so far, has not affirmed that States have a positive obligation to provide for it. See ibid 320.

> his possessions. Even in horizontal relations there might be public interest considerations involved, which may impose some obligations on the State (author's emphasis).[22]

Therefore, by means of the positive obligations doctrine the ECtHR has extended the scope of Article P1-1 far beyond its text making it a viable ground to claim the State's liability for interference with the peaceful enjoyment of possessions resulting from transactions between private individuals[23] and developing procedural obligations,[24] which include the obligation to provide both for adequate remedial actions[25] and for an effective system granting the enforcement of final judgments without undue delay.[26]

Furthermore, in its case law, the Court made reference also to some substantive obligation. Thus, for instance, in the *Budayeva* case, the ECtHR stated the 'positive obligation on the State to protect private property from natural disasters', making however clear that such an obligation 'cannot be construed as binding the State to compensate the full market value of destroyed property'.[27] Moreover, the State can be held liable only if and to the extent that, a causal link between its failure to take suitable measures to protect property and the material damage occurred is well-established. This is to say that Article P1-1 'does not go as far as requiring States to take preventive measures to protect private possessions in all situations and all areas prone to flooding or other natural disasters'.[28]

[22] App no 54522/00, *Kotov v Russia*, (2012) ECHR [G.C.], para 109.

[23] It is worth mentioning that a private act cannot be brought before the ECtHR as such, meaning that all alleged interference with a Convention right originated from private acts shall ultimately be attributable to the exercise of governmental authority, the judicial one first and foremost. Indeed, the Court has expressly stated that: 'it cannot remain passive where a national court's interpretation of a legal act, be it a testamentary disposition, a private contract, a public document, a statutory provision or an administrative practice appears unreasonable, arbitrary or blatantly inconsistent with the prohibition of discrimination established by Article 14 and more broadly with the principles underlying the Convention.' See, App no 16574/08, *Fabris v France*, (2013) ECHR [G.C.], para 60.

[24] In general terms, the Court has consistently held that: '[a]lthough Article 1 of Protocol No. 1 contains no explicit procedural requirements, the existence of procedural positive obligations under this provision was recognised by the Court both in cases involving State authorities … and in cases between private parties only … Thus, in a case belonging to the latter category the Court held that States were under an obligation to afford judicial procedures that offered the necessary procedural guarantees and therefore enabled the domestic courts and tribunals to adjudicate effectively and fairly any disputes between private persons.' See, App no 54522/00, *Kotov v Russia*, (2012) ECHR [G.C.], para 114.

[25] For instance, the Court has affirmed that States take on a duty of care in respect of sequestrate or seized properties and are thus liable for their damage and/or, loss. Accordingly, domestic legislation shall 'provide for the possibility of instituting proceedings against the State in order to obtain compensation for the damage resulting from the failure to keep such property in relatively good condition.' See, App no 49001/14, *Dabić v Croatia*, (2021) ECHR, para 55.

[26] For example, in the *Burdov* case, the Court has expressly stated that States have the obligation 'to guarantee to everyone the right to have a binding and enforceable judicial decision enforced within a reasonable time' and found a violation of Art P1-1 because of the public authorities' prolonged failure to comply with a binding and enforceable judgments that created an established right to payment in the applicant's favour, which amounted to a 'possession'. See, App no 33509/04, *Burdov v Russia (No. 2)*, (2009) ECHR, especially paras 70 and 87.

[27] App nos 15339/02, 21166/02, 20058/02, 11673/02, and 15343/02, *Budayeva et al v Russia* (2008) ECtHR, para 182.

[28] See, App no 58043/10, *Vladimir Slavov Vladimirov v Bulgaria* (2018) ECtHR (dec), para 41.

In a series of cases concerning planning restrictions, the ECtHR has instead stated the obligation to compensate all excessive interferences with property rights.[29] From the ECtHR case law can be inferred that regulation of property can be deemed excessive, first and foremost, when it affects the very substance of ownership, which encompasses the right to use and dispose of property.[30]

4. Bypassing the Temporal Scope of Article P1-1 in Property Restitution Cases

In the 1990s the political, economic, and social map of Europe changed dramatically under the impetus of democratic movements in Central and Eastern Europe. The new-born democratic countries managed in a very short time to fulfil statutory requirements to join the Council of Europe. Their membership, however, posed considerable challenges to the ECHR system itself,[31] which underwent very significant changes.[32]

Within a few years, the ECtHR was hit by waves of applications based on Article P1-1 brought by previous owners of property confiscated or nationalised during the communist era.

Even though Article P1-1 cannot be interpreted as granting any right of restitution of property that has been unlawfully or unjustly taken by former totalitarian governments,[33] the ECtHR quickly became the forum for complaints concerning

[29] See, App No 35332/05, *Anonymos Touristiki Etairia Xenodocheia Kritis v Greece* (2008) ECtHR, para 45; App no 40409/08, *Varfis v Greece* (2011) ECtHR, para 30.

[30] See, for instance, App nos 8803-8811/02, 8813/02 and 8815-8819/02, *Dogan et al v Turkey* (2004) ECtHR; App no 35859/02, *Housing Association of War Disabled and Victims of War of Attica et al v Greece* (2006) ECtHR; App no 33294/03, *Ayangil et al v Turkey* (2011) ECtHR.

[31] As remarked by MR Madsen, 'From Cold War Instrument to Supreme European Court: The European Court of Human Rights at the Crossroads of International and National Law and Politics' (2007) 32 *Law & Social Inquiry* 137, 155, '[t]he institution had to integrate a very substantial number of new member states into its institutional framework, as well as it had to monitor human rights in respect to legal systems that had only recently been refurnished.' It is worth recalling that the ratification of the ECHR is a prerequisite for joining the Council of Europe.

[32] Keeping in mind the words of the former ECtHR's president, Linos-Alexander Sicilianos, according to whom '[t]he reform of the Court is not a one-off exercise. It is a continuous process'; it can be said that this process started in 1998, with the entry into force of Protocol no 11 replacing the original structure – made up by the Court and the Commission on Human Rights – by a single full-time Court. See, the transcript of Siciliano's speech, *The reform and current challenges in the work of the European Court of Human Rights*, available at: rm.coe.int/speech-judge-linos-alexander-sicilianos-help-network-conference-2018/16808b8667.

[33] The ECtHR stated in general terms that the Convention does not impose any specific obligation on Contracting States to make reparation for injustices or damage caused by their predecessors. See, App no 24120/06, *Sfountouris et al v Germany*, (2004) ECHR (dec). More specifically with regard to property issues, the Court affirmed that: 'the Convention cannot be interpreted as imposing any general obligation on the Contracting States to restore property which was transferred to them before they had ratified the Convention … Nor is there any general obligation under the Convention to establish legal procedures in which restitution of property may be sought.' See, App no 7352/03, *Beshiri et al v Albania*, (2006) ECHR, para 61.

property lost under the communist regimes, despite the fact that the ECHR and its Protocols have no retroactive effect, thus they apply only to facts that have occurred after the date they entered into force in the respondent State.[34]

Restitution of private property to dispossessed owners has in fact been one of the most controversial and sensitive issues that post-communist States have had to deal with, and most of them, under domestic political pressure, addressed the issue passing specific legislation.

The ECtHR became then the warden of the proper implementation of the property restitution process,[35] as it considered that domestic legislation providing for the full or partial restoration of lost property:

> may be regarded as generating a new property right protected by Article 1 of Protocol No. 1 for persons satisfying the requirements for entitlement. The same may apply in respect of arrangements for restitution or compensation established under pre-ratification legislation, if such legislation remained in force after the Contracting State's ratification of Protocol.[36]

Given such legislation, the State has thus a positive obligation to implement it 'with reasonable clarity and coherence, in order to avoid, in so far as possible, legal uncertainty and ambiguity for the legal persons concerned'.[37]

However, the failure to comply with this obligation, resulting in a general legal uncertainty, is not in itself sufficient to constitute a breach of Article P1-1. Indeed, the Court will eventually declare a violation of Article P1-1 only after assessing whether the legal uncertainty has affected the applicant's protected interests in

[34] The ECtHR however resort to the concept of *continuing situation* to know of cases in which the alleged violation of the Convention began prior to its ratification and persisted after that date. As defined by the Court, 'the concept of a "continuing situation" refers to a state of affairs which operates by continuous activities by or on the part of the State to render the applicants victims.' See, App no 27824/95, *Posti and Rahko v Finland* (2002) ECtHR para 39. With respect to Art P1-1, the ECtHR applied the continuing violation doctrine in a series of cases against Turkey, which dealt with the continuous denial, since the 1974 *coup d'état*, for Greek Cypriots to accede their possessions in northern Cyprus. For the leading case, see App no 15318/89, *Loizidou v Turkey* (1996) ECtHR [G.C.]. With regard to the confiscation of private properties without compensation that occurred during the socialist era, the Court expressly ruled out that it could be considered as a continuing situation of deprivation of a right, because the taking of property is in principle an instantaneous act. See, App no 44912/98, *Kopecky v Slovaquie* (2004) ECtHR [G.C.] para 35.

[35] In other words, '[t]he judgments finding a violation of Article 1 of Protocol No. 1, in cases of property lost during the communist regime, are therefore related not to the very fact of the nationalisation or confiscation by the authoritarian power, but to the actual failure of the States to comply with their own legislation providing for compensation or restoration of property or with final judicial or administrative decisions restoring property or awarding compensation, rendered by domestic authorities in favour of the applicants, during the period following the ratification of the Convention.' See the study on *Private properties issues following the change of political regime in former socialist or communist countries Albania, Bosnia and Herzegovina, Bulgaria, Croatia, Romania and Serbia*, requested by the European Parliament, available at www.europarl.europa.eu/thinktank/en/document/IPOL-PETI_ET(2010)425609, 26.

[36] App no 44912/98, *Kopecký v Slovakia*, (2004) ECHR [G.C.], para 35.

[37] App no 63252/00, *Păduraru v Romania*, (2005) ECHR, para 92.

such a way as to upsetting the 'fair balance' between the demands of the public interest and the need to protect the applicant's right to the peaceful enjoyment of his possession.

Confiscation and nationalisation programmes varied significantly from state to state, and so did policies and legislation on restitution. Therefore, the case history on this issue is also very varied and the ECtHR consistently held that, being a subject matter involving consideration of economic and social issues, States enjoy a wide margin of appreciation.[38]

Restitution laws are nevertheless subject to the Court's 'quality' control, under the lawfulness principle,[39] and, furthermore, to the fair balance test that encompasses both procedural and substantive aspects of the legislation.

To conclude, it is worth noting that the choice of the ECtHR to make claims on restitution conditional on the existence of a specific domestic legislation tells us that the Court's function, as described by two eminent scholars, 'is not to make justice available to all victims of abuses of power, but more narrowly to secure the rule of law and the protection of human rights prospectively.'[40]

5. The Review of Justification for Interference with the Right to Peaceful Enjoyment of One's Possessions

In the previous paragraphs we have considered the first stage of judicial review, in which the ECtHR must answer to the cardinal question of what constitutes possessions within the meaning of Article P1-1; here, we turn the attention on the second stage of judicial review, in which the Court must decide whether there has been a breach of it.

The issue of what form of judicial control the ECtHR exercises is closely related to the question of how the Court interprets its role. There is an ongoing debate on whether it has overstepped its role as an international court, and exercises a power comparable to those of a constitutional court. The arguments put forward by various authors in support of the thesis that the ECtHR has developed certain

[38] For an outline of main issues and principles applied in the relevant case law, see Case-law of the European Court of Human Rights: summary of selected judgments and decisions on property restitution/compensation, available at: rm.coe.int/CoERMPublicCommonSearchServices/DisplayDCTMContent?documentId=0900001680592469. See also, Report of the Regional Conference on Protection of Property: The European Court of Human Rights and National Case-law in the Western Balkans, available at: rm.coe.int/property-rights-conference-coe-wb-december-2020-final/1680a256b1.

[39] As explained by the Court, '[t]he principle of lawfulness presupposes that the applicable provisions of domestic law are sufficiently accessible, precise and foreseeable in their application.' See, *ex multis*, App nos 32401/10 and 19 others, *Taganrog LRO et al v Russia*, (2022) ECHR, para 281.

[40] T Allen and B Douglas, 'Closing the door on restitution: the European Court of Human Rights' in A Buyse and M Hamilton (eds), *Transitional Jurisprudence and the ECHR: Justice, Politics and Rights* (Cambridge, Cambridge University Press, 2011) 208, 234.

characteristics proper to a constitutional court are different and pertain to the substance of the issues brought before the Court,[41] as well as to the canons of interpretation it has developed,[42] or the effects of its judgments in the legal systems of the contracting States.[43]

Leaving open the question of whether, and in what terms, the ECtHR could be considered as – or is evolving into – a sort of European constitutional court,[44] here the analysis is limited to giving an account of some foundational principles set by the Court to define the scope of its judicial review, as applied in cases dealing with Article P1-1.

From an analysis of the relevant case law it can be asserted that, as a rule, to be deemed compatible with Article P1-1, interference with the right to peaceful enjoyment of one's possessions must comply with the principle of lawfulness and pursue a legitimate aim by means that are reasonably proportionate to the goal sought to be realised.[45] In other words, when the Court finds that there has been

[41] See, for instance, R Ryssdal, 'On the road to a European constitutional Court' in F Emmert (ed), *Collected Courses of the Academy of European Law / Recueil des cours de l'Académie de droit européen Springer*, (Dordrecht, Springer, 1993) 3, 9, where embracing the thesis according to which the ECHR has become 'the embryo of a European Constitution', he remarks that 'the typical issue brought before the Commission and the Court is more of a constitutional nature: it embraces the age-long and sensitive problem of the balance to be struck between the general interest of the community and the protection of the individual's fundamental right.'

[42] For this perspective, see S Greer, 'Constitutionalizing Adjudication under the European Convention on Human Rights' (2003) 23 *Oxford Journal of Legal Studies* 405, 407, according to whom: 'some of these [principles of interpretation] are "constitutional" because they address three quintessentially constitutional questions: the "normative question" of what a given Convention right means including its relationship with other rights and with collective interests, the "institutional question" of which institution (judicial/non-judicial; national/European) should be responsible for providing the answer, and the "adjudicative question" of how, i.e., by which judicial method, the normative question should be addressed.'

[43] According to G Ulfstein, 'Transnational constitutional aspects of the European Court of Human Rights' (2021) 10 *Global Constitutionalism* 151, 152, the 'legal effects [of the judicial review undertaken by the ECtHR] should be considered constitutional because they affect the relationship between national constitutional organs and the individual, as well as the relationship between different constitutional organs.' See also pp 153–156 where the author traces back the doctrinal debate about the constitutional nature of the ECtHR.

[44] For more on this issue see S Greer and L Wildhaber, 'Revisiting the Debate about 'constitutionalising' the European Court of Human Rights' (2012) 12 *Human Rights Law Review* 655, where the authors outline both the institutional debate and the academic one. For a different framing of the debate, see K Dzehtsiarou, *Can the European Court of Human Rights Shape European Public Order?* (Cambridge, Cambridge University Press, 2022) 105, who criticizes the choice to make use of the constitutional paradigm to describe the role of the ECtHR and maintains that: '[t]he debate about the function of the ECtHR should be built around the cleavage between meta-function as opposed to technical function rather than between the constitutional and the adjudicatory nature of the Court'. In this perspective, '[t]he technical function of the ECtHR is rather straightforward: it has to resolve cases and put a legal end to conflicts between parties. The meta-function is much more complex and controversial: the Court's meta-function is to develop the body of law and bring about the version of international society it was designed to ensure. Although the meta-function is detectable on a high level of abstraction, it is much harder to pinpoint its precise content' (ibid 128).

[45] For a thorough examination of the three requirements, see S Praduroux, *The Protection of Property Rights* (n 18) 165 ff.

State interference with the right under Article P1-1, it addresses the three following key questions: first, was the interference, or limitation, prescribed by, or compliant with, law? Secondly, did it pursue an aim of general interest? Thirdly, with all the relevant circumstances taken into account, did it strike a fair balance between the general interest and the applicants' rights under Article P1-1?

The latter issue has gained central importance in the reasoning of the ECtHR and it is the gate through which the Court integrates non-economic and social considerations in the interpretation and application of the right to the peaceful enjoyment of one's possessions.

In general terms, it can be remarked that the Court takes a loose approach to the legitimate aim requirement generally allowing to national authorities a wide margin of appreciation in determining what is in the general interest and even assuming, when in doubt, the existence of a legitimate aim for the interference.

The fact that the general interest is rarely the subject of thorough consideration by the ECtHR affects the way in which it conducts the fair balance test, since it does not usually engage in the identification of a list of relevant public interest factors to be balanced against individuals' interests. It follows that the fair balance test in most cases amounts to an overall assessment of the factual circumstances of the case, rather than to a substantive evaluation of the relative importance of individuals' right against a given public interest.

One example is the case *Könyv-Tár Kft et al v Hungary*,[46] where the applicant companies complained of having lost their clientele, following the enactment of a new legislation which, essentially, established a state monopoly in their business sector.

The ECtHR explicitly stated that it did 'not need to determine whether the implementation of the impugned reform pursued a legitimate aim',[47] but it had to ascertain 'whether the circumstances of the case disclose[d] a violation of the applicant companies' rights under Article 1 of Protocol No. 1 in terms of proportionality'.[48]

Though, as the Court did not identify a specific public interest, the proportionality test it carried out was in fact an evaluation on the merits of the new legislation itself and on its impact on the applicant's business. Thus, considering, in particular, that the applicants were de facto prevented from continuing their commercial activity, without any measure to protect them from arbitrariness or to offer them compensation for their loss of business, the Court declared that there had been a violation of Article P1-1.[49]

[46] App no 21623/13, *Könyv-Tár Kft et al v Hungary* (2018) ECtHR.
[47] ibid para 46.
[48] ibid para 47.
[49] ibid para 59.

6. Reinterpreting the Scope of Article P1-1 Through the Prism of the Fair Balance Principle[50]

Some authors emphasise the importance of distinguishing between the definition of the scope of fundamental rights, and the review of justification for interference by the State, and criticise the ECtHR for not taking the distinction seriously. Indeed, there are cases in which the ECtHR fails to explain why the applicant's claim falls within the scope of a Convention right, but still rules on whether it has been violated, whereas in other cases the Court mixes the discussion of the scope of a right with references to elements concerning the justification for interference, more specifically the margin of appreciation and the fair balance test.[51]

In the cases in which a clear distinction between definition and application is missing, it is the very scope of Article P1-1 that is called into question.

As said the ECtHR defines the notion of possessions rather broadly to encompass, potentially, all and every economic interests. Nonetheless, not all economic interests that are recognised as possessions are protected alike, as the scope and the level of protection can significantly be reduced by the Court when scrutinising State restrictions on the right to peaceful enjoyment of possessions by means of the fair balance principle.

As a result, the guarantees provided by Article P1-1 can be expanded or narrowed depending on different factors, such as the kind of economic interest at stake,[52] or the public interest and non-pecuniary values involved.

Thus, for instance, dealing with rent-control schemes and restrictions, in the *Mellacher* case,[53] the Court found that legislation, which aimed at facilitating access to housing for the less well-off and that had the effect of substantially reducing the rent – by up to 80 per cent – perceived by the applicants, did not amount to a violation of Article P1-1. This is explained by the importance of the public

[50] As is well known, the fair balance principle is at the very core of ECtHR judicial review as, apart from the few rights that are absolute, the application of the Convention requires States to strike a fair balance between the rights and freedoms guaranteed by it and other competing rights and interests. On its origins and development, see A Mowbray, 'A Study of the Principle of Fair Balance in the Jurisprudence of the European Court of Human Rights' (2010) 10 *Human Rights Law Review* 289.

[51] See, JH Gerards and HCK Senden, 'The structure of fundamental rights and the European Court of Human Rights' (2009) 7 *International Journal of Constitutional Law* 619. According to these authors such an approach is undesirable as it 'causes serious problems from the perspective of the clarity of the Court's case law, the division of the burden of proof in (national) fundamental rights cases, and the application of the margin of appreciation doctrine', ibid 652.

[52] On this point we refer to L Mardikian, 'In-Between an Economic Freedom and a Human Right' (n 17) 370, who remarks that: '[t]he more risky and speculative the nature of the property in question is, the more the centre of gravity lies on its economic characteristics and therefore, the review of national measures potentially limiting the right is more lenient. On the contrary, measures that have a substantial impact on the social dimensions of property because of their impact on the subsistence, well-being or family home of the affected party, the more the courts [ie the ECtHR and the Court of the European Union] turn to the non-economic logic of property as a way of reading social obligations into the sphere of the economy.'

[53] App nos 10522/83; 11011/84; 11070/84, *Mellacher et al v Austria* (1989) ECHR.

interest pursued by the Austrian legislator. Whereas, in the *Bradshaw* case, based on the complaint that the amount of rent was very much lower than the market value, the ECtHR affirmed that since the applicant's property was used as a band club it involved 'a *degree of public interest which is significantly less marked* than in other cases and which does not justify such a substantial reduction compared with the free market rental value' (author's emphasis).[54]

In these two cases the public interest factor gathered prominence in the fair balance test affecting the level of protection granted to the applicant's possessions, but not the definition of the material scope of Article P1-1. In other cases, instead, the ECtHR brought into the fair balance test factors, which were able to undermine the very scope of Article P1-1.

For example, in the *Pine Valley* case the ECtHR found that the applicants' legitimate expectation, based on an outline planning permission, which had been recorded in a public register but subsequently declared void by the national courts, of being able to carry out their proposed land development project, felt within the scope of Article P1-1.[55]

Ruling out that the annulment of the planning permission could be regarded as a disproportionate measure in breach of Article P1-1, the ECtHR remarked that the applicants were engaged in a commercial venture which, by its very nature, involved an element of risk and, moreover, they were aware that the site was in an area zoned for the further development of agriculture and that the local authority opposed to any departure from it.[56]

In this case the applicant's conduct makes it questionable to claim that the applicants had legitimate expectations in the terms described by the ECtHR.

The applicant's conduct is therefore a factor that the Court should have assessed in the first stage of judicial review when it has to determine the existence of possession, rather than at the stage of the application of Article P1-1, when it has to rule on the justification for interference.

Likewise, in the *Ivanova and Cherkezov* case,[57] concerning the intended demolition of Ms Ivanova's house, which had been built without obtaining a building permit, the Court did not take into consideration the applicant's wrongful conduct to address the question of whether she could claim to have a possession within the meaning of Article P1-1. Rather, the Court skipped over the question of whether the applicant had a possession, considering that it was more appropriate to examine the case on the merits,[58] focusing on the 'salient issue' of 'whether the interference would strike a fair balance between the first applicant's interest to

[54] App no 37121/15, *Bradshaw et al v Malta* (2018) ECHR, para 58. The Court finally concluded that there had been a violation of Art P1-1 because of the extremely low rent and the lack of procedural safeguards in the application of the law.

[55] App no 12742/87, *Pine Valley Development Ltd et al* v *Ireland* (1991) ECtHR, especially para 51.

[56] Ibid, para 59.

[57] App no 46577/15, *Ivanova and Cherkezov v Bulgaria*, (2016) ECHR.

[58] See, ibid para 67.

keep her possessions intact and the general interest to ensure effective implementation of the prohibition against building without a permit.'[59]

In the ECtHR's reasoning the 'flagrant breach of the domestic building regulations' has to 'be regarded as a crucial consideration under Article 1 of Protocol No. 1'.[60] Thus it was enough for the Court to consider that the demolition order was issued a reasonable time after the construction of the house and its enforcement would have serve to deter other potential lawbreakers. Then, relying on 'the wide margin of appreciation that the Bulgarian authorities enjoy under Article 1 of Protocol No. 1 in choosing both the means of enforcement and in ascertaining whether the consequences of enforcement would be justified',[61] it concluded that the applicant's proprietary interest in the house didn't outweigh the public interest linked to the implementation of the demolition order, which was therefore not in breach of Article P1-1.

Considering that the ECHR is an instrument designed to promote the rule of law, one might wonder whether it would be desirable for the ECtHR to interpret Article P1-1 in a way such to exclude illegal property from its scope of application, departing from its current approach that gives precedence to facts over the law.[62]

It should however be noted that although in various cases the ECtHR has regarded illegal constructions as possessions,[63] it accords, under the fair balance test, significant weight to whether public authorities have tolerated the illegal situation for an appreciable amount of time, thereby failing to comply with their good governance obligations.[64]

Moreover, the Court has never considered their demolition as a deprivation of property, as opposed to cases concerning the demolition of legally constructed buildings.[65]

[59] Ibid para 72.

[60] Ibid para 75.

[61] Ibid.

[62] As I have discussed elsewhere, economic interest originated from a de facto situation that did not meet national legality requirements can be granted protection under Art P1-1. See, S Praduroux, 'Property and Expropriation: Two Concepts Revisited in the Light of the Case Law of the European Court of Human Rights and the European Court of Justice' (2019) 8 *European Property Law Journal* 172, 186.

[63] One of the most famous cases is *Öneryıldız v Turkey*, dealing with the accidental destruction of a dwelling which had been erected on public land by the applicant in breach of domestic law, the Court considered that 'the applicant's proprietary interest in his dwelling was of a sufficient nature and sufficiently recognised to constitute a substantive interest and hence a 'possession'" and examined the case "in the light of the general rule in the first sentence of the first paragraph, which lays down the right to the peaceful enjoyment of possessions.' App no 48939/99, *Öneryıldız v Turkey* (2004) ECtHR [GC], paras 129 and 133.

[64] In a number of cases, the ECtHR pointed up the importance of the principle of good governance in the context of property rights, stressing that 'where an issue in the general interest is at stake it is incumbent on the public authorities to act in good time, in an appropriate manner and with utmost consistency', this to avoid creating situations of legal uncertainty, contrary to the rule of law. See, App no 67412/14, *Britaniškina v Lithuania* (2018) ECtHR, para 47.

[65] See, App no 35179/97, *Allard v Sweden* (2003) ECtHR, concerning the demolition of the applicant's house that had been built without the consent of the other joint owners. The Court noted that the building of the house in issue was not illegal per se and regarded its demolition as a deprivation of possessions.

At first sight the different approach may appear irrelevant as, examining the compatibility with Article P1-1 of a State's action or omission, the Court considers whether the contested State's conduct meets the requirements of legitimacy and lawfulness, and complies with the fair balance principle, regardless of which of the three rules of Article P1-1 applies to the case. However, when carrying out the fair balance test the Court gives different weight to relevant factors such as, first and foremost, compensation terms. Indeed, while under the second rule a deprivation of property without payment of an amount reasonably related to its value would normally constitute a disproportionate interference, under the first and third rules the lack of compensation for restriction to the right granted by Article P1-1 acquires significant weight only when the very substance of ownership is affected.[66]

7. Article P1-1: A Right without Substance?

The judicial determination of the scope of Article P1-1 is based, as illustrated in the above paragraphs, on the search of an individual economic interest; but what is the very substance of the right to peaceful enjoyment of one's possessions?

The concept of the substance – or essence – of the right as a boundary to State interference with ECHR rights, has been referred to by the Court for the first time in the late 1960s and, as the ECtHR has neither developed a consistent methodological approach nor developed a clear definition of the concept, it is now a debated and controversial terms.[67]

As far as Article P1-1 is concerned, the ECtHR referred to the concept at hand in few cases, and never addressing the issue of what is the substance of the right to peaceful enjoyment of one's possessions. Indeed, in the well-known *Sporrong and Lönnroth* case, where for the first time the term appeared in the context of Article P1-1, the Court made use of the more specific formula: 'very substance of ownership'.[68]

The case has become one of the cornerstones of Article P1-1 jurisprudence, for as mentioned in the introduction to this chapter, it is the case in which the ECtHR has elucidated the scope of each of the three sentences contained in the Article. On the merits, the case concerned long-term expropriation permits and prohibitions on construction that, according to the Court, 'affected the *very substance of ownership* in that they recognised before the event that any expropriation would

[66] More broadly on compensation and the fair balance principle, see T Allen, 'Compensation for Property Under the European Convention on Human Rights' (2007) 28 *Michigan Journal of International Law* 287, 298 ff.

[67] Criticisms have been raised by both scholars and judges of the ECtHR's. See, S Van Drooghenbroeck, C Rizcallah, 'The ECHR and the Essence of Fundamental Rights: Searching for Sugar in Hot Milk?' (2019) 20 *German Law Journal* 904.

[68] App no 7151/75 and 7152/75, *Sporrong and Lönnroth v Sweden* (1982) ECtHR para 60.

be lawful and authorised the City of Stockholm to expropriate whenever it found it expedient to do so' (author's emphasis).[69] Thus having established that there was a State interference with the applicants' right under Article P1-1, the Court went on to examine whether it was justified in accordance with the fair balance test, and concluded that there had been a violation of Article P1-1, as the applicants had to bear 'an individual and excessive burden which could have been rendered legitimate only if they had had the possibility of seeking a reduction of the time-limits or of claiming compensation'.[70]

This ruling tells us therefore that ownership falls within the scope of application of Article P1-1, but it is not the substance of right to peaceful enjoyment of one's possessions. Indeed, a measure that affects very substance of ownership can nonetheless be compatible with Article P1-1.

In the same direction points the remark made by Judge Paulo Pinto de Albuquerque, according to which:

> What qualifies a measure as incompatible with the substance of the right to the peaceful enjoyment of one's possessions is not properly defined. However, the Court's jurisprudence provides some guidance as to what constitutes interference with the substance of ownership.[71]

To conclude, lacking a fairly clear answer to the question of what is the very substance of the right to peaceful enjoyment of one's possessions, it is however plausible to argue that it is not to be found in a minimum economic value, despite the said economic and pecuniary scope of Article P1-1.

This is because the ECtHR consistently stated that the taking of property without payment of any compensation can be considered justifiable under Article P1-1, even though only in exceptional circumstances; moreover, it expressly ruled out that Article P1-1 could give raise to 'any positive obligation for the State to maintain the value not only of deposits, but also of claims or any other asset'.[72]

8. The Search for a New Paradigm for Property Rights in the Climate Change Era

The criterion of economic utility, which informs the liberal notion of property, underpins as well – in the terms illustrated in the above paragraphs – the notion of possessions such as developed by the ECtHR.

[69] ibid.

[70] ibid para 73.

[71] App no 5294/14, *Albert et al v Hungary* (2019) ECtHR, dissenting opinion of Judge Pinto de Albuquerque, para 39.

[72] App no 35221/97, *O.N. v Bulgaria*, (2000) ECtHR (dec).

This understanding of property, which is instrumental to a capitalist economy, is increasingly being called into question, as environmental social awareness is increasing and the threat of climate change is becoming more acute.[73]

The doctrinal debate on the search for a new paradigm for property rights, which would internalise ecological interests into the very notion of property is thus gaining momentum.[74]

Property rights within national legal systems are indeed designed to protect the economic value of a given property, rather than its ecological value.[75]

This consideration holds true also with regard the right to peaceful enjoyment of one's possessions under Article P1-1. Suffice it to say that Article P1-1 may be invoked to protect the economic interests connected with land exploitation,[76] and the expropriation clause enshrined therein has been interpreted as to grant to the owner the market value of the expropriated property.[77] Moreover, the economic value of property is also protected against excessive interference that does not amount to deprivation of property, but affect the very substance of ownership.[78]

Article P1-1 can as well be invoked as a viable remedy for protecting property economic value against environmental nuisances. In the relevant case law, the ECtHR has consistently held that Article P1-1 does not guarantee the right to enjoy one's possessions in a pleasant environment and rejected the complaints

[73] In this regard, RM Ballardini, J Kaisto, and J Similä, 'Developing novel property concepts in private law to foster the circular economy' (2021) 279 *Journal of Cleaner Production* 1, 8, critically observe that: '[i]ssues related to environmental sustainability have largely been ignored in private law … This is especially due to heavy reliance by private law regimes on pure economic efficiency, utility and incentives, with the main focus on individual rights ownership.'

[74] See B Akkermans, 'Sustainable Property Law: towards a revaluation of our system of property law' *Maastricht Law, Faculty of Law Working Paper series*, 2020/01. Available at: www.maastrichtuniversity.nl/file/maastrichtlawworkingpaperseries2020-1bramakkermanspdf.

[75] Discussing the challenges posed by property law in the implementation of environmental sustainable policies, some suthors observe that it is '"ecologically blind" … and rigid, not easily accommodating changes due to environmental concerns'. See, A Lähteenmäki-Uutela, A Lonkila, S Huttunen, and N Grmelová, 'Legal rights of private property owners vs. sustainability transitions?' (2021) 323 *Journal of Cleaner Production* 1, 4.

[76] See, for example, App no 12033/86, *Fredin (No. 1) v Sweden* [1991] ECtHR, concerning the economic interests connected with the exploitation of a gravel pit; *Pine Valley Development Ltd et al* v *Ireland*, *supra* n 55, where the Court found that the applicant's expectation of realizing an economic interest from land development felt within the scope of Article P1-1; App no 46154/11, *Valle Pierimpiè Società Agricola S.p.a. v Italy*, (2014) EctHR, dealing with the exploitation of a fishing valley; App no 71130/13, *Gospodăria țărănească Chiper Terenti Grigore v the Republic of Moldova*, on minerals extraction.

[77] According to the principles settled by the Court: 'taking of property without payment of an amount reasonably related to its value will normally constitute a disproportionate interference and a total lack of compensation can be considered justifiable under Article 1 of Protocol No. 1 only in exceptional circumstances … Article 1 of Protocol No. 1 does not, however, guarantee a right to full compensation in all circumstances …' Moreover, '[l]egitimate objectives in the "public interest", such as those pursued in measures of economic reform or measures designed to achieve greater social justice, may call for less than reimbursement of the full market value.' See, App no 36813/97, *Scordino v Italy (no 1)*, (2006) ECtHR [G.C.], paras 95 and 97.

[78] See *Scordino v Italy (no 1)*, para 2.

whenever the applicant failed to prove that the value of her or his property had diminished.[79]

Having said that, it should not however be forgotten that the right to peaceful enjoyment of possessions is a qualified right,[80] therefore its very scope is, to some extent, conditional on the public interest served by the restrictions imposed by the State. Therefore, as far as the protection of the environment is a public-interest matter, environmental arguments can be used to justify the State's interference with property rights.

In this regard, the ECtHR has consistently held that economic imperatives should not be given precedence over environmental protection considerations and allowed a wide margin of appreciation to States with regard both to choosing the means for achieving environmental protection objectives and to ascertaining whether they meet the fair balance requirement.

To date the ECtHR has already handed down a significant number of decisions dealing with interference with Article P1-1 on environmental grounds. The measures challenged by the applicants range from revocation of planning permissions, to demolition orders on houses, from the revocation of a permit to exploit a gravel pit to a ban on building.[81]

These cases show the tension between the economic and environmental dimensions of property rights, as the ECtHR follows an economic rationality in deciding whether or not there is a protected possessions under Article P1-1, but then lets environmental interests prevail.

For a change of paradigm, the ECtHR should integrate the environmental value of property among the relevant factors to be considered when defining the scope of Article P1-1.

In the meantime, one may wonder whether the Court will be willing to consider the mitigation of climate change and / or the sustainable use of property to be assessed as a public interest.

Even though the ECtHR has never provided clear guidance to define the 'public interest' notion, merely repeating that it is 'necessarily extensive',[82] I think it is possible to argue that it will answer in the affirmative, by considering the growing scientific and societal consensus on the harmful effects of climate change.

[79] See, *ex multis*, App no 12853/03, *Ivan Atanasov v Bulgaria*, (2010) ECtHR. It should be said here that Art 8 (Right to respect for private and family life) provides a better ground for challenging the State's liability for environmental nuisances. Even though the Court never went so far as to affirm a right to a clean and quiet environment, in several cases it acknowledged that severe environmental pollution may affect individuals' well-being and prevent them from enjoying their homes in such a way as to affect their private and family life adversely. See, *Guide to the Case-law of the European Court of Human Rights. Environment*, 23 ff. Available at: echr.coe.int/Documents/Guide_Environment_ENG.pdf.

[80] According to the ECHR terminology qualified rights are those rights which may be interfered with in order to protect the rights of another or the wider public interest.

[81] For overview of the relevant cases, see the *Guide to the Case-law*, (n 79), 66 ff.

[82] This interpretation was first made by the Court in App No 8793/79, *James et al v The United Kingdom* (1986) ECtHR para 46.

This means that the ECtHR will be willing to justify restrictions on the right to the peaceful enjoyment of one's possessions for the sake of sustainability and sustainable development.

9. Conclusions

In the early case law, opposing to a 'scope-extending' interpretation of Article P1-1, Judge Gerald Fitzmaurice remarked that:

> the chief, if not the sole object of Article 1 of the Protocol (P1-1) was to prevent the arbitrary seizures, confiscations, expropriations, extortions, or other capricious interferences with peaceful possession that many governments are -or frequently have been- all too prone to resort to.[83]

More than four decades later, we can say that the Judge Fitzmaurice's advice went unheeded. The ECtHR has indeed engaged in a seemingly never-ending, expansive interpretation of Article P1-1 by defining the notion of 'possessions' rather broadly to encompass a wide range of economic interests and further extending its scope of material application through the positive obligations doctrine.

Over the years the ECtHR has also extended the scope of its judicial review. Stating that the principle of fair balance is 'inherent in Article 1 of Protocol No. 1 itself',[84] the Court added a third requirement for State interference and allowed itself to assess not only whether an alleged restriction on the right to peaceful enjoyment of one's possessions has some basis in domestic law and pursues a general interest, but also whether the fair balance between the requirements of the public interest and the need to protect the applicants' right has been respected.

When applied in cases falling within the scope of the third rule enshrined in Article P1-1, especially, the fair balance test allows the ECtHR to review the substantive fairness of both national legislation and domestic court decisions.

Given the wide judicial determination of scope of Article P1-1, the actions likely to amount to interference with Article P1-1 are various and different, such as: restrictions on freedom of contract;[85] the revocation of the authorisation, or the termination of a licence, to run a business;[86] the freezing of a

[83] See, App no 6833/74, *Marckx v Belgium*, (1979) ECtHR dissenting opinion of Judge Fitzmaurice, para 18. To briefly recall the case, the majority of the Court found that the Belgian inheritance law was contrary to Art P1-1 in conjunction with Art 14 (Prohibition of discrimination) ECHR, because discriminating against illegitimate children. Judge Fitzmaurice criticised the Court for relying on the term 'use to impart to Art P1-1 'a scope wider than the notion of possession, and extending to rights of inheritance and disposal', see ibid para 17.

[84] App no 33202/96, *Beyeler v Italy* (2000) ECtHR, para 111.

[85] See, for instance, cases dealing with rent control legislation, *cit. supra*.

[86] See, among others, App no 12033/86, *Fredin (No 1) v Sweden* (1991) ECtHR, concerning the revocation of the applicants' permit to exploit gravel on their property; App no 10873/84, *Tre Traktörer Aktiebolag v Sweden* (1989) ECtHR, on the revocation of a licence to sell alcoholic beverages.

bank account;[87] and so forth. It follows that the ECtHR's judicial review power covers today not only administrative acts and legislation, but also a wide range of private law areas, from inheritance law to contract law, from property law to tort law.

Therefore, and to conclude, Article P1-1, whose content is shaped by the ECtHR on criteria that are relevant to the rule of law, should be seen as a tool to enhance the rule of law in the domain of both public and private law.

More recently, see App no 38433/09, *Centro Europa 7 S.r.l. and Di Stefano v Italy* (2012) ECtHR [G.C.], concerning the exploitation of a licence for nationwide terrestrial television broadcasting; App no 21151/04, Megadat.com *SRL v Moldova* (2008) ECtHR, concerning the invalidation of the applicant's telecommunications licences; App no 49429/99, *Capital Bank AD v Bulgaria*, (2006) ECHR, dealing with the revocation of a banking licence.

[87] For references to cases see Guide on Art P1-1, (n 9), especially paras 339–340.

4

Access to Justice as an Integral Part of the Rule of Law in Western Balkan Countries

SVITLANA ZADOROZHNA

1. Introduction

Social and economic development are the main features of the contemporary world. Despite constant and universal change, the rule of law and access to justice remain the same, identically undefined and uncertain. However, we need a functional system to ensure democratic development and enable dispute resolution without disrupting cooperation and slowing down development. The rule of law forms the basis of all genuine democracy together with individual freedom and political liberty: these three values together ensure access to justice for all citizens including vulnerable ones. The implementation of the rule of law becomes a necessary condition for the admission of new European Union (EU) members, including the Western Balkan countries. The EU, together with the World Bank and the United Nations (UN), other international organisations promote the rule of law via its enlargement policy. Within the EU enlargement policy package, judiciary reform aiming to provide an independent, impartial, and efficient judiciary is considered to be the main component of the rule of law.

The EU not only defines the policy requirement, but also finances the rule of law and judiciary reforms of the Western Balkan countries, mainly via IPA programmes. The main conclusion of this audit of the effectiveness of EU support for the rule of law in the Western Balkans is that EU action has contributed to reforms in technical areas, such as the efficiency of the judiciary and the development of relevant legislation, but in a context of insufficient political will, it has had a limited overall impact in advancing fundamental rule of law reforms in the region.

Below we will discuss the understanding and meaning of the rule of law and access to justice as well as the role of the rule of law in judicial reform in the Western Balkan countries.

2. What is the Rule of Law and its 'Balkan' Peculiarities

To start, it is necessary to define the areas we study, i.e., what is 'the rule of law' and 'access to justice'? Neither of them are easy to define strictly, which leads to the increasing possibility of a more or less broad interpretation. For the purposes of this chapter we will be limited to defining their general features and their peculiarities for the Balkan countries if any. We will start with the first one, the rule of law.

2.1. The Rule of Law, Definitions to be Considered

Rule of law nowadays is mostly used in political discourse by international institutions. 'Good guys' are in support of the rule of law; it is a major source of legitimation for governments in the modern world.[1] Therefore, it is crucial to define the rule of law and even to find a definition that is shared by all, or at least most. Here we run into difficulties as there is no unique definition of the rule of law.

Brian Z Tamanaha gives perhaps the most basic definition: 'The rule of law means that government officials and citizens are bound by and abide by the law. I repeat: government officials and citizens are bound by and abide by the law.'[2] It provides for the minimum content of the rule of law.

Very similar definitions are provided by John Rawls and Marko Kmezić. According to Rawls, there are four elements of the rule of law concept, thus, a law must: a) be capable of being complied with by those to whom it is addressed; b) treat equally those who are similarly situated with respect to a given legal rule; c) be public; and d) provide a means for determining the truth of any facts needed for the application of a legal rule.[3] Kmezić notes that establishing a lasting and effective rule of law requires not only the presence of proper (independent) state institutions, but also a widely shared identification with the law in society – by citizens and political elites.[4]

These definitions do not include democracy and human rights as most other definitions do. For example, according to Prof Gome, the following are the requisites a country must have in order to operate under the 'rule of law': a legislature that enacts laws in accordance with the constitution and human rights; an independent judiciary; effective and accessible legal services; and a legal system guaranteeing equality before the law.[5] Both the quality of the laws, which should be clear, general,

[1] BZ Tamanaha, 'The History and Elements of the Rule of Law' (2012) *Singapore Journal of Legal Studies* 232.

[2] ibid 233.

[3] J Rawls, *A Theory of Justice*, 2nd edn, (Cambridge, Belknap Press, 1999) 237.

[4] M Kmezić, 'Rule of law and democracy in the Western Balkans: addressing the gap between policies and practice' (2020) 20(1) *Southeast European and Black Sea Studies* 183.

[5] TMRC Gome, 'Promoting the rule of law in Serbia. What is hindering the reforms in the justice sector?' (2017) 50 (4) *Communist and Post-Communist Studies* 331.

stable, and coherent and enforced; and the quality of the judicial system, which is to be capable, independent, accountable and impartial, are important to the rule of law,[6] especially when considering the rule of law in four dimensions: formal legality and substantive legality that refer to quality of rules and judicial capacity together with judicial impartiality that refer to quality of the judicial system.[7]

The same approach (including a human rights dimension) is used by international organisations and state governments while elaborating new legislation.

For instance, official documents of the United Nations, the Council of Europe, and the European Union include human rights and democracy as an integral part of the rule of law. Starting with the United Nations, the Universal Declaration of Human Rights provides that 'human rights should be protected by the rule of law'.[8] According to the 2005 World Summit Outcome, 'good governance and the rule of law at the national and international levels are essential for sustained economic growth, sustainable development and the eradication of poverty and hunger'.[9] The report of the Secretary General *The Rule of Law and Transitional Justice in Conflict and Post-conflict Societies* provides the understanding of the concept of the rule of law by the United Nations

> It refers to a principle of governance in which all persons, institutions and entities, public and private, including the State itself, are accountable to laws that are publicly promulgated, equally enforced and independently adjudicated, and which are consistent with international human rights norms and standards. It requires, as well, measures to ensure adherence to the principles of supremacy of law, equality before the law, accountability to the law, fairness in the application of the law, separation of powers, participation in decision-making, legal certainty, avoidance of arbitrariness and procedural and legal transparency.[10]

As for the Council of Europe, the Statute of the Council of Europe defines the rule of law as one of the principles which form the basis of all genuine democracy together with individual freedom and political liberty.[11] The same is reaffirmed by the Parliamentary Assembly of the Council of Europe in its Resolution 1594 (2007),[12] which adds that law in the 'rule of law' should not be considered as the statute of law, especially in young democracies with totalitarian pasts.

[6] H Haider, *Rule of Law Challenges in the Western Balkans*. K4D Helpdesk Report 464 (Brighton, Institute of Development Studies, 2018); M Mendelski, 'The Rule of Law (in Central and Eastern Europe)' in A Fagan and P Kopecký (eds), *The Routledge Handbook of East European Politics* (London, Routledge, 2018) 113.

[7] M Mendelski, 'Europeanization and the Rule of Law: Towards a Pathological Turn' (2026) 40 *Southeastern Europe* 346.

[8] Para 3 of the Preamble of the Universal Declaration of Human Rights, G.A. Res. 217 A (III) (10 December 1948).

[9] Para 11 of the G.A. RES/60/1, 2005 World Summit Outcome (24 October 2005).

[10] Para 6 of the Rule of Law and Transitional Justice in Conflict and Post-conflict Societies: Report of the Secretary-General, S/2004/616, 23 August 2004.

[11] Para 3 of the Preamble of the Statute of the Council of Europe, London, 4 May 1949.

[12] The Principle of the Rule of Law, Doc. No. 1594 (2007) available at: assembly.coe.int/nw/xml/XRef/Xref-XML2HTML-en.asp?fileid=17613&lang=en.

The principles of the 'rule of law', democracy and human rights are defined in the documents of the European Union and the Organization for Security and Co-operation in Europe (OSCE). Explicit reference to the 'rule of law' can be found, inter alia, in European Union/European Community treaties, the case law of the European Court of Justice, as well as in the Copenhagen criteria of 1993 for accession to the European Union.[13] In the European Union, "[t]he rule of law is the backbone of European liberal democracy and is one of the founding principles of the Union stemming from the common constitutional traditions of all Member States" and "respect for the rule of law within the Union is a prerequisite for the protection of fundamental rights".[14]

Liberty, democracy, respect for human rights and fundamental freedoms, and the rule of law are the principles on which the European Union was founded and which are common to all the Member States,[15] The mentioned principles were formally established as the structural and constitutional, cornerstones of the EU's legal system following the amendments introduced by the Treaty of Amsterdam in 1997.[16] This updated version of the Treaty[17] reconfirmed the same principles including the rule of law and established that their respect is the precondition for the new Member States to be admitted to the European Union. The Lisbon Treaty,[18] which supercedes the above two treaties, defines rule of law among the foundation values of the European Union: 'The Union is founded on the values of respect for human dignity, freedom, democracy, equality, the rule of law and respect for human rights'.[19] The same values (principles) are applied in relation to the countries that are admitted to the European Union, they should respect the values referred to in Article 1a and are committed to promoting them.[20]

Perhaps the widest understanding of the rule of law is offered by the World Justice Project, which in its 2022 report states that:

> Effective rule of law reduces corruption, combats poverty and disease, and protects people from injustices large and small. It is the foundation for communities of justice, opportunity, and peace – underpinning development, accountable government, and respect for fundamental rights. Traditionally, the rule of law has been viewed as the domain of lawyers and judges. However, everyday issues of safety, rights, justice, and governance affect us all; everyone is a stakeholder in the rule of law.[21]

[13] ibid.

[14] European Parliament resolution of 25 October 2016 with recommendations to the Commission on the establishment of an EU mechanism on democracy, the rule of law and fundamental rights, *OJ C 215*, 19.6.2018, p 162–177.

[15] Treaty on European Union (TEU), signed at Maastricht on 7 February 1992, *OJ C 191*, 29.6.1992, p 4–96.

[16] L Appicciafuoco, 'The Promotion of the Rule of Law in the Western Balkans: The European Union's Role' (2010) 11(8) *German Law Journal* 741.

[17] Consolidated version of the Treaty on European Union (CTEU), *OJ C 340*, 10.11.1997, 145–172.

[18] Treaty of Lisbon amending the Treaty on European Union and the Treaty establishing the European Community, signed at Lisbon, 13 December 2007, *OJ C 306*, 17.12.2007, 1–271.

[19] ibid Art 1a.

[20] ibid Art 49.

[21] The World Justice Project (WJP), Rule of Law Index® 2022 Report 13.

The rule of law is fundamental in advancing democracy if we consider it not solely an instrument of the government but as a rule to which the entire society (including the government) is bound. We should focus not only on the application of norms and procedures in order to strength the rule of law, but also emphasise its fundamental role in protecting rights and advancing inclusiveness, and in this way, framing the protection of rights within the broader discourse on human development.[22]

2.2. Rule of Law, Balkan Perspective

As previously indicated, the rule of law is a fundamental value that countries aspiring to join the European Union must uphold. The Treaty on European Union in Article 49 defines the conditions and in Article 1a values (previously – principles in Article 6) to which any country wishing to become a member of the European Union must conform. Such criteria (the Copenhagen criteria) were established by the Copenhagen European Council in 1993, strengthened by the Madrid European Council in 1995. These criteria include a stable democracy and the rule of law among other things.

The process of admission of the West Balkan countries demonstrates the importance of the implementation of the rule of law for the European future of the countries. The EU promotes the rule of law via its enlargement policy package, which provides that 'Accession candidates must give the rule of law, justice and fundamental rights utmost priority in the negotiations.'[23] The 2018 EU-Western Balkans strategy aims to build good neighbourly relations, especially taking into consideration the long-standing ethnic disputes in the region.[24] Therefore, the 2018 policy package defines six areas of common interest to both the EU and the Western Balkans, namely: (1) the rule of law; (2) security and migration; (3) socio-economic development; (4) transport and energy connectivity; (5) the digital agenda; and (6) reconciliation and good neighbourly relations.[25]

One of the main elements of the enlargement plan is the fulfilment of the mentioned Copenhagen criteria, as well as acquis communautaire, in particular chapter 23 thereof *Judiciary and Fundamental Rights*. And here it should be noted that according to World Justice Project, West Balkan countries have low rule of law index/score;[26] with even greater issues. Lasting problems with the rule of law in the

[22] M Tommasoli, 'Rule of law and democracy: addressing the gap between policies and practices' UN Chronicle, Dec. 2012, No. 4 Vol. XLIX, *Delivering Justice*. Available at: www.un.org/en/chronicle/article/rule-law-and-democracy-addressing-gap-between-policies-and-practices.

[23] European Commission, 'Communication on a Credible Enlargement Perspective for and Enhanced EU Engagement with the Western Balkans' COM (2018) available at: eur-lex.europa.eu/legal-content/EN/TXT/?uri=COM:2018:065:FIN.

[24] A Hoxhaj, 'The EU Rule of Law Initiative Towards the Western Balkans' (2021) 13 *Hague Journal on the Rule of Law* 143.

[25] European Commission (n 23).

[26] World Justice Project, Rule of Law index, <WJP Rule of Law Index | Global Insights (worldjusticeproject.org)> accessed 2 December 2023.

Western Balkans have already been pointed out by the Freedom House additionally. In its 2016 *Freedom in the World* report[27] there was observed an absence of the rule of law and an increase in patronage networks and clientelism, which threaten democratic institutions in the region. The 2021 report[28] pointed out countries that had experienced both setbacks (Serbia and Kosovo) and progress (Montenegro and North Macedonia).

Although the rule of law reform is a complex, expensive, and challenging issue, and despite a lack of shared and specific understanding of means, goals, opinions, and priorities between diverse stakeholders,[29] and although practitioners and legal experts do not share the same understanding of how rule of law can be established, the 2018 EU-Western Balkans strategy for the rule of law reforms in the Western Balkans should be considered as promising as it offers a platform for a productive dialogue between the EU and the countries of the Western Balkans. It can be seen as the EU's future engagement in the region.[30]

3. Access to Justice

International organisations, including the EU, the World Bank and the United Nations while promoting rule of law reforms focus on judicial reform as the primary objective.[31] Judiciary reform aiming to provide an independent, impartial, and efficient judiciary is considered to be the main component of the rule of law. Very often the concepts of 'rule of law' and 'judiciary reform' have been interchangeably used as having the same meaning.[32]

The reform of the judiciary can include many components, for instance, establishing independent judiciaries and modern justice and penitentiary systems, strengthening the capacity of justice institutions, promoting good governance and accountability (e.g., by fighting corruption), strengthening civilian control and oversight of justice systems, promoting and protecting human rights and freedoms, and improving access to justice.

This chapter will be focused on the last of the indicated components, access to justice.

[27] Freedom House, Freedom in the World report 2016 available at: freedomhouse.org/sites/default/files/FH_FITW_Report_2016.pdf.

[28] Freedom House, Freedom in the World report 2021, available at: freedomhouse.org/sites/default/files/2021-02/FIW2021_World_02252021_FINAL-web-upload.pdf.

[29] M Mendelski, 'The Rule of Law'.

[30] A Hoxhaj, 'The new EU rule of law initiative for the Western Balkans' in *Rule of Law in the Western Balkans: Exploring the New EU Enlargement Strategy and Necessary Steps Ahead* (Berlin, Aspen Institute, 2018), 23.

[31] A Memeti, 'Rule of Law Through Judicial Reform' (2014) 1(1) *Contemporary Southeastern Europe*, 58.

[32] ibid.

3.1. Notion and Substance

In contemporary democracies, justice systems occupy a central position among public institutions as autonomous and independent branches of the governments. The reason is that an independent and effective justice system not only provides a safeguard for human rights, but also, for example, regarding a number of other aspects of life in society that are crucial to the well-being of individuals and organisations, such as health, work, industrial relations, social security, family relations, civil rights, environmental rights, consumer rights, property rights, the enforcement of contracts.[33] It was well indicated by Kofi Annan in 2004 (Secretary-General of the United Nations that period), 'without a credible machinery to enforce the law and resolve disputes, people resorted to violence and illegal means'.[34] and 'The centrality of a strong justice mechanism lies in its essential contribution to fostering economic stability and growth, and to enabling all manner of disputes to be resolved within a structured and orderly framework';[35] therefore, it is crucial to analyse the justice system's functionality and define the factors that could strength or weaken it.

Scientific papers and official reports diagnose poor access to justice everywhere and warn of the consequences: growing caseloads, rising costs, and longer delays; scarce financial and human resources; an inefficient work organisation.[36] A state of 'crisis' is in place in large and small, rich and poor regions, regardless of their level of political and legal development.[37] For instance, the Action Committee on Access to Justice in Civil and Family Matters published the special report in 2013 that started with the words:

> There is a serious access to justice problem in Canada. The civil and family justice system is too complex, too slow and too expensive. It is too often incapable of producing just outcomes that are proportional to the problems brought to it or reflective of the needs of the people it is meant to serve. While there are many dedicated people trying hard to make it work and there have been many reform efforts, the system continues to lack coherent leadership, institutional structures that can design and implement change, and appropriate coordination to ensure consistent and cost effective reform. Major change is needed.[38]

[33] CEPEJ, 'The functioning of judicial systems and the situation of the economy in the European Union Member States: COMPILED REPORT' (CEPEJ, Strasbourg, 2013), available at: ec.europa.eu/justice/effective-justice/files/cepej_study_justice_scoreboard_en.pdf.

[34] Kofi Annan, 'Access to Justice' (UNDP Practice Note, 2004).

[35] UNODC, 'Judicial integrity' United Nations Office on Drugs and Crime, available at: www.unodc.org/unodc/en/corruption/judicial-integrity.html.

[36] See: Tommasoli (n 22), M Abregú, 2001 'Barricades or Obstacles: The Challenges of Access to Justice' in R V Puymbroeck (ed) *Comprehensive Legal and Judicial Development: Toward an Agenda for a Just and Equitable Society in the 21st Century* (The World Bank, Washington D.C., 2001) 53; National Center for Access to Justice available at: ncaj.org/what-access-justice; UNDP, Strengthening Judicial Integrity through Enhanced Access to Justice (2013); European Union Agency for Fundamental Rights, Access to Justice in Europe: an overview of challenges and opportunities (2011).

[37] H Fix-Fierro, *Courts, Justice and Efficiency: A Socio-legal Study of Economic Rationality in Adjudication* (Oxford, Hart Publishing, 2003) 1.

[38] 'Access to Civil & Family Justice: A Roadmap for Change Action Committee on Access to Justice in Civil and Family Matters' (2013) Available at: www.cfcj-fcjc.org/sites/default/files/docs/2013/AC_Report_English_Final.pdf.

In the USA, the Department of Justice talks about the 'access-to-justice crisis' and in March 2010, it established the Access to Justice Initiative (ATJ) to address it. According to the ATJ official site, 'ATJ's mission is to help the justice system efficiently deliver outcomes that are fair and accessible to all, irrespective of wealth and status'.[39] The ATJ's staff works within the Department of Justice, across federal agencies, and with state, local, and tribal justice system stakeholders to increase access to counsel and legal assistance and to improve the justice delivery systems that serve people who are unable to afford lawyers.

When we refer to the EU, according to the European Union Agency for Fundamental Rights (FRA), 'Access to justice is a core fundamental right and a central concept in the broader field of justice. However, it is a right that faces a number of challenges throughout the EU'.[40] According to another European authority, the European Commission, 'The EU recognises the need for better access to justice for individuals and companies'.[41]

Access to justice has traditionally been seen as access to the courts or the availability of legal assistance; however, this interpretation was extended significantly. Still, there is no unique definition of the access to justice, but among many offered by scientists and official documents we consider the more accurate the access to justice definition suggested by Linn Hammergren, formerly of the World Bank Poverty Reduction Group, who argues for a broader conception of access: 'the right of access, in its amplest sense, does not refer to specific cases and users, but rather to participation in the individual and collective benefits accruing from society's provision of the best, and most equitably delivered, justice service it can render'.[42]

Despite the absence of the unique interpretation, there are a number of measures elaborated by scientists and official organisations. Among them legal aid and mediation (ADR) are always indicated. Legal aid can be provided by state authorities or special foundations, like for example, the Access to Justice Foundation in the United Kingdom. One of the interpretations of the access to justice includes overcoming three groups of obstacles: economic, organisational, and procedural. Alternative dispute resolution is regarded as the measure to overcome procedural obstacles to access to justice.[43]

The United Nations Development Programme (UNDP) has defined the main barriers to access to justice to be overcome:[44]

[39] The U.S. Department of Justice official site Available at: www.justice.gov/atj.

[40] The European Union Agency for Fundamental Rights official site. Available at: fra.europa.eu/en/theme/access-justice.

[41] The European Commission official site. Available at: ec.europa.eu/justice/civil/access-justice/index_en.htm.

[42] V Maru, 'Access to Justice and Legal Empowerment: A Review of World Bank Practice' (2009) 9 *The Justice and Development Working Paper series*.

[43] M Cappelletti, 'Alternative Dispute Resolution Processes within the Framework of the World-Wide Access-to-Justice Movement' (1993) 3 *The Modern Law Review* 56.

[44] UNDP, 'Access to Justice: UNDP Practice Note' (2004).

- Long delays; prohibitive costs of using the system; lack of available and affordable legal representation, that is reliable and has integrity; abuse of authority and powers, resulting in unlawful searches, seizures, detention and imprisonment; and weak enforcement of laws and implementation of orders and decrees.
- Severe limitations in existing remedies provided either by law or in practice. Most legal systems fail to provide remedies that are preventive, timely, non-discriminatory, adequate, just and deterrent.
- Gender bias and other barriers in the law and legal systems: inadequacies in existing laws effectively fail to protect women, children, poor and other disadvantaged people, including those with disabilities and low levels of literacy.
- Lack of de facto protection, especially for women, children, and men in prisons or centres of detention.
- Lack of adequate information about what is supposed to exist under the law, what prevails in practice, and limited popular knowledge of rights.
- Lack of adequate legal aid systems.
- Limited public participation in reform programmes.
- Excessive number of laws.
- Formalistic and expensive legal procedures (in criminal and civil litigation and in administrative board procedures).
- Avoidance of the legal system due to economic reasons, fear, or a sense of futility of purpose.

One of the remedies that should overcome the mentioned barriers should be ADR according to the position of the World Bank, CEPEJ and other international institutions, as well as a number of scholars. In addition, the Green Paper defines that:

> One of the factors underpinning the development of ADR is of a practical and conjunctural nature. ADRs offer a solution to the problem of access to justice faced by citizens in many countries due to three factors: the volume of disputes brought before courts is increasing, the proceedings are becoming lengthier and the costs incurred by such proceedings are increasing. And the quantity, complexity and technical obscurity of the legislation also help to make access to justice more difficult.[45]

3.2. Access to Justice in Western Balkan Countries

While discussing access to justice in Balkan countries, the focus should be on entrenching the rule of law, effective fighting against corruption and organised crime, support for competent and independent judiciary, and the protection of

[45] Green paper on alternative dispute resolution in civil and commercial law, European Commission at 7 (19/04/2002), available at: eur-lex.europa.eu/legal-content/EN/ALL/?uri=CELEX:52002DC0196.

minority rights; these are the core of the EU and core goal of the Balkan region.[46] The rule of law needs a transparent legal system to exist; its main components are a clear set of laws that are freely and easily accessible to all, strong enforcement structures, and an independent judiciary to protect citizens against the arbitrary use of power by the state, individuals, or any other organisation. The administering of an independent judiciary is crucial for existing of the free society.[47] Therefore, it is not strange that the EU (together with different countries and international organisations) not only insists on necessity to strengthen the rule of law, but also is financing the required reforms. EU financial assistance is mainly channelled through the Instrument for Pre-accession (IPA), which supports the adoption and implementation of the reforms required for EU membership. During 2014–2020, EUR 690 million was allocated to the Western Balkans to support the rule of law and fundamental rights. The most funds were allocated to Serbia (EUR 246 million), and the lowest amount was given to Montenegro (EUR 42 million).[48]

The problem with judiciary reform in the Western Balkan countries is that there is no comprehensive approach and that the political context of each country is not taken into consideration. The EU does everything to establish in the Western Balkan countries an EU model of rule of law as well as judiciary compatible with EU Member States as the Western Balkan countries should become EU members in the future. Thus, the goal is to achieve a degree of similarity, or even parity, of standards between countries preparing to join the EU and current members, and not adjust to the countries' specifics.[49]

According to Hoxhaj,[50] the rule of law reforms should focus on three pillars: (1) increasing judicial capacity, (2) access to justice; and (3) digital justice.

1) In 'increasing judicial capacity' key changes can be made in culture, organisational structure, and good governance practice in the judiciary, thereby improving transparency and tackling corruption more effectively. Here a wide-reaching social transformation is also needed, not just a merely institutional approach to the rule of law and, in particular, in closing chapters 23 and 24 which pertain to *Judiciary and Fundamental Rights* and *Justice, Freedom and Security*. The EU should cooperate with the countries of the Western Balkans in seeking to change the inner substance of the judiciary. Like in most post-totalitarian countries, the judiciary in the Western Balkans is often highly corrupt. Therefore, changing the judiciary and more closely aligning it to the needs of ordinary citizens is crucial. Furthermore, it is important to ensure that judiciary is based on accountability, integrity, and openness. In addition,

[46] S Šelo Šabić, 'Fundamentals first: operationalizing the fight against corruption in the EU accession of the Western Balkan Countries', in *Rule of Law in the Western Balkans: Exploring the New EU Enlargement Strategy and Necessary Steps Ahead* (Berlin, Aspen Institute, 2018), 52.

[47] B Bara and J Bara, 'Rule of Law and Judicial Independence in Albania', (2017) 2(1) *University of Bologna Law Review* 23.

[48] European Court of Auditors (ECA), 'EU support for the rule of law in the Western Balkans: despite efforts, fundamental problems persist', Special Report 2022.

[49] Memeti (n 23).

[50] Hoxhaj (n 30).

it would be useful to adopt modern management practices, which would focus on results and a reliable accountability. All these initiatives should help to institutionalise the performance of judicial systems and, as a result, strengthen the judicial processes and potentially eliminate unethical practices and reduce the level of corruption. Due to limited investment into the judicial infrastructure, there are not a sufficient number of courts and citizens are forced to travel long distances following the cases moving to upper courts and tribunals. In such a way the citizens have limited access to justice. Therefore, paying attention to infrastructure development and increasing the capacity and resources of the judiciary should result in rendering the judiciary more accessible to the citizens of the Western Balkan countries.

2) According to the constitutions of the Western Balkan countries, all citizens have equal protection by law; everybody has equal 'access to justice'. However, in practice access to justice and free legal aid remain a challenge to citizens of the countries of the Western Balkans.[51] In this pillar, the rule of law initiative should be concentrated in taking effective steps towards reducing the obstacles that hinder public access to information, ensuring proximity and closer access to courts, as well as simplifying court procedures so that all parties can effectively participate in court processes. The initiative should ensure it enables citizens to be closer to the justice system via simplifying the court documents and procedures for all parties involved in the due process. This initiative ties closely to the above one and should be satisfied by establishing more courts and/or tribunals, in particular special courts for young offenders and other vulnerable groups. Court claims should be resolved in more effective and fairer way. This pillar also includes establishment of free legal aid centres and incorporate these into the judicial system. Such free legal aid is a very important element of access to justice for all the citizens, especially for marginalised and vulnerable groups. In addition, access to justice would be ensured through offering technical support and developing a digital case management system. Using the appropriate technology (including audiovisual recording and transcription of court proceedings) would not only ensure court efficiency, and make courts more transparent and easy to access, but also reduce the level of corruption in the judiciary.

3) Regarding 'digital justice', the use of technology should improve the administration of justice. As mentioned above, it can have a positive impact on enabling fair trials and further enhancing the effectiveness of administrative processes through data management, data processing, and secure archiving of the information of cases. The use of technology should guarantee more transparency and fairness in the adjudication of cases and due process, as well as facilitating better internal and external communication of the judiciary in the region. The use of technology can help to deliver more efficient, intelligent, and

[51] EU – Western Balkans Justice and Home Affairs ministerial forum – joint press statement (27 October 2017), available at: www.consilium.europa.eu/en/press/press-releases/2017/10/27/eu-western-balkans-justice-and-home-affairs-ministerial-forum-joint-press-statement/.

citizen-centric public services as well as encourage fairer decisions in courts. In a joint press statement EU – *Western Balkans: Ministerial Forum on Justice and Home Affairs, 3 December 2021*[52] the EU and the Western Balkans reaffirmed the importance of digitalisation in order to facilitate access to justice, improve its overall efficiency, and ensure the resilience of justice systems while also strengthening their integrity and accountability. The Western Balkan countries have made some progress on the establishment and generalised use of the Case Management System (CMS), the random allocation of cases, and public access to judgments. Among other things, digitalisation should reduce amount of long court delays as well as significantly cut some costs involved.

With regard to the mentioned areas for improvement, we would like to pay attention to judicial efficiency in Western Balkan countries. The judiciary is characterised by the long court delays and high backlog in cases.

Albania. A UNDP survey on access to justice in Albania[53] finds that the need for justice in the country is largely unmet. Almost half of the population has experienced legal problems; this is particularly true for members of disadvantaged groups. Court management in Albania remains poor. Albania is characterised by long delays in conducting judicial proceedings, a high backlog of cases, and lack of transparency in the judicial system, all of which further weaken it. Albania should undertake the following actions to improve the access to justice: 1) establish a functional legal aid system, 2) make legal representation and advice more accessible, 3) make the court system more accessible 4) build an effective mediation system.

Bosnia and Herzegovina. Bosnia and Herzegovina (BiH) has made some progress regarding the judicial system. The length of court proceedings has decreased in recent years.[54] The reduction of backlogs has contributed to making the courts more accountable. However, there is still a huge backlog and no effective mechanism to enforce court orders. Equal access to justice is also severely undermined by the fragmentation, politicisation, and inefficiency of the judicial system.[55] The EU also notes the necessity of implementing Alternative Dispute Resolution (ADR) methods, particularly mediation.[56]

Kosovo. The administration of justice in Kosovo is slow and inefficient. There is a large backlog of pending cases at court level. Judicial efficiency is constrained by the lack of physical, technical, and financial resources. Although a mediation system has been operational since 2008, it faces challenges such as low remuneration and insufficient funding, leading to the closure of three out of seven regional mediation centres. Public awareness or familiarity with alternative dispute resolution tools

[52] Joint press statement EU – Western Balkans: Ministerial Forum on Justice and Home Affairs, 3 December 2021, available at: www.consilium.europa.eu/it/press/press-releases/2021/12/03/joint-press-statement-eu-western-balkans-ministerial-forum-on-justice-and-home-affairs/.

[53] UNDP, Survey on Access to Justice in Albania (22 November 2017).

[54] European Commission, Bosnia and Herzegovina 2018 report. SWD (2018) 155 final.

[55] Haider (n 6).

[56] European Commission, Bosnia and Herzegovina 2018 report. SWD (2018) 155 final.

remains low, but the number of referred and solved cases has increased to about 1600 in 2017. Both the mediation and notary systems need further strengthening. Additionally, Kosovo needs to develop e-justice tools.[57]

North Macedonia. The government adopted the 2017–2022 Judicial Reform Strategy and a corresponding action plan. The efficiency of the judiciary in Macedonia has improved. Case backlogs have not been an issue for several years, although transparency remains an issue, even though it has improved with the publication of decisions on the courts' website.[58]

Montenegro. The key objectives of the Judicial Reform Strategy 2014–2018 include strengthening the independence, impartiality, and accountability of the judiciary. Montenegro, in general, is not affected by substantial court backlogs. The impact of alternative dispute resolution continues to be low and has even declined. The use of mediation needs to be promoted, further both among judges and parties to the disputes.[59]

Serbia. Serbia's judicial system performs at a lower standard than that of EU member states. Judicial efficiency and public confidence in the judiciary is undermined by a large backlog of cases, inadequate levels of competence, a high level of bureaucracy and red tape, and unchecked procedural abuses. There has been some progress, notably a reduction in the backlog of old enforcement cases and the adoption of measures to harmonise court practice. It should be noted that in the 2.5 years (2016–2018), almost 1 million cases were cleared from the backlog and efficiency measures were extended to courts covering more than 82 per cent of the Serbian population. However, access to justice is hindered by high legal fees, the lack of an efficient free legal aid system and delays in the adoption of the Law on Free Legal Aid, the poor availability and performance of appointed defence lawyers, delays in case processing, inefficient procedures for awarding compensation, and weak enforcement of final judgments. Little progress was made in introducing alternative dispute resolution mechanisms such as mediation. Awareness raising and promotion, including by relevant national associations, increased. In June 2017, the Supreme Court of Cassation, High Judicial Council, and the Ministry of Justice passed guidelines for enhancing mediation in Serbia. The use of mediation for alternative dispute resolution is still not satisfactory due to lack of systemic measures and support by all relevant institutions.[60]

4. Conclusions

The essence of the Western Balkans enlargement strategy towards the rule of law is to make certain the independence, quality, and efficiency of the judicial system.

[57] European Commission, Kosovo 2018 report. SWD (2018) 151 final.
[58] Haider (n 6).
[59] European Commission, Montenegro 2018 report. SWD (2018) 150 final.
[60] European Commission, Serbia 2018 report. SWD (2018) 152 final.

> The strategy not only requires the independence of the judiciary and of individual judges to ensure fairness and to hold the executive and legislative branches of the government to account, but it can also be translated as a crucial precondition for any democratic society based on the rule of law in the European Union.[61]

Strengthening the rule of law on paper, even by passing judicial reform packages as was done in all the Western Balkan countries, is not enough to strengthen and ensure the rule of law in practice. Despite more than 20 years of the EU support to reforms in the Western Balkans, fundamental problems persist. The EU Commission and other international organisations (e.g., the World Bank, the UN) report limited progress in the rule of law situation in the region. The suggested and financed reforms have clearly not been sufficient to effect real change in the rule of law, mainly because of the lack of domestic ownership and political will. The 2019 and 2022 evaluations of EU support for the rule of law recognised that EU support had inspired positive developments (including the one of access to justice); however, it also highlighted that progress was nevertheless limited and sustainability difficult to achieve. According to the evaluation, 'this is correlated to low levels of political will, institutional resistance to change, and inadequate participation or marginalisation of civil society'. The EU IPA has contributed to reforms in technical areas, such as the efficiency of the judiciary and the development of relevant legislation, but in a context of insufficient political will, it has had a limited overall impact in advancing fundamental rule of law reforms in the region. Some positive developments were noted mainly in Albania and North Macedonia, however, the EU Commission and other international organisations report limited progress in the rule of law in such areas as the independence of the judiciary, the concentration of power, political interference and corruption, which call for additional efforts in promoting reforms in these areas.[62] Overall, the EU Commission has found that, while EU action has contributed to reforms in technical and operational areas, such as improving the efficiency of the judiciary and the development of relevant legislation, it has had little overall impact on fundamental rule of law reforms in the region. A key reason for this is the insufficient domestic political will to drive the necessary reforms.[63]

However, the rule of law initiative for the Western Balkans is an encouraging new approach by the European Commission, and it has the potential to generate a more productive platform for the EU and the Western Balkans to engage in an evidence-based policy dialogue. Nevertheless, to be successful, the EU policy should also focus on institutional capacity building and investment in the judicial infrastructure to make it more accessible to the citizens of the Western Balkans.[64]

Thus, there should be a will from the Western Balkan countries, not only an order from the EU Commission to ensure the success of the rule of law and access to justice reforms.

[61] Hoxhaj (n 30).

[62] European Court of Auditors (ECA), 'EU support for the rule of law in the Western Balkans: despite efforts, fundamental problems persist', Special Report 2022.

[63] ibid.

[64] Hoxhaj (n 24).

PART 2

Substantive Rights, Such as Right to Property

5

The System of Consumer Protection and its Correlation with the Concept of Human Rights Protection in Southeast Europe

DARKO SPASEVSKI

1. Introduction

Almost every paper that analyses the development and protection of consumer rights usually includes two very famous quotations. The first one is the well-known statement made by President Kennedy when he introduced the Consumers Bill of Rights, stating that 'consumers, by definition, include us all'.[1] The second one is the equally famous quote by Mahatma Gandhi, who said:

> a customer is the most important visitor on our premises; he is not dependent on us. We are dependent on him. He is not an interruption in our work. He is the purpose of it. He is not an outsider in our business. He is part of it. We are not doing him a favour by serving him. He is doing us a favour by giving us an opportunity to do so.[2]

The discussion about the nature of consumer rights has become a very important issue since the formalisation of consumer rights through legislation and the enactment of national legislation for consumer protection. The process of legislating consumer rights has been time-consuming and full of dilemmas. The most controversial and challenging topic for discussion is the connection between consumer rights and human rights. The questions that need answering are: are consumer rights human rights? Or are consumer rights close to human rights but cannot be treated as human rights? It seems that the sensitivity of this discussion is an ongoing issue that is relevant not just for legal scholars but also for international and

[1] See EC Wacinkiewicz 'Consumer's Rights as a Special Category of Human Rights' (2013) 1(2) *International Journal on Consumer Law and Practice* 18 and M Durovic, 'International Consumer Law: What Is It All About?' (2019) *Journal of Consumer Policy* 127.

[2] See SN Mandal, 'Protection of Consumers' Rights: A Socio-Legal Challenge in India' (2010), *SSRN Electronic Journal* 1, available at: papers.ssrn.com/sol3/papers.cfm?abstract_id=1707568.

national governmental and non-governmental organisations, consumer associations, practitioners, and more.

This chapter will focus on the countries of Southeast Europe by analysing the relevant national legislation of the Republic of Macedonia, Albania, Serbia, Bosnia and Herzegovina, Montenegro, and Kosovo.

The research will cover the following very important aspects: i) the scope of protection of consumer rights within the so-called 'consumer rights directory' and the definition of consumer contracts, ii) the notion of the weaker contractual party as defined in the national legislation, iii) the public-law elements in consumer protection legislation, and iv) the constitutional approach towards consumer protection. These aspects are chosen because they are usually used to explain the correlation between consumer rights (protection) and human rights (protection).

2. Are Consumer Rights on the Way to Becoming Human Right?

On many occasions, in various works of legal literature, significant current developments, often of a global character, are cited as milestones in the development of consumer rights. Some authors refer to the financial crisis as an important milestone for the development of a more comprehensive system of consumer rights protection.[3] Other authors associate the development of a consumer rights protection system with certain:

> major global consumer law scandals, which simultaneously affected consumers in many different jurisdictions (eg Apple or Dieselgate) [and] have demonstrated the increasing relevance of international consumer law, highlighting the need for a response to these consumer law issues on a global level.[4]

Furthermore, according to the positioning of these authors, the development of consumer protection can be seen through its 'internationalisation' that will:

> focus on, first, the establishment of globally accepted minimum standards of consumer protection and, second, the development and facilitation of cooperation as a necessary pre-requisite for the efficient protection of consumers rather than on the harmonisation of substantive consumer law[5]

In addition, based on the findings of these authors, the internationalisation of consumer protection can be achieved through the 'UN Guidelines as the most

[3] See M Coakley and A Daniel, 'Improving Consumer Protection: Lessons from the 2008 Recession' (2019) *Minnesota Law Review*; M Melecky and S Rutledge, 'Financial Consumer Protection and the Global Financial Crisis' (2011) *Munich Personal RePEc Archive* available at: mpra.ub.uni-muenchen.de/28201/ and S Gojinetchi, 'Consumer Protection in the Shadow of the Global Financial Crisis – A study on the way forward of Consumer Protection in European Union, Republic of Moldova and P.R. of China' (2012) *Munich Personal RePEc Archive*, available at: mpra.ub.uni-muenchen.de/36630/.

[4] M Durovic (n 1) 137.

[5] ibid 126.

important source of international consumer law and, second, on the International Consumer Protection and Enforcement Network (ICPEN) as the most prominent global framework for cooperation in the area of consumer protection'.[6]

A very important trigger to re-examine the consumer protection legal framework was the COVID-19 pandemic. Of course, this is an event, the consequences of which are still ongoing, and it is still too early for more serious conclusions, but the fact is that a series of research has already analysed the situation in-depth and emphasised the need to increase consumer protection.[7]

When discussing whether there is a place for consumer rights on the list of human rights, different approaches can be seen. Essentially, both extremes are observed, as well several approaches that can be determined somewhere in between. This means that there are approaches according to which the character of consumer rights as a human right is contested, as well as opposing approaches that treat consumer rights as human rights. In the middle, there are approaches according to which consumer rights currently do not have the character of human rights but which leave room for them to acquire the character of human rights or at least soft human rights.

The main and dominant approach for describing the evolution of human rights is Vesak's three generations concept, according to which the first generation of human rights includes civil and political rights such as the right to life, freedom of expression, equality before the law, the right to vote, etc.; the second generation includes economic, social, and cultural rights such as the right to work, freedom of association, the right to education, etc., and the third generation of rights, which are in the process of embarking, known as solidarity rights including the right to development, the right to a healthy environment, the right to self-determination, etc.[8]

When discussing the reason for the development of the third generation of human rights, Sadeghi and others opine that the third generation is ascertained as a result of 'new needs of human'.[9]

Some authors notice that the introduction of new human rights will:

> create a damaging climate in terms of the value and validity of existing human rights' and furthermore, 'the proclamation of new human rights can be justified only when the need is sufficiently great and when the chance of acceptance by the international community is strong.[10]

[6] ibid.

[7] See OECD, 'The impact of the COVID-19 pandemic on financial consumers in Asia' (2022), available at: www.oecd.org/financial/education/the-impact-of-the-covid-19-pandemic-on-financial-consumers-in-asia.htm.

[8] See R Ariyaratna, 'Consumer Rights in the Context of Human Rights: A Legal Analysis' (2022) 2 *KDU Law Journal* 34.

[9] See SH Sadeghi, et al, 'Concept of 'Right' and its Three Generations' (2017) 5(4) *International Journal of Scientific Study* 38 available at https://www.ijss-sn.com/uploads/2/0/1/5/20153321/ijss-iran_jul_oa06_-_2017.pdf.

[10] See S Deutch , 'Are Consumer Rights Human Rights?' (1994) 32 (3) *Osgoode Hall Law Journal* 540 available at: digitalcommons.osgoode.yorku.ca/ohlj/vol32/iss3/4.

Many authors, when discussing the evolution of the development of human rights in general, express that:

> the recognition and operationalisation of a new human right is a long process that requires the consensus of international actors, the common accord of academics and experts in its conceptualisation and, last but not least, the willingness of governments to bind themselves to another human rights obligation.[11]

Although not closely related to the issue of interest of this paper, it is important to highlight the right to access the internet, and all the controversies related to it. In this regard, the intervention of the United Nations with the non-binding Resolution in 2016 should be underlined. This intervention declared internet access as a human right (even in a non-binding resolution). The non-binding resolution 'affirms also the importance of applying a comprehensive human rights-based approach in providing and in expanding access to Internet and requests all States to make efforts to bridge the many forms of digital divides'.[12] The essence of the resolution is an interpretation of Articles 19 of the Universal Declaration of Human Rights and the International Covenant on Civil and Political Rights with the intention that the same rights that people have offline must also be protected online, particularly freedom of expression.[13]

Furthermore, another example is the development of the right to water and sanitation. It took more than 25 years from launching the debate on the right to water and sanitation to the adoption of the separate General Comment by the Committee on Economic, Social and Cultural Rights (2002) and the General Assembly resolution on this matter (2010).[14] However, the process itself was quite challenging.[15]

One approach that tries to treat consumer rights as human rights is based on the assumption that the protection of consumer rights means protection of human dignity. According to some authors, 'protection of the individual consumer is perceived as part of maintaining human dignity-especially against big business organizations, monopolies, cartels, and multinational corporations'.[16]

Some authors emphasise the possibility for consumer rights to become human rights, using the argumentation of Deutch, according to whom 'consumer rights have the potential to become human rights because they contain a number of the characteristics of human rights. In particular, key elements are the wide

[11] See Ł Szoszkiewicz, 'Internet Access as a New Human Right? State of the Art on the Threshold of 2020' (2018) *Przegląd Prawniczy Uniwersytetu im Adama Mickiewicza* 49, available at: www.researchgate.net/publication/328290234_Internet_Access_as_a_New_Human_Right_State_of_the_Art_on_the_Threshold_of_2020.

[12] See United Nations, 'Internet Statement' (2016), available at: ap.ohchr.org/do cuments/E/HRC/d_res_dec/A_HRC_32_L20.docx.

[13] ibid.

[14] See Ł Szoszkiewicz (n 12) 49.

[15] ibid.

[16] See S Deutch (n 9) 537, 552.

recognition and universality of these rights, the promotion of human dignity and well-being, and the protection of individuals against more powerful entities such as governments'.[17]

3. The Notion of the Weaker Contracting Party in Legislation in Southeast Europe

Business-to-consumer relations are contractual relations between businesses and consumers. In general, the business as a party of the consumer contract is an entity of private law. However, in some cases, this entity can have a public-law character. This is the case with public-owned enterprises[18] which are not governed within the company law legislation and are providing services and goods to the general public by entering into contractual relations with consumers.

When analysing the legislation for consumer protection in Southeast Europe, it can be concluded that the legislative acts of the respective countries contain very similar definitions for business-to-consumer contracts and general clauses for protecting the weaker contracting party (the consumer). General provisions that tend to protect the weaker contractual party are visible in Articles 2(2) and 4(3) of the Law on Consumer Protection of the Republic of Macedonia.[19] Namely, Article 2(2) of the Law on Consumer Protection of the Republic of Macedonia contains a general clause which states that 'the consumer cannot waive his rights determined by this law', and Article 4(3) explicitly provides that 'when applying the provisions of this law, the position of the consumer as the economically weaker party, and especially the position of vulnerable consumers, must be considered'.

Provisions with the aim of providing balance and equality between the parties can also be found in the Serbian Law on Consumer Protection.[20] As a general clause in Article 3(1) of the Law on Consumer Protection of the Republic of Serbia, it is foreseen that 'the consumer cannot waive rights established by this law' and that 'contractual provision or other legal document which directly or indirectly denies or limits consumer rights recognized by this law are null and void'.

The Law on Consumer Protection of Montenegro,[21] in Article 4(10), contains a general provision according to which 'the consumer cannot waive any rights to

[17] See I Brendoher, *EU Consumer Law and Human Rights* (Oxford, Oxford University Press, 2013) 48.

[18] Eg, this is the case in the Republic of Macedonia, where most of the utility service providers are legal entities of public law known as public enterprises. They are state-owned or owned by local governments. A public enterprise is a specific type of legal form not included in the Law on Companies but regulated by the Law on Public Enterprises. See Law on Public Enterprises, ('Official Gazette of Republic of Macedonia' no 38/96, 9/97, 6/02, 40/03, 49/06, 22/07, 83/09, 97/10, 6/12, 119/13, 41/14, 138/14, 25/15, 61/15, 39/16, 64/18 and 35/19 and 'Official Gazette of Republic of North Macedonia' no 275/19, 89/22 and 274/22).

[19] See Official Gazette of Republic of North Macedonia, no 236/2022.

[20] See Official Gazette of the Republic of Serbia, no 88/2021.

[21] See Official Gazette of Montenegro, no 2/2014, 6/2014, 43/2015, 70/2017 and 67/2019.

which he is entitled by this law'. Additionally, in this case, similarly to the previously analysed countries from Southeast Europe, in Paragraph (2) of Article 4, it is provided that 'the contract provisions between the consumer and the business that are contrary to this law and which are causing damage to the consumer are null and void'.

As a general clause in Article 2 of the Law on Consumer Protection[22] of Bosnia and Herzegovina, it is stipulated that 'the consumer cannot waive or be deprived of the rights granted to him by this law'.

4. Consumer Rights Protection and the Human Rights Regime at the International Level

As a nascent process in the legislative development of the system of consumer rights protection through the system of human rights protection, it should be pointed out that although not explicitly mentioned, several international human rights agreements already implicitly protected consumers. In that sense, three important documents are mentioned: one by the United Nations in 1966, the International Covenant on Economic, Social and Cultural Rights (ICESCR); the second by the Council of Europe, the European Convention on Human Rights (ECHR) of 1950; and the third one, the European Social Charter (ESC) of 1961.[23] This finding is based on the argumentation of some authors that some of the economic and social rights in the ICESCR can be conceived of as consumer protection, such as 'the right to an adequate standard of living, established in Article 11(1), which includes the right to adequate food, clothing, housing, and to a continuous improvement of living conditions'.[24] Also, for example, these authors argue that:

> the right to physical and mental health in Article 12 of the ICESCR includes the improvement of environmental and industrial hygiene, and the prevention of diseases. As the protection of the individual from hazardous products is equally an aim of consumer law, this provision implicitly also protects consumers.[25]

Furthermore, it is a fact that the ECHR also provides implicit consumer protection through Article 6, Article 10, and Article 11.[26]

All of these documents preceded the great reform of the system of consumer rights protection carried out within the administration of President Kennedy, within the framework of the Bill of Consumer Rights. Namely, in 1962, in the

[22] See Official Gazette of Bosnia and Herzegovina, no 25/2006 and 88/2015.
[23] See I Brendoher (n 18) 49.
[24] ibid.
[25] ibid.
[26] ibid.

United States of America, four basic consumer rights were recognised: the right to choose, to information, to safety, and to be heard.[27] This was included in the concept of the Consumer Bill of Rights.

The United Nations Guidelines for Consumer Protection is a very important document for the international consumer protection regime. The guidelines were first adopted by the General Assembly in Resolution 39/248 of 16 April 1985, later expanded by the Economic and Social Council in Resolution E/1999/INF/2/Add.2 of 26 July 1999, and recently revised by the General Assembly in Resolution 70/186 of 22 December 2015.[28]

The meaning of the United Nations Guidelines for Consumer Protection is indisputably recognised as an established set of international consumer law principles.[29] As it is recognised, Guideline 5 of the Revised United Nations Guidelines for Consumer Protection indicates the very important legitimate needs such as:

a) Access by consumers to essential goods and services
b) Protection of vulnerable and disadvantaged consumers
c) Protection of consumers from hazards to their health and safety
d) Promotion and protection of the economic interests of consumers
e) Access by consumers to adequate information
f) Consumer education
g) Availability of effective consumer dispute resolution and redress
h) Freedom to form consumer and other relevant groups or organizations
i) Promotion of sustainable consumption patterns
j) Protection for using electronic commerce that is not less than the other form of commerce, and
k) Protection of consumer privacy.[30]

Many authors are considering the United Nations Guidelines for Consumer Protection as an upgrade of President Kennedy's Bill of Consumer Rights.[31]

The approach of widening the scope of the concept of consumer rights through interpretation of international documents can also be seen in the cases of the protection of consumers using e-commerce and consumer privacy within the United Nations Guidelines for Consumer Protection.[32]

At the international level, the United Nations Conference on Trade and Development (UNCTAD)'s Manual on Consumer Protection should be mentioned

[27] See SN Mandal (n 2) 1.
[28] The data is provided from the official site of UNCTAD available at: unctad.org/topic/competition-and-consumer-protection/un-guidelines-for-consumer-protection.
[29] See I Benöhr, 'The United Nations Guidelines for Consumer Protection: Legal Implications and New Frontiers' (2020), *Journal of Consumer Policy* 106, available at: link.springer.com/article/10.1007/s10603-019-09443-y.
[30] See: Ruwanthika Ariyaratna (n 8) 29.
[31] ibid.
[32] See R Ariyaratna (n 8) 29.

as one of the most important and vibrant documents that underlines the 'intrinsic disparities found in the consumer-supplier relationship such as bargaining power, knowledge, and other resources'.[33] Furthermore, consumer protection is a very important aspect of achieving the implementation of the Sustainable Development Goals (SDG) based on the fact that 'consumer protection measures contribute to equity and social justice by enhancing the bargaining equality between the interests of the consumer and producer'.[34] This should result in 'alleviating the problems of those who are particularly vulnerable in the marketplace such as children, the economically disadvantaged, and others who are illiterate and with specific needs or disabilities'.[35]

Some authors link democracy and basic democratic values with the development of consumer law by observing that this process can be seen as part of the democratisation process of countries, nations, and societies.[36]

Article 38 of the Charter of Fundamental Rights of the European Union (EU), which says that 'the Union policies shall ensure a high level of consumer protection'[37] is a foundational starting point of the system of consumer protection within the EU. This article is actually determinant for the whole regime of consumer protection at the EU level and national level of Member States of the EU. Next in line to this act are the relevant provisions for consumer protection placed within the Treaty on the Functioning of the European Union (TFEU).[38] Namely, in Article 4 (2) (f) of the TFEU, the issue about shared competence between the Union and the Member States is regulated. Article 12 of the TFEU is a general clause that stipulates that 'consumer protection requirements shall be taken into account in defining and implementing other Union policies and activities'. Article 114 (3) of the TFEU sets the important structural role of the Commission and the way of conduct regarding the protection of consumers. Namely, according to this provision:

> the Commission, in its proposals envisaged in paragraph 1 concerning health, safety, environmental protection, and consumer protection, will take as a base a high level of protection, taking account in particular of any new development based on scientific facts. Within their respective powers, the European Parliament and the Council will also seek to achieve this objective.

Article 169 of the TFEU defines specific objectives of the policies such as 'the health, safety, and economic interests of consumers, as well as promoting their right to information, education, and to organize themselves in order to safeguard their interests'.

[33] See R Simpson, 'Achieving the Sustainable Development Goals through Consumer Protection' (2017), UNCTAD 2, available at: unctad.org/system/files/official-document/ditccplp2017d2_en.pdf.
[34] ibid 3.
[35] ibid.
[36] See M Durovic (n 1) 127.
[37] Available at: www.europarl.europa.eu/charter/pdf/text_en.pdf.
[38] Available at: /eur-lex.europa.eu/LexUriServ/LexUriServ.do?uri=CELEX:12012E/TXT:en:PDF.

According to some authors, the position of the provisions for consumer protection within the Charter of Fundamental Rights of the European Union also has its own meaning. Namely, according to these authors, consumer protection is included in the 'Solidarity' chapter of the EU Charter of Fundamental Rights, along with other social provisions such as the right to preventive healthcare, environmental protection, and access to services of general interest what affirm a social European model formulated in response to a perceived need to create a stronger link between the EU and its citizens, and by that they have 'high-level status'.[39]

5. The Scope of Protection of the Consumer Rights and the Directory of Consumer Rights According to the Legislation of Southeast European Countries

According to Cała-Wacinkiewicz, 'the originally formulated consumer rights directory contained four basic rights: right to safety, right to information, right to choose products and services at competitive prices and right of expression of opinions influencing the development of consumer policy.'[40] The same author, in their explanation, continues with the statement that the following rights have been added or modified to the already mentioned four rights: the right to safety, protection of life and health, the right to information and education, the right to protection of economic interests, the right to access to an effective redress system, and the right to association, to be heard and represented.[41] The concept of the directory of consumer rights is introduced in this section as a kind of introduction to the analysis that follows, and it is focused on the directory of consumer rights set by the consumer rights legislation in the countries of Southeast Europe.

In the Republic of Macedonia, with the aim of transposing the relevant directives of the European Union in 2022, a new Law on Consumer Protection was adopted. The Law on Consumer Protection defines the contracting parties in the business-to-consumer relations. Namely, the consumer is defined as 'a natural person who procures goods or uses services for purposes that do not fall within the scope of their trade, business, craft or professional activity',[42] and the business is defined as 'a natural or legal person that supplies goods or provides services, ie offers them, including through other entities that are acting in the name or on behalf of the business, for purposes of its commercial, business, craft, or professional activity, regardless of whether it is state-owned or privately-owned'.[43]

[39] See I Brendoher (n 18) 71.
[40] See EC Wacinkiewicz (n 1) 21.
[41] ibid.
[42] See Art 3 (1) 34) of the Law on Consumer Protection of Republic of Macedonia (Official Gazette of Republic of North Macedonia, no 236/2022).
[43] See Art 3 (1) 53) of the Law on Consumer Protection of Republic of Macedonia, (Official Gazette of Republic of North Macedonia' no 236/2022).

The Law on Consumer Protection of Republic of Macedonia, in Article 2, lists the following consumer rights:

- The right to satisfaction of essential needs, which means the availability of essential goods and services, such as food, clothing, footwear, housing, healthcare protection, education, and hygiene;
- The right to safety, which means protection from goods and services that are harmful to life, health, property, or the environment, as well as from goods whose possession or use is prohibited;
- The right to be informed, which means the disposition of correct data and information that are necessary for a reasonable choice of the offered goods and services, and for making informed decisions;
- The right to choose, which means the opportunity to choose between more goods and services with affordable prices and appropriate quality;
- The right to participate, which means representing the interests of consumers in the processes of enacting and implementing policies for the protection of consumers, as well as the opportunity to represent the consumers in the processes of adopting and implementing new policies for the protection of consumers through associations for the protection of consumer rights;
- The right to legal protection, which means protection of the rights of consumers according to procedures foreseen with laws, in case of an injury to consumer rights, including compensation for the damage;
- The right to consumer education, which means the acquisition of basic knowledge and skills necessary for the correct and reliable choice of goods and services, as well as knowledge of the basic rights and obligations of consumers and the modalities for their realisation;
- The right to a healthy and sustainable environment, which means life and work in an environment that is not harmful and is protective towards life, health, and well-being of the present and future generations, as well as timely and complete information on the condition of the environment.

The scope of consumer rights in the Republic of Serbia is determined by Article 2 of the Law on Consumer Protection[44] as follows:

- The right to satisfaction of essential needs – availability of the most necessary goods and services such as food, clothing, shoes, residential space, health protection, education, and hygiene;
- The right to safety – protection from goods and services that are dangerous to life, health, property, or life or goods whose possession or usage is prohibited;

[44] See: Official Gazette of Republic of Serbia no 98/2006 and 115/2021.

- The right to be informed – provision of correct data that is necessary for a reasonable choice between the offered goods and services;
- The right to choose – the possibility of choice between more goods and services at affordable prices and with appropriate quality;
- The right to participate – representation of the interests of consumers in the procedure of creating and implementing policies for consumer protection and the possibility to participate through organizations and associations of consumers in the proceedings of adoption and implementation of consumer protection policies;
- The right to legal protection – protection of the rights of the consumer in the procedure determined by law in the case of damages to consumer rights and providing compensation for material damages and intangible damages that the consumer has suffered;
- The right to education – acquisition of basic knowledge and skills necessary for proper and reliable choice of products and services and knowledge about basic consumer rights and duties and the procedure for their enforcement;
- The right to a healthy and sustainable environment – life and work in an environment that is not harmful to health and welfare of the present and future generations and timely and complete information about the situation of the environment.

Article 5(1) of the Law on Consumer Protection of Serbia[45] defines the consumer as 'a natural person who obtains goods or services on the market for purposes that do not fall within their business or other commercial activities'. In the same article, in Paragraph 2, the business is defined as 'a legal entity, an entrepreneur or natural person who acts on the market within their own business activities or in other commercial purposes, independently or through other entities acting in the name or on behalf of the business.'

According to Article 2 of the Law on Consumer Protection of Albania, the law is applicable to all relationships between businesses and consumers regarding consumer commodities or services, without prejudice to provisions of *lex specialis* legislative acts.[46] The definition of a consumer in Article 3(6) of the Law on Consumer Protection of Albania states that 'consumer' is any person buying or using goods or services for meeting personal needs, for purposes not related to trade activity or practicing of the profession. The definition for a business included in Article 3(14) states that 'business' means any natural or legal person who is acting for purposes relating to their economic activity, trade, business, craft, or profession and anyone acting in the name or on behalf of the business.[47]

[45] See Official Gazette of Republic of Serbia, no 98/2006 and 115/2021.

[46] See Law no 9902, dated 17 April 2008, amending Law no. 10 444/20112, amending Law no 15/2013 and Law no 71/2018.

[47] See Law no. 9902, dated 17 April 2008, amending Law no 10 444/20112, Law no 15/2013, and Law no 71/2018.

Article 4 of the Law on Consumer Protection of Albania recognises the following basic consumer rights: the right to protect health, environment and safety of life, the right to protect economic interests, the right to complain, the right to compensation, the right to education, the right to information, the right to access public services, the right to legal defence, and the right to association or unions for the protection of consumers' interests, and the right to representation in their decision-making bodies.[48]

According to Article 2 of the Law on Consumer Protection of Montenegro,[49] a consumer is defined as 'a natural person who concludes legal transactions or acts in the market outside of their own commercial, business, craft, or professional activities' while a business is defined as 'a person who, independently or through other entities acting in the name or on behalf of the business, concludes legal transactions or works on the market within their own commercial, business, craft, or professional activities'.

Based on Article 1 (1) 3) of the Law on Consumer Protection[50] of Bosnia and Herzegovina, a consumer is defined as 'any natural person who buys, acquires, or uses products or services for their personal needs and for the needs of their household' while in Paragraph (5) of the same article, a business is defined as 'any person who directly or, as an intermediary between other persons, sells products or provides services to consumers'.

The consumer rights included in Article 3 of the Law on Consumer Protection[51] of Bosnia and Herzegovina refer to the following: a) the right of access to basic goods and services; b) the right to education on consumer issues; c) the right to safety and protection of life and health; d) the right to information; e) the right to choose; f) the right to be heard and represented; g) the right to damages and compensation; and h) the right to live and work in a healthy and sustainable environment.

Article 3 of the Law on Consumer Protection[52] of Kosovo defines a consumer as 'any natural person who buys and uses commodities or services to fulfil their needs, for purposes not related to commercial, business, craft, or professional activity' and a business as 'any natural or legal person who sells or engages in business or commercial activities, or acts on behalf of or for commercial, business, craft, or professional accounts of someone else, in relation to the subject matter covered by this law'. Furthermore, Article 4 of the Law on Consumer Protection[53] of Kosovo sets forth consumer rights including the following: the right to protect life, health, environment, and the economic interests of consumers, the right to

[48] See Law no 9902, dated 17 April 2008, amending Law no 10 444/20112, Law no 15/2013 and Law no 71/2018.

[49] See Official Gazette of Montenegro, no 2/2014, 6/2014 – amended, 43/2015, 70/2017 and 67/2019.

[50] See Official Gazette of Bosnia and Herzegovina, no 25/2006 and 88/2015.

[51] See Official Gazette of Bosnia and Herzegovina, no 25/2006 and 88/2015.

[52] See Official Gazette of the Republic of Kosovo, no 11/2018.

[53] See Official Gazette of the Republic of Kosovo, no 11/2018.

consumer information and education, the right to represent consumer interests, the right to organise consumers through consumer organisations, the right to protect consumers' interests, the right to complain, the right to legal protection of consumers, the right to compensation in certain cases for indemnity, the right to use public services, and the right to receive services in a language understood by consumers.

6. Constitutionalising of consumer rights – The Experience of Southeast European Countries

To some extent, certain legal scholars consider that the inclusion of consumer rights in the constitution is an expression of a strong guarantee that enables an increased degree of their realisation and protection, and furthermore, is 'another phase in the establishment of consumer rights as human rights'.[54] This would also mean the process of constitutionalising of consumer rights. The importance of establishing consumer protection within the constitutions is reflected in the fact that a constitution has legislative primacy in terms of hierarchy. However, while the inclusion of consumer rights and consumer protection in the constitution is important, so is the extent and content of these constitutional provisions.

In Europe, three systems of incorporation of consumer rights into national legal systems can be noticed: a protective model, a moderate model, and a liberal model, although they all overlap to some extent.[55]

Consumer protection as a constitutional principle is included in Article 90 of the Constitution of the Republic of Serbia. Article 90 of the Constitution of the Republic of Serbia contains two paragraphs. The first paragraph provides general protection of consumers, reading 'the Republic of Serbia protects consumers'. The second paragraph emphasises the specific values to which the Constitution of the Republic of Serbia gives priority: 'action directed against health, safety and consumer privacy, as well as all unfair market practices, are prohibited'.[56]

Article 70 of the Constitution of Montenegro contains two paragraphs regarding consumer protection. Both the first paragraph, which states 'the state is protecting consumers', and the second paragraph, which says 'actions that violate the health, safety and privacy of consumers are prohibited', are in line with the contents foreseen and proclaimed in the Constitution of the Republic of Serbia.[57]

The protection of consumer rights as a constitutional provision is also included in the constitution of Republika Srpska, which is one of the two entities

[54] See S Deutch (n 9) 574.
[55] See I Brendoher (n 18) 68.
[56] See Official Gazette of Republic of Serbia, nos 98/2006 and 115/2021.
[57] See Official Gazette of Montenegro, nos 1/2007 and 38/2013.

of Bosnia and Herzegovina. According to Article 53 of the Constitution of Republika Srpska, which consists of only one paragraph, 'the Republic provides consumer protection'.[58]

To understand the genesis of the inclusion of consumer protection in the constitutions of the countries of the former Yugoslavia, it should be emphasised that in a rudimentary form, consumer protection was included as a constitutional content in the Constitution of Yugoslavia from 1974. Article 43 (4) proclaims the principle of cooperation with consumer organisations, while Article 114 (2) encourages local forms of organisations (the most basic forms of local self-government) to cooperate in achieving consumer protection.[59]

Consumer protection is not included in the constitutions of Macedonia, Albania, Bosnia and Herzegovina, and Kosovo.

It can be concluded that the constitutions of the countries of Southeast Europe only contain minimum provisions regulating consumer protection. This conclusion is legitimate, for example, when compared to Article 60 of the Constitution of Portugal. Article 60 of the Constitution of Portugal contains three paragraphs that govern consumer protection. The first paragraph regulates the essence of protection, stating that 'consumers have the right to the good quality of the goods and services consumed, to training and information, to the protection of health, safety, and their economic interests, and to reparation for damages'. The second paragraph sets a constitutional criterion for advertising: 'advertising shall be disciplined by law, and all forms of concealed, indirect, or fraudulent advertising are prohibited'. The third paragraph of Article 60 of the Portuguese Constitution regulates the issue of organising consumer protection through consumer organisations. According to this provision, 'consumers associations and consumer cooperatives have the right, as laid down by law, to receive support from the state and to be consulted in relation to consumer-protection issues and are granted *legitimatio ad causam* in defence of their members or of collective or general interests'.

7. Public Law Elements in the Consumer Protection Regime of Southeast European Countries

Any approach towards the consumer protection regime should be, without any doubt, interdisciplinary. Many scholars point to the private and public law aspects, as well as the substantive and procedural law components.[60] Identification of this

[58] See Official Gazette of Republika Srpska, nos 21/92, 28/94, 8/96, 13/96, 15/96, 16/96, 21/96, 21/02, 26/02, 30/02, 31/02, 69/02, 31/03, 98/03, 115/05 and 117/05.

[59] See 'Official Gazette of Socialist Republic of Macedonia', no 7/74.

[60] See S Deutch (n 10) 542.

area as human rights might have a direct effect on the public aspect of consumer rights.[61] Considering that fact, the following section analyses the public law aspects of the consumer protection regime in Southeast Europe.

The Law on Consumer Protection of the Republic of Macedonia,[62] in Article 209, prescribes that 'the supervision of the implementation of the provisions of the law and the by-laws based on the law is performed by the Ministry for Economy'. In addition, administrative supervision according to Article 209(2) of the Law on Consumer Protection is provided by the State Market Inspectorate. Just one general remark: in principle, relations between parties within private law (for example, commercial contracts) are not exposed to state-organised supervision. While they have the right to judicial protection, that is within the concept of civil litigation. In contrast, business-to-consumer relations rely on the civil litigation procedure, but they also enjoy state-organised protection through different administrative entities.

Pursuant to Article 209(5) of the Law on Consumer Protection of the Republic of Macedonia, 'the inspector has the right, when conducting supervision, to request data from other state institutions or legal persons … and those entities are obliged to comply with the request of the inspectorate'. This provision clearly reflects the nature of the supervision done by the inspectorate within the administrative procedure. Unlike the litigation procedure, which is within the framework of a private-law mandate and regime, in this case, the public-law element is clearly manifested.

The Criminal Code[63] of the Republic of Macedonia, in Article 248, provides for a separate criminal indictment, 'defrauding buyers'. In accordance with the first paragraph of Article 248 of the Criminal Code, criminal liability is provided for the person who, with the intention of deceiving buyers, puts on the market products with a label in which data are entered that do not correspond to the content type, origin, or quality of the product or will put on the market products that, according to their weight or quality, do not correspond to what is regularly assumed for such products or products without a label on the content, type, origin, or quality of the product when such a label is prescribed. For this crime, a monetary fine or imprisonment of up to three years is prescribed. In addition, Article 285(1) of the Criminal Code of the Republic of Macedonia prescribes criminal liability for unlawful use of intellectual property rights, with the intention of deceiving buyers or users of services, infringing another's protected trademark, another's protected industrial design, or another's protected mark of product origin and geographical indication.

[61] ibid.

[62] See Official Gazette of Republic of North Macedonia, no 236/2022.

[63] See Official Gazette of Republic of Macedonia, nos 37/96, 80/99, 4/02, 43/03, 19/04, 81/05, 60/06, 73/06, 7/08, 139/08, 114/09, 51/11, 135/11, 185/11, 142/12, 166/12, 55/13, 82/13, 14/14, 27/14, 28/14, 41/14, 115/14, 132/14, 160/14, 199/14, 196/15, 226/15, 97/17 and 248/18.

In accordance with Article 18(1) of the Law on Consumer Protection[64] of the Republic of Serbia, supervision over the implementation of the law and by-laws is done by the governmental ministry. Furthermore, based on Article 181(3), the mandate of the state inspectorate is prescribed. Namely, according to Article 181(3) of the Law on Consumer Protection of the Republic of Serbia:

> the Ministry in charge of commerce, via the market inspectorate, and the Ministry in charge of tourism, via the tourism inspectorate, perform inspection supervision over the implementation of the law and by-laws, in accordance with the authorisations prescribed by this law and by-laws, and legislation that regulates inspection supervision in the areas of commerce and tourism.

In relation to the criminal protection of consumers, there is no particular criminal incrimination related to consumer protection in the Republic of Serbia.[65] However, there is a criminal incrimination for the unauthorised use of someone else's business names and other special markings of goods or services in Article 238 of the Serbian Criminal Code.[66]

The legal grounds for administrative protection in Montenegro are set in Article 173 of the Law on Consumer Protection,[67] which entitles the consumer to seek administrative protection through the state inspectorate.

In the Criminal Code of Montenegro, two criminal incriminations are provided that are related to the protection of consumers. The first one is the misleading (deceiving) of customers, prescribed in Article 285, and the second one is trademark counterfeiting, prescribed in Article 286.[68]

The Law on Consumer Protection[69] of Albania also includes administrative protection for consumers. This type of protection is included in Articles 48 and 49 of the Law on Consumer Protection. Article 48 of the Law on Consumer Protection of Albania determines the protection priorities that administrative protection should enable. Therefore, the competent state authorities should be the main responsible bodies for developing and implementing consumer protection policies to protect the basic rights of consumers, specifically with regard to sensitive groups of consumers, such as children, the elderly, the indigent, the disabled, the ill, and those with limited mental or physical abilities.

As the competent body for administrative protection of consumers, Article 49 of the Albanian Law on Consumer Protection[70] mandates the Ministry in charge

[64] See Official Gazette of Republic of Serbia, nos 98/2006 and 115/2021.

[65] See V Bošković, *Consumer Protection trough Criminal Law* (2022), available at: www.otvorenavratapravosudja.rs/teme/krivicno-pravo/zastita-potrosaca-kroz-kaznene-odredbe.

[66] Ibid.

[67] See Official Gazette of Montenegro, no 2/2014, 6/2014 – amended 43/2015, 70/2017, and 67/2019.

[68] See Official Gazette of Montenegro, no 70/2003, 13/2004 – amended 47/2006 and 'Official Gazette of Montenegro', no 40/2008, 25/2010, 32/2011, 64/2011–40/2013, 56/2013 – amended 14/2015, 42/2015, 58/2015 – Dr. Law, 44/2017, 49/2018 and 3/2020.

[69] See Law no 9902, dated 17 April 2008, amending Law no 10 444/20112, Law no 15/2013, and Law no 71/2018.

[70] See: Law no 9902, dated 17 April 2008, amending Law no 10 444/20112, Law no 15/2013, and Law no 71/2018.

of trade above all. Furthermore, Article 51 of the Law on Consumer Protection of Albania regulates the responsible body for market surveillance. It should also be noted that the establishment and functioning of the Consumer Protection Commission is regulated within the framework of Article 52 of the Law on Consumer Protection of Albania.

As in other countries in Southeast Europe, extensive administrative legal protection in terms of consumer rights is foreseen in Bosnia and Herzegovina. As bearers of consumer rights protection, Article 98 of the Law on Consumer Protection[71] of Bosnia and Herzegovina determines the following: a) Ministry of Foreign Trade and Economic Relations of Bosnia and Herzegovina; b) Ombudsman for Consumer Protection of Bosnia and Herzegovina; c) Council for Consumer Protection of Bosnia and Herzegovina; d) Competition Council of Bosnia and Herzegovina; e) responsible entities and organs of District Brčko; f) offices for competition and consumer protection of the Federation of Bosnia and Herzegovina and the Republic of Srpska; g) consumer associations; h) educational institutions and media; i) inspection and other organs.

One interesting concept included in the Law on Consumer Protection of Bosnia and Herzegovina is the concept of consumer ombudsman. Namely, in Article 100(1) of the Law on Consumer Protection[72] of Bosnia and Herzegovina, it is stipulated that the Ombudsman for Consumer Protection of Bosnia and Herzegovina is an independent institution established with the aim to promote good and efficient implementation of consumer protection policies in Bosnia and Herzegovina.

The duties and responsibilities of the Ombudsman for Consumer Protection are regulated within Article 101 of the Law on Consumer Protection[73] of Bosnia and Herzegovina. Furthermore, according to Article 103 of the Law on Consumer Protection of Bosnia and Herzegovina, the Ombudsman for Consumer Protection is authorised to: a) issue instructions to stop the implementation of activities that are in conflict with consumer legislation and to present those instructions before the court; b) initiate proceedings before the competent court; and c) initiate proceedings before the competent court in cases for compensation of damage caused to the collective interest of consumers, in accordance with the provisions of the Law.

In accordance with Article 118 of the Law on Consumer Protection[74] of Bosnia and Herzegovina, consumers have the right to request inspection supervision and exercise this right through the system of administrative protection. If a business unjustifiably rejects a consumer's request, the inspector will issue a decision asking the business to comply with the reasonable request of the consumer.

[71] See Official Gazette of Bosnia and Herzegovina, nos 25/2006 and 88/2015.
[72] See Official Gazette of Bosnia and Herzegovina, nos 25/2006 and 88/2015.
[73] See Official Gazette of Bosnia and Herzegovina, nos 25/2006 and 88/2015.
[74] See: Official Gazette of Bosnia and Herzegovina, nos 25/2006 and 88/2015.

Similarly, the consumer protection legislation of Kosovo also provides for administrative protection of consumer rights. According to Article 116 of the Law on Consumer Protection[75] of Kosovo, competent inspectorates provide administrative protection.

8. Conclusion – How Close or Far are Consumer Rights from Being Granted Status as Human Rights?

Today, 60 years after President Kennedy's legendary quote, 'consumers, by definition, include us all' and his Consumer Bill of Rights, the relevance of consumer rights is still apparent.

Since the first national legislation for consumer protection was developed and adopted, the question has arisen as to whether consumer rights are part of the list of human rights.

Based on the focus of this chapter, the main question raised is whether consumer rights are on their way to being considered within the framework of human rights. It is clear that the question of the essence of consumer rights becomes relevant every time significant developments occur, such as the global financial crisis of 2008, major global consumer law scandals, or the COVID-19 pandemic.

It can be concluded that the development of the list and coverage of human rights is an evolutionary process. The inclusion of a new right in the list of human rights is not a dogma and is not a one-time event. Furthermore, it is not only consumer rights that are exposed to this process, but the right to access the Internet as well. For example, the journey that took 25 years for the right to water and sanitation to be accepted as a human right is an example of this.

In addition, the theory considers the development of the third generation of human rights as a result of the 'new needs of human.' Therefore, there is a possibility for the inclusion of consumer rights in the third or even a new fourth generation of human rights. The research has shown that while expanded interpretations that extend the scope of human rights and enable the inclusion of consumer rights are noticeable, they cannot be treated as a comprehensive approach. Even though the extended interpretation was used several times within this chapter to explain its focus, it is not enough to consider it as the path for including consumer rights in the list of human rights.

Consumers enjoy additional protection compared to the usual protection afforded to contracting parties in other types of contractual relationships. This type of protection is usually based on the notion of the weaker party. This is undeniable, and it is very present in the legislation of the countries in Southeast Europe.

[75] See: Official Gazette of the Republic of Kosovo, no 11/2018.

The analysis based on the so-called 'consumer rights directory' approach acknowledges that the coverage of consumer rights in the legislation of the countries of Southeast Europe follows the concept and requirements set by the EU. It is completely understandable and is based on the obligation of these countries to transpose EU law. Such a high degree of compliance and transposition with the law of the EU is reflected in all the issues of interest discussed in this research.

This research noticed that the Republic of Serbia, Montenegro, and Republika Srpska have included provisions for the protection of consumer rights in their constitutions, while consumer protection is not included in the constitutions of Macedonia, Albania, Bosnia and Herzegovina, and Kosovo. Legal scholars, including those who advocate for the provision of consumer protection in the constitution, view it as 'another phase in the establishment of consumer rights as human rights.'

Assuming that identifying consumer protection as human rights might have a direct effect on the public aspect of consumer rights; this analysis showed that the legal framework for consumer protection in the countries of Southeast Europe is quite interdisciplinary, with a wide range of provisions of a public law character, such as administrative protection or criminal protection of consumer rights.

Based on the entire research and examination, the conclusion is clear. Until now, neither in the international nor regional context has there been a document that explicitly includes the rights of consumers in the list of human rights. This also applies to the countries of Southeast Europe.

6

Horizontal Application of Fundamental Rights and General Principles in Private Disputes: An Albanian Perspective

FJORALBA CAKA AND NADA DOLLANI

1. Introduction

Albania, as a South Eastern European country, had long suffered severe prevention of human rights protections by the state under communist regime. The collapse of communist regimes in East Europe inspired in Albania a Western aspiration to the enshrinement of human and fundamental rights. In 1996 the ECHR was ratified and two years later the Constitution of the Republic of Albania was adopted following a general referendum. The Albanian Constitution mirrors the ECHR on human rights including the right to property, and even refers to the ECHR explicitly, as it does not allow stricter limitations of human rights than the Convention itself. However, it was not until 2006 that the first Albanian cases came under scrutiny of ECtHR, which opened the door to examine state practices and private disputes under the framework of human rights protection. It was also in more recent years that the Albanian Constitutional Court envisaged a clearer guidance on how to incorporate fundamental rights into private law relationships and specifically to the most sensitive of all, property rights.

The question of impact of fundamental rights in private law is much-treaded by scholarly articles and has been extensively discussed in the last few decades. However more sophisticated issues on the interference of human rights in private law and the elaboration of a clear and certain balance scale to be used by judges in case law has still proven to be a rather challenging question.

The purpose of this chapter is to make a closer examination of property rights as a human right in Albania, protected by international instruments, namely the European Convention on Human Rights (ECHR), not only through the European

Court of Human Rights (ECtHR) jurisprudence, but also through case law of the Constitutional Court and the Supreme Court of Albania.

Following the case law in our country we have observed three main methods on the reflection of fundamental rights in private law relations as identified on the description of Dean Spielmann.[1] The first one is through 'state positive obligations doctrine'; the second one is the constitutional conforming (compatible) interpretation of legal provisions belonging to a lower hierarchy of norms such as Civil Code or other specific legal acts; and the third one pertaining to the balancing act the courts must conduct between fundamental rights and other public interests while deciding in private law cases. While the first method is elaborated by the ECtHR, for the second one we will refer to the Albanian Constitutional Court and for the third method we will analyse and consider the Albanian Supreme Court case law.

2. The Horizontal Application of the European Convention of Human Rights in Property Cases against Albania: The Initiation of a 'Cohabitation' with Article 6 of ECHR

There are scholars that the European Convention of Human Rights was not initially intended to have a third-party effect.[2] They argue that the legislative intention of the Convention did not provide any room either for direct or indirect effect. According to this view complaints about violations of the Convention can only be made against one of the Contracting States and complaints against legal persons are considered inadmissible *ratione personae*.[3] This narrow reading of the Convention is based on the provision of Article 34 of the Convention,[4] which poses a procedural obstacle to claims introduced against private parties.[5] However, the development of the ECHR case law, considering the Convention as a 'living instrument', has extended the application of the Convention indirectly also in private cases. In fact, a strict reading of Articles 33 and 34 of the Convention would lead to a situation where individuals would be victims of human rights

[1] D Spielmann, 'The European Convention on Human Rights. The European Court of Human Rights' in J Fedtke and D Oliver (eds), *Human Rights in the Private Sphere. A Comparative Study* (London and New York, Routledge-Cavendish, 2007) 427.

[2] E Engle 'Third party effect of fundamental rights (Drittwirkung)' (2009) 5 *Hanse Law Review* 165, 179. *Cf*: P van Dijk and CJH van Hoof, *Theory and Practice of the European Court of Human Rights* (Deventer – Boston, Kluwer Law and Taxation Publishers, 1990).

[3] Ibid.

[4] 'The Court may receive applications from any person, nongovernmental organization or group of individuals claiming to be the victim of a violation by one of the High Contracting Parties of the rights set forth in the Convention or the Protocols thereto.'

[5] D Spielmann (n 1).

violations both by the States and other individuals, but considered victims under the Convention, only with regards to the infringement of the Convention's rights by the Contracting States. To avoid a situation where the infringement of human rights would impact the Convention's value, the European Court of Human Rights expanded the application of the Convention also in private cases. The ECtHR was not just driven by the desire to have a Convention that is applied in practice, whose rights are 'effective' and 'practical', but also found its capacity to act, based on Article 1 of the Convention, as well as the open formulation of certain provisions that indicate that certain rights may be applied also in purely private cases. Moreover, the ECtHR not only created a theoretical framework to shape vast areas of private law by giving Convention rights indirect horizontal effects, but it also started to decide a number of cases in practice, acting as a final arbiter in disputes between private parties.[6] This has led to the growth of 'verticalisation' of horizontal conflicts before the ECtHR, where a conflict between two private parties which started before a domestic court, due to (in)action of the State, in situations where the state had a positive obligation to act, were found admissible for review under the ECHR.[7] However, as noted, the judicial review ECtHR in private cases oscillates from minimal, intermediates to striking itself an adequate balance between competing rights and policy concerns. The application of different standards of scrutiny in private law cases is done through the margin of appreciation and enables the Court to defer, to different degrees, assessments connected with the proportionality of state action to the Contracting Parties.[8]

This chapter will try to illustrate the instruments the ECtHR used to 'verticalised' horizontal cases and the judicial review of the Court in the property cases against Albania. Although there are almost 15 property cases against Albania judged before the ECtHR, since the ratification of the Convention, we have limited our research only to those cases that initiated as a horizontal conflict between two private parties over a certain property.

3. The State Positive Doctrine in Property Cases against Albania

In the property cases selected below against Albania, the ECtHR has employed the mechanism of state positive obligation to 'verticalise' the horizontal conflict before the ECtHR. In all the cases the issue was not whether the State has violated

[6] J Zglinski, 'Doing too little or too much? Private law before the European Court of Human Rights' (2018) 37 *Yearbook of European Law* 98.

[7] C Loven, '"Verticalised" cases before the European Court of Human Rights unraveled: an analysis of their characteristics and the Court's approach to them' (2020) 38 *Netherlands Quarterly of Human Rights* 246.

[8] J Zglinski (n 6) 109.

the fundamental rights of these individuals, 'but whether, by failing to act, it has prevented the individuals from effectively exercising their rights, in particular as a result of encroachments upon these rights by other private individuals'.[9] In particular, what is common in all the cases is that the state positive doctrine has offered to protect individuals from each other by holding the state responsible before the ECtHR for a failure to guarantee fundamental rights, especially the right of fair process before domestic courts.

The first property judgment against Albania was rendered in 2008, and like the majority of the cases that followed, it involved the return of a property appropriated by the state during Communist era (*Beshiri v Albania*).[10] The facts of the case are complex and similar with other cases of restitution of property in post-communist countries, going from one set of procedures to the other and involving facts and events occurring in different legal systems and periods. The facts of the case could be summarised as follow. One villa and two adjacent parcels of property belonged to the father of the applicants. During the communist era, between 1946 and 1978, the father of the applicants rented the villa to BN's father. In the second plot of land, BN's father constructed two buildings, which by a Decision of Tirana District Court in 1976 were declared to be his property. On the other hand, the applicants' father borrowed 16,204 ALL from the Communist Government to restore the villa, but due to his inability to repay the loan, the villa was nationalised by the government in 1978. The BN family with permission of the State continued to live in the villa, which since 1978 was considered state property. After the fall of communism in 1996 the applicants filed a claim with the Tirana Commission for Return and Compensation of Properties. After a long set of procedures back and forth in the Supreme Court and the Court Appeal, a final decision of the court acknowledged the applicants' property rights only over the two adjacent plots of land and ordered their compensation in one of the forms provided for by law. Nevertheless, the applicant neither took possessions over these two plots, nor was compensated in any form. Based on these circumstances the applicants brought the case before the European Court of Human Rights alleging infringement of Article1 Protocol1 and Article 6 of the Convention.

The ECtHR brought this private conflict under the scope of ECHR protections. As in other cases, the ECtHR used the state positive obligation doctrine, although in this case the Court did not refer at it explicitly. According to the Court it was the obligation of the state to ensure the enforcement of a decision of compensation in favour of the applicant. The failure of the State to enforce a court decision for compensation affected the effective exercise of the property rights, leaving the applicant in a state of uncertainty. Namely, the Court state that:

> [b]y failing to comply with the judgment of the Tirana Court of Appeal, the national authorities left the applicants in a state of uncertainty with regard to the chances of

[9] O Cherednychenko, 'Towards the control of private acts by the European Court of Human Rights?' (2006) 13 *Maastricht Journal of European and Comparative Law* 195.

[10] *Beshiri et al v Albania* App no 7352/03 (ECtHR, 22 August 2006).

> reacquiring their property rights. Furthermore, for a considerable period of time, they prevented them from having their compensation paid and from enjoying the possession of their money.[11]

The ECtHR in the two subsequent cases against Albania has made explicit reference to the state positive obligation in Article 1 of the Convention, read together with Article 1 Protocol 1. In the case *Marini v Albania*, the applicant, an American-Albanian national, and the Albanian Government (as a private party) established a joint-venture company Marini-Albplastik, specialising in the production of plastic materials. The state contribution in the joint venture was an old factory and its equipment, at a value of EUR 12,497, while the applicant's investment in the company consisted of capital amounting to 1,100,000 USD – approximately EUR 834,098, which was intended to be used for the renovation of the factory and future purchase of technology. When 60 per cent of the renovation of the factory had been carried out, unilaterally, without any legitimate cause, the State decided to rescind the agreement establishing the Marini-Albplastik company. Mr. Marini sued his partner (the State) in court for not upholding the obligation from the contract and reducing the value of his shares in the joint venture, but after a long calvary back and forth before domestic courts, going so far as an arbitrage procedure, the plaintiff failed to retrieve back the compensation required. In these circumstances the plaintiff brought the case before the ECtHR. With regards to the 'verticalisation' of this private conflict, the ECtHR responded:

> [the Court] reiterates that by virtue of Article 1 of the Convention each Contracting Party "shall secure to everyone within [its] jurisdiction the rights and freedoms defined in ... [the] Convention". The obligation to secure the effective exercise of the rights defined in that instrument may result in positive obligations for the State ... In such circumstances, the State cannot simply remain passive and "there is no room to distinguish between acts and omissions"
>
> As regards the right guaranteed by Article 1 of Protocol No. 1, **those positive obligations may entail certain measures necessary to protect the right of property ... even in cases involving litigation between individuals or companies**. This means, in particular, that States are under an obligation to afford judicial procedures that offer the necessary procedural guarantees and therefore enable the domestic courts and tribunals to adjudicate effectively and fairly any disputes between private persons.[12] (authors' emphasis)

In a similar vein, also in the case *Bushati v Albania*, the Court explicitly referred to Article 1 of the Convention and the state positive doctrine, as the basis to extend the protection of the Convention even in litigations involving private persons.[13] In case of *Mullai v Albania*, the State also was deemed to interfere, indirectly, in a private contract between two parties. On 30 April 1998, individual applicants

[11] *Beshiri et al v Albania* App no 7352/03 (ECtHR, 22 August 2006) 102.
[12] *Marini v Albania* App no 3738/02 (ECtHR, 18 December 2007) 170–171.
[13] *Bushati et al v Albania* App no 6397/04 (ECtHR, 8 December 2009) 93–94.

entered into an agreement with the applicant company for the construction of a tower block on their property. Under that agreement the applicant company was given authority to obtain the administrative authorisations needed for the construction. A final contract was to be concluded when the requisite permit had been obtained. The European Court of Human Rights noted that for:

> many years the individual applicants and the applicant company have been unable to enjoy and freely dispose of their contractual benefits as a result of the suspension of the construction work arising out of the disputed lawfulness of the building permit. The multiplicity of legal proceedings has failed to remedy the situation. There has accordingly been an interference with their right of property.[14]

In all the cases cited above, the ECtHR has read the positive obligations of the State under Article 1 Protocol 1 mainly as requirements to abide to procedural guarantees of Article 6 of the Convention. The Court has reiterated that it is a state positive obligation to guarantee a process and procedures that make it possible for private parties to defend their property rights before the domestic courts. A failure to guarantee a fair process for the protection of the right of property before the national court would amount to the infringements of the state positive obligations under Article 1Protocol 1 of the Convention. To illustrate it further, in the *Beshiri* case, the Court firstly emphasised that the Convention does not impose to the Contracting States any obligation to:

> return property which was transferred to them before they ratified the Convention. Nor does Article 1 of Protocol No. 1 impose any restrictions on the Contracting States' freedom to determine the scope of property restitution and to choose the conditions under which they agree to restore property rights of former owners.[15]

However, once the Contracting States decide to establish a procedure to restore property to former owners they have an obligation to honour all the guarantees of the Convention, especially Article 6.1.[16] In the case *Marini v Albania*, the Court defined the content of these positive obligations under Article 1 Protocol 1 as guarantees of 'judicial procedures that offer the necessary procedural guarantees and enable the domestic courts and tribunals to adjudicate effectively and fairly any disputes between private persons'.[17] In the case *Bushati v Albania*, the positive obligation was to 'ensure that the procedures enshrined in the legislation for the *enforcement of final judgments* … are complied with'.[18] Thus, the content of these positive obligations under Article 1 Protocol 1 are not fixed, but rather linked to procedural rights, fair trial guarantees that ensure the effective enjoyment of the right of property.

[14] *Mullai et al v Albania* App no 9074/07 (ECtHR 23 March 2010).
[15] *Beshiri et al v Albania* App no 7352/03 (ECtHR, 22 August 2006) para 80.
[16] ibid para 61.
[17] *Marini v Albania* (n 12) para 171.
[18] *Bushati v Albania* (n 13) para 93.

The interlink of the right of property with Article 1 Protocol 1 with Article 6 of the ECHR is embedded further in the judicial scrutiny process. For example, in case *Beshiri v Albania*, the Court found that the failure of the authorities to enforce the judgment in the applicants' favour, which was an infringement of Article 6.1, amounted to an interference with their right to the peaceful enjoyment of their possessions within the meaning of Article 1 of Protocol 1 to the Convention.[19] In *Bushati*, the Court states that as a consequence of the non-enforcement by the bailiff of the Supreme Court decision, the applicants 'were left in a situation of uncertainty and have been unable to fully enjoy their possessions. Accordingly, there has been a violation of Article 1 of Protocol No. 1.'

In the *Beshiri*, *Marini* and *Bushati* cases the Court engaged into a low level of scrutiny, establishing a two-step paradigm. The Court first acknowledged whether there was an infringement of the guarantees of Article 6 ECHR during the handling of the property conflict before the domestic court. Then the Court emphasised the positive obligations of the state under Article 1 Protocol 1, framed as procedural guarantees of a fair process. The Court then concluded that as result of the infringements of the fair process guarantees, the applicants were 'left in a situation of uncertainty and have been unable to fully enjoy their possessions', and as such there was an infringement of Article 1 Protocol 1. For illustration, in *Marini v Albania*, the Court, after noting the procedural shortcomings of Article 6.1 of ECHR in the case, stated:

> Having regard to the foregoing, the Court finds that the failure of the authorities to enforce the decisions in the applicant's favour, the manner in which the proceedings were conducted, and the uncertainty in which the applicant was left, upset the "fair balance" that has to be struck between the demands of the public interest and the need to protect the applicant's right to the peaceful enjoyment of his possessions. Consequently, the State failed to comply with its obligation to secure the applicant's effective enjoyment of his right of property as guaranteed by Article 1 of Protocol No. 1.[20]

However, in *Mullai*, although the Court again linked the infringement of Article 1 Protocol 1 with Article 6, did decide to leave out the 'fair balance test'. The Court ruled:

> The Court notes that this complaint is closely linked to the complaint under Article 6 § 1 of the Convention in which it found a violation of the principle of legal certainty (see paragraphs 79–88 above). In that connection, the Court notes that the case-law of the domestic courts has led to inconsistent decisions on the lawfulness of the building permit. The case-law lacked the required precision to enable the applicant company and the individual applicants to foresee, to a degree that was reasonable in the circumstances, the consequences of their actions and the State's interference.
>
> It follows that the interference with the applicant company's right and the proprietary rights of the individual applicants' who demolished their three-storey villa on the

[19] ibid para 101.
[20] *Marini et al v Albania* App no 3738/02 (ECtHR, 18 December 2007) 174.

> strength of the building permit issued by the authorities, cannot be considered lawful within the meaning of Article 1 of Protocol No. 1. This conclusion makes it unnecessary to ascertain whether a fair balance has been struck between the demands of the general interest of the community and the requirements of the protection of the applicants' fundamental rights …

Despite the lack of a consistency on the level of judicial scrutiny in these cases, the Court has created a 'double' link between the property right to the guarantees of Article 6 ECHR, one substantial, when examining the state positive obligations under Article 1 Protocol 1, and one procedural, when reviewing the lawfulness of the intervention in the peaceful enjoyment of the property right. Since the *Beshiri* case, the ECtHR, in almost every case against Albania, except *Kasmi*,[21] coupled the infringement of Article 1 Protocol 1 of the Convention with infringement of Article 6.1. Thus, the Court settled that Article 1 Protocol 1 will have been infringed any time that there is infringement of the guarantees of Article 6 of the Convention in a process of restitution and compensation of property. Despite the possibility that this double safeguard was not intentional or country-related, it undoubtedly increased the significance of the rule of law in Albania. The extension of the Convention in private cases and the verticalisation of horizontal private conflicts before the Court were important in order to avoid further infringement of property rights in practice. If the ECtHR would have not intervened, protection of the property rights would not be exercised at its fullest extent, since the State would not be rendered accountable for infringement of applicants' rights before the national courts. These 'messages' from the Court in Strasbourg, coupled with Constitutional provisions and special status of the ECHR in our domestic system, were received by the national judges, who started to pay much more attention to the ECHR and jurisprudence of the Court when handling private cases.

4. The Horizontal Application of Fundamental Rights in the Albanian Domestic System

4.1. Constitutional Clauses as a Front Door for the Horizontal Application of Fundamental Rights in Private Case

On a general note, it may be observed that the doctrine of horizontal application of human rights is not much advanced in the legal doctrine or the case law of the Albanian Courts. The national and international application of human rights in private cases has only recently been made the subject of scholarly interest with

[21] *Kasmi v Albania* App no 1175/06 (ECtHR, 23 June 2020).

only a few scholars addressing it.[22] On the other hand, as it would be discussed in part 3.1 and 3.2 of this chapter the Albanian judges still seem to seldom use the general principles of law or human rights to interpret or solve a conflict between individuals. Nevertheless, the legal framework is more advanced in this regard and has already established the tools and instruments that could be employed to advance the direct application of human rights or constitutional rights in private cases. For example, Article 4(3) of the Albanian Constitution foresees that 'The provisions of the Constitution are directly applicable, except when the Constitution provides otherwise.' This provision was seen as a decisive break from the communist past, where the human rights and constitutional protections were only rights written in paper but never enforced.[23] Similarly with other socialist countries, many fundamental rights were provided even at a Constitutional level, but there had merely a 'façade-like character', since there was neither the will to respect them, nor the instruments and procedure to enable their defence,[24] The drafters of the new democratic Constitution recognised that human rights and constitutional provisions are not practically enforceable if they are not directly applicable or accompanied with an independent and effective judicial system, that is why they acknowledged the direct applicability of the constitutional provisions in the basic act.[25] Article 4(3) of the Constitution has been subject of interpretation in different dicta of the Constitutional Court (CC). According to the CC, when there is an express rule or regulation in the Constitution, it cannot be evaded or exceeded it *but must be applied directly* (authors' emphasis).[26] Following this line of interpretation, the Constitutional Court has clarified that the High Court and other ordinary courts can interpret the Constitution, and this is a matter following under their own jurisdiction.[27] This means that the ordinary

[22] A Nuni, 'E drejta Private në Kushtetutë' (2008) 2 *Jus and Justicia* 73; N. Dollani, 'Konstitucionalizimi i të Drejtës Private. Zbatimi horizontal i Kushtetutës' (2011) *Studime Juridike* 293; N Dollani, 'The concept of property right under the European Convention on human Rights and its importance in the Albanian legal framework' in *New Perspectives of South East European Private Law* South East European Post-Doctoral Colloquium in Private Law – Proceedings, (Skopje, 2012) 60; N. Dollani 'Autonomy and Antidiscrimination in private law – the experience of the Western Balkans. Country Report Albania' in Civil Law Forum for South East Europe Collection of studies and analyses. Third Regional Conference (Tirana, 2013) 35; A. Vorpsi 'Konstitucionalizimi i të drejtës private dhe qasja e gjykatave shqiptare' (2015) 4 *Jeta Juridike* 4.

[23] N Dollani, 'The concept of property right under the European Convention on human Rights and its importance in the Albanian legal framework', 63.

[24] V Trstenjak and P Weingerl (eds), *The Influence of Human Rights and Basic Rights in Private Law* (Switzerland, Springer, 2016).

[25] N Dollani, 'Konstitucionalizimi i të Drejtës Private. Zbatimi horizontal i Kushtetutës' 293.

[26] *The only exception is when the Constitution has specifically charged the relevant state bodies to issue laws and other bylaws, in order to regulate relations in various fields* Decision of the Constitutional Court no 29, dated 9 November 2005.

[27] However, it has made it clear and stated in different decision that it is the CC that has the right of the final interpretation of the Constitution. Thus in Decision no 13, dated 12 July 2004 the CC has stated that: 'The high court acts within its jurisdiction even when it is interpreting the constitution, because this is a right [pertaining to] each court at every level of judgment as well as to anybody that applies the Constitution in its decision-making activity and beyond. The fact that the interpretation is

courts or the High Court when solving a case are called to apply the Constitution directly, even in private cases, unless the Constitution has a specific prohibition providing otherwise.

Moreover, thanks to the jurisprudence of the Constitutional Court the principle a conform interpretation is well established in domestic doctrine and legal practice. The Constitutional Court has reiterated in different decisions that:

> the ordinary courts within the scope of their jurisdiction, in respect of the principle of a court determined by law and the principle of constitutionality, during the review of disputes are obliged to make a conform interpretation with the constitutional standards of the law which is applied to resolve a specific case'.[28]

According to the Constitutional Court the conforming interpretation asks the court to evaluate the constitutional effects of different outcomes of the legal interpretation and choose the outcome that is in line with constitutional values, taking into account here the fundamental rights of individuals.[29] Thus, the direct applicability of the Constitution and its general principles by the ordinary courts seem to create a favourable ground for horizontal application of the constitutional/human rights even between private parties' litigations in court.

In addition, the Constitution of Albania has a very friendly approach towards international law and its application in the Albanian domestic legal system.[30] It provides for a monist system of the relationship between the international and national regimes. Article 5 of the Constitution provides that ratified international law is binding upon Albania. Moreover, apart this declaratory principle, other Articles of the Constitution elevate the international agreement above the domestic law. According to Article 116 of Constitution, international agreements are placed below the Constitution and above the laws and represent a second tier in the hierarchy of sources of law.[31] Moreover, according to Paragraph 1 of Article 122 of the Albanian Constitution, 'any international agreement that has been ratified is part of the domestic legal system, after it is published in the

made by the Joint Panels of the High Court, ie by the highest body of the judicial system, does not mean that it is final, because for such an interpretation, according to Article 124/1 of the Constitution, only the Constitutional Court is competent.'

[28] Decision no 19, date 1 April 2016. Moreover, the Constitutional Court stated that: 'The court, in order to resolve a case, has the functional duty to make different interpretations with regards to the meaning of the disposition, search for similar disposition in analogue cases and identify the general principles of constitutional jurisprudence.' Decision of the Constitutional Court 28/2008.

[29] The Constitutional Court in its Decision no 29, dated 31 May 2010, among other things has stated that: 'The Court considers that, in the present case, a confirming interpretation of the impugned law can be applied. This interpretation is possible when a law or legal provision can be interpreted in more than one way, and (at least) one of those is in accordance with the Constitution. This method evaluates the constitutional effects of different outcomes (of interpretations) and selects the outcome that is in line with constitutional values, taking into account here the fundamental rights of individuals.'

[30] E Alimehmeti and F Caka, 'The Relationship between International and Domestic Law in the Albanian Legal System' in Mezzetti, Luca, Carna Pistan, Alessandra Di Martino, Francesca Polacchini, and Justin O Frosini. *International Constitutional Law* (Torino, G Giappichelli Editore, 2015).

[31] N Dollani, 'Autonomy and Antidiscrimination in private law – the experience of the Western Balkans. Country Report Albania' 35, 44.

Official Journal of the Republic of Albania'. Article 122(2) provides for the supremacy of the international agreements ratified by law over the domestic law that is not incompatible with it. A special status is given to the ECHR by the Albanian Constitution, raising it at the constitutional level in cases of restriction of fundamental rights. The Constitution in its Art 17(2) provides that '... limitations of constitutional rights may not infringe the essence of the rights and freedoms and in no case may exceed the limitations provided for in the European Convention on Human Rights'. Therefore the Albanian Constitution invokes the ECHR directly and gives it a constitutional status, although only with regard to limitations of rights, a feature not usually found in other modern constitutions.[32]

The ECHR is consistently referred by the Albanian judges when they solve cases involving human rights allegations. However, the Constitutional Court has gone further, opening the front door an inch more, to allow the direct application of the Convention, even in private cases. Based on Article 5, 122 and 17 of the Constitution, the ECHR is considered an international act *directly applicable in the Albanian domestic* legal order and has *supremacy* over the domestic legislation.[33] In addition, not only is the European Convention directly applicable in the Albanian legal order, but so is its jurisprudence.[34] The Constitutional Court has expressly stated that:

> The [Constitutional] Court, in the interpretation of Articles 5, 116, 122 and 17/2 of the Constitution, has emphasized the special status of the European Convention of Human Rights in the internal legal order, and recognized the exclusive competence of the ECtHR in our legal system and the direct effect of its decisions in the interpretation of the constitutional standards of human rights, especially those referring to the right to a due process of law, enshrined in Article 42 of the Constitution ...
>
> The court has highlighted that in accordance with Article 122 of the Constitution and Articles 19 and 46 of the ECHR, judges at all levels should directly implement the decisions of the ECtHR, as complying with ECHR and the constitutional standards is a requirement not only for this Court but also for courts of ordinary jurisdiction, in particular the Supreme Court, due to its special reviewing competencies and its leading role in the unification of judicial practice.[35]

All the above provisions seem to create a favourable terrain for the application of the fundamental rights in every conflict, despite of the form of the law, being it public or private. It also seems to install 'a perpetual' hierarchy of norms, which judges should take into consideration when solving a case. The Constitutional

[32] ibid 44.

[33] In Decision of the Constitutional Court no16, dated 17 April 2000.

[34] In its Ruling no 20, dated 1 June 2011 the CC has stated that 'the European Court of Human Rights has in our legal system an exclusive competence. This competence is accepted by our internal legal system, for the purpose of implementing Article 122 of the Constitution, as well as Article 17/2 from which derives an obligation that the decisions of the European Court of Human Rights should be directly implemented.' Decision of the Constitutional Court no 20, dated 1 June 2011.

[35] Decision of the Constitutional Court no 18 dated 6 March 2017, paras 13, 14.

Court did not seem to make a difference in this regard between public or private law, or the nature of the cases, but asks the ordinary courts and High Court to directly apply the Convention and its jurisprudence in solving cases.

4.2. The Horizontal Application of Human Rights Doctrine in the Jurisprudence of the Constitutional Court in Albania: Consolidating the Cohabitation with Article 6 ECHR

The Constitutional Court is not considered as part of the Albanian judicial system. The Constitutional Court has jurisdiction to control the constitutionality of the legal acts of the Parliament, the executive, acts of local authority or compliance of the international agreements with the Constitution;[36] it is this Court which rules on the conflict of competences between different powers, or the constitutionality of elections of the President, Members of Parliament, or other public functionaries. Individuals have legal standing before the Constitutional Court only against a court decision, or a public act that infringes their fundamental rights guaranteed in the Constitution, and only after exhausting all the effective judicial remedies, unless provided otherwise.[37] The only space for individuals to address the Constitutional Court before 2016 amendments was the infringement of the individual rights of fair trial after all legal remedies for the protection of these rights have been exhausted.[38] The new legal amendment of this provision do not create, at least as is written, any legal basis to sue a private individual for infringement of fundamental rights. Article 131(f) of the Constitution provides that the Constitutional Court will have jurisdiction to review 'complaints by individuals against any act of public authority or judicial decision that infringes the fundamental rights and freedoms guaranteed in the Constitution, after all effective legal remedies for the protection of these rights have been exhausted, unless otherwise provided for in the Constitution.' Thus, it obviously follows that, as written in the formal law, conflicts among private parties cannot become issues of dispute before the Constitutional Court.

However, the strong influence of the European Convention of Human Rights in our internal legal order, as well as the progressive constitutional provision, has driven the Constitutional Court to cross formal boundaries and intervene even in conflicts between private parties. The readiness of the Constitutional Court to grant effect to fundamental rights embodied in national constitutions and international human rights, when solving a particular case, has given rise to horizontal application of fundamental rights.[39] This tendency in Albania was embraced without

[36] Art 131 of the Albanian Constitution.
[37] ibid.
[38] Art 131(f) of the 1998 Albanian Constitution.
[39] O Cherednychenko (n 9), 195.

difficulties by the Constitutional Court since it was considered the 'guardian' of the Constitution, including here also indirectly the protection of fundamental rights enshrined in the Constitution itself. As will be demonstrated in this section, the Constitutional Court in Albania has drawn inspiration from the ECtHR, to extend the application of human rights also in horizontal conflicts, changing somehow the institutional boundaries of the Constitutional Court itself. Similarly, as the ECtHR the Constitutional Court of Albania has coupled the infringement of property rights with the guarantees of a fair process. The intervention of the Constitutional Court in private conflicts is done indirectly, mainly through the control of guarantees of due process during the judicial proceedings.

We can cite some cases to illustrate the position of the Albanian Constitutional Court in this regard. In case 20/2008 of the Constitutional Court, an applicant brought a request before the Constitutional Court to declare void a decision of the Supreme Court, since it infringed on his right of fair process. The applicant (Mr Q. S.) was in a conflict over a property of land with another citizen (Mr N. H.). After losing all the judicial proceedings against the defendant in the civil court, the applicant filed criminal charges against him for forgery and criminal proceedings were opened. With a final decision of the court it was declared that in fact the father of Mr N.H. acquired property by forging a building permit. In light of this court ruling, the applicant reinvested the Supreme Court to reopen the case based on new evidence. The Supreme Court rejected to hear the case on the argument that this request was submitted beyond the preclusive deadline of one year, prescribed in Article 445 of the Code of Civil Procedure. The Constitutional Court had accepted jurisdiction over this case based on Article 131(f) of the Constitution and infringement of the right of fair process. The Constitutional Court engaged itself in the interpretation of the Article 445 and other provisions of the Code of Civil Procedure. By reading these provisions and the facts of the case in the light of due process and access to court, the Constitutional Court found that the Supreme Court has erred in the calculation of the deadline determined in Article 445 of the Code of Civil Procedure. The Constitutional Court ruled that the Supreme Court should have calculated the preclusive deadline of one year, not from the moment the applicant was aware of the forged document, but from the date the decision of the court on criminal charges was final. According to the Court since standards of Article 42 of the Constitution and Article 6 ECHR were not applied, the petitioner was denied in their constitutional right for access to justice and as a consequence also in his right of property.[40]

From a formalistic point a view this would be a transgression of the institutional boundaries and of the nature of constitutional review procedure before the CC. The Constitutional Court should not have engaged in the interpretation of the deadlines, and procedural aspects of the Civil Code of Procedure. However, despite the criticism, the Constitutional Court has clarified itself regarding how

[40] Decision of the Constitutional Court no 20, dated 29 September 2008, para 4.

and when it would engage in the interpretation of a (private) law in a specific conflict between private litigants. The Constitutional Court has noted that although the interpretation of the private (procedural) law is in the domain of the ordinary court, the Constitutional Court will step in, when the violations of the parties' fundamental rights result from issues of how the law is applied. Explicitly the Constitutional Court has clarified that:

> … the clarification of the meaning of each provision of the Civil Code of Procedure and its relationship with other related provisions in the judicial proceedings are in the competence of the ordinary court of the judicial system (see decision no.19 date 23.12.2004 of the CC). The [Constitutional] Court has stated that it will assess problems of interpretation and implementation of laws only when during this process fundamental constitutional rights are violated (See decision no 4, dated 28.02.2006 of the Constitutional Court).[41]

Thus, the Constitutional Court has indirectly applied the guarantees of the Convention and the fundamental rights of the Constitution in a private conflict. In the capacity of guarantor of human rights and under the auspices of a fair trial, the Constitutional Court has emerged in the interpretation of the civil law/civil law procedures. This interpretation of the private law has been in the light of the fundamental rights. Thus, the Constitutional Court has known itself to have the right to interpret the law and its application under the frame of due process, even when the conflict arises between private parties. According to the Constitutional Court:

> as long as the Constitutional Court makes the final interpretation of the Constitution and exercises the constitutional control of the legal norms, it cannot be prohibited from interpreting the laws in a specific case … Precisely, the interpretation made to the law in function of the constitutional principles constitutes constitutional jurisdiction and takes on the value of a final and binding interpretation for all. In this regard, the decision of the Constitutional Court becomes binding on the Supreme Court.[42]

Therefore, when the examination of concrete cases is related to the violation of the fundamental rights and freedoms of the individual and specifically, the due legal/fair right process, the Constitutional Court has jurisdiction to review the case and it falls under the CC competences. In this light the CC has struck down decisions of the Supreme Court with the argument that their reasoning was not clear, logical, and consistent,[43] that the Supreme Court have wrongfully applied Articles 130–132 of the Code of Civil procedures on the notification of the parties,[44] or because the lack of notification of third party.[45]

[41] ibid, para 3.
[42] Decision of the Constitutional Court no 5, dated 7 February 2001.
[43] Decision of the Constitutional Court no 33, dated 8 August 2005.
[44] Decision of the Constitutional Court no 92, dated 13 May 2002.
[45] Decision of the Constitutional Court no 34, dated 3 October 2007.

The CC has also further clarified that although the inconsistency between different laws does not in itself create anti-constitutionality, when the ambiguity created by this conflict of legal norms creates problems that lead to incorrect application of legal provisions and violation of the principle of the rule of law and legal certainty, the case also falls within the CC jurisdiction.[46] The same applies in cases when there is a conflict of jurisdiction/competences between different bodies. The CC has clarified that:

> problems of law enforcement and interpretation, including provisions on jurisdiction, are in principle the responsibility of the courts of the judiciary. However, the exceeding of competencies shall fall under the jurisdiction of the CC when there has been a violation of the procedural law that has infringed the constitutional rights for a due process of law.[47]

Based on the above observation it is clear that the doctrine of effective protection of human rights has not only been extended indirectly in private conflict cases, but has somehow affected also the physiognomy of the higher courts: we have a Supreme Court which in its interpretation of the law, in a specific conflict, also interprets and applies the Constitution, and a Constitutional Court which will also interfere in a private conflict to ensure the effective protection of human rights, especially the right of due process.

4.3. Selected Cases of Horizontal Application of General Principles and Fundamental Rights before the Supreme Court in Albania

The three cases of the Supreme Court detailed in this section illustrate the indirect application of general principles and fundamental rights in conflicts between private parties. These cases are isolated, and in none of them did the Supreme Court elaborate any doctrine of horizontal application of human rights or constitutional rights, or establish any theoretical framework with conditions and criteria when the principles or fundamental rights should be applied horizontally in private cases. There is no reference in the decisions of the Supreme Court to the *Drittwirkung* doctrine, or to the jurisprudence of any other country that would suggest that this application was an intentional exercise inspired by a comparative study on the horizontally application of fundamental rights and general principles in private cases. Even if this might have been the case, at least there is no clear reference throughout the decision. This leads us to the assumptions that justices of the Supreme Court, in reasoning these opinions were more driven by

[46] Decision of the Constitutional Court no 14, dated 22 May 2006.
[47] Decision of the Constitutional Court no 11, dated 23 April 2009.

distributive justice[48] in a contract or tort case to protect the weaker party, rather than the concern if the general principles of law or fundamental rights could be horizontally applied in a specific case.

4.3.1. The Horizontal Application of General Principles of Law in Private Contracts

One of the first cases where the Supreme Court applied general principles of law to construe the meaning of the civil law in a private conflict was related to the payment of interests in a loan contract. Although the Albanian Civil Code did not provide any maximum limit of allowed interest in a contract, the Supreme Court, based on the general principles of fairness and proportionality, declared invalid the part of the loan contract where high interests were provided. The Supreme Court stated:

> It is clear from the content of this provision and the articles defining the general terms contracts, that the freedom to enter an agreement is not absolute. In any case, it may be "restricted" by certain economic and moral considerations, … which the court should consider when deciding each specific case. Ignoring the aforementioned [economic and moral] considerations results in a lack of proportionality, or, as the legislator puts it, in a disproportionate harm to the interests of the contracting party, indicating that this party's will (consent) was not entirely free.
>
> According to Article 686/2 of the Civil Code "The general conditions that cause a loss or **disproportionate** harm to the interests of the contracting party are invalid, especially when they diverge significantly from **the principles of equality and impartiality** expressed in the general provisions of this Code that govern contractual relations. (authors' emphasis)[49]

Based in the above considerations, the Joint Panels of the Supreme Court, ruled that the part of the loan contract determining the interest rate is not in compliance with the 'economic logic' and 'moral reasoning', and declared that part of the contract invalid.[50]

[48] According to Cherednychenko the traditional view considers private law based on the principle of corrective justice, which considers parties entering a transaction 'mathematically' and 'geographically' as equal, *excluding the relevance of personal features of the parties to a transaction, such as their social rank, moral character, comparative wealth or needs*. On the other hand, Cherednychenko notes that in modern contract law, distributive justice is not totally excluded and does in practice influence many specific rules of general contract law. Distributive justice involves comparing the parties to a distribution by reference to a certain criterion and sometimes affects the rights and obligations of the parties in a certain contract, eg in many cases it is the obligation of the economically stronger party to remedy the weaker party's inexperience or lack of knowledge by informing and/or warning that weaker party about the particular nature of the intended transaction and the risks involved therein. However, she points out that distributive justice is only indirectly taken into account in the resolution of conflicts between the parties and the freedom to contract and private law instruments should have primacy in resolving conflicts between the parties. See: O Cherednychenko, *Fundamental rights, contract law and the protection of the weaker party: A comparative analysis of the constitutionalisation of contract law, with emphasis on risky financial transactions* Vol 5 (Munich, Sellier European Law Publication, 2007) 32.

[49] Supreme Court, Joint Panels, Decision no 932, dated 22 June 2000, Reg no 1800, p 5.

[50] ibid, p 6.

Another private case before the Supreme Court, which was resolved based on the application of general principles of law, was a case about the contingency fee in a legal service contract. The facts were as such: A.R. an Albanian citizen who has suffered an accident while working in Italy, opened a case for compensation for damages in the Court of Milan. Apart of an Italian lawyer, he chose to be represented also by two Albanian attorneys, who would assist him until the end of the trial and the execution of the court decision. With a notarial statement, the client A.R. had expressed the will to pay to the two Albanian attorneys the amount of 35 per cent of the total value of the compensation, which he would benefit after the decision of the Italian court. After the Court of Milan decided to award A.R a compensation of EUR 233,377, A.R. paid EUR 10,000 to the Italian legal representative and EUR 30,000 to the two Albanian attorneys. The latter were not satisfied with the compensation, claiming that their client should abide to the contract and pay them 35 per cent of the awarded compensation. After the refusal of the client to pay this amount, the two attorneys brought the case before the first instance court. The first instance court ruled that there was no agreement between the parties for the compensation of 35 per cent of the awarded compensation. The notarial statement signed by the defendant, is not an agreement between the parties, but rather a unilateral act and A.R. did not assume any obligation with it.

The appeal court overruled the first court decision with the argument that the notarial statement was in fact a contract, since both parties assumed rights and obligations: the client has declared to pay his attorneys 35 per cent of the compensation he would receive from the Italian Court, while the attorneys have committed to defend his rights until the execution of the final decision, assuming also the risk that in case of losing the trial they would receive no remuneration for the work performed. The Supreme Court overruled the decision of the Appeal Court and confirmed the decision of the First Instance Court, but on a different ground. The Supreme Court established that there is an agreement between the attorneys and the client. However, according to the Supreme Court, in this relationship the obligations of the client were unfair and not proportional in relation to the obligations of the plaintiff. The Supreme Court employed the principle of proportionality to construe the rights and obligations assumed by the parties in the contract.

According to the Supreme Court:

> … the terms of the lawyer-client contract should establish a proportional relationship between the value of the fee for legal services on the one hand and the specific service rendered, the clients objectives and interests on the other hand, which is assessed in light of the client's financial, social, and economic circumstances. Thus, the agreement should strike a fair balance between the demands and interests of the parties. The application of the principle of proportionality does not constitute an interference with the freedom of service provided, but puts the parties in a position so that no one is forced to bear an excessive burden.
>
> … For the case under consideration, the respondent A.R., as a user of legal services, has undertaken to pay the fee not from the resources in his possession, but from the resources that would be created from these services. It is clear that there is no reasonable

> link of proportionality between the services rendered by the plaintiff party in the interest of the defendant and the value or charge for the purportedly performed services in the agreement made between the parties or in the request of the plaintiffs. We do not have a situation where the plaintiff's fee request and the services they provided are fairly balanced in the matter at hand.[51]

Based on these arguments, the Supreme Court decided to annul the decision of the Appeal Court and leave in force the decision of the first instance court.

In both cases illustrated above the general principles of equality, fairness, and proportionality have construed the economic freedom of the parties in favour of the protection of the weaker contracting party. The Supreme Court has employed general principles of law to declare void an agreement or part of an agreement concluded with the free will of the parties. The general principle to prevent abuse of a stronger party is provided in Article 686 of the Civil Code of Albania, which clearly provides that the general conditions of a contract which lead to a loss or a disproportionate damage to the contracting party's interests, especially when they differ substantially from the principles of equality and impartiality as defined in the Civil Code, are void. Similar solutions that opt for the protection of the weaker contracting party are reported in different jurisdictions. Fundamental rights and general principles are indirectly applied in cases of onerous or one-sided contracts. For example, in the *Bürgschaft* case the German Constitutional Court held that a civil court must intervene on the basis of the general clauses of private law (like the provisions on contracts contrary to good faith or good morals) if a structural imbalance in bargaining power led to a one-sided onerous contract. If a civil court does not do so, it may violate human dignity as protected by Article 1 of the German constitution.[52] In some countries the principles of protecting the weaker party is expressly considered a general principle of contract law, or there are even cases such as in Brazil, were the social function of a contract requires parties to promote not only their own interests but also socially useful interests.[53] These general principles may serve as 'the gateways to the effect of fundamental rights in contractual relationships', and serve for the fundamental rights in private cases, contributing in striking a balance between the conflicting rights and interests of the individuals.[54] Smits notes that vague concepts like good faith, good morals, or public policy are filled-in by fundamental rights and lead to the application of fundamental rights in relationships between private parties.[55]

However, despite the fact that we encourage the horizontal application of general principles when resolving the case, we are against advising the Albanian judges to use the general principles as a legal foundation each time they interpret

[51] Supreme Court of Albania, case no 241, date 12 May 2011.

[52] J Smits, 'Private Law and Fundamental Rights: a Sceptical View' in T Barkhuysen and S Lindenbergh (eds), *Constitutionalisation of Private Law* (Leiden, Brill Nijhoff, 2006) 9, 11.

[53] V Trstenjak and P Weingerl (eds), *The Influence of Human Rights and Basic Rights in Private Law* (Switzerland, Springer, 2016) 11, 12.

[54] ibid 11.

[55] J Smits (n 49) 12.

a contract, isolated from the will of the parties. Private law should be interpreted in compliance with fundamental rights but not absorbed by the latter.[56] Although fundamental rights should be respected – and as per Constitution they stand above every law, being it public law or private law – the specific (private) law has detailed rules to regulate a relationship and the judge should solve the case based on them. If a judge, in solving a case, would abandon the interpretation of private law and recourse to the general principles or fundamental rights, and decide against what the private parties have agreed, they would be infringing not only a party's autonomy, but also the principle of rule of law. Especially in countries such as Albania, where corruption is high and the rule of law is considered still weak, a judge that solves cases based solely on the notions of distributive justice, irrespective of the parties' agreement, might lead to risky and problematic scenarios; it might generate more corruption and less rule of law. These considerations bring us to the conclusion that 'practical' and 'effective' protection of fundamental rights also in the private realm, are realised not only by the horizontal application of general principles and fundamental rights, but also through a strong and independent judiciary that acts in compliance with rule of law, who abides to the law, independence, and impartiality. Therefore, instead of a blind and automatic subordination of private law towards fundamental rights, dialogue between to legal domain seem the best option.[57] Further than a dialogue, we would suggest collaboration, where the two legal realms should not walk separately, but give and share in achieving the purpose for which they were established.

4.3.2. The Horizontal Application of Constitutional Rights in Private Conflicts

One of most well-known decisions, where the Supreme Court used the Albanian Constitution directly to interpret civil law provision, was in a judgment regarding the right for compensation for damages. Three people, respectively 31, 12 and 13 years old, were killed in a car accident on the national highways in 2002. After administering technical and forensic evidence the Court declared guilty the author of the accident, for the criminal offence of violation of traffic rules causing the death of three persons.[58] The parents of the victims filed six lawsuits in civil court seeking damages related to the accident. They claimed that after the accident they have experienced severe mental and emotional distress, ongoing physical health issues which had a negative impact on the quality of their lives. Therefore, they requested reimbursement for not only financial costs (funeral costs and legal defence), but also maintenance, living, and healthcare compensation for family members.[59]

[56] ibid, p 14.
[57] O Cherednychenko (n 45) 509.
[58] Supreme Court of Albania, case no 12, dated 14 September 2007, p 83.
[59] Supreme Court of Albania, case no 12/2007, p 84.

The Court of First Instance made a narrow interpretation of Article 608 of the Civil Code. According to this Court, Article 608 of the Civil Code provides compensation for non-contractual damages caused to the injured person only, meaning 'to his person or property', and not damages caused to the health or property of third parties.[60] The court of appeal upheld the decision of the First Instance Court, based on the same arguments. The Supreme Court decided to withdraw the case in a Joint Panel and do a unification of the judicial practice with regards to the rights of compensation caused in car accidents.

The Joint Panels of the Supreme Court, employed the general principles of law and fundamental human rights to construe broadly Article 608 and 625 of the Civil Code. With regards to the legal standing of family members for compensation for damages, the Supreme Court ruled that they were eligible to request compensation for damages in case of a car accident based on Article 608 of the Civil Code, not only as heirs of the victim of the accident, but also as individuals who as a consequence of the accident have suffered pecuniary and non-pecuniary damages. According to the Supreme Court:

> [o]ne of the fundamental principles of coexistence in human society is the prohibition to cause harm to others (alterum non laedere or neminem laedere) and whoever violates the rights and legal interests of another is obliged to compensate him ... Through compensation, it is intended precisely the full restoration of the injured party (restitutio in integrum) in the previous state (status quo ante), in which the person would have been if the illegal fact had not occurred.[61]

Secondly, the Supreme Court employed Articles 3 and 15 of the Constitution to construe that Articles 608 and 625 of the Civil Code requires the full repair of every damage done illegally, that is, not only towards assets in the narrow economic sense, but also non-pecuniary interests. The Supreme Court referred to the Constitution to reach the conclusion that compensation for non-pecuniary damages in Article 625 of the Civil Code stands as an independent claim *vis a vis* the claim of compensation for pecuniary damages and compensation for the reduction of the ability to work, provided for in Article 641 of the Civil Code.[62]

[60] Moreover, the court read the Civil Code provisions together with the Decree No. 295, date 15 September 1992 'On vehicles compulsory liability insurance damages caused to third parties' and ruled that: 'Article 17 and 18 of the Decree provides only for the compensation of death, health damage and property damage caused to the injured person in a car accident. These provisions explicitly ... cover only compensation for pecuniary damages and exclude the compensation for non-pecuniary damages, provided in article 625 of the Civil Code.' ibid, para 87.

[61] Ibid, para 87.

[62] Namely, the Supreme Court has stated: 'The right to life and health is an objective right that derives from a person's existence and is unbreakable and separate from it. Therefore, the Constitution (Articles 3, 15/1, and 21) protects and guarantees them as fundamental human rights. The protection of human health is covered by several legal provisions, including the requirement that the state provides healthcare (Articles 15/2 and 56), the right to enforce this protection in court (Articles 42/2), and others. These provisions require anyone who violates a person's physical or mental integrity to make amends for the harm they have caused .... For the above reasons, the Joint Panels of the Supreme Court reach the unifying conclusion that: Damages to health (biological harm) consists, in essence, of the violation

This non-pecuniary damage, provided by the letter "a" of Article 625 of the Civil Code, is the object of search and compensation independent from other non-pecuniary damages suffered by the victim due to the same illegal fact.[63]

Another issue of interpretation was whether the parents of a victim in a car accident should have the right of compensation for food and living expenses or not, when the victim was a minor, respectively 13 and 12 years old. According to Article 643 of the Civil Code in case of death of a person, the damage that must be compensated consists of:

> a) expenses for food and maintenance of his minor children, his wife and parents not able to work who were in charge of the deceased, fully or partially, as well as persons who lived in the family of *the deceased and who enjoyed the right of maintenance from him* (authors' emphasis).

The Supreme Court referred to Articles 3 and 15 of the Constitution, Articles 8 and 12 of the ECHR, and the Albanian Family Code provisions and made a very broad reading of Article 643 of the civil code. According to the SC, the death of a minor child, apart from the serious emotional and moral sufferings, presupposes also the loss of a potential economic support and care, which would have come, if the child would have reached the age of adulthood.

> In particular, with the loss of life the minor victim can no longer contribute, with the income that he would provide in the future, to the support of the surviving family members with whom he had a very close (family) relationship and a stable, economic and affective cohabitation (Article 163 of the Family Code).[64]

The Supreme Court elevated the right of a family as a fundamental right in a society, for which the state has an obligation to defend it and that in case of disturbance should be compensated. The Court ruled:

> From the above, stems not only the reality but also the need of the society to recognize that family, apart from being a unit that generates income, is above all the unit of the society that produces services and mutual care for its members. Therefore, as such, the invasion in the family in any form, legitimizes the right of the state to defend it, but also the right of family members to be compensated in the event that these fundamental rights are breached …
>
> … According to articles 608 and 643/a of the Civil Code, surviving family members who had a close and long-lasting relationship with the minor who died as a result of an illegal act are entitled to compensation for pecuniary damages, in the form of lost earning, because they were not able to capitalize on the minor's solidarity and mutual support, which included not only care for the family as a whole but also his financial support for

of the good health, of the physical and/or mental integrity of the person. This non-pecuniary damage, provided for by the letter "a" of Article 625 of the Civil Code, is the subject for a claim and compensation independent from other non-pecuniary damages suffered by the injured party due to the same illegal fact.' Supreme Court Decision No 12/2007, p 96.

[63] Ibid.

[64] Supreme Court Decision No 12/2007, p 93.

> the family. Whether or not the minor's parents and other family members have enough money to support them at the time of the death is irrelevant for the purpose of their eligibility to claim such compensation.[65]

Finally, the Supreme Court used the prohibition of discrimination, Article 18 of the Constitution to rule that the right to profit this compensation should not be related to the age of the victim.

This decision of the Supreme Court is a reflection of the jurisprudence of the Constitutional Court, who calls the lower courts, including the Supreme Court to directly apply the Constitution in solving a case. Without engaging in a longer discussion on different legal aspects of this case, which would go beyond the space and limits of this chapter, there are some final general remarks we would like to bring forth. Firstly, after the ratification of the ECHR and the new Constitution in 1988 an increase in focus of the fundamental rights was witnessed among judges of different court levels, including the Supreme Court. Gradually a professional awareness of the obligation to respect the fundamental rights was established, especially the guarantees of Article 6 of the Convention, and that the courts had an important role to play in this regard. The control of the guarantees of fair process by the Constitutional Court and ECtHR and the overturning of some decision of the Supreme Court by the former, have further contributed to increase the awareness of the insurances that individuals have in the system against public authorities, including the court itself. Secondly, despite these developments, the doctrine of horizontal effect of human rights is far from settled in Albanian law and judicial practice. Fundamental rights, even when they are used in a horizontal conflict before the Supreme Court, are currently used mainly to construe the interpretation of the existing private legal provisions, rather than as sources of subjective rights which individuals could enforce in court. In all the three cases above, the judges of the Supreme Court were more driven by the principles of distributive justice, or protecting the weaker party, or human dignity, rather than abstract consideration on application of fundamental rights horizontally. Thirdly, fundamental rights are and will be increasingly invoked before the ordinary courts and the Supreme Court by the parties. In fact, many of the arguments in this case with regards to the application of fundamental rights were brought ahead by the plaintiff and the Supreme Court had to respond about the alleged violations. This means that in the future, judges should be prepared for similar requests from the parties, who will use fundamental rights instruments to advance their rights and procedural position before the court. On the other hand, this requires judges to acquire the relevant knowledge on the content of fundamental rights as developed by the ECtHR and the Constitutional Court, understand the limits and the nature of different disciplines of law, and above all be fair, independent and impartial. Finally, since the developments of the judicial practice in ECtHR has a snowball effect on the domestic courts of the contracting state, the ECtHR should be careful and clear when deciding on these cases.

[65] Supreme Court Decision No 12/2007, pg 93.

5. Conclusions

The property cases against Albania before the ECtHR where the Convention was applied horizontally were based on the doctrine of positive obligation and Article 1 of the Convention. The European Court of Human Rights has construe Article 1 Protocol 1 as entailing not only negative obligations, but also positive obligations, of a procedural nature that enable the peaceful enjoyment of the property rights. In almost all the cases against Albania, the Court has employed a double layer of application of Article 6 in relation to Article 1 Protocol 1. Firstly, the guarantees of Article 6 were deemed as part of the positive obligation of the Contracting States; in a conflict about property rights between private parties, the State has the obligation to ensure a judicial system that respect the procedural rights of the parties, is independent and impartial and guarantees a fair process. Secondly, Article 6 of the ECHR was used in the judicial scrutiny phase, to assess the lawfulness of the state intervention. This coupling of Article 6 with the horizontal application of fundamental rights in private conflicts, seem to have rescinded also in the Constitutional Court of Albania. However, the logic and the general framework are different. As illustrated in this chapter, the Constitutional Court vested with the power to review the standards of the fair process before the domestic courts, even in individual cases, used this leverage to 'constitutionalise' private law by interpreting the private law provisions in the light of constitutional principles. This had led not only to situations where the Constitutional Court has interpreted provisions of the Civil Code of Procedures itself, but has also somehow changed the institutional character of the Constitutional Court, which in certain cases seem to act as a 'fourth' court of appeal for private cases litigations. With regards to the application of general principles and fundamental rights by the Supreme Court, we have noted that we are far from an established practice. The cases illustrated in this paper are rather isolated and they do not amount in any settled practice about horizontal application of fundamental rights by the Supreme Court. However, since there is a general awareness of the judges on the ECHR and its jurisprudence, as well as more cases are being invoked before the national courts with regards to fundamental rights, there is a need of a clearer, well elaborated doctrine by the ECtHR itself on the horizontal application of fundamental rights and its limits.

7

The Role of the Rule of Law in Croatian Private Law Relationships

EMILIA MIŠĆENIĆ*

1. Introduction

As important pillars of the European Union (EU), the rule of law and respect for human rights are enshrined in Article 2 of the Treaty on European Union (TEU).[1] Together with respect for human dignity, freedom, democracy and equality, the rule of law and respect for human rights present common values upon which the Union is founded and which form part of the constitutional traditions of the Member States. There is a positive duty of the Union and of its institutions, as well as of the Member States, to protect and secure the observance of and respect for these values. The Court of Justice of the European Union (CJEU) ensures that the rule of law is respected in interpretation and application of the Treaties (Article 19(1) of the TFEU).[2] As established in *Les Verts v Parliament*, the Union is a community based on the rule of law, 'inasmuch as neither its Member States nor its institutions can avoid review of the question whether the measures adopted by them are in conformity with the basic constitutional charter, the Treaty'.[3]

In the case of a risk of a serious breach of the values protected under Article 2 of the TEU, the sanction mechanism under Article 7 of the TEU can be invoked under certain conditions.[4] Besides the potential infringement proceeding as a

* This work has been partially supported by the University of Rijeka project Transparency and Fairness in the Digital Environment (uniri-iskusni-drustvo-23-101).

[1] Consolidated versions of the Treaty on European Union (TEU) and the Treaty on the Functioning of the European Union (TFEU) [2016] OJ C 202/1.

[2] D Kochenov and P Bard, 'Kirchberg Salami Lost in Bosphorus: The Multiplication of Judicial Independence Standards and the Future of the Rule of Law in Europe' (2022) 60 *Journal of Common Market Studies* 1–19.

[3] Judgment of 23 April 1986, C-294/83, *Les Verts v Parliament*, ECLI:EU:C:1986:166, para 23.

[4] European Commission, Communication, A New EU Framework to Strengthen the Rule of Law, COM (2014) 158, 11.3.2014; Council of Europe, European Commission for Democracy Through Law (Venice Commission) Rule of Law Checklist, Venice, 11–12 March 2016.

sanctioning mechanism, there are many other steps that protect the rule of law in the EU.[5] The protection of the rule of law, democracy and of fundamental rights is operated through a far more complex mechanism, involving European and international bodies and experts, such as the EU Rule of Law Commission; the European Commission for Democracy through Law (the Venice Commission) of the Council of Europe; and the UN Human Rights Treaty Bodies. Similarly, as with the protection of human rights and fundamental freedoms under the European Convention for the Protection of Human Rights and Fundamental Freedoms (ECHR)[6] and the Charter of Fundamental Rights of the European Union (EU Charter),[7] this duty relates primarily to public law relationships between the Union, the states and the citizens. By respecting the duties arising under the ratified international agreements and EU law, the Member States – meaning the courts, legislators and executive powers as emanations of the state – are required to protect the rule of law and respect human rights in their relationships towards the citizens ('staatliche grundrechtliche Schutzpflicht').

Traditionally, legal scholarship was more focused on observing the rule of law as a key principle dominating public law relationships.[8] However, for the past decade, the rule of law has been getting more and more attention from private law scholars, who are exploring how, and to what extent, the rule of law impacts private law relationships.[9] In particular, this approach was inspired by the legal research on the constitutionalisation of private law[10] and different legal doctrines on the impact of the constitutionally protected human rights and fundamental freedoms on private law relationships.[11] The latter include the legal doctrines and methods on the radiating effects (*Ausstrahlungswirkung*) of the constitutionally protected values in private law relationships, such as the principle of equality

[5] D Kochenov and L Pech, 'Monitoring and Enforcement of the Rule of Law in the EU: Rhetoric and Reality' (2015) 11 *European Constitutional Law Review* 512–40.

[6] European Convention for the Protection of Human Rights and Fundamental Freedoms, Rome, 4 November 1950, as amended by Protocols Nos 11 and 14, supplemented by Protocols Nos 1, 4, 6, 7, 12 and 13.

[7] Charter of Fundamental Rights of the European Union [2016] OJ C 202/391.

[8] See, eg FC Decost, 'Review Essay Redeeming the Rule of Law: *Constitutional Justice: A Liberal Theory of the Rule of Law*, T.R.S. Allan (Oxford, Oxford University Press, 2001)' (2002) 39(4) *Alberta Law Review* 1004–30; P Craig, 'Formal and Substantive Conceptions of the Rule of Law: An Analytical Framework' in R Bellamy (ed), *The Rule of Law and the Separation of Powers* (London, Routledge, 2005); J Raz, 'The Rule of Law and Its Virtue' in J Raz, *The Authority of Law: Essays on Law and Morality* (Oxford, Oxford Scholarship Online, 2012); GK Hadfield and BR Weingast, 'Is Rule of Law an Equilibrium Without (Some) Private Enforcement?' in J Knight and M Schwartzberg (eds), *Privatization* (Nomos, 2019) 246–75; J Habermas, 'On the Internal Relation between the Rule of Law and Democracy' in C Cronin, P Greiff, *The Inclusion of the Other, Studies in Political Theory* (Frankfurt am Mein, Suhrkampf Verlag, 1998) 253.

[9] LM Austin and D Klimchuk (eds), *Private Law and the Rule of Law* (Oxford Scholarship Online, 2015).

[10] HW Micklitz, 'Introduction' in HW Micklitz (ed), *Constitutionalization of European Private Law* (Oxford, Oxford University Press, 2014); S Grundmann (ed), *Constitutional Values and European Contract Law* (Austin, Wolters Kluwer, 2008).

[11] H Collins, 'Private Law, Fundamental Rights, and the Rule of Law' (2018) 121(1) *West Virginia Law Review*, 1–25, and therein cited literature.

and non-discrimination, or on the indirect effects of these rights in private law (*unmittelbare Drittwirkung*), and interpretation of private law rules consistent to the constitution (*verfassungskonforme Anwendung*), as some of the examples.

One particular aspect of EU law, which contributes significantly to constitutionalisation of private law and observance of constitutionally protected rights and values in private law relationships, are the sources of EU secondary law, such as the prominent EU anti-discrimination directives. Together with other relevant EU directives and regulations addressing the protection of human rights and fundamental freedoms, these important EU legal acts enter the Member States' laws by way of approximation. In doing so, they often emphasise the pre-existing duty under the national laws related to the respect of constitutionally protected fundamental rights in private law relationships. As a consequence of harmonising with EU anti-discrimination directives, the Member States' laws, including the Croatian ones, contain provisions prohibiting discrimination in private law relationships. These harmonised national rules offer direct protection and guarantee equality and human rights in private law relationships.

Furthermore, one can also argue that approximation of the Member States' laws in this area has contributed significantly to the diminishing of the widespread division between the public and private law.[12] This is not solely because of the mixture of private and public law provisions in EU directives, but mostly because of the substantive impact that some of these directives have had on private laws. By allowing compensation of damage under private law rules due to violation of equality and non-discrimination, and by recognising that discrimination violates the personality rights of the affected persons, these rules alleviate the strict distinction between public and private law, and enables them to work together in protecting private individual rights.[13] And it is precisely this division, when accepted and applied *stricto sensu*, that stands in the way to proper and better understanding of the impact of fundamental rights and the rule of law on private law and private law relationships.

2. General Remarks on the Rule of Law

The doctrinal debates about the rule of law should not miss the key point of the rule of law, which is to guarantee the rule of the 'law' that incorporates all areas of law, both public and private. When talking about the rule of law, one often tends to

[12] On public/private division in EU law, see HW Micklitz, 'Rethinking the Public/Private Divide' in MP Maduro et al (eds), *Transnational Law: Rethinking European Law and Legal Thinking* (Cambridge, Cambridge University Press, 2014) 271–306; D Leczykiewicz and S Weatherill (eds), *The Involvement of EU Law in Private Law Relationships* (Oxford, Hart Publishing, 2013); O Cherednychenko, 'Rediscovering the Public/Private Divide in EU Private Law' (2019) *European Law Journal* 27–47; and many others.

[13] N Reich, 'Effective Private Law Remedies in Discrimination Cases' in R Schulze (ed), *Non-Discrimination in European Private Law* (Tübingen, Mohr Siebeck, 2011) 57.

focus on the role of the government and public law institutions in protecting the rule of law.[14] As rightly emphasised by *Habermas*, academia is 'accustomed to consider law, the rule of law, and democracy as subjects of different disciplines',[15] while in fact this is not so. Although these are not the same notions or legal concepts, they are closely related and should be observed together. As properly stated by *Waldron*, the rule of law is only one star in a constellation of ideals that includes, among others, democracy, human rights and economic freedom.[16] Democratic processes cannot be separated from the law and its enforcement, in the same manner as the rule of law cannot only be observed only from the perspective of public law.

The very basic idea of the rule of law is to prevent the exercise of power beyond what is allowed or necessary under the law, ie the prevention of arbitrariness through assertion of power. Furthermore, the citizens should have access to the law, and the law should guide them in their decisions and transactions.[17] Another key part of the rule of law is effective enforcement, which provides the people access to justice and legal procedures that protect them from the abuse of powers – both public and private. However, as emphasised by a number of scholars, there is much controversy regarding the exact meaning of the rule of law and its reach.[18] Some of the main features of the rule of law, such as publicity, stability, generality, neutrality, etc., are observed through the lens of public law. In light of a more formalist approach, the legal norm should offer guidance to its addresses and enable compliance with the law, while the state must ensure its effective enforcement.[19] This of course raises concerns with respect to private law rules, which can be changed at any moment by the legislator. This is especially the case in SEE states such as Croatia, where democracy, the rule of law and respect of human rights are still not satisfactory, and enforcement of law is not effective enough.[20]

According to *Raz*, in legal systems that do not possess certain characteristics of the legal norm, it does not mean that the law does not exist, but it is not characterised by the rule of law.[21] This question certainly needs to be addressed and

[14] See, eg W Lucy, 'The rule of law and private law' in LM Austin and D Klimchuk (eds), *Private Law and the Rule of Law* (Oxford Scholarship Online, 2015) 41–66; L Austin, 'What's "Private" about the Rule of Law?' (2016) 1 *JOTWEL Journal of Things We Like (Lots).*

[15] Habermas (n 8) 253.

[16] J Waldron, *The Rule of Law and the Measure of Property* (Cambridge, Cambridge University Press, 2012) 12.

[17] ibid, 6.

[18] On different interpretations of the rule of law, see Hadfield and Weingast (n 8) 259; L Austin, 'Property and the Rule of Law' (2014) 20 *Legal Theory*; H Dagan, 'Private Law Pluralism and the Rule of Law' in H Dagan, *Reconstructing American Legal Realism & Rethinking Private Law Theory* (New York, Oxford Academic, 2013) 168; and other selected online reading on the rule of law available at European Parliament EP Library.

[19] Decost (n 8) 1006; Raz (n 8) 212.

[20] S Rodin, 'Croatia: Developing Judicial Culture of Fundamental Rights' in R Arnold (ed), *The Universalism of Human Rights. Ius Gentium: Comparative Perspectives on Law and Justice 16* (Dordrecht et al, Springer, 2013) 391–404.

[21] Hadfield and Weingast (n 8) 260; Raz (n 8) 211, 221–22.

examined within the Croatian legal framework and the presented case law. As a SEE country with a turbulent and dynamic political, economic and legal history, Croatia has struggled with the enforcement of the rule of law.[22] After the dissolution of the Socialist Federal Republic of Yugoslavia (SFRY), Croatia became an independent state,[23] went through a transition period, signed the Stabilisation and Association Agreement with EU and the Member States (SAA) in 2001,[24] and joined the EU in 2013.[25] The transition to a legal system observing the rule of law and a democratic society was not an easy task, as it will be demonstrated in the next section.

3. The Enforcement of the Rule of Law in Croatia

In the Croatian legal framework, the rule of law is guaranteed by the Constitution, the ECHR, EU Treaties, EU Charter and many other valuable international agreements, which form part of the legal system and are hierarchically positioned above the statutory acts.[26] The ECHR has formed part of the Croatian legal system since 1997,[27] and plays a crucial role in the national case law and jurisprudence.[28] In one of its earlier decisions, the Constitutional Court found that the application of the law contrary to international agreements in general, and in particular contrary to the ECHR, represents a violation of the obligations assumed under international law and of the rule of law under Article 3 of the Constitution.[29] Pursuant to Article 3 of the Constitution 'freedom, equal rights, national and gender equality, peace-making, social justice, respect for human rights, inviolability of ownership, conservation of nature and the environment, *the rule of law* and a democratic

[22] S Rodin, 'Croatian Accession to the European Union: The Transformation of the Legal System' in K Ott (ed), *Croatian Accession to the European Union* (Institute of Public Finance and Friedrich Ebert Stiftung, Zagreb, 2003) 223–48.

[23] Constitutional Decision on Sovereignty and Independence of the Republic of Croatia, OG No 31/91; Decision of the Croatian Parliament on severing all state-building bonds with the states forming Yugoslav federation, OG No 53/91.

[24] Act on Confirmation of the Stabilization and Association Agreement of 29 October 2001 between the Republic of Croatia and the European Communities and their Member States, OG IA Nos 14/01, 15/01, 14/02, 1/05, 7/05, 9/ 05 and 11/06.

[25] Treaty between Member States of the European Union and the Republic of Croatia concerning the Accession of the Republic of Croatia to the European Union, OJ L 112, 24.04.2012 in force from 1 July 2013.

[26] Art 141 of the Constitution (Art 134 of the consolidated version).

[27] Act on the Confirmation of the ECHR and Protocols Nos 1, 4, 6, 7 and 11, OG IA Nos 18/97, 6/99 and 8/99; Protocol No 13, OG IA Nos 14/02 and 13/03; Protocol No 12, OG IA Nos 14/02 and 9/05; Protocol No 14, OG IA Nos 1/06 and 2/10.

[28] K Turković and J Omejec, 'Croatia – Commitment to Reform: Assessing the Impact of the ECtHR's Case Law on Reinforcing Democratization Efforts in Croatian Legal order' in I Motoc and I Ziemele (eds), *The Impact of the ECHR on Democratic Change in Central and Eastern Europe: Judicial Perspectives* (Cambridge, Cambridge University Press, 2016) 110–35.

[29] Conclusion of the Constitutional Court of the Republic of Croatia of 11 March 1998, Nos U-I-920/95 and U-I-950/96.

multiparty system are *the highest values of the constitutional order of the Republic of Croatia* and the ground for interpretation of the Constitution' (author's emphasis).

The strong corelation between the protection of human rights and fundamental freedoms arises from Chapter III and its Article 14(1), according to which 'everyone in the Republic of Croatia has the rights and freedoms, regardless of their race, skin colour, gender, language, religion, political or other conviction, national or social origin, property, birth, education, social status or other characteristics', while according to paragraph 2 '*everyone is equal before the law*' (author's emphasis).[30] There are other provisions that guarantee the rule of law, such as the constitutional provision requiring the Supreme Court of the Republic of Croatia, as the highest court, to ascertain the uniform application of law and equality of everyone in its application.[31] Furthermore, the constitutional provisions of Chapter VIIA, on the European Union, require Croatia's active participation in the creation of European unity and ensuring lasting peace, liberty, security and prosperity, as well as achievement of common objectives, such as the protection of EU fundamental principles and values. In accordance with these constitutional provisions, in Croatia, all EU citizens enjoy the rights guaranteed by the *acquis* and the Croatian courts protect the subjective rights arising from the *acquis*.[32]

The normative guarantee of the rule of law, however, differs from enforcement in practice. Even prior to becoming a Member State, Croatia struggled with the enforcement of the rule of law, as one of the main preconditions for entering the EU. Under the Copenhagen criteria, Croatia was required to demonstrate respect of human rights and the rule of law. According to conclusions of the European Council in 1993, the 'associated countries in central and eastern Europe that so desire shall become members of the EU', once they have ensured democracy and the rule of law, respect of human rights and protection of minorities.[33] The SAA signed with the EU and the Member States contained several provisions on the rule of law, such as Article 75 requiring reinforcement of institutions and consolidation of the rule of law. The emphasis was on the improvement of law enforcement and the justice system as a whole, and this is precisely where the Croatian legal system has proven to be weak.

Over the years, various reports have pointed out different issues in the Croatian judicial system, such as violation of the right to a fair trial, the reasonable time requirement, arbitrability in decision making, and non-transparency, as well as the lack of education, in particular with respect to EU law and consistent

[30] Art 14 of the Constitution.

[31] Art 119 of the Constitution (Art 116 of the consolidated version). Pursuant to Art 20 of the Courts Act, OG Nos 28/13, 33/15, 82/15, 82/16, 67/18, 126/19, 130/20, 21/22 and 60/22 the Supreme Court ensures the uniform application of law and the equality of everyone in its application.

[32] Arts 145 and 146 of the Constitution (Arts 141.c and 141.d of the consolidated version).

[33] Decision of the European Council in Copenhagen in 1993, Bulletin of the European Communities, No 6, 1993, 8 and 13.

interpretation.[34] The reports also warn about the issues related to the human rights protection and discrimination.[35] Despite human rights and fundamental freedoms being protected by the ECHR and a number of international agreements that are an integral part of the Croatian legal order, the enforcement is not satisfactory.[36] The most affected groups are the Roma and Serbian minorities, the LGBTIQ, but also disabled persons and women.[37] The first European Commission report in 2002 emphasised the ineffectiveness of the judiciary and demanded 'radical reforms' aimed at strengthening the rule of law. It accentuated serious organisational problems, inefficiency of procedures, a lack of expertise and long delays in proceedings, which affect the enforcement of the rule of law.[38] Twenty years later, in the 2022 Rule of Law Report, Croatia was given recommendations on how to improve the judicial system and its effectiveness.[39]

4. The Rule of Law and Protection of Fundamental Rights in Croatian Private Law

Increasing guarantee of constitutionally protected human rights and fundamental values in private law relationships plays the principal role in the effective enforcement of the rule of law. *Nota bene*, these concepts are not the same and should not be equated, but they are all parts of the same 'constellation of stars' and undoubtedly affect each other. Legal scholarship and practice have raised several objections against the increasing acceptance of the role of the rule of law in the area of private law and alignment with fundamental rights.[40] In some of the cases, the resistance is explained by the different features of public and private law, while in others by

[34] A Uzelac, 'The Rule of Law and the Judicial System: Court Delays as a Barrier to Accession' in K Ott (ed), *Croatian Accession to the European Union* (Zagreb, Institute of Public Finance and Friedrich Ebert Stiftung, 2003) 105–30.

[35] European Implementation Network and Democracy Reporting International, Justice Delayed and Justice Denied: Non-Implementation of European Courts Judgments and the Rule of Law, April 2022.

[36] F. Miscenic and D Kesonja, 'The Enforcement and Effectiveness of Anti-Discrimination Law: Chapter 8 Croatia' in M Mercat-Bruns, DB Oppenheimer and C Sartorius (eds), *Enforcement and Effectiveness of Discrimination Law in a Global World* (Cham, Springer, 2018) 129–51.

[37] Council of Europe, Advisory Committee on the Framework Convention for the Protection of National Minorities (ACFC), Fifth Opinion on Croatia, June 2021, emphasised the need for 'increasing the impact of human rights and non-discrimination training for law enforcement and the judiciary, as such measures would improve outreach to vulnerable groups and fight under-reporting of discrimination cases'.

[38] Commission Staff Working Paper, Croatia, Stabilisation and Association Report, COM (2002) 163, Brussels, 4 April 2002.

[39] Communication from the Commission to the European Parliament, the Council, the European Economic and Social Committee and the Committee of the Regions, 2022 Rule of Law Report, The rule of law situation in the European Union, Luxembourg, 13.7.2022 COM (2022) 500 final, 5, 9 and 24. According to the Commission Staff Working Paper, 2022 Rule of Law Report, Country Chapter on the rule of law situation in Croatia, Luxembourg, 13.7.2022 SWD(2022) 511 final.

[40] As noted by Collins (n 11) 8–12, and Austin and Klimchuk (n 9) 1–14.

the unpredictability that could be caused by private law rules, such as the good faith requirement.[41] There is also a developed discussion on the possible conflict between the basic civil law principles, such as private autonomy and freedom of contract, and fundamental rights and freedoms, such as non-discrimination and equality.[42] Where some legal scholars see the connection, others see the friction between the private law rules and the rule of law.[43]

In this chapter, the author argues that these rights and freedoms do not necessarily need to be seen as opponents and their proper exercise would not necessarily result in a conflict. Rather the opposite, the rule of law should and could be used to promote the fundamental rights in private law, and vice versa. The protection of fundamental rights upholds the rule of law through protection of the right to equality before the law, prohibition of retroactivity, entitlement to a fair and public hearing, etc. Certain private law rules have the strong potential to promote the rule of law in the sense that they set the boundaries and limits to excessive use of power by stronger parties and guarantee equality.

The Croatian legal system has many rules that provide at least an indirect effect regarding constitutionally protected fundamental rights and values in private law relationships. Some of the key provisions of the Croatian Obligations Act (OA)[44] require direct compliance of obligations relationships with the Constitution.[45] Under Article 2 of the OA the parties are free to regulate their obligation relationships, but these cannot be regulated in contravention of the Constitution, mandatory laws or the morals of society. Articles on the nullity of contracts (Article 322(1) of the OA), performance (Articles 270–271 of the OA) and condition (Article 298(1) of the OA) prescribe the nullity of the contract when one of these legal institutes is in violation of the Constitution, mandatory laws or the morals of society.[46] Under these private law provisions, the conduct of parties resulting in violation of fundamental rights is sanctioned with nullity.

Moreover, the equality that establishes the foundations of the rule of law can be found in a number of private law provisions. The rules of the Obligations Act, Family Act, Inheritance Act, Consumer Protection Act, Competition Act, Labour Act, Act on Ownership and Other Real Rights, and many others contain different provisions granting parties equality. Article 3 of the OA on the equality of the

[41] Collins (n 11) 9–10.

[42] See, eg N Reich, 'The Impact of the Non-Discrimination Principle on Private Autonomy' in D Leczykiewicz and S Weatherill (eds), *The Involvement of EU Law in Private Law Relationships* (Oxford, Hart Publishing, 2013) 253–78; J Basedow, 'Grundsatz der Nichtdiskriminierung im europäischen Privatrecht (2008) 2 *Zeitschrift für Europäisches Privatrecht*, 230–51; and many others.

[43] On the interaction of the rule of law and various fields of private law, such as contracts, torts, and property, see Austin and Klimchuk (n 9).

[44] Obligations Act, OG Nos 35/05, 41/08, 125/11, 78/15, 29/18 and 126/21.

[45] The Constitution of the Republic of Croatia, OG Nos 56/90, 135/97, 8/98 (consolidated text), 113/00, 124/00 (consolidated text), 28/01, 41/01 (consolidated text), 55/01 (correction), 76/10, 85/10 (consolidated text).

[46] For other examples see E Mišćenić, 'Autonomy and Antidiscrimination in Private Law, Country Report for Croatia' in South East European Law School Network, *Civil Law Forum for South East Europe – Collection for Studies and Analyses* (Skopje, Centre for SEELS 2014) 100.

parties to the obligation relationship is interpreted as prohibiting any discrimination that places one party in a less favourable position than the other party.[47] The content of these provisions undoubtedly serves the same purpose as the rule of law, by prohibiting the use of excessive power or creation of an imbalance and inequality in private law relationships.

The presented legal norms therefore provide strong potential for the enforcement of the rule of law and protection of human rights and fundamental freedoms in private law and relationships. However, what often stands in the way to the achievement of these goals is the lack of the effective enforcement of the existing legal norms. In countries such as Croatia, Romania, Serbia, and other SEE countries, but also other Member States, such as Poland or Hungary,[48] the rule of law is often difficult to achieve due of the poor enforcement of the existing legal rules.[49] So, even if the law is in place and it possesses all the necessary qualities, the rule of law can be and very often is affected by the ineffectiveness of the enforcement, as it will be demonstrated in the following sections of the chapter.

The presented Croatian case law on anti-discrimination and consumer protection confirms that the line between the rule of law and fundamental rights in private law is becoming thinner. Although there is no developed legal scholarship, or cases in which the direct effect of fundamental rights in private law relationships is explicitly recognised, there are rulings confirming the strengthening of the constitutionalisation of the private law.[50] The courts are undoubtedly aware of the importance of the constitutionally protected human rights and fundamental freedoms in private law relationships and beyond. However, they see it strictly as their duty to enforce the law and protect the rule of law as public authorities, rather than a tool for allowing a direct effect of fundamental rights in private law relationships. This can be supported normatively and by the case law, which is especially focused on the so-called conventional rights arising under the ECHR.[51] While the enforcement of the conventional rights is recognised, the same cannot be said for the protection of fundamental rights arising from the EU law and the EU Charter.[52] The next two sections demonstrate to what extent the rule of law is recognised and guaranteed in private law relationships.

[47] Z Slakoper, G Mihelcic, L Belanic and I Tot, *Obvezno pravo, Opći dio s uvodom u privatno pravo* (Zagreb, Novi informator, 2022) 48–50; N Gavella, *Privatno pravo* (Zagreb, Narodne novine, 2019) 14–15.

[48] D Kochenov and P Bárd, 'Rule of Law Crisis in the New Member States of the EU: The Pitfalls of Overemphasising Enforcement' (2018) 1 *RECONNECT – Reconciling Europe with its Citizens through Democracy and Rule of Law Working Paper* No 1, 3–28.

[49] C Dallara, *Democracy and Judicial Reforms in South-East Europe: Between the EU and the Legacies of the Past* (Cham, Springer, 2014) 44–54.

[50] T Josipović, 'The Role of Human Rights and Fundamental Freedoms for the Development of Croatian Private Law' in V Trstenjak and P Weingerl (eds), *The Influence of Human Rights and Basic Rights in Private Law* (Cham, Springer, 2016) 199–246.

[51] Turković and Omejec (n 28) 110.

[52] H Majić, 'The Croatian Constitutional Court and the EU Charter of Fundamental Rights: A Limbo Between the Charter, The ECHR and National Constitution' (2021) 5 *EU and comparative law issues and challenges series (ECLIC)*, 198–219.

4.1. Anti-Discrimination Cases

The enforcement of the rule of law might prove particularly challenging in cases in which private law principles collide with the constitutionally protected values. This is even more so in cases in which constitutionally protected rights and freedoms collide with each other. In this respect one should mention several cases concerning hate speech and discrimination. In these cases, which are related to violations of fundamental rights in employment and labour relationships, private law provisions on personality rights were also affected. Personality rights, such as the right to life, physical and mental health, reputation, honour, dignity, name, privacy of personal and family life, freedom and other rights, are protected under Article 19 of the OA. The violation of personality rights can result in damage compensation, in particular of the non-material damage. Under the Croatian civil law, the definition of 'non-material damage' is equated with the violation of personality rights (Article 1046 of the OA).

The Croatian case law related to violation of personality rights recognises the indirect effect of the constitutionally protected fundamental rights, such as equality and non-discrimination. For instance, the County Court in Varaždin found that the violation of personality rights to honour, dignity and reputation was caused by a respondent's discriminatory behaviour, which violated fundamental human rights.[53] The Court relied on the constitutionally protected values and fundamental rights protected by the Constitution and the ECHR, as well as on private law provisions, in order to ensure the fair damage compensation to the plaintiffs: 'the act of the respondent violated their dignity, reputation and honour, which are the values protected by provisions of the European Convention on Human Rights and the values equally recognised for every person'.[54] Such an interpretation is in line with national anti-discrimination law,[55] which provides the right to compensation (material and non-material) in cases of discrimination.[56]

Nonetheless, there are private law cases, in which the essential elements of the rule of law are affected by inconsistent interpretation of the existing legal rules. In 2010, two high-ranking officials at a prominent Croatian football club and the Croatian Football Federation made discriminatory and offensive statements to the newspapers. They discouraged gay persons from applying for jobs or employment at football clubs, by stating that 'luckily, only healthy people play football' and that gays should not play in the Croatian national team.[57] Several proceedings that were initiated by anti-discrimination associations resulted with different outcomes.

[53] Judgment of the County Court in Varazdin of 25 October 2011, Gž.3123/11-2.

[54] ibid (translated by author).

[55] Anti-Discrimination Act, OG Nos 85/08 and 112/12; Gender Equality Act, OG Nos 82/08, 125/11,20/12, 138/12 and 69/17 and 138/12 and Act on the Life Partnership of the Same-sex Persons, OG Nos 92/14 and 98/19.

[56] Arts 11 and 17(1)(3)–(4) of the Anti-Discrimination Act; Art 30 of the Gender Equality Act.

[57] E Mišćenić, 'The Impact of the Croatian Anti-discrimination Law on Private Law Relations' in N Bodiroga-Vukobrat et al (eds), *New Europe – Old Values? Reform and Perseverance* (Cham, Springer, 2015) 97–135.

In one of the proceedings, the court concluded that there is no 'real' victim or damage caused by the given statement and therefore direct discrimination had not been proven by plaintiffs.[58] The first instance court argued that the respondent's statement did not present any unfavourable treatment and it was a *hypothetical statement* by which the respondent did not, and could not, have treated plaintiffs less favourably on grounds of sexual orientation.[59] As confirmed by the Supreme Court, 'in the given case, there are no circumstances on the grounds of which it could be concluded that the homosexuals have been unable or restricted in access to the football representation on the ground of the sexual orientation, and in particular that this would result from the respondent's statement.'[60]

The courts also argued that statements represent the respondent's expression of his own personal values and that he has the right to express them due to the constitutionally guaranteed freedom of expression. The first instance court found that accepting the claims in this case would result in the violation of respondent's freedom of expression, guaranteed in Article 10 of the ECHR and Article 38 of the Constitution. The Court concluded that 'the case at hand does not present discrimination in the sense of the ADA provisions; it presents the respondent's opinion, which he stated publicly by using the freedom of expression, which is not only an individual but also a civil right and freedom that guarantees the right to different opinions, which is a fundamental precondition for maintaining and developing a democratic society.'[61] By using the same reasoning, the first instance court dismissed the claims in another anti-discrimination case, but differently in this case, the Supreme Court, as the court of appeal, concluded that the statement is a 'clear example of direct discrimination' and prohibited such behaviour in the future.[62] It also reached the conclusion that the statement is a violation of dignity and intends to humiliate persons of the same sexual orientation.

An important turnaround occurred in 2015, when the Supreme Court released a renewed judgment in the cases, upholding the discriminatory statements by freedom of expression.[63] Upon revision, the Supreme Court reversed the above presented findings in the judgements from 2011 and 2012[64] and found that the respondent discriminated persons of the same-sex orientation. This time, the Court observed the CJEU interpretation in the *Feryn* case[65] and mistakenly referred to it as the ECtHR case: 'In this case the factual state corresponds to the one in the Feryn case and it is therefore founded to apply the legal reasoning of the European

[58] Judgment of the County Court in Zagreb 24 March 2011, 15 Pnz-6/10-27 (translated by author).
[59] ibid.
[60] Judgment of the Supreme Court of the Republic of Croatia of 18 April 2012, Gž 12/11-2 (translated by author).
[61] Judgment of the County Court in Zagreb (n 58) (translated by author).
[62] Judgment of the Supreme Court of the Republic of Croatia of 28 February 2012, Gz-41/11-2 (translated by author).
[63] Judgment of the Supreme Court of the Republic of Croatia of 17 June 2015, Rev 300/13-2.
[64] Judgment of the County Court in Zagreb (n 58); judgment of the Supreme Court of the Republic of Croatia (n 60).
[65] Judgment of 10 July 2008, C-54/07, *Feryn*, EU:C:2008:397.

Court of Human Rights in the Feryn case in the context of the M case.'[66] In *Feryn*, the CJEU interpreted Directive 2000/43/EC and concluded that the person in a comparable situation can be hypothetical and that 'direct discrimination is not dependant on the identification of a complainant who claims to have been the victim'.[67] A corresponding conclusion can be found in the *Asociaţia Accept* case,[68] where the CJEU confirmed that discrimination can arise from statements by a person who is publicly perceived as playing a leading role in the club.[69] However, this interpretation was not taken into account in the reversed ruling.

When it comes to the conflict between two constitutionally protected rights, such as the right to equality and non-discrimination and freedom of expression, this argument was dismissed by decision of the Constitutional Court in 2017.[70] The Court confirmed that the disputed statement is not a value judgement and that it presents direct discrimination on the grounds of sexual orientation of homosexual football players. Although not expressly, the Constitutional Court touched upon the rule of law. By analysing the constitutional and conventional right to freedom of expression, the Court emphasised that the realisation of this freedom can be subject to limitations, which are necessary in a democratic society. The reasons to limit freedom include *inter alia* the impartiality of courts, reputation or rights of others, etc. (Article 10 of the ECHR). The Court applied the proportionality test and concluded that the Supreme Court interference was 'necessary in democratic society'.[71]

One of the most intriguing Croatian anti-discrimination cases that can be related to the rule of law is the *Krešić* case. Besides the violation of equality as one of the main features of the rule of law, this case features arbitrariness and abuse of power in an employment relationship. The case is also important for the constitutionalisation of the private law, since it demonstrates the violation of constitutionally protected fundamental rights and of civil law provisions protecting personality rights, such as dignity and honour. The case refers to sexual harassment and discrimination of the scientific assistant Krešić at his workplace at the Faculty of Organization and Informatics (FOI). Krešić was repeatedly insulted by his co-workers and prevented from professional advancement due to his homosexual orientation. He initiated the first individual antidiscrimination proceeding in Croatia against his employer and won the case at all court instances, although not on all points of the claim.[72]

[66] Judgment of the Supreme Court of the Republic of Croatia of 17 June 2015, Rev 300/13-2 (translated by author).

[67] *Feryn* (n 65), para 25.

[68] Judgment of 25 April 2013, C-81/12, *Asociaţia Accept*, EU:C:2013:275, para 36.

[69] ibid, para 53.

[70] Decision of the Constitutional Court of the Republic of Croatia of 22 March 2017, U-III/872/2016.

[71] ibid 8.3 (translated by author).

[72] Judgment of the Municipal Court in Varaždin of 12 July 2012, P-3153/10-89 (not publicly available); judgment of the County Court in Varaždin of 9 July 2013, Gž-5048/12-2 (not publicly available); order of the Supreme Court of the Republic of Croatia of 20 August 2014, Revr 1330/13-2. See also the order of the County Court in Varaždin of 26 May 2011, Gž.2923/11-2 and the order of the Municipal Court in Varaždin of 28 April 2011, No 20 P.3153/10-11.

This proceeding triggered yet another civil law proceeding in which discriminators claimed that their dignity and reputation was violated by the victim. They sued Krešić and demanded damage compensation due to violation of their mental health, reputation, honour and dignity. The first instance court found that Krešić was discriminated, but he violated the personality rights of the plaintiff by talking about the case publicly and ordered a payment of damage compensation in the amount of 30.000,00 Croatian Kunas (HRK) with interest.[73] Upon appeal, the action was dismissed together with the claim for damage compensation.[74] In the antidiscrimination proceeding mentioned above, the court ordered Krešić's former employer FOI (in the meantime Krešić quit his job) to compensate damages in the amount of 75.000,00 HRK.[75] The ruling was reversed in 2018 and the amount was lowered to 40.000,00 HRK.[76] Krešić initiated a proceeding before the Constitutional Court in 2018, and in 2020 a proceeding before the ECtHR for violation of the right to a fair trial.[77]

The ECtHR application is related to the issue of the applicant's right of access to the Supreme Court and of the overall fairness of the proceeding related to damage compensation. Since the Supreme Court declared his appeal inadmissible on point of law in the subsequent compensation proceeding, the applicant invoked the violation of the right to a fair trial under Article 6(1) of the ECHR. In particular, he has asked whether the decision of the Supreme Court was arbitrary, unforeseeable or excessively formalistic so as to unduly restrict the applicant's access to the court, and/or was it the consequence of the Supreme Court's inconsistent practice on the matter, in breach of the principle of legal certainty? While awaiting the ECtHR decision, one can establish that all these questions relate to the rule of law in private law relationships and its enforcement. The case demonstrates that the rule of law plays a key role in the relationship between the employer and the worker, whose fundamental rights were violated by sexual harassment and discrimination, on the one hand, and whose right to an effective legal remedy was not guaranteed, on the other.

4.2. Consumer Protection Cases

The correlation between the rule of law and private law is very strong in consumer relationships. The rule of law upholds equality and prevents the abuse of power, and consumer relationships are characterised by parties' inequality. As described by the settled CJEU case law, the consumer 'is in a weak position vis-à-vis the seller

[73] Judgment of the Municipal Court in Varaždin of 31 January 2013, P-1802/11 (not publicly available).

[74] Judgment of the County Court in Varaždin, June 2016 (not publicly available) and judgment of the Supreme Court of the Republic of Croatia of 2 June 2016 (not publicly available).

[75] Judgment of the Municipal Court in Varaždin, October 2015 (not publicly available).

[76] Judgment of the Municipal Court in Varaždin of 10 September 2018 (not publicly available).

[77] ECtHR case *KREŠIĆ v CROATIA* and 1 other application lodged on 31 October 2019 and 22 January 2020, Applications Nos 58090/19 and 6689/20.

or supplier, as regards both his bargaining power and his level of knowledge.'[78] The rule of law can therefore prevent attempts by the more powerful parties, such as businesses, to manipulate the law in a manner that benefits them. The mandatory nature of the consumer law and the duty of the courts to observe the application of certain consumer provisions on their own motion, correspond to the goal of the rule of law, which is designed to prevent the abuse of law and assertion of power.

As an example of consumer disputes in which the rule of law played a role, one should mention the first Croatian collective redress proceeding against the use of unfair contractual terms in Swiss Franc (CHF) loans and legislative interventions related to these contracts.[79] The issue was not only inequality and abuse of power, but also other features of the rule of law, such as retroactivity and legitimacy. The case law touched upon the main features of the rule of law, such as transparency, judicial independence and above all, the integrity of judicial proceedings. The abuse of power in consumer relationships started with violations of the Croatian consumer law during the 2003–2009 period, when credit agreements expressed or denominated in foreign currency (CHF and HRK/CHF) were offered and concluded in the Croatian market. The extensive Croatian case law confirmed the violation of provisions transposed from relevant EU consumer directives,[80] such as those on pre-contractual and contractual informing, creditworthiness assessment, advertising, and unfair contract terms.[81] The severe economic consequences manifested themselves in the aftermath of the global financial crisis, when due to the increase of instalments from 50% to 80%, consumers became unable to repay their debts. In 2016, the Constitutional Court confirmed that the debt crisis caused by the CHF loans has led to a 'grave social conditions in which hundreds of thousands of Croatian citizens live.'[82]

During the collective redress proceeding, the Commercial Court in Zagreb found both disputed contractual terms to be unfair and invalid, in the first instance ruling from 2013.[83] A year later, the ruling was overturned by the judgment of the High Commercial Court, which established that the variable interest rate was unfair, but the currency clause denominating the loan in the foreign currency (CHF)

[78] Judgment of 27 June 2000 in the joined cases C-240/98 to C-244/98, *Océano Grupo and Salvat Editores*, ECLI:EU:C:2000:346.

[79] E Miscenic, 'Croatian Case "Franak": Effective or "Defective" Protection of Consumer Rights?' (2016) V *Harmonius Journal of Legal and Social Studies in South East Europe*, 184–209.

[80] Council Directive 87/102/EEC of 22 December 1986 for the approximation of the laws, regulations and administrative provisions of the Member States concerning consumer credit, OJ L 42/48, amended by the Council Directive 90/88/EEC, OJ L 61/14 and Directive 98/7/EC of the European Parliament and Council, OJ L 101/17; Council Directive 84/450/EEC of 10 September 1984 concerning misleading and comparative advertising, OJ L 250; Directive 2005/29/EC of the European Parliament and Council of 11 May 2005 concerning unfair business-to-consumer commercial practices in the internal market, OJ L 149; Council Directive 93/13/EEC of 5 April 1993 on unfair terms in consumer contracts, OJ L 95.

[81] E Mišćenić, 'Currency Clauses in CHF Credit Agreements: A "Small Wheel" in the Swiss Loans' Mechanism' (2020) 6 *Journal of European Consumer and Market Law (EuCML)* 226–35.

[82] Decision of the Constitutional Court of the Republic of Croatia of 13 December 2016, U-I-392/2011 et al, 84 (translated by author).

[83] Judgment and order of the Commercial Court in Zagreb of 4 July 2013, P-1401/12, 118 *et seq.*

was excluded from the unfairness test.[84] Upon revision, the Supreme Court confirmed this ruling in 2015.[85] The reasoning in the background of these court decisions was the transparency of the currency clause, which was, unlike the variable interest rate, 'very well known to consumers, including all the legal consequences it produces'.[86] On the other hand, the Supreme Court recognised the abuse of power in regard to the variable interest rates, 'which remained completely unintelligible to consumers', due to incomplete and unintelligible contractual formulations.[87] In 2016, the Constitutional Court decided to revoke the part of the Supreme Court's ruling related to the transparency and fairness of currency clauses in CHF and HRK/CHF consumer credit agreements.[88] The plaintiffs considered that the invoked courts decisions were arbitrary and violated legal certainty, trust in the judiciary, and equality before the law.[89] The Constitutional Court concluded that the courts were treating disputed contractual terms unequally: 'the Supreme Court interpreted the concept of intelligibility of disputed contractual terms … differently'.[90] It also emphasised that 'it remains unclear by which criteria the Supreme Court was guided when it established that the contractual term on the currency clause, differently than the contractual term on the variable interest rate, does not undergo the fairness test'.[91]

The Constitutional Court required a renewal of the proceeding due to the violation of the right to a fair trial: 'In light of the foregoing, it remains up to the Constitutional Court to establish that in the concrete case … the right to a fair trial has been violated, as guaranteed by Article 19, paragraph 1 of the Constitution and Article 6 of the Convention in its aspect of the right to a reasoned judicial decision'.[92] The Constitutional Court found the lack of judicial decision reasoning to be one of the 'first and essential sign indicating arbitrary judicial decision making'.[93] Although the violation of Article 6 of the ECHR has been recognised, Article 47 of the EU Charter on the right to an effective remedy has not been invoked in order to remove obstacles to the effective consumer protection under the UCTD.[94] Moreover, the Supreme Court explicitly refused to apply the interpretation of transparency requirements from *Kásler and Káslerné Rábai* due to factual

[84] Judgment and order of the High Commercial Court of the Republic of Croatia of 13 June 2014, Pž-7129/13-4, 50 and 53.

[85] Judgment and order of the Supreme Court of the Republic of Croatia of 9 April 2015, Revt-249/14-2 (translated by author).

[86] ibid, 18.

[87] ibid, 34.

[88] Decision of the Constitutional Court of the Republic of Croatia of 13 December 2016, et al. (translated by author).

[89] ibid, 45 and 75.

[90] ibid, point 17.

[91] ibid, point 19.

[92] ibid, point 22.

[93] ibid, point 13.2.

[94] A van Duin, 'Metamorphosis? The Role of Article 47 of the EU Charter of Fundamental Rights in Cases Concerning National Remedies and Procedures under Directive 93/13' (2017) 6(5) *Journal of European Consumer and Market Law (EuCML)* 190–98.

differences between the Hungarian case and the Croatian case.[95] Therefore, the Constitutional Court concluded that: 'The Supreme Court did not give sufficient and relevant reasons for arriving at the conclusion that the facts are so different that it is not possible to apply the general legal viewpoints of the CJEU (from the Hungarian case) when interpreting the meaning of the intelligibility of a contractual term, despite both cases dealing with the contractual term on the currency clause linked to the Swiss franc'.[96]

In 2017, the Supreme Court ordered a retrial with respect to the part related to the transparency of the currency clause and sent the case to the High Commercial Court.[97] This time, the High Commercial Court relied on EU consistent interpretation and the CJEU case law and overturned the outcome regarding the transparency and unfairness of the currency clause.[98] The ruling found the currency clause to be unintelligible and non-transparent, therefore causing a significant imbalance to the detriment of consumers: 'The imbalance between rights and obligations that existed when the relevant term was contracted is undoubtedly to the detriment of consumers and is significant.'[99] There are several connections to the rule of law that should be noted. The first one relates to the imbalance and inequality in the private law relationship between banks and consumers. Here it was obvious that the stronger party is creating its own law through a violation of harmonised national provisions and is positioning herself both above the law and above the other party, therefore causing inequality in the private law relationship. Another important connection to the rule of law arises from the supremacy of law, which, according to legal scholarship, prevents arbitrariness and wide discretionary powers.[100] By giving its own interpretation to the legal norm that 'must normally be given an autonomous and uniform interpretation throughout the European Union',[101] the Supreme Court actually violated the supremacy of law. The confirmation came also from the Commission, which stated that the 'Croatian courts, including the Supreme Court still do not see themselves as European courts'.[102]

The High Commercial Court ruling from 2018 and the following decisions in the collective redress proceeding attempted to alight the two sides of the rule of law, namely the substantive one and the enforcement. By applying the interpretation of

[95] Judgment and order of the Supreme Court (n 85), 22.

[96] Decision of the Constitutional Court (n 88), 20.

[97] Order of the Supreme Court of the Republic of Croatia of 3 October 2017, Revt 575/16-5.

[98] E Miscenic, 'Uniform Interpretation of Article 4(2) of UCT Directive in the Context of Consumer Credit Agreements: Is it possible?' (2018) 3 *Revue du droit de l'Union européenne* 127–59.

[99] Judgment of the High Commercial Court of the Republic of Croatia of 14 June 2018, 43 Pž-6632/2017-10, 62 (translated by author).

[100] See, eg M Harris, 'The Rule of Law in Private Law: A New Animating Ideal for Employment Law?' (2011) *SSRN Electronic Journal* 1–25, 6–8 referring to the work of *Dicey*, *Fallon*, *Thomson*, *Bingham*, and many others.

[101] Judgment of 26 February 2015, C-143/13, *Matei*, ECLI:EU:C:2015:127, para 50.

[102] European Commission, An evaluation study of national procedural laws and practices in terms of their impact on the free circulation of judgments and on the equivalence and effectiveness of the procedural protection of consumers under EU consumer law, Strand 2 Procedural Protection of Consumers, JUST/2014/RCON/PR/CIVI/0082, 2017, 61.

the substantive transparency requirements from the UCTD, the Court found that the currency clauses in CHF and HRK/CHF loans 'were unintelligible to clients, since the consequences and reach of such contractual terms were not explained to them in a valid manner'.[103] The Court abided by the law by respecting the above presented constitutional duty, according to which the Croatian courts protect the subjective rights arising from the *acquis*.[104] The findings of the High Commercial Court were supported on appeal in the judgment of the Supreme Court from 2019,[105] and in the decision of the Constitutional Court in 2021,[106] both of which confirmed the non-transparency and unfairness of disputed currency clauses in CHF and HRK/CHF credit agreements.[107] The abuse of power in business-to-consumer (B2C) relationships was emphasised in the Supreme Court ruling from 2019, according to which the banks 'consciously omitted to inform clients about it', despite being aware of the risks to consumers.[108]

Even more relevant for the rule of law debate are the legislative interventions and the following case law, by which the legislator attempted to intervene in the created imbalance in consumer relationships. From 2012 onward, the Croatian legislator intervened several times into the consumer credit law in order to strengthen the transparency and information requirements in consumer credit agreements.[109] However, after the Swiss National Bank announcement in 2015 that it would no longer hold the CHF at the fixed exchange rate against the euro (EUR), the legislator intervened directly in the concluded contracts. First, it fixed the CHF exchange rate at 6.39 HRK for 1 CHF,[110] and several months later it introduced a measure that enabled consumers to convert the HRK/CHF and CHF loans into HRK/EUR and EUR loans.[111] The banks were legally required to offer the conversion to consumers, and consumers could opt for this one-time offered conversion, under legally prescribed terms. As emphasised by the Constitutional Court, the offered conversion contracts were not based on the free will of both contractual parties and 'could hardly be seen as regular private law contracts that are used to form the regular obligations law relationships'.[112] One of the most discussed issues

[103] Judgment of the High Commercial Court (n 99) 53.
[104] Arts. 145 and 146 of the Constitution (Arts. 141.c and 141.d of the consolidated version).
[105] Judgment and order of the Supreme Court of the Republic of Croatia of 3 September 2019, Rev-2221/2018-11, 24.
[106] Decision and order of the Constitutional Court of the Republic of Croatia of 3 February 2021, U-III-4150-2019 et al, 103.
[107] T Josipović, 'Kroatische Verbraucher vs. Kredite in CHF – ein Drama in fünf Akten ohne Schlussakt' (2020) 6 *Osteuropa Recht* 4–33.
[108] Judgment and order of the Supreme Court (n 105) 24.
[109] T Josipović and H Ernst, 'Recent Crisis-Motivated Reforms in Croatian Private Law' (2015) 13(1) *European Lawyer Journal* 73–97.
[110] Act on Amendments of Consumer Credit Act, OG No 9/15; Act on Amendments of Credit Institutions Act, OG No 19/15.
[111] Act on Amendments of Consumer Credit Act, OG No 102/15; Act on Amendments of Credit Institutions Act, OG No 102/15.
[112] Decision and order of the Constitutional Court of the Republic of Croatia of 11 October 2015, U-I-2780-2015 et al, 35 (translated by author).

was the retroactivity of the introduced measure, which required the conversion of loans from the moment of the contract's conclusion. The European Central Bank (ECB) requested the Croatian authorities to assess the constitutionality of the conversion measure and noted that 'introducing measures with retroactive effect such as the draft law will undermine legal certainty and is not in line with the principle of legitimate expectations'.[113]

The rule of law was extensively discussed in proposals for the evaluation of constitutionality of the legislative amendments introducing the conversion, submitted to the Constitutional Court by different banks, attorneys and individuals.[114] The applicants considered that the rule of law was violated by the state's intervention in contractual relationships, which was discriminatory, retroactive, not in the public interest and in violation of the principle of legal certainty. Some other features of the rule of law were invoked too, such as the lack of the clarity and precision of the legal norm. After a detailed analysis of the introduced legislative amendments and their goals, as well as of the functioning mechanism and economic and legal consequences for credit institutions and consumers, the Constitutional Court dismissed the proposals for the evaluation of constitutionality in 2017.[115] The Court found that the conversion was a proportional and necessary measure that intended to protect the public order, social justice and consumers: 'The aim of the conversion model was to enable consumers to ensure a free and dignified life for themselves and their family from their earnings, to protect the *fundamental human right to a dignified life*, since the significant part of instalments was higher than the monthly income and due to repayment of credit they did not have the financial means to meet essential life needs, *the right that is guaranteed by provisions of the Constitution, the Charter of Fundamental Rights of the European Union, and the Treaty on the Functioning of the European Union*'.[116]

When applying the proportionality test, the Constitutional Court established that the credit institutions misused the civil law institute on which the currency clause is based. The goal of the institute is to preserve the equal value of contractual obligations in the case of realisation of risks that could arise under the contract.[117] By misusing the clause that should guarantee a contractual balance and equality between the parties and by earning on the appreciation of the CHF foreign currency '… the credit institutions undoubtedly realised a significant gain and obviously violated the principle of equal values of contracted performances and the equality of contractual parties'.[118] This particular sentence and the following reasoning accentuate the violation of the rule of law in the Croatian private law

[113] ECB Opinion of 18 September 2015 on the conversion of Swiss franc loans in Croatia (CON/2015/32).

[114] Order of the Constitutional Court of the Republic of Croatia of 4 April 2017, U-I-3685/2015 et al. (translated by author).

[115] ibid.

[116] ibid, 49 (emphasis by author).

[117] Art 22 of the Obligations Act.

[118] Order of the Constitutional Court (n 114) 90.

and consumer relationships.[119] Another contribution to the rule of law discussion is a decision of the Constitutional Court from 2021.[120] Once the Supreme Court confirmed the unfairness of the currency clauses in 2019, banks made several claims, including those related to the violation of the rule of law. They argued that the court's decision making was arbitrary and that the access to justice and the right to a fair trial under Article 6 of the ECHR and Article 47 of the EU Charter had been violated.[121] The banks also questioned the substantive conclusions of the courts related to unintelligibility and unfairness of the currency clauses, claiming that they were arbitrary and unreasonable. The Constitutional Court concluded that the court's findings relied on extensive and relevant argumentation and reasoning that cannot be considered unreasonable or arbitrary.[122]

The case got its final closure in the ECtHR decision related to the application of *OTP BANKA d.d. v Croatia* and 4 other applications submitted against Croatia due to 'alleged unfairness of civil proceedings before commercial courts concerning a collective consumer dispute'.[123] Five different banks as applicants lodged complaints with the ECtHR due to alleged violation of Article 6(1) of the ECHR. They claimed that the ordinary courts refused to refer questions for a preliminary ruling to the CJEU, violated the principle of equality of arms, and committed other violations of the civil law proceedings. The Court examined jointly the applications and found that the Croatian courts gave reasons why they considered it unnecessary to ask for a preliminary ruling, therefore complying with the obligations under Article 6(1) of the ECHR. The Court considered that these reasons were not arbitrary or manifestly unreasonable,[124] and therefore rejected the complaint as inadmissible under Article 35 of the ECHR. As regards the other alleged violations of Article 6(1) of the ECHR, such as the principle of equality of arms, the Court found 'that it cannot be said that applicant banks were placed at a substantial disadvantage *vis-à-vis* their opponent'.[125] The Court stated that nothing in the domestic rulings suggests that the banks were treated unfairly and unequally in courts proceedings, and that the factual and legal reasons of courts decisions, 'do not appear arbitrary or manifestly unreasonable'.[126] According to the Court, 'there is nothing to suggest that the domestic courts lacked impartiality or that the proceedings were otherwise unfair'.[127]

[119] See also decision of the Constitutional Court of the Republic of Croatia of 13 December 2016, U-III-2521/2015 et al, 89–90: 'such a contract clause should not, however, turn a loan agreement into a risky speculative transaction … the consumer … has a legitimate expectation that … the use of currency clause (as a safeguard, not a profit clause) when fulfilling the contractual obligation of loan repayment will not make them poor and bankrupt'.

[120] Decision and order of the Constitutional Court of the Republic of Croatia of 3 February 2021, U-III-4150-2019 et al.

[121] ibid, 57–64.

[122] ibid, 86.1.

[123] ECtHR case *OTP BANKA d.d. AND OTHERS v CROATIA* of 8 November 2022, Applications Nos 38541/21, 39015/21, 39063/21, 39167/21 and 41145/21.

[124] ibid, 13.

[125] ibid, 15.

[126] ibid, 16.

[127] ibid.

5. Conclusion

The acceptance of the idea that the rule of law is not strictly a public law concept, allows its entrance into the private law and private law relationships. As emphasised by *Austin* and *Klimchuk*, in their coedited book *Private Law and the Rule of Law*, one needs to 'explore the idea that the perception of the rule of law as an essentially public law doctrine is in fact a misperception'.[128] Private parties are subjects to law, and as such they are capable of violating and abusing the law.[129] In a private law context, the rule of law therefore needs to be understood as a tool that will prevent or sanction the circumventing of private law rules that prohibit such violations. The rule of law strengthens the enforcement of private law rules in the very same way that certain private law rules contribute to the rule of law by requiring equality and preventing the circumvention or abuse of the law. The rule of law also strengthens the effects of constitutionally protected fundamental rights in private law relationships. Differently than the relation of the rule of law and private law, this topic has been recognised by the case law and intensively discussed by legal scholars.[130]

The author of this chapter agrees with views of legal scholars and in particular with *Collins*, who emphasised years ago that EU contract law demands the shift from *Dworkin's* rule-book concept of the rule of law towards a rights-based version of it.[131] The latter, which is based on citizens' moral and political rights under positive law, is reflected in the CJEU case law involving values and fundamental rights guaranteed by the EU Charter and ECHR.[132] This shift, however, does not always come easy to national courts, and, as seen in this chapter, particularly not to those from the SEE countries. While the Croatian anti-discrimination and consumer protection cases obviously indicate the strengthening of the constitutionalisation of private law, the link between the rule of law and private law is still not recognised.

In spite of not being explicitly recognised by the Croatian legal scholarship or case law, the link is there. The presented Croatian private law provisions indicate that they share common values with the rule of law, such as the prohibition of abuse of power and promotion of equality. In that respect, one can easily argue that some of the private law rules serve the same purpose as the rule of law. It can also be argued that certain features of the rule of law, such as publicity and prevention of arbitrability, are not at odds with the private law rules. This can particularly

[128] Austin and Klimchuk (n 9).

[129] Harris (n 100) 8.

[130] See the chapter on Fundamental Rights in the book authored by J Basedow, *EU Private Law, Anatomy of a Growing Legal Order* (Cambridge, Intersentia, 2021) 203–23.

[131] H Collins, 'The Revolutionary Trajectory of EU Contract Law towards Post-national Law' in S Worthington et al (eds), *Revolution and Evolution in Private Law* (Hart Publishing, 2018), 326, quoting R Dworkin, *A Matter of Principle* (Oxford, Clarendon Press, 1986) 9.

[132] ibid, 328.

be discussed with respect to the main elements and principles that form the very essence of the rule of law, such as legal equality, legitimacy, and legal certainty. Nonetheless, some of these features are undermined by poor enforcement of private law rules and this chapter represents an attempt to change the way the rule of law is understood in the Croatian legal system. By broadening horizons and recognising the role of the rule of law in private law and private law relationships, one actually strengthens the enforcement of the rule of law in general.

8

ECHR and the Derogation in a Time of Emergency – The Case of the Republic of North Macedonia

JULIJA BRSAKOSKA BAZERKOSKA AND ALEKSANDAR SPASOV

1. Introduction

Derogation clauses are an important part of the international human rights instruments. Like most human rights treaties,[1] the European Convention on Human Rights contains an emergency derogation clause in Article 15. This clause defines the conditions of derogation from the human rights obligations in case of emergency. It is also designed to limit the suspension of rights in those particular times of emergency. The importance of this clause rests within the need to effectively protect the right to life, without contradicting the mere notion of human rights in the context of a public emergency, as was the COVID-19 pandemic.[2]

The complexity of the situation created by the COVID-19 global pandemic in European societies, brought numerous challenges when it comes to implementation of Article 15 of the Convention. The exceptional circumstances brought by the COVID-19 pandemic led to more extensive restrictions of human rights than in normal times – both in duration and in scope.[3] According to the ECHR, states can

[1] See eg: International Covenant on Civil and Political Rights (ICCPR), American Convention on Human Rights (ACHR), Arab Charter on Human Rights.

[2] C Binder, M Nowak, JA Hofbauer and P Janig (eds), *Elgar Encyclopedia of Human Rights* (Cheltenham, Elgar Online, 2022); F Cowell, 'Sovereignty and the Question of Derogation: An Analysis of Article 15 of the ECHR and the Absence of a Derogation Clause in the ACHPR' (2013) 1 *Birkbeck Law Review* 135; A Buyse and M Hamilton (eds), *Transitional Jurisprudence and the European Convention on Human Rights: Justice, Politics and Rights*, (Cambridge, Cambridge University Press, 2011); E Hafner-Burton, L Helfer and C Fariss, 'Emergency and Escape: Explaining Derogations from Human Rights Treaties' (2011) 65 *International Organization* 673, 707.

[3] A Lebret, 'COVID-19 pandemic and derogation to human rights', (2020) 7(1) *Journal of Law and the Biosciences* available at: doi.org/10.1093/jlb/lsaa015; VV Horodovenko, LG Udovyka, and HO Dichko, 'Ensuring Respect for Human Rights and Freedoms in the Context of States' Measures Introduction to Combat the COVID-19 Pandemic: European Experience' (2020) 73 *Wiadomości Lekarskie* (12 cz 2)

limit the exercise of most human rights if it is necessary to protect the rights of others or collective interests. During the COVID-19 pandemic, it was a real challenge to establish conditions for a legitimate derogation and to ensure that the general measures adopted by the states do not disproportionally harm vulnerable people.

This chapter will examine the case of the Republic of North Macedonia and its use of Article 15 of the ECHR in an attempt to limit some of the rights of its citizens because of the public emergency created by the COVID-19 pandemic. It will elaborate on the manners and procedures used by the Republic of North Macedonia in defining the public emergency, in outlining the extent of derogation and the manner of informing the Secretary General of the Council of Europe. The analysis should provide insight whether the interference in the case of the Republic of North Macedonia in its attempt to limit the human rights in the case of COVID-19 pandemic could be justified by the state of emergency, and whether the Convention was implemented in a proper manner.

The following part of this chapter will provide an analysis of the ECHR derogation clause under Article 15 along with the connected case law of the European Court for Human Rights. The third part will look into the challenges in defining the COVID-19 pandemic as a public emergency, while the final part will examine the case of the Republic of North Macedonia, elaborating on the specific cases of derogation in times of emergency in the country.

2. European Convention on Human Rights: The Importance of Article 15

The European Convention on Human Rights contains a powerful derogation clause under Article 15 of the Convention. This is a complex legal provision comprised of various components. Article 15 gives, in exceptional circumstances, the possibility of derogating, in a limited and supervised manner, from the contracting states' obligations to secure certain rights and freedoms under the Convention. The article defines the circumstances under which states can validly derogate from their obligations under the Convention. It also limits the measures they may take in the course of any derogation. At the same time, it protects certain fundamental rights in the Convention from any derogation and sets out the procedural requirements that any state making a derogation must follow.[4]

2773, 2779; J Dos Santos, P Stein Messetti, F Adami, I Bezerra, P Maia, E Tristan-Cheever, and L de Abreu, 'Collision of Fundamental Human Rights and the Right to Health Access During the Novel Coronavirus Pandemic' (2021) *Frontiers in Public Health* 8; RO Alsawalqa, AS Al Qaralleh, and AM Al-Asasfeh, 'The Threat of the COVID-19 Pandemic to Human Rights: Jordan as a Model' (2022) 7(3) *Journal of Human Rights and Social Work* 265, 276.

[4] See more in: A Mokhtar, 'Human rights obligations v. derogations: Article 15 of the European Convention on Human Rights' (2004) 8(1) *The International Journal of Human Rights* 65, 87; S Wallace, 'Derogations from the European Convention on Human Rights: The Case for Reform' (2020) 20(4) *Human Rights Law Review* 769, 796.

Three important conditions for a valid derogation are set out in Article 15:

1. it must be in time of war or other public emergency threatening the life of the nation;
2. the measures taken in response to that war or public emergency must not go beyond the extent strictly required by the exigencies of the situation; and
3. the measures must not be inconsistent with the state's other obligations under international law.

According to the European Court of Human Rights,[5] the natural and customary meaning of 'public emergency threatening the life of the nation' is clear and refers to 'an exceptional situation of crisis or emergency which affects the whole population and constitutes a threat to the organised life of the community of which the State is composed'.[6] The Court's case-law has never indicated that the emergency should be temporary in its duration.[7] On the contrary, the cases demonstrate that it is possible for a 'public emergency' to continue for many years.[8] As the Court stated in *Ireland v the United Kingdom*:[9] 'it falls in the first place to each Contracting State, with its responsibility for "the life of [its] nation", to determine whether that life is threatened by a "public emergency". Since national authorities are in direct and continuous contact with the pressing needs of the moment, they are in a better position to decide whether there is an emergency and what should be the nature and scope of the derogations necessary to prevent it. Considering this matter, there is a wide margin of appreciation that is left to national authorities.

[5] See more on case law connected to Art 15 ECHR in: AR Gil, 'Derogation Clauses of International Human Rights Instruments: protecting rights at the maximum possible extent in times of crisis', (2021) 1 *Catolica Law Review* 11, 42. In the past, the ECtHR and the ECHR bodies have dealt with declarations of 'state of emergency' in two important cases connected with the United Kingdom, regarding the situation in Northern Ireland, and Turkey, as regards the Kurdish Separatist Movement (PKK) in the south-east region of the country. Generally, it was considered that these measures were adequate, bearing in mind the seriousness of the threats concerned. The decision was different in the so-called *Greek Case*, where a revolutionary government, relying primary on considerations of power, declared the state of emergency after a takeover. The European Commission agreed with the applicant's argument, who affirmed that a revolutionary government could hardly justify a derogation based on an emergency which it had created itself. Moreover, contrarily to the other cases, the *Greek Case* involved the suspension of an extensive group of human rights – not only the protection against arbitrary detention, but also the rights to a fair trial, private home, freedom of expression, freedom of thought, conscience and religion, freedom of assembly and association, free elections, and to a remedy against human rights violations. Also, there were interferences with non-derogable rights.

[6] *Lawless v Ireland* no. 3 (1961) 1 EHRR 15. The case *Lawless v Ireland*, was the first case in which it was ruled what constitutes an emergency by the ECtHR. The emergency, defined in this case as an 'exceptional situation of crisis or emergency which affects the whole population and constitutes a threat to the organised life of the community of which the State is composed' is determined by the state which makes the derogation according to Art 15. With regards to this element, the Court most often accepts the assessment of the state, even though this assessment may be sometimes too broad.

[7] More on the relevant case law in: Guide on Art 15 of the Convention – Derogation in time of emergency, Council of Europe, latest update on 31 August 2022.

[8] *Ireland v the United Kingdom*, 1978, *Brannigan and McBride v the United Kingdom*, 1993, *Marshall v the United Kingdom*, 2001.

[9] *Ireland v the United Kingdom*, 1978.

Mainly because of the jurisdictional nature of the ECtHR, the judges in Strasbourg rely heavily on the arguments and information given by the states. There is very rarely an in-depth examination by the Court. Moreover, the ECtHR recognises the margin of appreciation to states during the emergency in order to show certain respect to the state.[10] This is connected to the previously stated fact that states have direct and continuous contact with the pressing needs of the moment. Therefore, Strasbourg judges do not make autonomous enquiries in order to know whether a state of emergency should have been declared in the first place.[11]

Nevertheless, as it is emphasised by the Court, it is not an unlimited discretion, since the ECtHR can observe it.[12] Subsequently, since the purpose of Article 15 is to permit states to take derogating measures to protect their populations from future risks, the existence of the threat to the life of the nation must be assessed primarily with reference to those facts which were known at the time of the derogation.

The role of the ECtHR is important in the evaluation of whether the state has exceeded the strictly required by the exigencies of the situation, proportionality of the exceptional measures. In these cases, the Court takes into account all relevant factors, such as the nature of the rights affected, circumstances leading to the declaration, its length; as well as the strength of the country's democratic system. It is the state which has the responsibility of providing a reasoned justification for the measures adopted.[13] And it is important for states to justify that those measures fully respect the principle of proportionality, meaning that the basic principle of human rights is still applicable in the context of derogation. It must be properly justified that the human rights represent 'the rule' and derogations represent the 'exception'.[14] The states need to carefully weight balance between the needs of the state and the community, on the one hand and the right of individuals to have most of their rights and freedoms effectively protected in public emergencies, on the other.

Additionally, the Court found that the crisis or danger should be exceptional, which means that all regular measures or restrictions permitted by the ECHR for maintaining public safety, health and order are plainly inadequate.[15] It is important to emphasise, that the derogation clauses should not contradict the notion of human rights. They should, on the contrary, contribute to their effective protection.

[10] AR Gil (n 5) 11, 42.

[11] ibid. When assessing whether the measures are strictly necessary, the ECtHR evaluates whether they are necessary to counter the threat to the life of the nation; whether they are proportionate (meaning that they are not exceeding the demands of the specific situation), and whether the measures are with adequate duration (meaning that once the need for introduction of the measures expires, the measures should be revoked). In addition, it is necessary for the introduced measures to be undertaken in response to the state of emergency and therefore justified, as well as to have measures against possible abuse of the newly introduced measures.

[12] *Brannigan and McBride v the United Kingdom*, 1993; *Mehmet Hasan Altan v Turkey*, 2018; *Şahin Alpay v Turkey*, 2018.

[13] AR Gil (n 5) 11, 42.

[14] Ibid.

[15] *Denmark, Norway, Sweden and the Netherlands v Greece* (the '*Greek case*'), 1969.

States have positive obligations to protect the right to life, which might justify derogations to some other human rights.[16] However, there need to be guarantees that the exercise of other rights will not be subjected to undue limitations.

Each measure taken during times of emergency must be in accordance with other obligations of the state according to international law. Article 15 of the ECHR emphasises this obligation of the states, since it is important to respect the other existing obligations the state has taken in accordance to international law, or the customary norms of this law.

While providing the circumstances of derogation, Article 15 also provides that certain rights in the Convention are always protected from derogation. According to the text of Article 15, Paragraph 2, these are: Article 2 – which refers to the right to life, except in respect of deaths resulting from lawful acts of war, Article 3 – which refers to the prohibition of torture and other forms of ill-treatment, Article 4, Paragraph 1 – which refers to the prohibition of slavery or servitude, and Article 7 – which refers to no punishment without law.

Another set of clauses which prohibit derogation is contained in the three of the additional protocols to the Convention. These are: Protocol 6, which refers to the abolition of the death penalty in time of peace and limiting the death penalty in time of war, Protocol 7, referring to the *ne bis in idem* principle only, as contained in Article 4 of that protocol, and Protocol 13 – the complete abolition of the death penalty.

The effect of these exceptions from derogation is that the rights to which they refer continue to apply during any time of war or public emergency, irrespective of any derogation made by the state.[17]

Finally, Article 15 Paragraph 3 provides that:

> any High Contracting Party availing itself of this right of derogation shall keep the Secretary General of the Council of Europe fully informed of the measures which it has taken and the reasons therefore. It shall also inform the Secretary General of the Council of Europe when such measures have ceased to operate and the provisions of the Convention are again being fully executed.

The process of informing the Secretary General is important within this derogation clause because of the need to provide a mechanism for the derogation to become public. Moreover, it has to be emphasised that the ECHR is primarily a system of collective enforcement and it is through the Secretary General that the other states are informed of the derogation. There is an obligation for the state to write a letter and attach copies of the legal texts under which the emergency measures will be taken, with an explanation of their purpose. The information passed to the Secretary General in pursuance of Article 15 Paragraph 3 must be communicated by him as soon as possible to the other states parties of the ECHR.[18]

[16] A Lebret (n 3).

[17] More on the relevant case law in: Guide on Article 15 of the Convention – Derogation in time of emergency, Council of Europe, latest update on 31 August 2022.

[18] *Greece v the United Kingdom*, 1958.

In the case of *Greece v the United Kingdom*, 1958, the Commission found that it was clear from the wording of Article 15 Paragraph 3 that the notification does not have to be made before the measure in question is introduced. However, the wording of this provision does not provide guidance for the time within which the notification must be made. In this particular case, the three-month period between taking the derogating measure and its notification had been too long and could not be justified by administrative delays resulting from the alleged emergency. In the case of *Denmark, Norway, Sweden and the Netherlands v Greece* (the '*Greek case*') 1969, the fact that the notification of certain measures came four months after they were taken could not be justified. On the other hand, the Court found that notification twelve days after the measures entered into force was sufficient.[19]

While derogations from the ECHR are not uncommon, the series of notifications for derogation that came during the COVID-19 pandemic were different in terms of the number of countries that resorted to this step, as well as the short time span in which the notifications arrived. The following section will attempt to distinguish the COVID-19 pandemic from other types of emergencies arising in the past.

3. The COVID-19 Pandemic as a Public Emergency

Since March 2020, with the beginning of the COVID-19 pandemic, the world faced one of its most severe public health crises. Moreover, using the words of Dunja Mijatović, Council of Europe's Commissioner for Human Rights – 2020 was a disastrous year for human rights in Europe. According to her: 'While commitment to upholding human rights standards has been faltering all over the continent for several years, the COVID-19 pandemic has accelerated the erosion of the democratic fabric of our society, on which protection of human rights ultimately depends.'[20]

The European Convention on Human Rights contains a list of rights, most of which can be limited for valid purposes, including public health. If those measures for limitations are recognised to be necessary in a democratic society, they can be acceptable in normal times.[21] However, the COVID-19 crisis was not a normal time.[22] According to the French President Macron, in his address to the nation in March 2020, France was 'at war not against another army or another nation, but against an enemy that is invisible, elusive, and is making progress.'[23]

[19] *Lawless v Ireland*, 1961.

[20] D Mijatović, *Commissioner for Human Rights of the Council of Europe, Annual Activity Report 2020*, available at: www.rm.coe.int/annual-activity-report-2020-by-dunja-mijatovic-council-of-europe-commi/1680a2150d.

[21] C Schreuer, 'Derogation of Human Rights in Situations of Public Emergency: The Experience of the European Convention on Human Rights', (1982) 9 *The Yale Journal of Word Public Order* 113.

[22] A Lebret (n 3).

[23] Michel Rose, '*We are at war*': *France imposes lockdown to combat virus* (Reuters, Mar. 16, 2020), available at: www.reuters.com/article/us-health-coronavirus-macron-restriction/we-are-at-war-france-imposes-lockdown-to-combat-virus-idUSKBN2133G5.

In these particular circumstances caused by the COVID-19 pandemic, Article 15 of the ECHR seemed to be the right clause to be at states' disposal to implement certain derogations. Similar provisions like Article 15 of the ECHR can be found in Article 4 of the International Covenant on Civil and Political Rights (ICCPR), Article 27 of the American Convention on Human Rights (ACHR), or Article 4 of the Arab Charter on Human Rights. According to Lebret, the possibility to derogate in times of emergency does not substitute itself to permissible limitations of human rights, and if states can attain their public policy objectives without using derogatory measures, they should do it.[24]

Very often, during normal times, the exercise of fundamental rights can conflict with each other or with collective interests. Therefore, it is states' obligation to balance those interests and limit some of those rights if necessary. When the circumstances are exceptional, more severe restrictions and derogations can be admitted.[25]

The states were walking the thin line of balancing the derogations regarding the measures that would treat individuals differently on the grounds of their age or nationality. It was especially important that emergency declarations based on the COVID-19 pandemic are not used as a basis to target particular individuals or groups, including minorities or certain nationalities. Additionally, the importance of adopting positive actions to guarantee an equal protection of all human beings, was emphasised. These positive actions were predominantly significant for vulnerable persons. All of these measures would be highly substantial in the context of any public health crisis, mainly for the purpose of guaranteeing of an equal access to medical care.

During the COVID-19 pandemic, considering the fact that hospitals lacked essential resources, such as ventilators and masks for medical staff, the quarantine measures appeared necessary means to limit the spread of the virus. Depending on different factors in a given country, the imposition of fines for persons not respecting social distancing or curfews might also be considered as strictly required if really dissuasive. The extent of the quarantine that was imposed in the early stages of the COVID-19 pandemic was unprecedented. Therefore, the risk that the state of emergency, together with serious restrictions to human rights, might become the norm, was high.

The COVID-19 pandemic has caused numerous problems for the state of the rule of law in many countries. During the pandemic, the police violence against peaceful protesters was on the rise, together with the undermining of national human rights structures and attacks on journalists and human rights defenders.[26]

[24] A Lebret (n 3).

[25] Ibid.

[26] D Mijatović, *Commissioner for Human Rights of the Council of Europe, Annual Activity Report 2020*, available at: www.rm.coe.int/annual-activity-report-2020-by-dunja-mijatovic-council-of-europe-commi/1680a2150d; VV Horodovenko, LG Udovyka and HO Dichko, 'Ensuring Respect for Human Rights and Freedoms in the Context of States' Measures Introduction to Combat the COVID-19 Pandemic: European Experience' (2020) 73 *Wiadomości Lekarskie*, (12 cz 2), 2773–2779; RO Alsawalqa, AS Al Qaralleh and AM Al-Asasfeh, 'The Threat of the COVID-19 Pandemic to Human Rights: Jordan as a Model' (2022) 7(3) *Journal of Human Rights and Social Work* 265, 276.

The COVID-19 pandemic added to the already existent structural discrimination in the societies, especially in employment, health, education, housing, and the criminal justice system. Not all people were equal in the face of the pandemic. As noted by Ms Mijatović, in her Annual Activity Report 2020, those who were poor before the pandemic became poorer, while those who were disadvantaged faced even greater disadvantages.[27] The inequalities affecting older people, women, LGBT+ people and ethnic minorities grew starkly in 2020.

The countries in the Western Balkans were not an exception to this trend. Moreover, all the countries in the region, including the Republic of North Macedonia imposed very strict restrictions at the beginning of the pandemic and struggled to keep up with the multiple human rights challenges arising during the COVID-19 pandemic. The pandemic extended the already existing gap between legislation and reality in human rights protection in the country. All these issues and challenges to human rights protection in the case of the Republic of North Macedonia will be elaborated below.

4. The Case of the Republic of North Macedonia

The number of notifications for the use of Article 15 ECHR that arrived at the Council of Europe during the COVID-19 pandemic was significant and all arrived in a very short time span.[28] What is more important to note is the unprecedented nature of 'public emergency' that the Member States of the Council of Europe invoked during the crisis. There was a huge discrepancy between the different Council of Europe Member States in resorting to the derogation mechanism of Article 15. The fact is that despite facing a similar or even larger number of COVID-19 cases and having imposed similar emergency measures, there were numerous ECHR High Contracting Parties that chose not to use Article 15. The Republic of North Macedonia was one of the countries that used Article 15 of the ECHR to derogate some of the basic human rights during the COVID-19 pandemic.

Following the announcement of the World Health Organization on 11 March 2020 confirming the COVID-19 pandemic, on 18 March 2020, the President of the Republic of North Macedonia brought a decision to establish the existence of the state of emergency on the entire territory of the Republic of North Macedonia. The state of emergency was established for a period of 30 days with a main goal to prevent the spread of the COVID-19 virus.

[27] D Mijatović, *Commissioner for Human Rights of the Council of Europe, Annual Activity Report 2020*, available at: www.rm.coe.int/annual-activity-report-2020-by-dunja-mijatovic-council-of-europe-commi/1680a2150d.

[28] As can be seen on the CoE website – www.coe.int/en/web/conventions/derogations-covid-19, ten of the ECHR High Contracting Parties have used ECHR Art 15 during COVID-19 pandemic. Nine of them (Albania, Armenia, Estonia, Georgia, Latvia, North Macedonia, Republic of Moldova, Romania, and Serbia) are countries that are either former members of the Communist Bloc (either as part of the USSR or as members of the Council for Mutual Economic Assistance), or countries part of the former SFRY.

The most distinguishing thing about this decision was the fact that it provided an opportunity for the Government of the Republic of North Macedonia to adopt decrees with the force of law during the state of emergency. Those decrees needed to be in accordance with the Constitution and relevant laws in the country. After the presidential decision was enacted, the Government publicly announced that certain human rights and fundamental freedoms guaranteed under the Constitution might be temporarily suspended or restricted for the duration of state of emergency.[29]

The first case of COVID-19 in the country was detected on 26 February 2020, and from that moment on, the Government gradually adopted a set of decisions, conclusions and took preventive measures to protect the public health. Those measures included, among others, the suspension of regular classroom instruction in primary, secondary, and vocational schools and universities, replacing it with distance home learning; restriction of public assemblies; cancelling all public events, meetings, and gatherings; closing of museums, theatres, and cinemas for visitors; cancellation of performances and conferences; suspension of international passenger air traffic; establishing special rules of isolation and state-organised quarantine for citizens entering the country; ban on and special regime of movement in parts and on the entire territory of the country; as well as additional movement restrictions.

The application of these measures influenced the exercise of certain rights and freedoms provided with the ECHR. These refer particularly to Article 8 (Right to respect for private and family life) and Article 11 (Freedom of assembly and association) of the Convention; Article 2 of the Protocol to the Convention (Right to education) and Article 2 of Protocol 4 to the Convention (Freedom of movement).

Since the Government of the Republic of North Macedonia used the possibility for derogation under Article 15 of the European Convention on Human Rights, on its thirtieth session it adopted the 'Information on the need to notify the Secretary General of the Council of Europe on the Republic of North Macedonia's derogation from certain articles of the European Convention on Human Rights

[29] The list of decisions and decrees enacted during the COVID-19 pandemic in the Republic of North Macedonia: Decision to establish the existence of state of emergency (Official Gazette of the Republic of North Macedonia No 68/20); Decision on the measures to prevent the introduction and spread of coronavirus COVID-19 (Official Gazette of the Republic of North Macedonia Nos 62/20, 63/20, 64/20, 66/20, 70/20 and 72/20); Decree with the force of law on the application of the law on public gatherings during state of emergency (Official Gazette of the Republic of North Macedonia No 71/20); Decision on carrying out mandatory state quarantine for nationals of the Republic of North Macedonia returning from abroad by humanitarian flights (Official Gazette of the Republic of North Macedonia No 71/20); Decree with the force of law on the application of the Law on the protection of the population against infectious diseases during state of emergency (Official Gazette of the Republic of North Macedonia Nos 72/21 and 76/20); Decree with the force of law on the application of the Law on primary education in state of emergency (Official Gazette of the Republic of North Macedonia No 76/20); Decision supplementing the Decision banning and introducing special regime of movement on the territory of the Republic of North Macedonia (Official Gazette of the Republic of North Macedonia Nos 76/20 and 78/20).

as a consequence of the COVID-19 pandemic.'[30] The Government restated the grounds for introduction of a state of emergency – the COVID-19 pandemic, and it also explicitly provided that the:

> protection of health … [as] legitimate grounds to restrict those rights in order to enable the undertaking of measures to address the serious risks to the health of the population or to certain sections of the population, provided that they are: based on the law, necessary in a democratic society and specifically targeted to the prevention of illness or care for sick people.[31]

After the Government adopted the 'Information on the need to notify the Secretary General of the Council of Europe on the Republic of North Macedonia's derogation from certain articles of the European Convention on Human Rights as a consequence of the COVID-19 pandemic' the first notification to the Secretary General of the Council of Europe that Republic of North Macedonia was invoking Article 15 of the ECHR to face the ongoing pandemics was submitted on 2 April 2020. Since the decision of the president to establish the existence of the state of emergency on the entire territory of the Republic of North Macedonia was limited to 30 days, with every new decision to extend the state of emergency, the Republic of North Macedonia was notifying the Secretary General on the use of Article 15 of the ECHR. The final notification referring to the withdrawal of the derogation was submitted on 30 June 2020.[32]

In terms of timeline, while the notifications of the other nine countries were made in a matter of several days, in the Republic of North Macedonia there was a two-week period between declaring a state of emergency and notifying the Secretary General. What can be concluded from the cases of the ECtHR elaborated in the first part of this chapter,[33] most probably, delays in notifying the Secretary General would not appear as an issue before the Court. If requested, however, the Republic of North Macedonia should be prepared to justify the time difference.

4.1. The Specific Political and Legal Context in the Country

The political and the legal context in the case of the Republic of North Macedonia was very unique at the beginning of the COVID-19 pandemic. The country had a caretaker government established to lead the country until the early parliamentary elections scheduled for 12 April 2020. Because of the pandemic, the elections were postponed until 15 July 2020. When the pandemic broke out in the country, the Assembly was already dissolved and there was not a functional legislative body.

[30] 'From the 30th session of the Government of the Republic of North Macedonia: 'The countries in the region and the EU have agreed on green corridors for facilitating transport and trade with primary products' (27 March 2020) available at: vlada.mk/node/20774.

[31] Ibid.

[32] All the notifications are available at: www.coe.int/en/web/conventions/derogations-covid-19.

[33] *Lawless v Ireland*, 1961; *Greece v the United Kingdom*, 1958.

Therefore, it was indispensable to give legitimacy to the Government to implement certain measures and bridge the gap created by the pandemic to the time when it would be safe again to hold elections. Since the Assembly was dissolved and not in a position to validate the decisions of the president of the Republic of North Macedonia, as laid down in the Constitution, the Constitutional Court decisions were of fundamental importance to determine the legal framework for further functioning of the Government and other institutions in the country. In its Decision no 55 – of 12 May 2022, when evaluating the Decision of the President, the Constitutional Court decided that the decision to establish the existence of the state of emergency on the entire territory of the Republic of North Macedonia was constitutional.[34]

What can be noted is that at the very beginning of the COVID-19 pandemic, similarly as in other countries across the continent and in the world, there was a need for derogation of the obligations to secure certain rights and freedoms in the Republic of North Macedonia. The notification of the derogations was done according to Article 15 Paragraph 3 of the ECHR. However, we could argue that there was not a proper estimation of the derogation of rights under the specific circumstances of the pandemic, especially when it comes to situations in which already existing discrimination could be further increased. The next part will elaborate on these issues and the manner the country attempted to correct the wrong that was done at the very beginning of the COVID-19 pandemic.

4.2. The Proportionality of the Derogations in the Case of Republic of North Macedonia

This section of the chapter will elaborate on the proportionality and the manner in which the derogation in times of emergency was put in practice in the case of the state of emergency in the Republic of North Macedonia, taking into consideration several cases that are inconsistent with the spirit of the Convention and especially with Article 15 ECHR.

At the very beginning of the pandemic, the first misstep the Republic of North Macedonia made was the fact that it had announced the COVID-19 pandemic based only on the announcement coming from the World Health Organization on 11 March 2020. The domestic legislation – the Law on the Protection of the Population against Communicable Diseases,[35] although containing provisions on announcing pandemics, was not used in this particular case, without any

[34] More info in: Ministry of Justice of the Republic of North Macedonia, Analysis of the Experiences of the State Institutions during the Time of Emergency, 23 February 2021, available at: www.pravda.gov.mk/Upload/Documents/Анализа.pdf.

[35] The Law on the Protection of the Population against Communicable Diseases was enacted in 2004 and has been changed several times throughout the years (Official Gazette of the Republic of North Macedonia Nos 66/2004, 99/2009, 149/2014, 150/2015 and 37/2016).

viable explanation. The Law was changed in October 2020 in order to be in line with the need for wearing mask as one of the most effective measures during the COVID-19 pandemic.

The measures for distancing did not affect everyone in the same way. The measures were general and rarely tailored to the needs of specific groups.[36] In the publicly available documents published during the pandemic, it was hard to identify whether and how the assessment of the impact of the measures was made, both in general, and on specific groups. This made it difficult to monitor whether the introduced measures were strictly necessary.

Moreover, another difficult task in the case of Republic of North Macedonia's derogation from ECHR was to determine, at the very beginning of the COVID-19 pandemic, the proportionality of the measures it has taken. Explicitly, the measures were taken in relation to COVID-19 and in order to protect the public health. Nevertheless, there was very rarely an explanation for the individual measures as to why they were taken and what the assessment of the decision makers had been with regards to the impact they should have had.[37]

The assessment of proportionality was made even more difficult because of the fact that COVID-19 was a new virus. At the beginning of the COVID-19 pandemic, there was not sufficient data on the ways in which the virus was spread, although there were some initial scientific findings about how long it could survive without a host. Therefore, it has been easy to rely on a general justification of any measure that would keep people away from each other.[38] These kind of general measures bring with them the danger that they may disproportionately affect specific groups, such as care recipients on a variety of grounds. Additionally, the general measures may also restrain the community's potential for assistance and support. The community assistance and support is vital in cases when the other measures to prevent the spread of the infection are complied with. As a most prominent example, we should mention the assistance in the provision of food and medicine for the elderly through community support.

[36] For example, the general measures to restrict movement may not take into account the health status of certain groups of people. They need to be sensitive to those people for whom daily walks may be part of a prescribed therapy for a particular health condition. Additionally, taking into consideration of the ethnic and gender perspectives, as well as the perspective on disability were even more important in the situation of COVID-19 pandemic. The social, the personal and the societal status of the people when imposing the measures should have been taken into account, mainly because of the major consequences the COVID-19 crisis had on the economy of the country. Moreover, there is a need to take into consideration the need of certain groups of people, such as the migrants, regardless of how low the number of people estimated to be affected may be. The assessment of the proportionality of the measures in the country is of particular importance, not only to identify those people or groups of people who are more affected by the measures introduced compared to others, but also because the proportionality of the measures would be one of the criteria based on which the derogation would be assessed in the event of possible future cases that would reach the ECtHR.

[37] B Kotevska, 'On Shaky Ground: Human Rights and COVID-19 in North Macedonia after the derogation from the European Convention on Human Rights', (2020) European Policy Institute – Skopje. Available at: https://epi.org.mk/post/14727?lang=en.

[38] Ibid.

The case of the right to education during the COVID-19 pandemic in the Republic of North Macedonia is particularly important to observe, predominantly because of the inconsistencies in the implemented policies. Within the first months of the state of emergency, the whole burden of online education was left on the children and their parents, while the state was very slow in its reaction. The start of the home schooling was hectic and disorganised, mainly because there was no common online platform to be used by the schools and the students. It was at the beginning of autumn 2020 when the Government secured a stable subscription for Microsoft Teams platform for primary and secondary education, as well as for the universities. This caused significant delays in the start of the new school year and placed extra burden on both parents and students.[39]

Furthermore, the issue of freedom of movement and its derogation posed many troubles to everyday life of Macedonian citizens. The derogation of the freedom of movement was done in a manner that did not take into account the specific circumstances of different categories, which further broadened the already existing discrimination in different areas. Numerous people that were self-employed, such as farmers and the craftsmen, were in a position where they were not able to secure their already modest incomes. Additionally, the exemptions for these categories to move freely were difficult obtain. The need to have adaptation of the general measures in some cases where there is a specific situation was not noticed by the Government, making the situation of these categories of people very difficult.

There were certain cases in the Republic of North Macedonia, connected with the right to respect private and family life, which questioned whether the specific restrictions were indeed strictly needed. Because they needed to take care of elderly family members, numerous people were punished for breaking the rules, sometimes with disproportionate fines. In a situation of a public health emergency like in normal times, human rights compliance might require the adoption of specific measures that make the basic rights of vulnerable people as effective as the rest of the population.[40] This has to be taken into the account even more during a global crisis, such as the one caused by the COVID-19 pandemic. Any decision or measure taken in this context must take into account the respective situations of women, detainees, and elderly people, as they are emblematic of vulnerability in time of crisis. The need for affirmative measures in times of restrictions or suspensions of rights, is emphasised in order to ensure that the impact of those restrictions on the most vulnerable groups is not disproportionate. In the Republic of North Macedonia, this approach was not taken into account. The Government re-evaluated its actions after the state of emergency was over and the derogation of certain rights and freedoms was ended. To correct the injustice done, the Ministry of Justice drafted a Law on amnesty, aimed at correcting the unequal prosecutorial and judicial practice in different regions of the country, the fact that

[39] More info at: Ministry of Education of the Republic of North Macedonia web page. Available at: www.mon.gov.mk.

[40] See more in: A Lebret (n 3).

different personal circumstances of fined people were not taken into account, and also because of the fact that statistically an overwhelmingly large number of fined people are in a very dire social and economic position. Although the initiative was fair, the Law is still in parliamentary procedure and is not enacted. The more time passes without this Law, the injustice done to different vulnerable categories of people during the pandemic, will be harder to correct.[41]

Finally, the restrictions put in place on the freedom of assembly and association in the Republic of North Macedonia, have had a significant effect on the early elections held in the country on 15 July 2020. There are numerous smaller parties in the country that affect the forming of government during the elections, but that usually do not have many means at their disposal to present their programmes. Therefore, the freedom of assembly is crucial for these parties to gather stronger support. The restrictions to this freedom during the COVID-19 times put the small parties in a rather disadvantageous position in comparison to the larger parties, which used mainly their media presence to address the public.

All these elaborated cases during the COVID-19 pandemic in the Republic of North Macedonia, need to serve as a lesson for a possible future health crisis. They are examples that should guide future actions that need to be very sensitive of the possibility of a disproportionately negative effect on those who are most disadvantaged in society. It is extremely necessary for possible future health crisis to introduce an intersectional approach to the planning, implementation, monitoring, evaluation and termination of measures aimed at the derogation of certain rights guaranteed under the European Convention on Human Rights.

5. Conclusions

In the aftermath of the COVID-19 health crisis, which was an emergency threatening the life of the nations around the globe, countries are trying to draw

[41] At the moment of writing of this chapter, the Law on Amnesty was in parliamentary procedure and there was a huge public pressure for it to be enacted very soon. There were numerous reports in the news of people being fined disproportionately. Moreover, there were around 150 people that were not able to pay their fines and according to the law and the fact that all the deadlines have passed their fines have been transformed into prison sentences.

The case that got most attention, and was reported in the news several times, was the case of a mother of a six-year-old boy who was sentenced to prison because she didn't have the money to pay the fine that has been determined. She got fined because she was out on the street in the time of the curfew. To make the situation more absurd is the fact that she was on her way home before the curfew and her car broke, so she could not make it home on time. Now she faces three months in prison because she could not afford to pay the fine (see more at kanal5.com.mk/majka-na-malo-dete-treba-da-odi-za-zatvor-poradi-prekrshuvanje-na-policiski-chas-vo-pandemijata/a568898).

There were numerous cases reported in the news of people being fined because of not respecting the measures imposed to restrict the freedom of movement and them not being able to pay the fine and having to serve sentence in prison. In most cases, those were people whose livelihoods depended on them being able to move at certain time, or the older members of the family depended on them.

conclusions on how to manage these types of emergencies in the future. In the hindsight, the main question that needs to be answered is – what are the lessons that we have learnt from this crisis? States should try to learn how to pay particular attention in the future to the vulnerable population in order to ensure they are not disproportionally affected. There is a strong necessity to adopt the measures by applying the principle of proportionality. Beyond the management of the COVID-19 emergency, this crisis shows the fragility of health systems. It should be a lesson urging governments to review their strategies and to invest massively in the healthcare sector.

The same lessons apply in the case of the Republic of North Macedonia. What has been learned from the COVID-19 pandemic is that the society and the Government need to show greater flexibility and understanding when dealing with another crisis. The legal framework for emergencies like the COVID-19 crisis was deprived and therefore should be remodelled. Steps were made in that direction with the drafting of the new Law on State of Emergency aiming at regulating all aspects of the state of emergency, connecting the decisions of the Constitutional Court with the future legal framework for Government functioning in future cases of emergency.[42]

Additionally, the country needs to earnestly deal with the issues connected to the fragility of its health system. The health protection of the general population connected with other health issues than COVID-19 has been hugely undermined in the Republic of North Macedonia during the pandemic. Since the health system was in a very bad condition, it was not able to deal effectively with the other health issues in the times of health emergency like the one caused by COVID-19.

When it comes to derogations of human rights in times of emergency, the COVID-19 pandemic forced the Republic of North Macedonia, like many other countries in the world, to learn as they act. Claims arising from the measures or the lack of measures in the country, will most likely surface in the next couple of years. What has to be remembered for the future is that the derogation from human rights instruments does not protect human rights abuses. The thin line between necessary measures and abuses in times of crises needs to be reassessed over and over again.

[42] More info in: Ministry of Justice of the Republic of North Macedonia, Analysis of the Experiences of the State Institutions during the Time of Emergency, 23 February 2021, available at: https://www.pravda.gov.mk/Upload/Documents/Анализа.pdf.

9

Property Rights and the Secularisation of the State: Challenges of North Macedonian Pluralism

FEDERICA TORTA

1. Introduction

The Balkans – observes Mark Mazower – have not always existed.[1] The mountain range has always existed, but the historical-geographical category has only emerged since the 1880s. At the end of the nineteenth century, the Balkans were seen as a place of political instability and violent conflicts between the different nationalities in the region. After World War I, the expression Balkanisation became a generic term for the reduction of a state to 'perpetual political disorder'.[2]

The Balkans continues to be considered as a land of conquest between the West and the East, a region marked by millennia-old fracture lines, overwhelmed by the burden of an oppressive past and as an eternal hotbed of the 'ancestral hatreds' of its various ethnic groups.[3]

In this context, the territory of North Macedonia stands as an extreme of the Balkan model mainly for two reasons. First, because of the strategic location of the North Macedonian territory: controlling North Macedonia means controlling the East-West axis of communications in the Balkans, the ancient Egnatia route. Second, because North Macedonia is a mosaic of different national or ethnic identities (a '*macedonia*'"as the famous dish of French cuisine was called, inspired precisely by the miscellany that this country represents).

[1] M Mazower, *The Balkans: A Short History* (New York, Modern Library, 2000).
[2] G Franzinetti, *The Balkans from 1878 to the present* (Rome, Carocci Editore, 2001).
[3] ibid.

In such a social framework, consisting of a Slavic-North Macedonian Orthodox population in demographic crisis and a fast-growing Muslim Albanian minority, the religious issue also becomes a political agenda.[4]

2. Religious Freedom and Private Property Legislation, National Jurisprudence, and ECtHR

The decades between 1945 and 1990 gave North Macedonia the opportunity to develop certain areas of the country and strengthen its weak national identity. For the first time in their history, North Macedonians had their own republic and their own government, which, despite being part of the Federation, has wide autonomy. Forty five years of autonomous government is enough for a country to create a ruling class capable of managing public services and governing an independent state. Following the example of Slovenia and Croatia, North Macedonia held the first elections in its history in which more than 20 political parties participated.[5] Four parties formed a coalition opposed by the nationalist IMRO, a minority party. In January 1991, the North Macedonian Assembly declared the country's independence.[6] By Referendum on 8 September 1991, the Republic of North Macedonia was proclaimed as the national and historical state of the people of North Macedonia.

The first Constitution of the Republic of North Macedonia as an independent and sovereign state was promulgated in 1992. It provides for the equality of citizens in their freedoms and rights, regardless of sex, race, colour, national and social origin, political and religious beliefs, property and social status.[7]

[4] Census of Population, Households and Dwellings in the Republic of North Macedonia, 2021 – first dataset. Available at: https://www.stat.gov.mk/PrikaziSoopstenie_en.aspx?rbrtxt=146#:~:text=In%20the%20total%20resident%20population%20in%20the%20Republic,Vlachs%2C%201.30%25%20as%20Serbs%20and%200.87%25%20as%20Bosniaks.

[5] D Nohlen and DP Stover, *Elections in Europe: A Data Handbook*, (Baden-Baden, Nomos, 2010).

[6] J Tagliabue 'Macedonians vote for independence from Yugoslavia', *New York Times*. Available at: https://www.nytimes.com/1991/09/10/world/macedonians-vote-for-independence-from-yugoslavia.html.

[7] *Introduction to the Constitution of the Republic of North Macedonia 1992*. Available at: licodu.cois.it/?p=1254.

> 'Taking as the points of departure the historical, cultural, spiritual and statehood heritage of the North Macedonian people and their struggle over centuries for national and social freedom as well as the creation of their own state, and particularly the traditions of statehood and legality of the Krushevo Republic and the historic decisions of the Anti-Fascist Assembly of the People's Liberation of North Macedonia, together with the constitutional and legal continuity of the North Macedonian state as a sovereign republic within Federal Yugoslavia and freely manifested will of the citizens of the Republic of North Macedonia in the referendum of September 8th, 1991, as well as the historical fact that North Macedonia is established as a national state of the North Macedonian people, in which full equality as citizens and permanent co-existence with the North Macedonian people is provided for Albanians, Turks, Vlachs, Romanics and other nationalities living in the Republic of North Macedonia, and intent on:
>
> the establishment of the Republic of North Macedonia as a sovereign and independent state, a well as a civil and democratic one;

Regarding religious freedom, the Constitution of 1992 declares citizens free, guaranteeing *forum internum* and *forum externum*, privately and publicly, individually, or collectively.[8]

For this reason, communities and religious groups in North Macedonia are free to establish schools and other social and charitable institutions, deferring to the Law for the practical application of the aforementioned principles.[9]

However, to regulate the constitutional principles enshrined in 1992, five years later, in August 1997 the Parliament of North Macedonia approved the Law on Religious Communities and Groups.[10]

This Law regulates the entire religious organisation of the country, from the establishment of religious communities to their functioning and practice of worship[11] by prescribing that religious affairs and religious rites can only be practised by a registered religious community or a registered religious group[12] and thus, introducing for the first time the mechanism of single denomination.

This is an instrument through which the State de facto imposes the registration of only one organisation for each religious denomination, so that registered religious groups that have in their denomination an identifying component of an already registered organisation cannot coexist, nor that use for their registration the word 'North Macedonia' and those deriving from it.[13]

On registration, however, many rights depend, including property rights.[14]

the establishment and consolidation of the rule of law as a fundamental system of government;

the guaranteeing of human rights, citizens' freedoms and ethnic equality;

the provision of peace and a common home for the North Macedonian people with the nationalities living in the Republic of North Macedonia;

and on the provision of social justice, economic wellbeing and prosperity in the life of the individual and the community'

[8] Art 19, Constitution of the Republic of North Macedonia, 1992.

'The freedom of religious confession is guaranteed.

The right to express one's faith freely and publicly, individually or with others is guaranteed.

The North Macedonian Orthodox Church and other religious communities and groups are free to establish schools and other social and charitable institutions, by ways of a procedure regulated by law.'

[9] ibid.

[10] RM Gazette no 35/97, 23 July 1997. Available at: licodu.cois.it/?p=1253.

[11] Law on Religious Communities and Groups, (Official Gazette of RM no 35/97, July 1997), art 1 "Со овој закон се уредува положбата на верските заедници, основањето и работата на религиозните групи, верската поука и верските училишта, како облик на остварување на слободата на вероисповеста и на изразување на верата".

[12] Law on Religious Communities and Groups (n 11), Art 3 "Верски работи и верски обреди во Република Македонија може да врши само регистрирана верска заедница, односно религиозна група. Верските заедници и религиозните групи својата дејност ја вршат во согласност со Уставот, законите и другите прописи."

[13] For a discussion of the unique denomination issue, see F Torta, 'The Bektashi discriminated against in North Macedonia' (2019) 4 *Il Dialogo Al Hiwar* 33.

[14] Torta (n 13).

This defines a mechanism that, by making the government the arbiter between religious factions[15] prevents minorities from owning ecclesiastical properties and claiming state-owned property under the socialist era.[16]

Thus emerges the ban on worship for the Serbian Orthodox Church of the Archdiocese of Ohrid[17] and the Bektashi Community,[18] present in the country for four centuries.[19]

The absence of clarity on the meaning of the term religious groups leaves discretion to the executive with regard to granting recognition to minor cults, which prevents them from owning property and thus from acquiring the land necessary for the construction of houses of worship, from owning buildings to be used for worship, renovating or expanding them, submitting applications for the construction of places of worship within the town plans, when they do not directly proceed to the demolition of buildings dedicated to worship of non-recognised Churches, as was the case for the Serbian Orthodox Church.[20]

For these reasons, in 1998, the North Macedonian Constitutional Court, on the initiative of some religious minorities[21] declared unconstitutional several articles of the Law on Religious Communities and Religious Groups of 1997, basing its

[15] G Grigorita, 'Autonomie et synodalité dans l'Eglise ortodoxe (les prescriptions des saints canons et les réalités ecclésiastiques actuelles)' (2009) 1 *Studii Theologice*. Available at: www.studiiteologice.editurapatriarhiei.ro/.

[16] Torta (n 13).

[17] Unlike the Catholic Church, whose structure is unique with archdioceses referring to Rome, in the Orthodox world there are currently many autocephalous, i.e. independent, local Churches. Although it is not the norm, local Churches usually correspond to nations.

> Particularly regarding North Macedonia, in 1961, a part of the then-Yugoslav Republic of North Macedonia's Orthodox Church separated from the mother Church to create a new 'Orthodox Church', without the consent of the ecclesiastical authorities. The new Church proclaimed its autocephaly on 19 July 1967, citing ethnic difference as the only reason for independence. Since the mother church did not recognise the Orthodox Church of North Macedonia, the self-proclaimed Orthodox Church of North Macedonia was considered schismatic. On the other hand, however, in 1991, with the independence of the state of North Macedonia from Yugoslavia, the Orthodox Church of Serbia, the only one recognised in the territory, began the reorganisation of this Church within an exarchate, from which the Archbishopric of Ohrid derives.

[18] Bektāšīya in E Yarshater (ed), *Encyclopaedia Iranica* (15 December 1989).

[19] For a discussion of the Bektashi issue, see Torta (n 13).

[20] Torta (n 13).

[21] The Court was called upon at the joint initiative of the Baptist, Evangelical, Evangelical-Congregational, and Pentecostal Churches to decide on the constitutionality or otherwise of Arts 3, 10, 11, 13, 14, and 22 of that Law and declared them inadmissible:

- Art 3, which grants the right to conduct religious activities only to registered religious communities, thus violating the constitutional principle of religious freedom;
- Art 10, which requires a minimum number of 50 adult citizens or permanent residents for the establishment of a religious group and provides for the registration of the personal information of the 50 founders;
- Arts 13 and 14 and part of Article 22 as contrary to the principle of separation of church and state.

The Constitutional Court based its decision not only on the articles of the Constitution, but also on the norms on freedom of thought and belief contained in the Universal Declaration of Human Rights and the European Convention for the Protection of Human Rights and Fundamental Freedoms.

decision not only on the articles of the Constitution, but also on the norms on freedom of thought and belief contained in the Universal Declaration of Human Rights and the European Convention for the Protection of Human Rights and Fundamental Freedoms.[22]

The government's openly favourable attitude toward the North Macedonian Orthodox Church and the Sunni Muslims also raised concerns from the Organization for Security and Cooperation in Europe (OSCE)[23] and the Advisory Council on Freedom of Religion and Belief,[24] as well as the Venice Commission.[25]

The basic principles of relations between the state and religious communities contained in the North Macedonian Constitution and the Law on Religious Communities and Groups can be summarized as follows:

- Freedom of religion implies the right of everyone to freely express his or her beliefs, either publicly, individually or as a member of a specific religious community. Denominations are separate from the state and equal to each other before the law.
- Freedom of religion implies, in addition, the right to profess one's religion, if one has one.
- No one can be forced to profess any religion against his or her will. Freedom of belief is an individual and strictly personal matter and part of the private sphere.
- Freedom of religion implies the right not to be forced by any authority to join a church or official religion. In addition, no one can be forced to go to religious facilities or attend religious ceremonies against his or her will.
- It is forbidden to hold religious ceremonies, give religious teaching, organize religious meetings and gatherings, as well as carry out other religious activities for political purposes or to incite religious, national or other intolerance.
- Religious communities and religious groups have the right to access the mass media and publish materials in print media in the context of their activities.
- In accordance with the internal regulations of the various religious communities, religious officials and other persons engaged in the performance of religious ceremonies and activities have the right to accept donations or monetary contributions for the performance of religious services upon specific request of groups of citizens.

[22] Decision of the Constitutional Court of the Republic, 64, in *Official Bulletin of the Republic of North Macedonia*, 3324, 31 December 1998.

[23] 'With 57 participating states from North America, Europe and Asia, the Organization for Security and Cooperation in Europe (OSCE) is the world's largest regional security organization. The OSCE works to ensure stability, peace, and democracy for more than a billion people through political dialogue on shared values and practical activities that aim to have lasting effects. The OSCE is a forum for political dialogue on a wide range of security issues and a platform for joint action to improve the lives of individuals and communities. The Organization takes a comprehensive approach to security, encompassing the politico-military, economic and environmental, and human dimensions. Through this approach and its inclusive composition, the OSCE helps overcome differences and build confidence among states through cooperation in the fields of conflict prevention, crisis management, and post-conflict reconstruction.' Available at: www.osce.org/it/who-we-are.

[24] This assessment was prepared by Alan Page, Professor of Public Law at the University of Dundee, of the Society for Advanced Legal Studies, as well as and by the ODIHR Legislative Support Unit, *Department in cooperation with the Rule of Law Unit of the OSCE Spillover Monitor Mission to Skopje*. Available at: https://www.osce.org/files/f/documents/3/6/34685.pdf.

[25] Venice Commission 22/0[3/2007] CDL-AD (2007)005, *Opinion on the Draft Law on the Legal Status of a Church, a Religious Community and a Religious Group of "the former Yugoslav Republic of North Macedonia" adopted by the Venice Commission at its 70th Plenary Session* (Venice, 16–17 March 2007). The European Commission for Democracy through Law, known as the Venice Commission after the name of the city where it meets, is an advisory body of the Council of Europe. Established in 1990, the Commission has played a key role in the adoption of constitutions that conform to the standards of the European constitutional heritage.

Nevertheless, the government proposed and received approval for in 2007 a new Law on Religious Communities, Organisations and Groups as the result of a lengthy drafting process that began in 2005 and concluded with its entry into force in May 2008, which increased the criticism expressed by international institutions.[26]

Below are the key steps in the legislative process that led to the approval of the Law of 2008.

At the beginning of 2007, Minister of Justice of the Republic of North Macedonia Mihajlo Manevski[27] was asked to analyse the Draft Law 'On the Legal Status of Churches, Religious Communities and Religious Groups.'[28] The members of the Venice Commission F. Flanagan and Hans-Heinrich Vogel and the deputy Hubert Haenel were therefore instructed to analyse the draft and express an opinion on it, also analysing its compatibility with the European Convention on Human Rights[29] and the general principles of the *Guidelines for Review of Legislation Pertaining to Religion or Belief.*[30]

In the Opinion No 424/2007[31] it emerged that the religious situation and the regulations concerning its organisation were, and still are,[32] particularly complex

Initially conceived as an emergency constitutional engineering tool in a context of democratic transition, the Commission has seen its activities gradually evolve to become an internationally recognized body of independent legal reflection.

The Commission contributes significantly to the dissemination of Europe's constitutional heritage, which is based on the continent's fundamental legal values, and provides states with "constitutional support." In addition, the Venice Commission, by developing standards and advice on constitutional matters, plays an essential role in conflict management and prevention.' Available at: www.venice.coe.int/WebForms/pages/?p=01_Presentation&lang=IT.

Relative to the North Macedonian case see: HDIM.NGO/400/08 7 October 2008, p 1 'On March 6, 2007, a meeting was held in Skopje with North Macedonian authorities, ODIHR delegates, the Venice Commission, and representatives of major religious communities. On March 16 and 17, 2007, the Venice Commission adopted an official plenary opinion illuminating several important issues that violated international human rights standards.' Available at: www.osce.org/odihr/34234?download=true.

[26] K Ivanova Petrova, *La Bulgaria e l'Islam: Il pluralismo imperfetto dell'ordinamento bulgaro* (Bologna, Bononia University Press, 2015).

[27] Minister of Justice and former chairman of the Anti-Corruption Commission. For more details www.balcanicaucaso.org/aree/NorthMacedonia/Nuovo-governo-in-North Macedonia-a-caccia-di-posti-di-lavoro-34372.

[28] CDL(2007)015). See the Third Bill since 2005. Opinion no 424/2007, Ch II, Para A, Pun – to 8, Strasbourg. 'The present draft constitutes the third version since 2005. OSCE/ODIHR Advisory Council had been involved in this process and had already provided two sets of comments.'

[29] The Republic of North Macedonia adopted the jurisdiction of the ECtHR in 1994 and the ICCPR in 1991. Ch III, Para 13. 'The following opinion addresses the compatibility of the draft law on "The legal status of a church, religious community and religious group" in "the former Yugoslav Republic of North Macedonia" with the European Convention on Human Rights as it concerns religious freedom. It also takes into account the main principles of the Guidelines for Review of Legislation Pertaining to Religion or Belief, prepared by the OSCE/ODIHR Advisory Panel of Experts on the Freedom of Religion or Belief in consultation with the Venice Commission (CDL- AD (2004)028).'

[30] These are guidelines prepared by OSCE/ODIHR with the consultation of the Venice Commission (CDL-AD(2004)028). For further discussion, see www.osce.org/odihr/13993 (n 29).

[31] For the full text see https://www.venice.coe.int/webforms/documents/default.aspx?pdffile=CDL-AD(2007)005-e.

[32] HDIM.NGO/400/08 7 October 2008, p 1. 'This document provides an analysis of the Law and a suggested approach to enforcement of the law in order to ensure that its implementation complies with international human rights norms.' (n 31).

and controversial.[33] In fact, although some changes were made based on Opinion No 424/2007 before the Law came into force, the problems and critical issues of the single denomination remain, as raised in the opinion expressed in the autumn of 2008 by the OSCE.[34,35]

According to international standards, in fact, the guarantees of religious freedom are not subordinated to any kind of specific registration system and all entities must benefit from them without conditions of affiliation or registration.[36] The Venice Commission also emphasises that the approval of a law referring only to religious entities that wish to acquire a legal personality and consequently take advantage of the principles and rights enshrined in the law could be interpreted as an impediment for unregistered religious entities to freely practise their faith[37] in violation of Articles 9, 10, and 11 of the ECHR.[38]

[33] Para B (n 31).

> '10. The situation in the country concerning religion and the legislation governing its organization is complex and controversial. There are approximately 35 religious communities in the country, regulated by the existing law; 26 of them are registered. The different religious groups have learned over the centuries to live together in the same country; the Orthodox can be considered as the majority in the whole country, whilst specific regions or areas of the country are composed in majority of Muslims.
>
> 11. Historically, religious entities have always had an important role in the society, its edu- cation and well – being, even though they are separate from the state. 12. Religious issues have always been closely linked to political issues.'

[34] HDIM.NGO/400/08 7 October 2008, p 2' 'Major modifications were laudably made to the draft Law by the North Macedonian authorities in order to comply with the Venice Commission's Opinion and ODIHR's comments, but some issues have not been addressed and remain problematic in the final version of the Law.'

[35] *Draft Law on the Legal Status of a Church, a Religious Community and a Religious Group of* 'The Former Yugoslav Republic of North Macedonia' Arts 3–8.

[36] Item 35 'Furthermore, the Venice Commission reminds the drafters that, ac- cording to international standards, the guarantees of freedom of religion are not subordinate to any kind of specific system of registration or religious entities; they must benefit any religious entity without any conditions of affiliation or registration.'

[37] Ibid 'The Venice Commission considers that passing a law which refers only to religious entities which want to acquire legal personality and consequently benefit from the principles and rights enshrined in the law might be understood as aiming to prevent the religious entities which do not want to be registered, from freely exercising their faiths.' cf (n 31).

[38] Para 37 'This is a matter of considerable importance that requires clarification, since limitations on the freedoms guaranteed by Articles 9, 10 and 11 ECHR must comply with one of the legitimate purposes set out in those Articles.' See: ECHR Arts 9,10, 11. 'Article 9. Freedom of thought, conscience and religion.

1. Everyone has the right to freedom of thought, conscience and religion; this right includes freedom to change his religion or belief and freedom, either alone or in community with others and in public or private, to manifest his religion or belief, in worship, teaching, practice and observance.
2. Freedom to manifest one's religion or beliefs shall be subject only to such limitations as are prescribed by law and are necessary in a democratic society in the interests of public safety, for the protection of public order, health or morals, or for the protection of the rights and freedoms of others.

Article 10. Freedom of expression.

1. Everyone has the right to freedom of expression. This right shall include freedom to hold opinions and to receive and impart information and ideas without interference by public authority

One of the most controversial points of the Law is precisely the single denomination, which as always gives a public authority[39] the discretionary power to evaluate and compare similarities or differences among religious bodies and therefore also to enter theological issues,[40] creating interference of state bodies in freedom of religion and faith.[41]

The North Macedonian legislator, called upon to explain the meaning of the rule[42] at the meeting of 6 March 2007 organised with international institutions, replied that a church or religious entity could not be allowed to confuse believers by adopting a name identical to that of another church.[43] The drafters then considered that the State should protect the people from confusion and should therefore

and regardless of frontiers. This Article shall not prevent States from requiring the licensing of broadcasting, television or cinema enterprises.

2. The exercise of these freedoms, since it carries with it duties and responsibilities, may be subject to such formalities, conditions, restrictions or penalties as are prescribed by law and are necessary in a democratic society, in the interests of national security, territorial integrity or public safety, for the prevention of disorder or crime, for the protection of health or morals, for the protection of the reputation or rights of others, for preventing the disclosure of information received incondence, or for maintaining the authority and impartiality of the judiciary.

ARTICLE 11. Freedom of assembly and association

1. Everyone has the right to freedom to peaceful assembly and to freedom of association with others, including the right to form and to join trade unions for the protection of his interests.
2. No restrictions shall be placed on the exercise of these rights other than such as are prescribed by law and are necessary in a democratic society in the interests of national security or public safety, for the prevention of disorder or crime, for the protection of health or morals or for the protection of the rights and freedoms of others. This Article shall not prevent the imposition of lawful restrictions on the exercise of these rights by members of the armed forces, of the police or of the administration of the State.' (n 31).

[39] The Court in charge of the registry.

[40] Item 60 'Moreover this draft would leave to a public authority – i.e. the Court in charge of the Register – the discretionary power to assess and compare similarities or differences between religious entities and consequently enter into theological questions. This would be considered under international understanding as an unnecessary interference of state bodies into the freedom of religion or belief. In addition, the Commission considers that the mention, for instance, in draft Article 9.4 of "same identity" would leave to a public authority the assessment of similarities of two faiths, and this cannot be considered as a neutral or impartial position but more likely as an *infringement* of the freedom of religion.'

[41] Para 61 'A quite similar lack of clarity, of undue interference and hence matter of serious concern applies to the wording of draft Article 9.4, which provides that "a church, religious community and religious group that does not have the same identity or that does not use the same name or a name similar to an already registered church, religious community or religious group will be entered in the competent register' (n 31).

[42] Item 62 'At the meeting of March 6, the delegation asked the drafters to explain the meaning of both these articles.' (n 31).

[43] Item 63 'Whilst it was acknowledged and recalled that everybody has the right to express his/her beliefs, as for registration issues and possibilities it was considered that a church or a religious entity could not be allowed to confuse the believers by having an identical name to another church. The drafters consider that the State has the duty to protect the public from confusion and therefore could refuse registration to any religious entity which would not sufficiently distinguish itself from already registered religious entities.' (n 31).

be authorised to refuse registration of religious entities that were not sufficiently distinct from those already registered.[44]

In fact, if more than one denomination of a church, religious community, or religious group were allowed to register, there would be significant controversy in the country and in particular the registration of the Archbishopric of Ohrid would conflict with the already existing and registered Orthodox Church of North Macedonia.[45] In addition to this element, the delegation's attention was brought back to the fact that this particular issue involves historical and political aspects, which are fundamental,[46] and in particular it emerged that, given the positive relations with the Orthodox Church of North Macedonia, it would have been a danger to the state, its integrity and the interests.[47]

Finally, the formal procedures required for registration[48] also raised concerns.[49]

Doubt has arisen particularly in the part that stipulates that the religious entity must apply to Court II Skopje for registration by submitting an 'action program'[50] and proving citizenship or permanent residence of the founder of the religious entity[51] for its registration, a provision again linkable to the conflicts between the North Macedonian Orthodox Church and the Archbishopric of Ohrid and the Sunni Community against the Bekstashi.

Despite multiple calls from the international community for changes to the text of the Law, the government proposed and obtained the new Law on Churches, Communities and Religious Groups, which came into effect in May 2008, introducing some formal changes, which, although improving the law, do not change its substantially discriminatory content towards undesired minorities.[52]

[44] Ibid.

[45] Forum 18 New Service, Oslo, Norway wwwforum18.org, 2 February 2007. See Item 64 'Indeed, whether more than one denomination or community of a church, religious community or religious group can be registered is a matter of significant public controversy in the country. In particular, the drafters consider that the registration of the "Orthodox Church of Serbia" would conflict with the already existing "Orthodox Church of North Macedonia.'

[46] Item 65 'In addition to this element, the attention of the delegation was drawn to the fact that this particular issue also entails both historical groundings and political aspects in the country.' (n 31).

[47] Point 66 'Moreover, according to the discussions the relations between the State and the Church have always been very close. It would therefore constitute a danger for the State, its integrity, and the interest of its citizens to see a religious entity which might support foreign interests having a legal personality in the country.' (n 31).

[48] Para C (e), Item 76 'Articles 12 and 13 of the draft law enumerate the necessary procedures.' (n 31).

[49] Point 77 'The requirements seem to be both far-reaching, unclear in their purposes and would need simplification. Moreover, here again the Venice Commission wonders about the lawfulness under international standards of some of those procedures. Indeed, the religious entity should present a "program of exertion." Even though the delegation was told that this requirement was of a formal nature and that the court would not look into the components of this program, the Commission recommends deleting this mention. It is likely to be seen as an unlawful infringement for the freedom of religion, all the more so since the formal nature of this requirement or all procedures is not clearly specified in the draft law' (n 31).

[50] Ibid.

[51] Para 78 'The same applies to the necessity to prove the nationality or the permanent residence of the founder of the religious entity. Moreover the Commission wonders why a founder should be designated or even exist in every religious entity.'

[52] K Ivanova Petrova, (n 26).

3. The North Macedonian Orthodox Church and the Archbishopric of Ohrid

The history of the North Macedonian Orthodox Church spans about twelve centuries, from the period AD 886–916 to the present. Between AD 886 and 916, 3,500 students attended the Ohrid School, also known as the first University of the Balkans, engaging in religious proselytising activities.[53] The history of the North Macedonian Orthodox Church is closely linked to the spread of the teaching of St. Clement and St. Naum of Ohrid.[54] Clement was the first Slavic bishop in the Balkans: unlike the Greek bishops he celebrated religious services and preached in the language of the North Macedonian Slavs.[55] His diocese of Velica became a patriarchate at the time of King Samoil in the 10th century.

According to historical sources, in the late 9th and early 10th centuries, Clement and Naum of Ohrid laid the foundation for the diffusion of education and culture among the North Macedonian Slavic populations.[56] Their cultural, educational, and religious mission lasted for three whole decades and was then continued by others, even among populations outside North Macedonian borders.[57] The development of the famous Ohrid literary school was intricately connected with the religious, cultural, and educational activities carried out by the two scholars.[58] The period of greatest activity is defined as the 'Golden Age of Slavic literature'. Their knowledge was transmitted by disciples, and following the establishment of the independent Ohrid Archbishopric, the literary and spiritual teachings of Clement and Naum were introduced as subjects of study in the institutes of higher theological education founded at monasteries.[59] After the fall of the Samoil kingdom in 1018 the Archbishopric joined the Byzantine state.[60]

Despite the imposition of Greek-Byzantine high clergy on the Ohrid Archbishopric, the latter managed to preserve its independence for nearly eight centuries and retained its cultural background until Sultan Mustafa III abolished the Ohrid Archbishopric in 1767,[61] under the Archbishopric of Constantinople.[62]

[53] S Kostovski, 'Church and State' in S Ferrari, W. Cole Durham Jr and EA Sewell (eds), *Law and Religion in Post-Communist Europe* Law and Religion Studies Series 1 (Leuven, Peeters, 2011).

[54] Ibid.

[55] Ibid.

[56] Ibid.

[57] On the work of St. Clement and St Naum and the creation of the Slavic Archbishopric Of Ohrid, see DS Dimevski, *History of the North Macedonian Orthodox Church* (Skopje, Makedonska Kniga, 1989) 44; J Belovski, *The North Macedonia Autocephalous Orthodox Church* (Skopje, Studentski Zbor, 1986) 7; D Ilievski, *The North Macedonian Autocephalous Orthodox Church* (Skopje, George Fox University Press, 1972) 16.

[58] S Kostovski (n 53).

[59] S Kostovski (n 53).

[60] On the position of the Ohrid Archbishopric in Byzantine times and during Bulgarian, Serbian, and Turkish rule, see n 57 and C Grozdanov, Ohrid and the Ohrid Archbishopricin the 14th Century (1980) VI *History*.

[61] J Belovski (n 57).

[62] S Kostovski (n 53).

Members of the Greek clergy systematically attempted to eliminate the Slavonic language from religious services in North Macedonian monasteries and to destroy works in the Slavonic language.[63] However, the Ohrid Archbishopric carried on the Slavic tradition of manual transcription and translation of religious texts as well as secular literature in Slavic language. With the creation of the Bulgarian Exarchate in 1870, the North Macedonian Orthodox Church was subjected to a second religious power[64] and during this unstable historical period, there were numerous uprisings protesting the restoration of the Ohrid Archbishopric. The Balkan Wars and the end of World War I lead to a further territorial, and religious, division of North Macedonia among the neighbouring countries and their eparchies-Greece, Serbia, and Bulgaria. Since 1944, Orthodox North Macedonians aspired to make the Archdiocese of Ohrid independent.[65]

After World War II, North Macedonia became a federal state of the Yugoslav Federation, and in 1945 the first National Assembly of the North Macedonian Church was held in Skopje, which adopted a resolution in favour of the re-establishment of the Ohrid Archbishopric as an independent North Macedonian Church.[66] For its part, however, the Serbian Orthodox Church, which considers the Ohrid Archbishopric as its own and sees in it a representation of its historical roots and traditions, refused to consider the Assembly's resolution.[67]

In 1958 following various failures of the restoration of the Archbishopric, the second National Assembly of the North Macedonian Church[68] was held, this time in Ohrid: the restoration of the Ohrid Archbishopric as an independent North Macedonian Church was proclaimed and Dositej[69] nominated as its head.[70]

The Serbian Orthodox Church recognises the independence of the North Macedonian Church but tries to impose its own control and jurisdiction on it.[71]

In the 1960s, when the Assembly of the Archbishops of the Serbian Orthodox Church was held, it emerged that the independence of the North Macedonian Orthodox Church was only illusory; the Holy Synod of the North Macedonian Orthodox Church proclaimed the latter as an autocephalous Church[72] and in 1967 adopted the Statute of the North Macedonian Orthodox Church and Archbishopric of Ohrid.[73]

[63] Ibid.

[64] S Kostovski (n 53).

[65] B Stasiewski, in *History of the Church, The Church in Absolutism and the Enlightenment* (Milan, Jaka Book, 1978).

[66] S Kostovski (n 53).

[67] S Kostovski (n 53).

[68] Y Chiron, *History of the Church* vol X (Milan, aka Book SpA, 1995) 433. 'Serbian Patriarch Germano had to approve in 1958–59 the declaration of autonomy of a North Macedonian ecclesial assembly and the election of its suffragan bishop Dositej and archbishop of Ohrid and North Macedonia.'

[69] Ibid.

[70] Ibid.

[71] Ibid.

[72] 'Proclamation of the Autocephalous *Status* (Tomos) of the North Macedonian Orthodox Church,' in 'Vesnik' no 4/67, archives of the North Macedonian Archbishopric. Cf S Kostovski (n 53) and n 57.

[73] For the full text see licodu.cois.it/?p=3141.

It stated that all churches, monasteries, chapels, orthodox cemeteries and places of worship, movable and immovable property in general, such as the canonical and spiritual jurisdiction of the North Macedonian Orthodox Church, were property of the North Macedonian Orthodox Church.[74] The properties of the North Macedonian Orthodox dioceses in North Macedonia and outside its territory were governed by the law and regulations of the dioceses of the North Macedonian ecclesial communities, confirmed by the Holy Synod and in accordance with the Statute.[75] In addition, the following administrative matters were under the jurisdiction of the Authorized Economic Organization of North Macedonia (AEO): ensuring that churches, monasteries and all other religious institutions hold legal proofs of ownership of places of worship; control of contracts concluded for the purchase and sale and leasing of local churches, monasteries and dioceses and approval of the final sale of the property of the entire North Macedonian Orthodox Church; settlement of debts of churches, monasteries, dioceses and the Archbishopric.[76]

The authority of the Diocesan Assembly, on the other hand, included deciding on the purchase and sale of movable and immovable property of the diocese.[77]

The authority of the Eparchies, instead, included the following administrative matters: issuing guidelines for the management and control of diocesan properties and other institutions, decisions and solutions for the sale and indebtedness of churches, monasteries, and diocesan properties, and finally deciding on the purchase of churches, monasteries, and diocesan properties.[78]

[74] Statute of the North Macedonian Orthodox Church and the Archbishopric of Ohrid,

Art 173 co 1 'Член 173

точка 1. Сите цркви, манастири, параклиси, црквишта, оброчишта – свети води, гробишта и православни култни места, со целокупните движни и недвижни имоти, што се под канонска и духовна јуриздикција на МПЦ, се сопственост на МПЦ.' For the English text Constitution of the North Macedonian Orthodox Church seelicodu.cois.it/?p=7939.

[75] Art 173 co 2 'точка2. Имотите на македонските православни епархии во Македонија и надвор од нејзината територија, се уредуваат со статут на епархии и правилник на македонските црковни општини, потврдени од Светиот Синод, кои се во согласност со овој Устав.' (n 74).

[76] Art 64 'Член 64 Во надлежност на АУО спаѓаат и следниве црковно – управни работи:

[…]

9) се грижи и настојува црквите, манастирите и сите други црковно – верски установи да имаат законски докази за сопственоста на своите имоти;

10) врши контрола на склучените договори за земање и давање под закуп на црковно – општински, манастирски и епархиски имоти;

12) одобрува конечно отуѓување на имоти во целата Македонска Православна Црква и отпишување на за должувања на црквите, манастирите, епархиите и Архиепископијата.' (n 74).

[77] Art 83 'Во надлежност на Епархиското Собрание спаѓа:
ж) одлучува за купување и отуѓување на движни и недвижни имоти на Епархијата;' (n 74).

[78] Art 92 'Во надлежност на ЕУО спаѓаат следниве црковно – управни работи:

4) издава упатства за управување, раководење и контролирање со епархиските имоти, фондови, задужбини и други институции;

In 1975 the North Macedonian Church gave itself a constitution, but its development was hindered by Yugoslav legislation, which in 1976 intensified anti-religious provisions in the Constituent Republic of North Macedonia.[79]

4. The History of the Ohrid Archbishopric After the Fall of the Socialist Bloc

Following the fall of the socialist bloc, the regained autonomy of the ethnic and linguistic communities in the territories of North Macedonia has given vigour to the public space of the North Macedonian Orthodox Church which, despite the proclaimed separation between the state and religious denominations, has been recognised as a traditional and established church:[80] it is part of the nucleus of Eastern European religious denominations to which the legal systems grant greater rights precisely because they are part of the tradition and history of the peoples and have contributed in the past and still contribute today to shaping their national identity.[81] It has preserved and transmitted the language and has been a point of reference for national culture.[82]

In 1994 the North Macedonian Orthodox Church gave itself a Statute.[83] In it, it is established that Ohrid is the centre of the North Macedonian Orthodox Church[84] and that North Macedonian is the official language of worship.[85] The head of the Church is the Archbishop of Ohrid and North Macedonia:[86] in the ceremony of his inauguration, elements of connection with the North Macedonian

5) донесува одлуки и решенија за отуѓување и задолжување на црковни, манастирски и епархиски имоти и за тоа гоо известува Епархиското Собрание, кое ги доставува предметите на конечно одлучување на АУО;

6) конечно решава за закупи на црковни, манастирски и епархиски имоти;' (n 74).

[79] Y Chiron (n 68).

[80] G Cimbalo, in *Religion and Human Rights in the Transitional Societies of Eastern Europe*, in *Human Rights and Religious Freedom* edited by POSSENTI V., Rubbettino, Catanzaro, 2010, p. 141. (n. 81).

[81] ibid.

[82] ibid.

[83] *Statute of the North Macedonian Orthodox Church 1994*, for the full text see licodu.cois.it/?p=7939.

[84] Ibid Art 4 'The North Macedonian Orthodox Church has its own flag: red coloured cloth, with the proportion of 1 x 2m. In accordance with the coat of arms of the North Macedonian Orthodox Church the picture of the temple of "Saint. Clement of Ohrid" in Ohrid is imprinted at its centre. The picture is in golden colour with the proportion of 30 x 40 cm.'

[85] Ibid Art 5 'In the North Macedonian Orthodox Church the official language is the North Macedonian language and its Cyrillic letter; public-worship languages are the Church-Slavic and North Macedonian. Into the parts of the Church-services other languages may be used too, under the conditions and in a way determined by a decision of the Holy Bishop's Synod (hereinafter referred to as "Holy Synod").'

[86] Ibid Art 9 'At the head of the MOC is the Archbishop as its Governor. The title of the Archbishop is Archbishop of Ohrid and North Macedonia and he is addressed with "Your Beatitude.'

state emerge such that not only he must promise to be loyal to his Church, but also to his motherland: the Republic of North Macedonia.[87]

In 2005 the Serbian Orthodox Church claimed recognition of the Ohrid Patriarchate as autonomous and under the full liturgical and canonical unity of the Patriarchate of Pec, namely of the Serbian Orthodox Church and its movable and immovable property.[88] This remains an open question, as evidenced by both the 2005 ruling of the North Macedonian Supreme Court on the appeal of the Orthodox Archbishopric of Ohrid against the Government of the Republic of

[87] Ibid Art 53 'The following morning, after the formal ascending at the throne, the newly elected Archbishop, after the receiving of the Archbishoprical "insignia" (panagia and scepter), from the oldest ordained Bishop, takes an oath:

> "We N.N. elected and ascended Archbishop of Ohrid and North Macedonia swear to Almighty God; that we shall be loyal and devoted to the North Macedonian Orthodox Church and to our Motherland, the Republic of North Macedonia; that we shall guard the purity and teachings of the Holy Orthodoxy, the Holy Canons and Church regulations, and we shall keep canonical unity with all other local Orthodox Churches; we shall respect the North Macedonian Orthodox Church in every aspect, especially its Constitution and regulations which arise from
>
> the Constitution; in all our deeds and actions we shall act only in accordance with the interest of our Holy Church and Motherland; and we shall not agree with any change contrary to their interest. As we believe, confess and work, thus the Almighty God, the Holy Mother, the Holy North Macedonian and Pan-Slavic even to the Apostles, the Holy brothers Cyril and Methodius of Solun, Saint Clement and Saint Naum, the Miracle-Workers of Ohrid, the North Macedonian s and all other Saints shall help us."

The Archbishop publicly signs the text of the oath personally and it is entered in the Council's Minutes and, the original of the oath is kept at the Holy Synod's archives.

As a specific characteristic, the Archbishop wears a white "panakamilavka" with a diamond cross and, during the divine-services "panagia" of the Holy Mother, of the Saint Clement of Ohrid and a Cross.

The Archbishoprical "panagia" which is left as a heritage from one Archbishop of the MOC to another, is with the figure of Saint Clement of Ohrid and, the figures of the North Macedonian Saints are ensued on the necklace.'

[88] *Tomos of the 2003–2005 recognition of the Ohrid Patriarchate*, 'The Holy Synod of Bishops of the Orthodox Ohrid Archbishopric was constituted on the 25th of December in the year of our Lord 2003, who had elected His Eminence, the Metropolitan of Veles and Vardar Valley kyr John to be the Chairman thereof. The aforesaid has had the title of Our Exarch for all the dioceses of the autonomous Orthodox Ohrid Archbishopric awaiting final canonical settlement of the situation in the above named ancient and glorious church district, and in accordance with the provisions of the aforesaid Agreement signed in Nish on 17th of May in the year of our Lord 2002, from now on he shall have the title of Blessed Archbishop of Ohrid and Metropolitan of Skopje.

Therefore, We officially certify and proclaim the aforesaid with this Patriarchal and Assembly's Tomos. By the grace of our Lord, the autonomous Orthodox Ohrid Archbishopricremains in full liturgical and canonical unity with our Patriarchate of Pec, i.e., with the Serbian Orthodox Church, and therefore with the fullness of the Most Holy Catholic Orthodox Church, being canonically expressed with the confirmation of the election of the Prelate thereof by Our humbleness. All the property of the Serbian Orthodox Church, movable and immovable, situated in the region of the aforesaid holy dioceses, i.e., eparchies, is hereby given to possession to the Orthodox Ohrid Archbishopric.

As a proof, confirmation and permanent testimony of all that has been constituted and established canonically with regard to the aforesaid dioceses becoming parts of the Orthodox Ohrid Archbishopric, hereby we issue to His Beatitude, the Archbishop of Ohrid and Metropolitan of Skopje Kyr John, our beloved brother in Christ our Lord and fellow minister of Our humbleness, with all the Eminent Bishops of the Orthodox Ohrid Archbishopric, our beloved brethren and fellow ministers in the Holy Spirit, our following.' For the integral text see: licodu.cois.it/?p=5371.

North Macedonia[89] and the rejection decision of the Skopje Court of Appeal on 15 December 2010.[90]

The Orthodox Archdiocese of Ohrid then appealed against North Macedonia[91] to the European Court of Human Rights, of which the North Macedonian government was informed on 22 February 2013.

The ECtHR issued its judgment on the case on 16 November 2017, which became final on 9 April 2018.

It reads:

> in view of the foregoing, it cannot be said that the reasons provided by the national authorities, taken as a whole, were "relevant and sufficient" to justify the interference in this case. It further considers that the way the domestic authorities refused the recognition of the applicant association as a religious organisation cannot be accepted as necessary in a democratic society. It follows that there has been a violation of Article 11 of the Convention, interpreted in the light of Article 9.[92]

Following the measure, at its assembly held in Strasbourg from 12–14 March 2019, the Council of Europe's Committee of Ministers discusses the supervision of the implementation of the aforementioned judgment of the European Court of Human Rights. The Committee welcomeed that the Skopje Registration Court, with reference to the ECtHR judgment, accepted the reopening of the contested case and that the re-registration procedure is proceeding.

In addition, on 22 February 2019, the registration judge acknowledged the obligation to consider the findings of the European Court of Human Rights and relevant case law and to provide compensation to applicants in accordance with the Convention and current remedies, and to make efforts to assist applicants in overcoming the obstacles they faced.[93]

However, the ECtHR ruling never led to a practical application of the registration of the Greek Orthodox Archbishopric of Ohrid.[94]

[89] For the full text see licodu.cois.it/wp-content/uploads/2014/11/Arcivescovado-di-Ohrid-contro-il-governo-della-Repubblica-di-North Macedonia.pdf.

[90] For the full text see licodu.cois.it/wp-content/uploads/2014/11/Arcivescovado-di-Ohrid-culto greco-ortodosso-Patriarcato-di-Pec.pdf.

[91] For more details see European Court of Human Rights, Appeal No. 3532/07 by the Orthodox Archdiocese of Ohrid v Former Yugoslav Republic of North Macedonia filed 25 December 25 2006 – hudoc.echr.coe.int/eng#{%22appno%22:[%223532/07%22],%22itemid%22:[%22001-117472%22].

[92] European Court of Human Rights, Case *Ohrid Orthodox Archdiocese (Ohrid Greek Orthodox Archdiocese of the Patriarchate of Peć) v Former Yugoslav Republic of North Macedonia* (Application No. 3532/07), Judgment, Strasbourg, 16 November 2017, FINAL 9 April 2018 – hudoc.echr.coe.int/eng#{%22itemid%22:[%22001- 1 78890%22]}, Para 121.

[93] Council of Europe, Deputies of Ministers, 1340th Meeting, 12–14 March 2019 (DH), H46-22 *Orthodox Archdiocese of Ohrid (Greek Orthodox Archdiocese of Ohrid of the Patriarchate of Peć) v Former Yugoslav Republic of North Macedonia* (Appeal No. 3532/07), Supervision of the Enforcement of European Court Judgments, Reference Document: CM/Notes/1340/H46-22, 14 March 2019 – search.coe.int/cm/Pages/result_details. aspx?ObjectID=090000168093755d.

[94] O Oehring, 'Der Streit zwischen der Mazedonisch Orthodoxen Kirche und der Serbisch Orthodoxen Kirche – Hypothek für Nordmazedonien?' (2021) 426 *Konrad-Adenauer-Stiftunge*. Available at: www.kas.de/ro/analysen-und-argumente/detail/-/content/der-streit-zwischen-den-orthodoxen-kirchen-in-mazedonien-und-serbien.

Nevertheless, where state policy has not come, ecclesiastical policy has come, demonstrating the great temporal power of Orthodox hierarchies.

The North Macedonian church was one of the issues left unresolved by the Pan-Orthodox Synod of Crete of 16–27 June 2016[95] and was certainly one of the major issues on which the mediation ability of the Ecumenical Patriarchate had to be measured in order to reaffirm and confirm its role between the Orthodox Churches in the Balkan area, Orthodoxy's main area of presence and scenario of action in which the Patriarchate claims the right to exercise its hegemony and, in so doing, confirms its primacy over all other Patriarchates.[96]

As showed by the Patriarch Bartholomew's arguments for the rejection of the North Macedonian Orthodox Church's recognition of autocephaly in November 2018, the name conflict between North Macedonia and Greece was also creating an impasse.[97]

In fact, Greece, after the dissolution of the Yugoslav federation, opposed giving the country the name Macedonia, claiming exclusive use of this name for a region of its country long disputed by Turks, Greeks, and Macedonian peoples, located north of its borders.

After lengthy negotiations that went through several stages, the Prespa Agreement was signed in June 2019, giving the country the name Republic of North Macedonia. Although the referendum held to confirm the pre-agreement on 30 September 2018 did not achieve a quorum, in January 2019, the North Macedonian Parliament approved a constitutional amendment ratifying the agreement, in order to be able to join the European Union and, on 27 March 2020, NATO.

Today, North Macedonia is a candidate country to join the European Union, despite a setback suffered on 18 October 2019, when the Council of Europe stopped the opening of accession negotiations for North Macedonia and Albania.[98]

With the name issue resolved, negotiations with the Patriarchate of Constantinople and the Serbian Orthodox Church resumed, in part to stem the North Macedonian Orthodox Church's attempt to obtain autocephaly through the Bulgarian Orthodox Church.[99]

After a series of lengthy meetings involving even high state officials and numerous difficulties compounded by the recognition of the autocephaly of the Ukrainian Orthodox Church, the Covid-19 pandemic, the death of Patriarch Irinej of Serbia, and the tensions that the Russian-Ukrainian crisis brought to the pan-Orthodox world, on 9 May 2022, the decision came.[100]

[95] G Cimbalo, 'Orthodox Autocephaly and Confessional Pluralism in North Macedonia' (2022) 13 *State, Churches, and Confessional Pluralism, Telematic Journal*. Available at: www.statoechiese.it.

[96] Ibid.

[97] Ibid.

[98] Ibid.

[99] Ibid. For further discussion see also *Kirchenstreit Nordmakedonien Der lange Weg der Makedonischen Orthodoxen Kirche zur Autokephalie* (2022), available at: www.noek.info/bilder/dossier/N%C3%96K_dossier_nordmakedonien_autokephalie3.pdf.

[100] Kirchenstreit Nordmakedonien (n 100).

The Patriarchate of Constantinople would have accepted the hierarchy, clergy, and laity of the North Macedonian Orthodox Church, under the name of the Church of 'Ohrid', thus 'healing the wound of schism'; the canonical territory of the Ohrid Orthodox Church would, however, be limited to the territory of the state of North Macedonia, although the Church has dioceses and hierarchs in North America, Europe and Australia. The words 'North Macedonia' or any variation thereof could not have been used in the name of the Church.[101]

This brings the rich American Canadian eparchies, the European eparchies, the eparchies of Australia and New Zealand, and the eparchies of Camberra, Australia and Tasmania under the direct management of the Patriarchate of Constantinople.[102]

After a few days the Moscow Patriarchate's reaction came, in the words of Nikolai Balasov, who defines the Constantinople's recognition of the North Macedonian Orthodox Church 'a blatantly politically motivated invasion of the competence of the Serbian Orthodox Church.'[103]

However, a few days later, in the sermon delivered during a joint liturgy held at St. Clement's Church of Ohrid in Skopje on 24 May 2022, the Serbian Orthodox Church, Mother Church of the North Macedonian Orthodox Church, unanimously recognised the autocephaly of the North Macedonian Orthodox Church – the Archbishopric of Ohrid.[104]

Less than a month later came Bulgaria's turn, although its synod left open the question of the name[105] and on 25 August 2022 the decision came from Moscow during the synod's regular session at the Stavropegial Danilov Monastery, chaired

[101] Cimbalo (n 96).

[102] ibid. Cimbalo explaining the phenomenon of direct management of eparchies abroad is quoted in full. 'The assignment of jurisdiction over the eparchies abroad of the North Macedonian Church to the Ecumenical Patriarchate constitutes for the latter a rich recompense for its efforts in recomposing the schism and supporting the granting of autocephaly. Indeed, it must be considered that the Ecumenical Patriarchate – lacking its own territory, and therefore its own members – claims jurisdiction over all the Orthodox of the Diaspora outside the canonical territory of its own national Church.

It is worth remembering that North Macedonia is a land of emigration, and that in the numerous and populous communities of migrants, ecclesiastical structures have been created over time that have provided the Church of the motherland with substantial remittances in foreign currency, coming from the donations of the believers, who were certainly financially in a better position than those who had remained in their homeland to live in a territory that is notoriously one of the poorest in the Balkan Peninsula. The proceeds of the operation and the conditions imposed by the Ecumenical Patriarchate thus constituted an undoubted economic advantage for its finances and an example of how to make the exercise of ecclesiastical power economically advantageous.

Moreover, this condition seems to be a constant in the Ecumenical Patriarchate's conduct when granting autocephaly. In fact, it was previously schismatic, in communion as an independent This decision creates an entirely new situation in the country and provides a solution to one of the "historical" controversies of Orthodoxy.' (Serbian and North Macedonian primates and hierarchs to concelebrate this week – orthochristian.com/146183.html).

[103] Orthodox Times, 25 May 2022. orthodoxtimes.com/patriarchate-of-moscow-the-recognition-by-the-serbian-orthodox-church-of-the-autocephaly-of-the-church-in-north-NorthMacedonia-is-a-joyful-event/.

[104] L Tano, 27 May 2022 *Serbian Patriarch Grants Independence to North Macedonian Church* (eastjournal.net).

[105] The Bulgarian Orthodox Church has some concerns on the name of the North Macedonian Orthodox Church, because it believes that the Ohrid Archdiocese is part of its ecclesiastical history, cf *The Battle*

by Patriarch Kirill. During that occasion, the members expressed hope that the North Macedonian Orthodox Church would firmly preserve the holy Orthodox faith in purity and integrity and observe fidelity to the Orthodox canonical tradition, deciding to notify Patriarch Porfirije of Serbia and Archbishop Stephan of North Macedonia of the decision of the Holy Synod,[106] which arrived to the latter on 8 September 2022.[107]

There is no doubt that this ecclesiastical-diplomatic dynamic should not be seen outside of the Russian invasion of Ukraine. In fact, in these months in which the autocephaly of the Ukrainian Orthodox Church is being debated in Orthodox world, the autocephaly of the Macedonian Orthodox Church appears as a laboratory.[108] Some analysts ask: why did the Russian Orthodox Church take this decision only now and not ten or fifteen years ago? And why did the Moscow Patriarchate quickly recognise the North Macedonian Orthodox Church in 2022?[109]

Belgrade, Moscow, and Constantinople seem to be fighting for supremacy in Balkan Orthodoxy, maintaining their established places as major players.[110]

The North Macedonian Church issue has thus already become central to this battle for supremacy, and in what manner, and how quickly, it is resolved and how quickly will determine what Balkan Orthodoxy will look like.[111]

In addition, the Serbian Patriarchate's granting of autocephaly to the North Macedonian Church, renamed the Orthodox Church of Ohrid, is taking place with a succession of rapid events on the canonical and liturgical level that have overshadowed the legal problems involved in the changes introduced in the status of the Orthodox Churches in North Macedonia.[112]

According to the current legislation, it is reasonable to assume that the Archbishopric of Ohrid will start procedures for the liquidation of its assets and activities, providing for the destination of the assets pertaining to the confession, which were conferred at the time of the signing of the Tomos that established it as a structure of the Serbian Orthodox Church, with authority over the entire North Macedonian territory. This heritage consists of monuments of inestimable value to the entire nation.[113]

of the Faith: The North Macedonian Church Question between the Moscow and Ecumenical Patriarchates at https://www.europeantimes.news/2022/09/the-battle-of-the-faith-the-North Macedonian -church-question-between-the-moscow-and-ecumenical-patriarchates/.

[106] Pan Orthodox Christian Society, 27 August 2022, ocpsociety.org/russian-orthodox-church-recognizes-the-autocephaly-of-the-North Macedonian -orthodox-church-ohrid-archbishopric/.

[107] *Преспанско – Пелагониска Православна Епархија* available at: www.pppe.mk/2022/pismo-od-ruskiot-patrijarh-kiril-do-arhiepiskopot-ohridski-i-makedonski-stefan/.

[108] Religious Information Service of Ukraine, 14 December 2022 available at: risu.ua/en/bulgarian-orthodox-church-recognized-the-serbian-pseudo-tomos-of-church-in-republic-of-north-macedonia_n134814.

[109] *The Battle of the Faith: The North Macedonian Church Question between the Moscow and Ecumenical Patriarchates* available at: https://www.europeantimes.news/2022/09/the-battle-of-the-faith-the-North Macedonian -church-question-between-the-moscow-and-ecumenical-patriarchates/ (n 106).

[110] *The Battle of the Faith* (n 106).

[111] Ibid.

[112] Cimbalo (n 96).

[113] Ibid.

In turn, the North Macedonian Orthodox Church will also have to provide notice of the cessation of its activities, using the same standards, communicating its return to communion with the Serbian Mother Church, in turn proceeding to inventory its property, which will be donated to the Mother Church.[114]

After that, the Synod of the Serbian Church and its Patriarch must grant the Eparchies located on the territory of North Macedonia to constitute themselves as the Ohrid Orthodox Church, to which the Serbian Church recognises autocephaly, through the issuance of a Tomos that will contain the definition of the canonical territory of the new religious entity and the indication of the goods attributed to it.[115]

Only at this point will the new religious entity be able to arrange for the registration of its denomination in the register of religious denominations, entering the full disposition of property, in accordance with the provisions of the North Macedonian law on religious freedom.[116]

To understand the complexity of the problem, it is enough to consider that in Ohrid alone there are 365 churches, several monasteries and ecclesiastical buildings of different nature and function, belonging to the two confessions, most of which preserve frescoes, artefacts, books and religious objects of historical and artistic value. In addition, there are currently around thirty active monasteries in the whole of North Macedonia, rich in works of art, and to which are connected the country's most important economic activities of guest accommodation and tourist services.[117]

5. The Bektashi Order and the Harabati Baba Teqqe

On the other hand, in Tetovo, North Macedonia, there is a large monastery nestled in the mountains that divide the small Balkan state from Kosovo. This religious complex is among the most important places of worship of one of the last Dervish communities of Europe, the Bektashi. The Islamic confraternity, headquartered in Albania, where they found refuge after being banned by Atatürk in 1925, is what remains of the Order of the Janissaries and has been a bridge between the Western Christianity and Eastern Islam for centuries.[118]

Representing both secular and modern Islam, the Bektashi have as their place of worship the *teqqe*, a walled complex that encloses prayer chapels, the dwelling of the Baba (their spiritual leader) and the graves of deceased clerics.[119]

Inside the *teqqe*, unlike a normal mosque, there are no minarets, and women and men meet and pray together, not disdaining a glass of rakija in moments of conviviality.

[114] Ibid.
[115] Ibid.
[116] Cimbalo (n 96).
[117] Ibid.
[118] Torta (n 13).
[119] Ibid.

Like all liberal and progressive Sufi confraternities, the Bektashi are very avowedly opposed by Wahhabi Islamism, which condemns them even more than Christians and Jews. If in Albania, the Order enjoys secular protection, gained actively since the second half of the nineteenth century for having taken part in the history of Albanian nationalism and the national liberation of the State, the same is not true in neighbouring North Macedonia, where it is opposed by the radical Islam brought in in the 1990s to fight the wars in former Yugoslavia.[120]

The Wahhabis in fact use the ethnic division of North Macedonia, where the Slav-North Macedonian, Orthodox community contrasts with the remaining 30 per cent of the population, Albanian and Muslim, to gain institutional ground. The difficulties in claiming a strong national identity make North Macedonia, historically torn apart by its neighbouring states, easy prey to the transnational interests of Islamic extremist fringes and the powers that use these movements.[121]

The episodes of violence against the Bektashi community have been numerous in the country's history. The worst one occurred after the brief war of 2001 when, in 2002, the historic Harabati Baba Teqqe in Tetovo was vandalised and partially occupied by Muslim radicals associated with the NLA (a North Macedonian group of the Uck, a paramilitary organisation active during and after the Kosovo conflict). Still in 2021, the Report on International Religious Freedom Report, denounced acts of vandalism at the Harabati Baba Teqqe and threats against the Bektashi community, which is strenuously fighting, also internationally, for institutional recognition.[122]

The government of North Macedonia, in fact, with a series of laws on the status of religious organisations that have followed one another since the end of the 1990s and culminated in the Law on the Status of Churches, Communities and Religious Groups of 2008, has taken an attitude of open favour towards Sunni Muslims, to the detriment of the Bektashi. In particular, through the mechanism of the single denomination, it denies recognition as a religious organisation to the Sufi Order.[123]

Through this instrument, the State de facto imposes the registration of only one organisation for each religious denomination, so that no registered religious groups can coexist that have in their name an identifying component of an already registered organisation, nor that use the words 'North Macedonia' and those derived from them for registration.[124]

However, many rights depend on registration, including even property rights.[125]

[120] Ibid.
[121] Ibid.
[122] *North Macedonia Report on International Religious Freedom*, (2021) available at: www.state.gov/wp-content/uploads/2022/05/NORTH-MACEDONIA-2021-INTERNATIONAL-RELIGIOUS-FREEDOM-REPORT.pdf.
[123] Ibid p 4.
[124] Torta (n 13).
[125] Ibid.

In practice, this extremely complex mechanism prevents the Bektashi Order from owning ecclesiastical property and from claiming that which was state-owned during the socialist era. In fact, by requisitioning it in 2002, the government gave the Islamic Community of North Macedonia (ICM), the only registered Islamic religious organisation in the country, a pro-government organisation with radical Islamist fringes within it, ownership of two Bektashi *teqqas*, including the one in Tetovo.[126]

At the international level, the case, as well as attracting strong criticism from organisations such as OSCE and the Helsinki Committee, came to the table of the European Court of Human Rights in 2013, which only in April 2018, given the political complexity of the case, issued a historic ruling in favour of the Order, accusing the government of violating the Edu Convention and obliging it to compensate the community.[127]

The Court's ruling came into effect on 10 September 2018 and the Bektashi community has reapplied for registration with the relevant institutions which to date have not yet proceeded with its recognition.[128]

It reads that 'there has been a violation of Article 11 of the Convention, read in the light of Article 9 in respect of the applicant association'.[129]

Also in 2018, on the occasion of the 480th anniversary of the Haraabati Baba Teqqe in Tetovo, the CMI signed a new agreement in Ankara with the Turkish International Cooperation Agency to renovate the monastery complex, without the consent of the Bektashi community.

Representatives of the Sufi Order continued to express concerns about its renovation, fearing that it was a tool for their definitive ouster from the monastery, but they were not given a voice, as it is an unregistered religious organisation.

Today, at the entrance of the Harabati Baba Teqqe there is a banner with the insignia of the ICM in Arabic and Albanian, which presents the international community with a grim reality: religious freedom, although loudly acclaimed, is still not sufficiently guaranteed. In North Macedonia, there are two main reasons for this crisis. Due to the economic difficulties that the country has had to face, the Muslim community has acted as a vehicle for international aid, sometimes of a fundamentalist Islamic matrix, sacrificing its own internal freedom; in addition, due to ethnic fragmentation, the Albanian community has also tried to find strength in radical Islamic identity, attracted by the wealth of Middle Eastern countries, which thus share very little ground with European Islam.[130]

However, beyond the reasons for this crisis of progressive Islam, which does not only involve North Macedonia, how can we be promoters of fundamental

[126] Ibid.

[127] Case of *Bektashi Community et al v The Former Yugoslav Republic of Macedonia*, at hudoc.echr.coe.int/fre#{%22itemid%22:[%22001-182170%22]}.

[128] See also www.state.gov/wp-content/uploads/2022/05/NORTH-MACEDONIA-2021-INTERNATIONAL-RELIGIOUS-FREEDOM-REPORT.pdf.

[129] Case (n 129).

[130] Ibid.

freedoms, protecting those communities, such as the Bektashi Order in front of the disapplication of ECtHR rulings and numerous international reports? Especially when representing minorities means addressing politics and international relations that are frequently difficult.

6. In Conclusion

In light of what has been observed, the transfer of ecclesiastical heritage and especially of the places of worship to the new orthodox confessional organisation in the country appears to be very articulated and complex. This is even more so if considering that it must be done in compliance with Article 22 of the North Macedonian Law on Religious Freedom, which states that:

> religious communities, i.e. religious groups, may, in accordance with the law, own and acquire ownership of real estate and other means necessary to carry out their activities. For the construction or acquisition of a structure intended for the performance of religious works and rites, in addition to the conditions determined by law, the religious community, that is, the religious group, is obliged to provide a positive opinion of the organisation in charge of religious community and religious group affairs.[131]

It is difficult, especially in the present historical moment, to predict how and when such bureaucratic procedures will be implemented and who will benefit from the steps that ecclesiastical property will have to go through before being conferred to the newly formed Orthodox Church.

On the other hand, there is an imbalance whereby an important part of the North Macedonian Islamic tradition is still not recognised. In fact, from the Orthodox point of view, even if only thanks to ecclesiastic policies, the division is getting resolved.

Instead, on the Islamic side, there is a progressive isolation of progressive and laic Bektashi Order that, besides being worrying, risks exacerbating the ethnic conflict between Macedonians and Albanians.

Hopefully, in a short time, the Republic of North Macedonia and religious communities will find an effective solution to these divisions, which are a laboratory for international conflicts, avoiding the discrimination of minority communities that results from them. It would thus find greater internal political stability to such an extent that it would finally become independent of external interference in the country, thus making its entry into the European Union possible as a country pacified in its ethnic and religious conflicts.

[131] North Macedonian Religious Freedom Law of su licodu.cois.it/?cat=14&paged=18&lang=en, Database ed by G Cimbalo.

PART 3

Procedural Rights – Access to Justice

10

Blast from the Past – Consumer Collective Redress in Serbia

BRANKA BABOVIC VUKSANOVIC

1. Introduction

This chapter will examine the relationship between the rule of law principle and the human rights underpinning it, using consumers' right to a fair trial in the Republic of Serbia as an example. The Constitution of the Republic of Serbia defines that the rule of law is underpinned by inalienable human rights, including the right to a fair trial. It will also analyse whether legislative changes concerning consumer collective redress have affected how the right to a fair trial is exercised and the effects on the rule of law principle and the relationship between individuals.

The problem of mass claims before Serbian courts is identified as a symptom of procedural inadequacies. A lawsuit deluge occurred in various cases before Serbian courts, causing a huge backlog that jeopardises exercising the right to a trial within a reasonable time in litigation proceedings. In light of this reality, there will be analysis of whether the Republic of Serbia is acting upon the interpretation of the right to a fair trial contained in the European Court of Human Rights (ECtHR)'s judgments. According to the ECtHR's jurisprudence, states are responsible for organising their judiciary so as not to give rise to any infringement of the right to a trial within a reasonable time due to an excessive influx of cases.[1] One of the reasons for the problem with the mass claims could be the elimination of existing collective redress mechanisms from the Serbian judiciary and deterrence from introducing new (different[2]) ones.

Namely, the first legal concept which expanded consumer access to justice to be introduced into civil proceedings was the organisational claim. However, the provisions of the Civil Procedure Act (CPA) stipulating organisational claims were

[1] *Zimmermann and Steiner v Switzerland* App no 8737/79 (EHRR, 13 July 1983), para 22. The court excludes temporary backlog in the courts provided 'that they take with the requisite promptness, remedial action to deal with an exceptional situation of this kind'. In the Republic of Serbia, the courts' backlog due to mass claims has been a reality for years.

[2] Judicial associations in Serbia are promoting the test case proceedings as a possible resolution to the mass claims problem instead of the organisational claim which was once part of the Serbian law.

subsequently abolished by a Constitutional Court decision. Later on, the legislator introduced administrative proceedings for the protection of the collective interests of consumers before the Ministry of Trade, Tourism and Services (the Ministry). This created difficulties in the pending litigation proceedings because the courts have been dismissing organisational claims due to the unconstitutionality of the procedural law. Furthermore, the collective redress before the Ministry, which is not an independent body, is not as effective as in the litigation proceedings.

Even though the provisions of the CPA concerning the organisational claim had many flaws, the Constitutional Court Decision was neither right nor appropriately reasoned. This chapter will also assess if these legislative changes have negatively affected the obligation of the Republic of Serbia to adjust its acts with the ECtHR's jurisprudence in terms of the extent to which the right to a fair trial is applied in the administrative proceedings. According to the jurisprudence of the ECtHR, it would be deemed contrary to the spirit of the European Convention on Human Rights (ECHR) if states shifted competence from one type of proceedings to another where the guarantee of the right to a fair trial would not apply to the same extent. Finally, the chapter assesses how exercising the right to a fair trial in the light of consumer collective redress legislative changes reflects on the relationship between consumers and traders. It will show that that relationship has tilted in favour of traders and to consumers' detriment.

2. Overburdened Judiciary

In recent years one of the most apparent problems of the Serbian judiciary has been the issue of mass claims. In the first instance courts in Belgrade in 2021, each judge was assigned an average of 2,500 cases with a monthly influx of 200 new cases.[3] The collective redress mechanisms, which are the usual procedural tools for mass claims, did not take root in the Serbian legal system. The only existing mechanism to enable deciding on several such claims in a single proceeding is the joinder of proceedings. However, a joinder is suitable only for several claims and not for mass infringement resulting in thousands of cases.

Mass claims drew public attention for the first time in the famous case of Swiss Franc (CHF)-indexed loans. This case concerns actions to terminate CHF-indexed loan agreements due to unfair contractual terms. Loans indexed in stable foreign currency, usually CHF, were very popular in many Central and Eastern European countries, and occasionally in Western Europe because the interest rate was lower than for the same loans expressed in national currency.[4] However, the problem arose when the CHF exchange rate started to go up, thereby driving an increase in

[3] According to the information provided by the Association of Judges and Prosecutor in Serbia (www.ust.rs/saopstenja-za-javnost-21-03.html).

[4] European Parliament Research Service, '*Unfair terms in Swiss Francs Loans- Overview of the European Court of Justice Case Law- Briefing for the European Parliament*', March 2021, (www.europarl.europa.eu/RegData/etudes/BRIE/2021/689361/EPRS_BRI(2021)689361_EN.pdf) 1–2.

loan obligations. Due to a huge influx of these cases in Serbia, the association of financial service users Efektiva filed an organisational claim regarding loan agreements in CHF. This case was completed on a procedural matter.[5]

Following the Constitutional Court decision repealing the entire chapter governing collective redress, the Court dismissed the claim in this case.[6] Resolution of the cases derived from the CHF-indexed loans followed in individual proceedings. Even though there was no collective redress mechanism in place, the borrowers who were parties to the individual disputes came together and protested in the streets of Belgrade. The protest took place in front of the Supreme Court of Cassation, demanding that this court resolves their problem in a consistent manner.[7]

The troubles did not end there. A series of mass claims occurred before Serbian courts. What followed was a deluge of more than 13,000 claims for damage compensation due to unlawfully overpaid kindergarten fees filed by parents against the City of Belgrade and kindergartens.[8] In these cases, the disputable issue was how to qualify the claim, and hence what limitation period would apply. Should the claims be qualified as damage compensation, the shorter limitation period applies and the parents could be compensated only partially. The Supreme Court of Cassation had taken the position that all these claims had been founded and qualified as claims for damages.

This case also identifies the need for action by associations rather than individuals. In this case, the parents addressed the public, noting that they had not had timely information on whether the fee had been unlawful. Following the position of the Supreme Court of Cassation, the kindergartens did offer settlements. However, the settlements were not widely accepted because the parents brought actions for unjustified enrichment, trying to gain full compensation for the period for which the compensation of damages would be time-barred. Afterwards, the Serbian judiciary dealt with several mass claims and some courts were almost blocked constantly.[9]

Some of the mass claims were between consumers and traders, but not all. Mass claims were present in different areas of law. The most remarkable cases were lawsuits of army retirees for incomplete payment of pensions, lawsuits against the National Employment Agency for the incomplete payment of unemployment benefits, lawsuits for the reimbursement of the unlawful loan processing fees, and lawsuits against the Post of Serbia for unlawfully collected fees from the retirees.[10]

[5] B Babović, 'Zaštita kolektivnih interesa potrošača' (2014) 2 *Anali PFB* 216.

[6] For example, in Croatia, the first organisational claim was also the action to ascertain the unfair contractual terms in CHF-indexed loan agreements as null and void: E Mišćenić and S Petrić, *Nepoštenost valutne klauzule u CHF I HRK/CHF kreditima*, (Zagreb, Narodne novine, 2020).

[7] Just how high a pressure was put on by the public is also attested to by the fact that the Serbian President talked to these protesters in the streets of Belgrade (www.bbc.com/serbian/lat/balkan-47659600).

[8] Information available at the legal news portal Paragraf Lex (paragraflex.rs/dnevne-vesti/160118/160118-vest10.html).

[9] The biggest backlog occurred in Belgrade because of the wide jurisdiction of its basic courts, information provided by the Association of Judges and Prosecutor in Serbia (www.ust.rs/saopstenja-za-javnost-21-03.html).

[10] The data is available at the website of the Association of Judges and Prosecutors in Serbia (http://ust.rs/saopstenja-za-javnost-21-03.html).

Many of these lawsuits were filed by socially endangered categories of citizens against public entities. The amounts claimed were often small. This clearly shows a need for legal aid, which could be provided by associations or ombudsmen entitled to file a claim in the collective redress proceedings.

Instead of associations, ombudsmen, or other entities, the claims are now usually filled by attorneys attracted to the prospect of easy money. In practice, for some attorneys-at-law, the collection of compensation of costs became easy money in litigations that required a mere reproduction of previous cases. That launched specific 'guerrilla' tactics[11] aimed at nothing other than multiplying the claims through various cases of abuse of procedural law, for example bringing several actions for each of the claims that can otherwise be accumulated. This led to the set-up of various associations for representations in mass disputes, with a mission to encourage citizens to lodge lawsuits in mass cases. The idea was to have as many reimbursements of the costs of proceedings collected once the judgments are final.[12] The parties to reimburse the costs of the proceedings if the case is won were the banks, large companies, or the government. One could also note procedural frauds using fake powers of attorney[13] of individuals who were not aware of being a party to a proceeding. Apart from that, the same court experts usually multiplied their opinion in many cases benefiting from the fact the same- type cases are dealt with separately.

All of this resulted in mass claims being the major problem of the Serbian judiciary, causing court inefficiency.[14] At the same time, the provisions concerning collective protection in litigation were gradually abolished, at first from the Civil Proceedings Act, and then from the Consumer Protection Act. The Gender Equality Act is the most recent one that has undergone amendments in that respect.[15]

3. Introduction of Consumer Collective Redress into Serbian Law

In order to understand the dynamics of mass claims in Serbia, context is needed on the introduction of collective redress into Serbian law. The emphasis was put on consumer protection.

[11] The term is relatively new, see G Horwath and S Wilske (eds), *Guerilla Tactics in International Arbitration*, (Alphen aan den Rijn, Kluwer, 2013).

[12] There are proposals to combat these guerrilla tactics through legislative changes in Serbia which are focused on reforming the cost reimbursement system in small claims proceedings.

[13] This was brought up by the Judges' Association of Serbia in their Recommendations for the draft Law on amendments to the Civil Procedure Act in 2021, available at www.sudije.rs/Dokumenta/Objave/2021%2003%2003%20Dru%C5%A1tvo%20sudija%20Srbije%20-%20sugestije%20u%20vezi%20sa%20izmenama%20ZPP.pdf.

[14] According to the information provided by the Association of Judges and Prosecutors in Serbia, judges in Belgrade based courts were assigned with more than 2,500 cases, while there was a monthly influx of 200 cases (in 2021), available at: www.ust.rs/saopstenja-za-javnost-21-03.html.

[15] The 2009 Act provided for an organisational claim and was changed in 2021.

The 2010 Consumer Protection Act[16] (2010 CPA) introduced collective redress into litigation proceedings. It authorised 'those associations whose aim of association or activity' concerns the issues of interest for a greater number of consumers[17] to seek an injunction in litigation proceedings,[18] provided that these proceedings are subject to the provisions of the Civil Procedure Act mutatis mutandis. At the time when the 2010 CPA was adopted, the Civil Procedure Act did not contain any provision concerning collective redress, but it was introduced into litigation proceedings in 2011. Specifically, in the Civil Procedure Act, a special chapter on collective redress[19] was included providing for the 'claim for the protection of collective rights and interest' which was an organisational claim. However, after sparse case law[20] in this area, the Constitutional Court repealed the provisions of the Civil Procedure Act governing the organisational claim.

The rationale of the Constitutional Court Decision contains many unusual statements. First of all, the reason for the Constitutional Court's conclusion that the provisions on the organisational claim are vague, and as such imprecise and unconstitutional, is that the precise nature of the collective interest that should be protected by such a claim is not legally defined.[21] In this decision, the Constitutional Court first states that the definitions of collective rights and interests do not exist in the stated provisions and that there are no references to other acts which would define this term. Nevertheless, in order to find the definition of collective rights and interests in Serbian legislation, the Constitutional Court attempts to equate this term with some of the existing ones, such as the term 'group' in the context of anti-discrimination legislation. Since analogy with the term 'group' is impossible, the Constitutional Court concludes that the provisions concerning the organisational claim are vague, unspecific and therefore unconstitutional.[22] Based on the statement that the term 'collective rights and interests' is vague, the Constitutional Court also finds that the provision authorising the associations to file the organisational claim is unconstitutional because the associations 'do not organise to exercise collective rights, but to achieve goals that are non-profit, i.e. that are of common interest'. It is clear that the Constitutional court supports the decision of unconstitutionality with the notion that the term 'collective rights and interest' was neither regulated nor clear to the court.[23]

Furthermore, the Constitutional Court states that it arises out of the Civil Procedure Act that litigation protects individual subjective rights, therefore it excludes the protection of collective rights and interests (however defined) from

[16] Serbian 2010 Consumer Protection Act.
[17] Art 129(2) of the 2010 CPA.
[18] Art 137 of the 2010 CPA.
[19] Serbian Constitutional Court Decision IUz. 51/2012 of 23 May 2012.
[20] According to available information there were only two proceedings: B Babović (n 5) 215–218.
[21] For more information see: B Babović (n 5) 215–218.
[22] Serbian Constitutional Court Decision IUz. 51/2012 of 23 May 2012.
[23] As opposed to that, Serbian legal litarature already had scholarship that tried to provide the definition of 'collective rights and interest', M Jovanović, 'Opšti pogled na koncepte' in M Jovanović (ed), *Kolektivna prava: Pozitivna diskriminacija u ustavnopravnom sistemu Republike Srbije*, (Belgrade, Sluzbeni glasnik, 2009).

civil proceedings.[24] In addition to this, the Constitutional Court also states in its findings that the entire chapter governing the organisational claim is not clear, specific, or predictable enough to provide guidelines to citizens on the required conduct. For the same reason the Constitutional Court finds that the provisions concerning collective redress contained in the 2011 Civil Procedure Act do not comply with the ECtHR. The Constitutional Court stated that these provisions do not have those characteristics which, according to the case law of the ECtHR, all acts must contain to comply with the rule of law principle. At the same time, the Constitutional Court cites out of context[25] the case law of the ECtHR, applying the conclusions from the decisions *Silver et al v United Kingdom* (1983)[26] and the judgment in the case *Sunday Times v The United Kingdom* (1979)[27] to support its stance that the provisions concerning collective citizens' interests and rights are not clear enough. Throughout the decision of the Constitutional Court, the prevailing argument is that the term 'collective citizens' rights and interests' is vague. Furthermore, the Constitutional Court pointed out that the litigation proceedings are reserved for the protection of individual citizens' rights. The Constitutional Court is not alone in that perspective.

Following the adoption of this decision, the Consumer Protection Act was also amended. The 2010 CPA contained provisions concerning the protection of collective citizens' rights and interests in litigation proceedings. However, soon after the Constitutional Court Decision, the 2010 CPA was amended to prescribe the protection of the collective interests of consumers in administrative proceedings instead of the protection of the collective interests of consumers in litigation proceedings. Within the statement of reasons attached to the Draft Law, it was stated that provisions on collective redress were drafted in line with the Directive 2009/22/EC,[28] but in a way that is in accordance with the characteristics and needs of Serbia's legal system.[29]

As a result of such an approach, consumer collective redress was implemented in an unusual way. The competence was conferred on the Ministry of Trade, Tourism and Services. It was provided that the proceedings were to be instituted either *ex officio* or by authorised parties or consumer associations duly registered with the Ministry. On the issue of competent authority, the law diverged from the provisions of the Directive 2009/22/EC without specifying which interest of the Serbian legal system it served. One can conclude from the statement of reasons within the Consumer Protection Act 2014 (2014 CPA) that the protection of the collective interests of consumers helps in reaching a higher level of consumer protection in practice. In that same *actit* is emphasised that these provisions put in place a

[24] ibid.

[25] For more information see A Jakšić, *Građansko procesno pravo* (Belgrade, Pravni fakultet Univerziteta u Beogradu, 2018) 774–775.

[26] *Silver et al v United Kingdom* App no 5947/72 (EHRR, 24 October 1983).

[27] *Sunday Times v The United Kingdom* App no 6538/74 (EHRR, 6 November 1980).

[28] Ministry of Justice of the Republic of Serbia, *Statement of Reasons to the Draft Consumer Protection Act of the Republic of Serbia* (Belgrade 2014), 120.

[29] Directive 2009/22/EC of the European Parliament and the Council of 23 April 2009 on injunction for the protection of consumer interests.

system that uses a wide range of institutions in charge of consumer protection.[30] As an advantage of the administrative proceedings over the previously applicable court proceedings, CCP 2014 states the administrative proceedings being faster and more efficient than the court proceedings.[31] These provisions also introduce the definition of the collective interest of consumers, and a positive one at that.[32]

Even though the 2014 CPA statement of reasons does not say so, it seems that these provisions complied with the requirements in the statement of reasons in the Constitutional Court Decision declaring the Civil Proceedings Act provisions unconstitutional. At first, the notion of collective interest was defined through a definition, unlike the provisions of the directive that was complied with. However, a positive definition was subsequently also introduced into EU law.

What followed was the introduction of the administrative proceedings instead of litigation. However, the claims being decided in these proceedings, such as the nullity of unfair contractual terms, are by their legal nature such as to be decided by a court in litigation.[33] Apart from that, the directive does note that the proceedings for the protection of collective citizens' rights and interests may also be conducted as administrative proceedings, but this issue has not been further specified. Looking at the text of Directive 2009/22/EC, Recital 9 of the Preamble, we can see that the administrative authority means 'administrative authorities competent to rule on the proceedings referred to in this Directive.' Such competence should be statutory, but primarily it must by its nature correspond to the competence of the authority which is stipulated to rule. From the experience in comparative law, it will most frequently be an ombudsman or other independent body. The exercise of such function by a ministry is not found in any EU country.

The authorities that rule on administrative proceedings are normally competent for regulatory redress. These are commonly a sectoral regulatory authority or a consumer law enforcement authority. From the experience of the EU countries these bodies rarely impose any measures, but they usually act to have a deal brokered between the trader and the consumer.[34] Such bodies are often authorised to institute a class action before the court.[35] They are seldom authorised to impose civil sanctions. There are exceptions to this rule, though. The Environment Agency and the English Nature which were the first agencies in the UK on which such authority was conferred in 2010.[36]

[30] Ministry of Justice of the Republic of Serbia, *Statement of Reasons to the Draft Consumer Protection Act of the Republic of Serbia* (Belgrade 2014) 120.

[31] ibid 121.

[32] The then-applicable Directive 2009/22/EC contained a negative definition. This definition was subsequently criticised, and a positive definition was introduced into EU law within the 'New Deal for Consumers', H Missiak, 'The Collective Interest of Consumers: New Definition, New Weaknesses', (2019) 6 *European Review of Private Law* 1329.

[33] M Karanikić Mirić, 'Kolektivna zaštita potrošača u srpskom pravu' (2014) 14 *Anali Pravnog fakulteta Univerziteta u Zenici* 57.

[34] C Hodges, S Voet, *Delivering Collective Redress – New Technologies*, (Oxford, Hart Publishing, 2018) 289.

[35] It is the case with Consumer Ombudsman in Denmark or Finland, ibid 160–166.

[36] ibid 207.

While the provisions of the 2011 Civil Procedure Act concerning the organisational claim were applicable, only two proceedings were instituted. The most notable proceedings were conducted for the claim filed by the association of financial service users Efektiva regarding loan agreements in CHF. This case was completed on a procedural matter.[37] Following the Constitutional Court decision repealing the entire chapter governing *collective redress*, the Court dismissed the claim in this case. It is noteworthy that the first instance court, as well as the court deciding on the appeal against dismissal of the claim, demonstrated a misunderstanding of the term 'collective redress' in consumer law.

The court dismissed the claim filed by Efektiva on the grounds of the unconstitutionality of the organisational claim. This decision was based on the provisions of the Law on Constitutional Court, which prescribes that the law cannot apply after the declaration of its unconstitutionality. The only exception to this rule is a situation in which the judgment based on that law has become final already. However, this exception could not apply because the proceedings were at their initial stage. Efektiva appealed against the decision of the first instance court, and the appeal was rejected. This decision was never challenged on the grounds of violating the right to a fair trial. Furthermore, the proceedings before the ECtHR were never instituted. According to the case law of ECtHR, infringement of Article 6(1) exists when legislative changes affected the course of the proceedings before a national court. The changes in the law while the case is pending, which make the case unwinnable, could be considered a reason for the infringement of Article 6(1) ECHR. However, the research could not identify a case law similar to this one when the Constitutional court declared the unconstitutionality of the procedural law.

Many flaws can be found in the provisions of the 2011 Civil Procedure Act the introduced the organisational claim. Nevertheless, the Constitutional Court decision that established the noncompliance of the 2011 CPA provisions with the Constitution and the ratified international agreements was based on the misunderstanding of 'collective redress', and also contains other flawed wording and contradictions. The legislative changes that followed, have affected both the role of the consumer associations in protecting the collective rights and interests of consumers as well as the effectiveness of collective redress in the Serbian legal system.

4. The Role of Consumer Associations in Protecting the Collective Interests of Consumers in Serbia

The decision of the Constitutional Court stated that the consumer associations are neither organised to file the claims for the protection of collective rights and interest, nor is the litigation suitable for the protection of the collective rights of consumers, while the term 'collective rights and interests' remains unclear.

[37] Babović (n 5) 216.

Following this decision, consumer collective redress became administrative while consumer organisations are entitled to initiate the proceedings before the Ministry. The Constitutional Court made its decision based on the tradition, and the legislator based on the 'characteristics' of the Serbian law.

There is, indeed, a tradition in the field of consumer protection in Serbia. The protection of the common interests of consumers in the Republic of Serbia dates back to the 1970s. Consumer organisations[38] were in charge of consumer protection as early as the 1970s in then Socialist Federal Republic of Yugoslavia (SFRY). The 1974 SFRY Constitution was the first in the world to prescribe that consumer organisations are the ones that protect consumer interests, inter alia, by entering into statutory prescribed types of agreements with other organisations and communities regarding transactions of common interest.[39] This principle was specified by means of laws so that consumer organisations were to agree with traders not only on product ranges and product and service prices, but also on other major issues, including mutual relationships between consumer organisations and traders.[40] In peoples' democracies, as defined by socialist elites, law required that legally binding agreements be made regarding social needs, including consumer needs.

Namely, in the SFRY era, both property and interests were common, social, and the economy was planned. Therefore, in a planned economy and one-party system, consumer organisations were in charge of protecting the common interests of consumers but had no *locus standi* before the court. Their activities fell under the domain of socialist self-management and administrative law. This was, also, in line with the national procedural law tradition, according to which a claim in litigation proceedings was filed for the protection of subjective civil rights in a two-party dispute.

Following the break-up of the SFRY, there was no mention of the protection of the collective interests of consumers in Serbia until as late as 2010. During the 1990s in Serbia, as well as other countries resulting from the breakup of the SFRY, the transition process started, followed by European integration. These changes brought about an influx of concepts foreign to the legal tradition of a country undergoing transition. The legal practice of the EU countries on representative actions in litigation proceedings,[41] particularly the organisational claim began to be replication by post-socialist countries.[42]

The idea of such legal concepts in western democratic capitalist societies, that Serbia transitions into, is to use procedural law to ensure that, after the proceedings,

[38] In the socialist self-management era these were organisations in charge of protecting consumer interests.

[39] 1974 SFRY Constitution.

[40] For more information see D Denković, *Zaštita potro,šača u pravu SFRJ* (Belgrade, Pravni fakultet, 1974).

[41] M Cappelletti, *International Encyclopaedia of Comparative Law, Volume XVI, Civil procedure*, (Tübingen, Mohr Siebeck, 2014) 66.

[42] In Serbian legislation, the representative actions were firstly introduced in the antidiscrimination acts in 2009.

'policies sought to be accomplished by law' are implemented.[43] Finally, it was back in the 1970s when it became obvious that the consumers and other beneficiaries of the law in the Western welfare state, were the ones who would least frequently resort to bringing an action before the court to protect their rights. It was established that there was a disproportion between the need for redress and meeting that need, i.e. access to justice'[44] This led to the change in the rules of the civil procedure through derogations from previously applicable principles. For this very reason, consumer associations have been granted *locus standi* before the court as the most appropriate method to protect collective rights and interests.

As opposed to that, in socialist Serbia, as already described, even though consumer associations, had a role in governing relationships with traders, consumer associations did not have *locus standi* before the court.[45] However, in the chaotic process of Serbia's transition, the idea to extend the right of access to justice (of consumers) by means of the organisational claim has taken on a different form. The Republic of Serbia first saw the introduction of the organisational claim for the protection of the collective interests of consumers. What followed was the finding of the Constitutional Court that such provisions were unconstitutional. The legislator, upon this finding, introduced administrative proceedings for the protection of the collective rights and interests of consumers.

In Serbia, *locus standi* was first extended to consumer associations only to be revoked due to tradition in procedural law. Returning to a tradition that was shaped in a different kind of society has resulted in losing what is perhaps the most significant advantage of consumer collective redress – extending access to justice. That way, Serbia is denied what the main advantage of the organisational claim is. As part of the 'access to justice movement'[46] the organisational claim allows consumers and environmentalists improved access to justice, even though such a method often encroaches upon the traditional setting of the litigation proceedings.

According to the current legislation, Consumer organisations are not entitled to initiate litigation proceedings for the protection of collective rights, but they are entitled to initiate administrative proceedings before the Ministry. However, the scope of the protection is not the same, and neither are the effects of the final administrative decision and the final judgment. The guarantees contained within the right to a fair trial are not exercised to the same extent.

5. Right to a Fair Trial

The fact that the proceedings for the protection of the collective rights and interests of consumers are now defined as administrative proceedings does not mean that

[43] Cappelletti (n 41) 66–67.
[44] ibid 67.
[45] ibid.
[46] ibid.

they are excluded from the scope of application of the right to a fair trial. As early as the 1970s, the ECtHR took the position that Article 6(1) of the ECHR shall be applied every time when it is decided on human rights and obligations, irrespective of the type of proceedings deciding on it.[47] The condition for the application of Article 6(1) of the ECHR is that a dispute regarding civil rights and obligations exists; in this case, a dispute exists between consumers and a trader. It is clear that disputes of this type fall under the scope of Article 6(1) ECHR, but it is not clear whether the legislative changes in Serbia affected the scope of the guarantees to the right to the fair trial. Furthermore, since the case *Golder v United Kingdom*[48] it would be deemed contrary to the spirit of the ECHR if states shifted competence from one type of proceedings to another where the guarantee of the right to a fair trial would not apply to the same extent. It remains that we examine whether any of these proceedings provided a broader scope of rights than another,[49] i.e. whether the proceedings for the protection of collective citizens' rights and interests in the administrative proceedings have been written in compliance with the guarantee of the right to a fair trial.

5.1. Access to Justice

The provisions of the Civil Procedure Act on consumer collective redress extended the scope of the right of access to justice, in that associations were authorised to file the organisational claim. That way the scope of remedies protecting consumer rights and interests was expanded. Furthermore, their abolition by the Constitutional Court as unspecific and insufficiently clear for citizens to be able to align their conduct with them is neither right nor appropriately reasoned.[50] The change in the type of proceedings that followed also included a change in the scope of claims that could be filed.

In proceedings before a civil court, it was provided that a plaintiff may seek: 1) prohibition of undertaking any activities threatening to infringe citizens' rights and interests which the plaintiff is legally authorised to protect; 2) remedy of an existing infringement of collective citizens' rights and interests or adverse effects from the defendant's conduct, and restoration to a previous state, a state where such infringement could no longer occur or a state closely corresponding to the state prior to such infringement; 3) ascertaining impermissibility of the activity having infringed collective citizens' interests and rights; 4) publication of the

[47] *Ringeisen v Austria* App no 2614/65 (EHRR, 22 June 1972), *König v Deutschland* App no 6232/73 (EHRR, 10 March 1980).

[48] *Golder v United Kingdom* App no 4451/07 (EHRR, 21 February 1975), para 18.

[49] A Uzelac, 'Pravo na pošteno suđenje: opći i građanskopravni aspekti čl.6 st.1 Europske konvencije za zaštitu ljudskih prava i temeljnih sloboda', in I Radačić (ed) *Usklađenost hrvatskog zakona i prakse sa standardima Europske konvencije za zaštitu ljudskih prava i temeljnih sloboda* (Zagreb, Centar za mirovne studije, 2010) 92.

[50] A Jakšić, *Građansko procesno pravo* (Belgrade, Pravni fakultet Univerziteta u Beogradu, 2018) 774–775.

judgment adopting the statement of claim for the reasons referred to in points 1) to 3) of this Article in the media, at the defendant's expense.[51]

For administrative proceedings, the scope of measures to be imposed is also broadly prescribed. Therefore, an administrative authority may order that the person against whom proceedings have been conducted adopt specific behaviour or that such person be prohibited specific behaviour, in particular that such person: 1) cease infringing the provisions of the Consumer Protection Act jeopardising a collective interest of consumers and refrain from any such future infringement; 2) remedy any irregularity found; and 3) without delay, suspend contracting any unfair contractual provisions. The administrative authority's decisions are also published if a measure has been imposed. If a claim is not meritorious or a trader has remedied its behaviour, the decision is not published.

The current provisions of the Consumer Protection Act relate solely to the rights contained within that act. That way, the entire categories of consumers like the consumers of financial services are denied access to collective redress mechanism, because their rights are regulated by the Law on the Protection of Financial Service Consumers,[52] and not by the Law on Consumer Protection.[53]

5.2. Right to be Heard before an Independent Tribunal

The issue of independence is more challenging since the competence was shifted from litigation proceedings before the civil court to administrative proceedings before the Ministry. Comparative law contains examples of the protection of the collective rights of consumers in administrative proceedings. The example is the Directive of the European Parliament and of the Council on representative actions for the protection of the collective interests of consumers, which refers to a court or an administrative authority interchangeably. Thus, the protection of the collective interests of consumers is usually brought before the court or ombudsman or regulatory body. However, when quasi-judicial powers are conferred on other authorities and organisations, those authorities and organisations must be independent from the executive.[54] The Ministry is not independent from the executive and it is not a regulatory body. Even though a ministry has a regulatory role in different situations, such a role is not identical to that of an independent agency.

The independence of the executive branch is also a condition for applying the provision of Article 6(1) of the ECHR. To allow for the provision protecting the right to a fair trial to be applied to administrative proceedings, it is necessary that

[51] Art 498 of the 2011 Civil Procedure Act.

[52] The 2011 Law on the Protection of Financial Service Consumers.

[53] Art 4 of the CPA explicitly stipulates that the protection of financial services consumers is regulated by the separate law.

[54] M Allena, F Goisis, 'Full jurisdiction under article 6 ECHR: Hans Kelsen v the principle of separation of powers' (2020) 26(2) *European Public Law* 288.

the acting authority is independent from the executive.[55] A ministry, by its nature, is anything but independent. In practice, the proceedings are conducted before the Consumer Protection Department. However, this department is a functioning unit within the Ministry of Trade, Tourism, and Services, managed by an Assistant Minister. Therefore, an independent tribunal is not guaranteed.

5.3. Effectiveness of the Collective Redress in Administrative Proceedings

It is questionable whether the administrative proceedings described above are effective in addressing the challenges of collective redress and consumer protection. Access to justice is effective if the court decision is properly enforced.[56] The situation with the enforcement of the Ministry's decision in collective redress proceedings is a bit more complicated. The Ministry is entitled to impose administrative measures against the trader. If a trader fails to act on the measure imposed by the Ministry, the misdemeanour proceedings are instituted by the Ministry, However, the injured party, under the Misdemeanour Act, is also entitled to initiate the misdemeanour proceeding. Even though the Ministry is obligated to inform the injured party if it institutes the proceedings, the party does not influence the course of the proceedings.

Contrary to the enforcement of the judgment rendered in litigation proceedings, a three-year limitation period may apply.[57] According to the Serbian Misdemeanour Act and the CPA,[58] the limitation period could be in the course of misdemeanour proceedings. It is often the case when the service of process is not successful.[59] Therefore, it is possible that if the court is not efficient enough that the imposed measure is never enforced, and the fine is never paid. If the trader acts contrary to the measure for the protection of the collective interests of consumers, it commits an infringement subject to a fine ranging from RSD 300,000 to 2,000,000 (approximately EUR 2,500 to EUR 17,000). Even if the fine is paid by the trader, the sums in question are not big enough to prevent the traders from mass infringement of consumer law. There is no data about whether misdemeanour penalties have ever been imposed for this type of infringement.

Another reason why misdemeanour courts in Serbia are not a good choice for the enforcement of consumer collective redress is that these courts do not have specialised departments. Instead, any judge may be assigned any case which

[55] ibid.

[56] B Rainey, P McCormick, C Ovey, *Jacobs, White, and Ovey: The European Convention on Human Rights* (Oxford, Oxford University Press, 2020) 298.

[57] Art 190(1) of the 2014 CPA.

[58] Art 190 (2) CPA.

[59] I Vuković, *Prekršajno pravo*, (Belgrade, Pravni fakultet Univerziteta u Beogradu, 2015) 142.

could be a cause of procedural inefficiency.[60] Therefore, the measures for infringing collective citizens' rights and interests, which are quite rare and untypical cases, are adjudicated by a judge usually competent for any of the typical misdemeanour cases.[61] The sparse case law does not provide enough information about the quality of decisions in this area of law which is quite uncommon in the misdemeanour courts.

5.4. Right to a Trial within a Reasonable Time

Excessive length of the proceedings is one of the most frequently claimed aspects of the right to a fair trial before the ECtHR.[62] The length of the proceedings is not just an occasional problem for the Serbian judiciary, but a systemic one.[63] The court that is overburdened with a series of mass claims cannot process any case efficiently. According to the case law of the ECtHR, backlog before a national court as a symptom of systemic judicial inefficiency does not justify the unreasonable length of the proceedings.[64] One of the reasons stated in the Statement of reasons to the Draft 2014 CPA was that administrative proceedings for the protection of collective rights and interests are not as long as litigation proceedings.[65]

However, Serbia failed at dealing with a deluge of same-type cases before civil courts. Thus, the litigation proceedings are blocked due to an enormous backlog of cases with identical claims,[66] and often the same defendant, resulting in overloaded courts and an inability to act within a reasonable time. An example of such mass cases was the claim by borrowers against banks seeking a refund of the loan processing fee. Even though it pertains to consumers, the protection of the collective interests of financial services consumers is not regulated since the CPA does not apply.

An excessive length of proceedings due to overloaded courts in these situations does not comply with the right to a fair trial according to the ECtHR's case law. As per ECtHR's case law, the states have a responsibility to organise their judiciary so as not to give rise to an infringement of a right to a trial within a reasonable time

[60] A Uzelac, 'Croatia: Omnipotent Judges as the Cause of Procedural Inefficiency and Impotence', in CH van Rhee and F Yulin (eds), *Civil Litigation in China and Europe* (Dordrecht, Springer, 2014).

[61] Eg misdemeanour traffic violations, customs misdemeanour violations, or tax misdemeanour violations.

[62] B Rainey, P McCormick and C Ovey in Jacobs, White, and Ovey (eds), *The European Convention on Human Rights* (Oxford, Oxford University Press, 2020) 308.

[63] Venice Commission, *Can excessive length of the proceedings be remedied*? (Venice, Venice Commission, 2006) 13.

[64] *Lukenda v Slovenia* App no 23032/02 (ECHR, 6 October 2005), paras 93–94.

[65] Ministry of Justice of the Republic of Serbia, *Statement of Reasons to the Draft Consumer Protection Act of the Republic of Serbia* (Belgrade, 2014) 120.

[66] The World Bank Group, *Serbia Judicial Functional Review*, (Belgrade, The World Bank Group, 2014) 116.

due to an excessive influx of cases.[67] The opposite conclusion was reached by the Court only in the case *Buchholz v Germany*.[68] The Court concluded that the state was not responsible for the duration of the proceedings caused by a sudden surge of disputes. According to the Court, the state could not have reasonably foreseen the huge influx of cases, which was a result of an economic recession, even if it had acted straight away.

5.5. Implications of the Legislative Changes in the Area of Consumer Collective Redress to the Rights to the Fair Trial

The state has transferred the competence and changed the type of proceedings in the cases that, by its nature, are better suited for litigation rather than administrative proceedings. Independence is not guaranteed in this type of proceeding since the proceedings are conducted before the organisational unit of the Ministry. Furthermore, the sanctions imposed by the misdemeanour court are monetarily small and as such, do not represent a genuine penalty for the trader. Therefore, it is not very likely that the trader will refrain from infringing the collective rights and interests of the consumers. On the one hand, the proceedings for the protection of collective rights and interests are not effective enough. On the other hand, consumers are rationally uninterested in lodging lawsuits for their small claims arising out of the infringement of consumer rights. Consequently, the consumers are left on their own or to the guerrilla lawyers that will represent them in small claim courts in those disputes. Instead of having associations or ombudsmen that protect the consumers in proceedings with established rules on cost allocation, the rule-violating attorneys will represent the parties in return for the cost compensation in case of a win over a major corporation or the state. To conclude, the scope of the right to a fair trial was narrowed after the competence for the consumer collective redress was shifted to the Ministry.

6. The Outcome

As a country in transition, Serbia has gone down a winding road adopting the collective redress mechanism that diverged from the Serbian legal tradition. The final outcome was unsatisfactory as consumer collective redress began to be applied within the administrative proceedings before the Ministry, which failed to serve its purpose.

[67] *Zimmermann and Steiner v Switzerland* App no 8737/79 (EHRR, 13 July 1983) para 22, *Guincho v Portugal* App no 8990/80 (EHRR, 10 July 1984), para 41; A Uzelac, 'Pravo na pošteno suđenje: opći i građanskopravni aspekti čl.6 st.1 Europske konvencije za zaštitu ljudskih prava i temeljnih sloboda', 97.

[68] *Buchholz v Germany* App no 7759/77 (EHRR, 6 May 1981), para 51.

The original idea of the collective redress mechanism is to bring the following benefits: procedural economy in access to justice, upholding the law, and deterrence.[69] However, for the past several years in Serbia, the focus is on the idea of employing judicial protection through the aggregation of claims in order to resolve mass litigations. Doing so would reduce a backlog in courts.

Namely, the issue of efficiency is the ultimate problem of the Serbian judiciary.[70] A large number of applications against Serbia have been lodged with the ECtHR claiming a violation of the right to a trial within a reasonable time. Judicial reform is being implemented to a large extent in order to increase its efficiency.

The problem was addressed by proposals to reintroduce the collective redress mechanism into litigation so as to reduce the problem of mass claims. The specific proposals for the types of claims to be introduced were often lacking. In instances where such proposals were specified, they principally concerned the introduction of a test case.[71] However, the preliminary version of the Act amending the Civil Proceedings Act does not contain such a proposal.

What the proposals normally lack is the proposal to extend the right of access to justice by consumers through extended *locus standi*. The segment of weaker party protection is completely overshadowed by the issue of mass claims and backlog in the Serbian judiciary, and by the judicial system problems. It seems that the problems of the judiciary outweigh the interest of individuals. Apart from that, the collective redress mechanism is often deemed foreign in Serbian civil procedural law since it is not part of the civil procedure tradition.[72] As previously stated, the tradition was usually analysed only partially.

7. Influence on the Consumer-Trader Relationship

Legislative changes concerning consumer collective redress, i.e. absence of consumer collective redress instruments, have affected the consumer-trader relationship. Let us take, as an example, the mass claims regarding loan processing costs filed before

[69] They are set as the objectives of a class action by Supreme Court of Canada, See C Piché, 'Empirical Data and the Powerful Lessons Learnt about Class Action in Quebec', in A Uzelac and S Voet (eds) *Class Actions in Europe: Holy Grail or a Wrong Trail* (New York, Springer, 2021) 325. Hodges discusses such set objectives from the perspective of collective redress in general, C Hodges, 'Evaluating Collective Redress: Models, Evidence, Outcome, and Policy' in, A Uzelac and S Voet (eds) *Class Actions in Europe* 21.

[70] Ministry of Justice of the Republic of Serbia, *National Strategy for Judicial Reform – preliminary version 2019–2024* (Министарство правде Републике Србије (mpravde.gov.rs)), 24.

[71] During 2021, the working group of the Ministry of Justice of the Republic of Serbia drew up amendments to the Civil Proceedings Act and was delivered a proposal by the Association of Judges and Prosecutors to introduce such claim in order to resolve the issue of backlog due to mass claims (www.ust.rs/saopstenja-za-javnost-21-03.html).

[72] The Constitutional court in its 2013 decision cited only part of the statement of reasons of the 2011 CPC which is the information that the introduction of the collective redress mechanism in the CPC was an obligation towards the EU in the process of Serbia's EU integration.

Serbian courts. Back in 2019, there were more than 200,000 claims against Serbian banks for the compensation of the loan processing costs. The consumers claimed that they were dealing with the unfair contractual term while the banks defended themselves claiming that the terms were in compliance with the law. Even though the Supreme Court of Cassation gave an interpretative opinion on the issue of the legality of the loan processing costs clause, what followed was the inconsistent legal practice of the courts. This caused the Supreme Court of Cassation to give a supplementary interpretative opinion. Afterwards, the courts aligned their case law on this issue and rejected the claims. As a result, many plaintiffs withdrew their claims, and the costs of the more than 200,000 proceedings were generated. Those who filed their claims earlier were more fortunate since the judgements in their favour were rendered before the reaction of the Supreme Court of Cassation.

The consumers who withdrew their claims, after the supplementary interpretative opinion, could have been obliged to bear all costs of the proceedings. In practice, the banks offered to forgive the costs of the proceedings to those plaintiffs who withdrew their claims soon after the reaction of the highest court in the country. That way, each party bore its own costs of the proceedings. Instead of the collective redress leading to a single judgment, the mass claim was resolved through an interpretative opinion of the highest court in the country. This opinion subsequently affected the decisions in all cases.

The interpretative opinions of the Supreme Court of Cassation in this and other mass claims cases are a clear indication that mass claims are dealt with centrally, by one court. This method proved flawed as the position of claimants is weakened since each claimant is dealing with the case individually and paying the costs of the proceedings individually. The interpretation of the Supreme Court of Cassation, in practice, follows the fact that numerous proceedings are pending. In contrast, the collective redress allows the claimants to be engaged in one court proceeding (for example, class action) or initiate individual proceedings after the judgment is rendered (for example, organisational claim). This distinction comes to the fore when dealing with small claims because, in these claims, the consumers are not interested in filling the claim.

Another example is a surge of claims that threatened Elektroprivreda Srbije, the sole supplier of electricity in the country. As of 2014, the monthly electricity bill for the individual consumer was increased by RSD 140 (approx EUR 1.20) for 'the guaranteed supplier's cost.' The collection of these bills was challenged as unlawful and compensation was demanded for the entire period in which the fee was charged. Most claims for a compensation of around RSD 15,000 (approx EUR 120) have been rejected. However, the proceedings were, again, instituted before the Supreme Court of Cassation to resolve the contentious legal issue. This court has also found that the provision is lawful and that the claims should be rejected.[73]

[73] Interpretative opinion of the Serbian Supreme Court of Cassation- Civil Law Department, 16 September 2021. (Pravni stav – dopuna stava o troškovima obrade kredita sa obrazloženjem_0.pdf (sud.rs)).

In the meantime, attorneys-at-law, informally 'specialised' in mass claims, invited citizens to represent them in another mass case, hoping to collect the court fees that exceed the amount of the claim.

Therefore, the existing litigation mechanisms failed to provide effective protection of consumer rights. Citizens are at risk of incurring additional costs as a result of uncertain dispute resolution. At the same time, some attorneys take advantage of such situations and cause the highest possible costs to be subsequently reimbursed if the consumer wins against the trader. It can be concluded from the last example that citizens make uninformed decisions due to mixed messages by opportunistic attorneys. The citizens alone bear the risks of suing for their paltry sums. Furthermore, when infringement of consumer law causes small claims, the lawsuits would most probably not be filed and the position of consumers is weakened. The only way to protect the collective rights of the consumers would be in administrative proceedings. However, it remains uncertain if those proceedings are effective since the problem of mass consumer claims before the courts still exists.

As a result of such diminished guarantees in the right to a fair trial and the disrupted rule of law principle, such relationships develop between individuals where the position of the trader grows stronger and that of the consumers grows weaker.

8. Conclusion

This chapter analysed the impact of the legislative changes in the area of consumer collective redress to the exercising of the right to the fair trial and the rule of law in Serbia. This analysis shows that problems that emerge when the institute of collective redress is not present in the country's judiciary, particularly in the post-socialist judiciary, are significant and systemic. Firstly, the judiciary is overburdened with mass claims since there is no appropriate procedural tool to avoid this. Secondly, 'guerrilla' tactics are developed by some attorneys who pursue easy money by replicating identical claims and hoping for the reimbursement of the costs from the banks, traders, or the state.

The organisational claim was the only collective redress mechanism in Serbian law to deal with these issues. In comparison to other collective redress mechanisms, the organisational claim would not be the best choice to avoid problems of mass claims. Furthermore, the provisions on collective redress were not drafted without flaws. However, the organisational claim was revoked by the Constitutional Court on the grounds that are applicable to each collective redress tool. When it revoked the organisational claim, the Constitutional Court invoked the tradition of procedural law and stated that collective redress is not in line with it.

However, this 'blast from the past' is incomplete because neither the past of the Serbian legal system nor the tradition of similar legal systems was fully analysed. Instead, consumer collective redress was introduced in administrative proceedings before the Ministry. This way, the scope of the right to a fair trial is not properly applied and the goals of collective protection of consumer rights could not be achieved. To conclude, implementing collective redress in post-socialist countries is a challenge,[74] but the absence of it is a problem.

[74] A Uzelac, 'Why No Class Actions in Europe? A View from the Side of Dysfunctional Justice Systems' in V Harsági and CH van Rhee (eds), *Multi-Party Redress Mechanisms in Europe: Squeaking Mice?* (Cambridge, Intersentia, 2014).

11

Rule by Law, Excessive Length of Proceedings, and Property Rights in Slovenia

MITJA KOVAC*

1. Introduction

Ever since Adam Smith, economists and lawyers have known that commerce and manufacturing rarely flourish when the rule of law is missing. The importance of the rule of law for economic growth and development can thus hardly be overstated.[1] Creating prosperity, institutional stability, social progress, and wealth under the rule of law – whereby the law is, as Corstens states, more than 'flimsy words on paper, where government action is genuinely bound by the rules of law where citizens have genuine access to the courts – demands time, integrity and constant commitment'.[2] In order to generate and preserve the fragile rule of law, the judiciary and executive and legislature branches must make constant efforts. Namely, the 'viability and the quality of the rule of law ultimately depends for the most part on the people'.[3] For example, if citizens elect politicians who cut off access to the courts, judges' self-selection leads to a nepotistic guild, or the legislature abolishes the judicial review of legislation, the rule of law might decline substantially and rapidly. Corstens notes that even in a democracy the rule of law is not completely self-evident.[4] In reality, the rule of law exists in various degrees and

* The author acknowledges financial support from the Slovenian Research Agency (research core funding No P5-0128).

[1] See DC North and RB Weingast, 'Constitutions and Commitment: The Evolution of Institutions Governing Public Choice in Seventeenth-Century England' (1989) 49(4) *The Journal of Economic History* 803, 832; S Knack and P Keefer, 'Institutions and Economic Performance: Cross-country Tests using Alternative Institutional Measures' (1995) 7(3) *Economics and Politics*, 207, 28; D Acemoglu, S Johnson and JA Robinson, 'Institutions as a Fundamental Cause of Long-Run Growth' in P Aghion and S Durlauf (eds), *Handbook of Economic Growth* (Amsterdam, Elsevier, 2005); and A Rodríguez-Pose, 'Do Institutions Matter for Regional Development?' (2013) 47 (7) *Regional Studies* 1043, 1047.

[2] G Corstens, *Understanding the Rule of Law* (Oxford, Hart Publishing, 2017) 4.

[3] Corstens (n 2).

[4] Corstens (n 2).

institutional embodiments and once high quality is achieved it does not continue to exist without the constant effort and support of ordinary citizens who should benefit from such a rule of law.

The utmost significance of the rule of law and the commitment to it by all stakeholders – judges, legislatures, executives, politicians, and citizens – must be constantly nurtured and embedded in all parts of society and passed down from generation to generation. Justice Learned Hand famously wrote 'liberty lies in the hearts of men and women; when it dies there, no constitution, no law, no court can save it; no constitution, no law, no court can do much to help it'.[5] Tamanaha defines the rule of law as a principle meaning that government official and citizens are bound and abide by the law.[6] Yet, Alvazzi del Frate and Torini argue the current meaning of the rule of law has increasingly changed to become broader, more symbolic, and full of emotion.[7] They add that it is very difficult to properly define the content of this principle since it is associated with vague, sometimes misleading, different meanings.[8] The rule of law therefore includes a multitude of different legal and political principles glued together by the intention of establishing government by laws, not by individuals.[9] In contrast, Craig believes the rule of law concept can be summarised by referring to the guarantee of the rights of freedom and the principle of equality of people before the law.[10] However, Spac et al argue that the rule of law should not be confounded with complete judicial self-governing because such self-governing could actually result in the capture of the judiciary from the inside, then also undermining the operation of the rule of law.[11]

Following the above-mentioned critical debate, this chapter seeks to examine whether the rule of law in Slovenia is also shown or realised in the domain of private law. Relevant judgments issued by the ECtHR with respect to Slovenian cases of property rights and access to justice are examined. The chapter describes both how the rule of law concept is materialised in the area of property law and how it concerns relationships among citizens. It is also argued that the biggest threat to the rule of law in both private law and the relationships among citizens might be its

[5] I Dilliard, *The Spirit of Liberty: Papers and Addresses by Learned Hand* (New York, Knopf Publishers, 1952).

[6] BZ Tamanaha, 'The History and Elements of the Rule of Law' (2012) *Singapore Journal of Legal Studies* 233, 247.

[7] P Alvazzi del Frate and A Torini, 'Rule of Law between the Seventeenth and Nineteenth Centuries' in G Amato, B Barbisan and C Pinelli (eds), *Rule of Law vs Majoritarian Democracy* (Oxford, Hart Publishing, 2021) 12.

[8] Alvazzi and Torini (n 7).

[9] According to Alvazi del Frate and Torini, this means that the replacement of the 'government of individuals', considered arbitrary and potentially despotic, with the 'government of laws', characterised by the compliance with formal legal rules,' Alvazi and Torini (n 7).

[10] P Craig, 'Formal and Substantive Conceptions of the Rule of Law: An Analytical framework' (1997) 21 *Public Law* 467, 487.

[11] They show that the Slovak example displays the dangers of establishing judicial self-governance in countries where an internal ethical culture and a strong sense of judicial duty are still lacking; S Spáč, K Šipulová and M Urbániková, 'Capturing the Judiciary from Inside: The Story of Judicial Self-Governance in Slovakia' (2018) 19 (7) *German Law Journal* 1741, 1768.

transformation into rule by law, even into rule by judges. The challenges concerning how to improve the quality of the judiciary and consequent quality of the rule of law itself are shown not be overcome by the simple transfer of complete power to the judiciary, especially with respect to careers in that branch. Namely, a considerably autonomous judiciary in an immature-low-human-capital-post-socialist society might empower judicial elites, bringing rule by judges, not rule by law. Such reduced democratic accountability of the judiciary, compartmentalising it from society, might enable it to promote its own interests. The selection processes could move away from being merit-based and instead be abused to fill judicial benches with judges closely tied to the system (i.e. adverse selection problem, a 'market for lemons' problem, opportunism, and nepotism). Accountability mechanisms such as promotions, disciplinary procedures, or remuneration schemes might be used to reward allies of those on top of the hierarchy (nepotism, particularism) and to punish critics. Finally, the chapter offers some substantive policy recommendations for an improved institutional framework that could further strengthen the rule of law as experienced by Slovenian citizens.

In this chapter, the analysis is both positive and normative. The analytical approach employs classic law and economics methodology.[12] Further, the law and economics methodology relied on follows the standard comparative law and economics approach.[13] This approach provides a bridge between facts and normative conclusions, and between economic theory and policy proposals for improving the legal system considered.[14] In addition, it seeks to complement other legal disciplines by revealing the underlying economic logic and the social effects of the assessed legal institutions.[15] In looking for transparency in the law, the approach adopted is part of what 'the best traditional legal scholarship aims to do: clarifying the underlying order of law as it is; offering tools for fashioning law to cope with novel situations'.[16] Still, several caveats are warranted. First, the chapter aims not to offer the final word on the matter but, via an exploratory analysis, to consider whether the rule of law concept is also both materialised in the domain of property law and concerns inter-citizen relationships. The text exclusively focuses on Slovenian ECtHR property law cases and omits the discussion of other potential significant variables.

[12] For a synthesis of law and economics scholarship, see G De Geest, *Contract Law and Economics – Encyclopaedia of Law and Economics*, Volume 6, 2nd edn (Cheltenham, Edward Elgar, 2011). Also see RA Posner, *Economic Analysis of Law*, 8th edn (New York, Wolters Kluwer Law Publishers, 2011).

[13] R Bergh Van den, *The Roundabouts of European Law and Economics* (The Hague, Eleven International Publishing, 2018).

[14] Bergh Van den (n 13) 27.

[15] This methodology complements traditional legal disciplines by bringing to light a logic that decision-makers follow without necessarily expressing it in their reasons for judgment, yet which constrains their results. It also seeks to make this logic transparent to outside observers; A Ogus, *Costs and Cautionary Tales: Economic Insights for the Law*, (Oxford, Hart Publishing, 2006) 11–16. See also G Calabresi, *The Future of Law & Economics* (New Haven, Yale University Press 2016); and RA Posner, *Divergent Paths: The Academy and the Judiciary* (Cambridge, Harvard University Press, 2016).

[16] E MacKaay, *Law and Economics for Civil Law Systems* (Cheltenham, Edward Elgar, 2013) 6.

The structure of this chapter is as follows. Section two presents the main facts about the Slovenian legal system and its performance. Section three is concerned with both Slovenian EctHR property law cases and the lengths of court proceedings. Section four addresses problems with the rule of law, rule by law and rule by judges before offering some policy recommendations. Section five concludes.

2. The Slovenian Judicial System: In Facts and Figures

Slovenia is a small country that gained independence from Yugoslavia in 1991, joined the EU in 2004, and adopted the euro as its currency in 2007.[17] After becoming independent in 1991, Slovenia established liberal democratic institutions, enshrined respect for human rights, and enjoyed a period of strong, robust economic growth and macroeconomic stability. It is noted that, as shown by Tables 1–4 (in the appendix), this solid economic performance came despite many inefficiencies and backlogs with regard to enforcing property rights and contracts (creating systemic uncertainty and instability). The country also managed to rapidly integrate into the European Union, the OECD, NATO, and the European Monetary Union (EMU). In 2021, with GDP per capita similar to that of Spain and its inequality-adjusted HDI, the country was ranked 9th worldwide together with Sweden and the Netherlands.

In its Constitution adopted on 23 December 1991, Slovenia expressly states that the judiciary is an independent branch of government and that all matters pertaining to judges and judicial work must be prescribed by law. Based on the new Constitution, three acts legislating the judiciary were introduced in 1994, namely the Constitutional Court Act, the Judicial Services Act, and the Judiciary Act, each amended several times thereafter.

The uniform judicial system of the Republic of Slovenia includes courts of general and specialised jurisdiction, with the latter holding jurisdiction only in the fields of labour and social law and administrative law. The courts of general jurisdiction are found on four levels:

a) 44 local courts are courts of first instance and vested with jurisdiction for less serious criminal cases; civil cases concerning claims for damages or property rights up to a certain value, all civil cases concerning disturbance of possession, easement of real estate, hire, lease or tenancy relationships; the legal obligation to pay maintenance if the disagreements are not dealt with in conjunction with marriage disputes or disputes to establish or contest fatherhood; probate and other non-litigious matters; the keeping of land register; sand civil enforcement;

[17] Slovenia has a population of 2 million people, its GDP is around EUR 35 billion (91% of EU average), GDP per capita in 2021 is EUR 29,201 and the territory measures 20,273 km2.

b) 11 district courts are courts of first instance as well. They hold jurisdiction over criminal and civil cases which exceed the competency of the local courts; juvenile criminal cases; enforcement of criminal sentences; the trial of violations of human rights and fundamental freedoms; family disputes, except regarding maintenance; confirmation of foreign court rulings; commercial disputes; bankruptcy, forced settlements and liquidation; copyright and intellectual property cases; company register entries;
c) four higher courts are courts of appellate jurisdiction. Alongside determining appeals against decisions of the local and district courts in their territories, they rule over disputes of jurisdiction between local and district courts;
d) the Supreme Court, as the highest court in the country;
e) there are another four specialised courts of first instance (three competent in the area of labour disputes, one also for social security disputes. They share a common court of appeal); and
f) the Administrative Court of the Republic of Slovenia, with the status of a higher court.[18]

The independence of Slovenian judges is guaranteed by the Constitution of the Republic of Slovenia (*Ustava Republike Slovenije*).[19] The status of judges (*sodniki*) is governed by Articles 125–134 of the Constitution as well as the Judicial Service Act (*Zakon o sodniški službi*).[20] Judges are elected by the National Assembly (*Državni zbor*; ie the Parliament) based on a proposal from the Judicial Council (*Sodni svet*) as a separate constitutional body. The office of judge is permanent while the age limit and conditions for election are set out in law.[21] Pursuant to the State Prosecution Service Act (*Zakon o državnem tožilstvu; ZDT-1*),[22] a person meeting the conditions to be elected to a judicial office under the act regulating the judicial service (general conditions) and specific conditions for appointment to the position of a state prosecutor as laid down in this Act may be appointed a state prosecutor (*državni tožilec*).

[18] Sodni Svet, Republika Slovenija, *Response Questionnaire Project Group Timeliness* (Brussels, European Network of Councils for the Judiciary, 2022).

[19] Constitution, Art 125, The Independence of the Judges: 'The judges shall independently exercise their duties and functions in accordance with this Constitution and with the law'; Constitution of the Republic of Slovenia (Official Gazette of the Republic of Slovenia Nos 33/91-I, 42/97 – UZS68, 66/00 – UZ80, 24/03 – UZ3a, 47, 68, 69/04 – UZ14, 69/04 – UZ43, 69/04 – UZ50, 68/06 – UZ121,140,143, 47/13 – UZ148, 47/13 – UZ90,97,99 and 75/16 – UZ70a).

[20] Judicial Service Act (Official Gazette of the Republic of Slovenia, Nos 94/07 – official consolidated text, 91/09, 33/11, 46/13, 63/13 in 69/13 – corrigendum, 95/14 – ZUPPJS15, 17/15, 23/17 – ZSSve and 36/19 – ZDT-1C).

[21] Constitution, Art 130, The Election of Judges provides that: 'The National Assembly shall elect judges upon the proposal of the Judicial Council,' Constitution of the Republic of Slovenia (Official Gazette of the Republic of Slovenia Nos 33/91-I, 42/97 – UZS68, 66/00 – UZ80, 24/03 – UZ3a, 47, 68, 69/04 – UZ14, 69/04 – UZ43, 69/04 – UZ50, 68/06 – UZ121,140,143, 47/13 – UZ148, 47/13 – UZ90,97,99 and 75/16 – UZ70a).

[22] State Prosecution Service Act (Official Gazette of the Republic of Slovenia, Nos 58/11, 21/12 – ZDU-1F, 47/12, 15/13 – ZODPol, 47/13 – ZDU-1G, 48/13 – ZSKZDČEU1, 19/15, 23/17 – ZSSve and 36/19).

State prosecutors in the Republic of Slovenia operate on four levels: local state prosecutors, district state prosecutors, higher state prosecutors and supreme state prosecutors. The term of office of a state prosecutor is permanent.

The office of a judge is permanent and normally ends upon retirement which is compulsory only at age 70. The grounds for terminating the office of a judge must be determined by statute.[23]

The Judicial Council is a state authority that in line with the Constitution does not fall under any branch of power. In the process of appointing judges, the Council ensures the cooperation of the legislative, executive, and judicial branches. Its tasks include protecting the independence of judges and the judiciary, and promoting and ensuring its accountability, efficiency, and quality of work. The Judicial Council's primary responsibility is to select candidates for judicial offices in the candidate-selection process and to propose a single candidate for a judicial office to the National Assembly. In addition, it adopts the Code of Judicial Ethics and appoints members of the Ethics and Integrity Commission, adopts qualitative criteria for assessing judges' work, decides on the promotion of judges, may lodge a request for an evaluation of a judicial service with respect to a particular judge, and may request that the work of a certain judge be officially supervised. The Council gives opinions to the National Assembly and the ministry on laws governing the courts and the judicial service, and appoints and dismisses presidents of courts and gives its opinion to the National Assembly regarding the appointment of the President of the Supreme Court (the National Assembly appoints the President of the Supreme Court on the proposal of the minister responsible for justice) and decides on appeals made by judges who believe that their independent position or the independence of the judiciary has been violated. The Constitution guarantees that judges have a majority in the Judicial Council and that members of this body who come from their ranks are elected by their peers.[24]

[23] For example, Constitution, Art 132, para 1 states that: 'The circumstances in which a judge shall no longer hold office shall be specified by statute'. Moreover, the Judicial Service Act, Art 74 provides: 'Judges shall have their judicial office terminated pursuant to law: 1. if they fail to make an oath no later than sixty days from the day of being elected to judicial office, unless the failure of not making an oath is a result of factors beyond their control; 2. if they lose the citizenship of the Republic of Slovenia; 3. if they lose the capacity to contract or cease to be in sufficient health to perform judicial service; 4. if they resign from judicial service via a written application sent to the Judicial Council by the president of the court; 5. if the court is abolished and it cannot be guaranteed that they will continue to perform judicial service at another court; 6. if they accept an office, begin to perform activities, conclude an employment relationship or despite a prohibition perform work that is incompatible with judicial office (Article 41, third paragraph of Article 42 and third paragraph of Article 43); 7. if it proceeds from assessment of their service that they are unsuited to judicial service (Article 33); 8. if a disciplinary sanction of termination of judicial office is pronounced upon them'.

[24] Constitution, Art 131, The Judicial Council: 'There shall be a Judicial Council composed of eleven members. Five members shall be elected by vote of the National Assembly on the nomination of the President of the Republic from amongst practicing lawyers, professors of law and other lawyers. Six members shall be elected from amongst judges holding permanent judicial office. The President of the Judicial Council shall be chosen by the members of the Judicial Council from amongst their own number'.

A judge is bound by the Constitution and the law. Pursuant to the Constitution, a judge is also bound by the general principles of international law as well as ratified and published international treaties (Article 3 of the Courts Act). Judges are accountable since they face either impeachment or disciplinary procedures. A disciplinary sanction may not be imposed upon a judge except under the conditions and according to the procedures described in the Judicial Service Act. Disciplinary proceedings are fast-tracked. Criminal liability and liability for a misdemeanour shall not exclude a disciplinary liability on the part of a judge (Article 80 of the Judicial Service Act).[25]

Within the framework of court management and exercising supervision over the implementation of court management tasks, one may not interfere with the independent position of a judge in decision-making regarding cases assigned to them (Paragraph 2, Article 60 of the Courts Act). In the course of official supervision, it is not permitted to interfere with the independence of a judge in the performance of their judicial office (Paragraph 2, Article 79a of the Judicial Service Act). As part of disciplinary proceedings, it is not permitted to interfere with a judge's independence in the performance of their judicial office (Paragraph 4, Article 80 of the Judicial Service Act). In the exercise of its powers, the Service for the Supervision of Court Administration may not interfere with a judge's independence in the performance of their duties of judicial office, with the presumption of innocence, with the secrecy of legal proceedings or with the guarantee of a fair trial, and may not examine case files except in parts relating to a review of court fees and an administrative review (Paragraph 5, Article 65a of the Courts Act). While exercising its powers, the ministry responsible for justice may not interfere with the independence of a judge in the performance of their judicial duties, with the presumption of innocence, with the secrecy of legal proceedings or with the guarantee of a fair trial (Paragraph 3, Article 67a of the Courts Act).

The Judicial Council adopts the Code of Judicial Ethics and appoints members of the Ethics and Integrity Commission. The Code of Judicial Ethics (*Kodeks sodniške etike*)[26] establishes rules for the professional and personal conduct of judges with a view to protecting their independence, impartiality and honesty, and the good reputation of the judicial branch.[27]

[25] See the Judicial Service Act, Chapter VII – Disciplinary Proceedings and Suspensions from Judicial Service, Judicial Service Act (Official Gazette of the Republic of Slovenia, Nos 94/07 – official consolidated text, 91/09, 33/11, 46/13, 63/13 in 69/13 – corrigendum, 95/14 – ZUPPJS15, 17/15, 23/17 – ZSSve and 36/19 – ZDT-1C).

[26] Sodni Svet, *The Code of Judicial Ethics with commentary* (Ljubljana, Sodni Svet, 2017) available at: www.sodnisvet.si/images/stories/Kodeks_sodniske_etike_komentar_ang_sept_2017.pdf.

[27] Moreover, judges are obliged to comply with the Code of judicial ethics both in the performance of judicial office and outside of it. The Ethics and Integrity Commission has the following powers: a) to adopt principled opinions on conduct constituting violation of the Code of Judicial Ethics; b) to issue recommendations regarding compliance with the rules on judicial ethics and integrity pursuant to the Code of Judicial Ethics; c) to adopt guidelines in the area of judicial ethics and integrity in compliance with the Code of Judicial Ethics; and d) to provide education and training of judges in the field of ethics and integrity in cooperation with the Judicial Training Centre.

2.1. Judicial Backlogs and Inefficiencies

Even when Slovenia was part of Yugoslavia, its judicial system struggled with backlogs.[28] As Zajc notes, backlogs and unresolved cases in Slovenia are thus not a recent occurrence.[29] Already in the 1980s and 1990s, backlogs started to accumulate and by 1992 there were 199,893 unresolved cases, among which 100,049 'important' cases were before first-instance courts. Moreover, 40 per cent of the unresolved cases were commercial and half of these were commercial enforcement procedures.[30] Zajc also shows that matters became worse up until 1998 when the judiciary faced 597,587 unresolved cases at the year's end, 213,559 of which were 'important', an almost a threefold increase since 1990 when 199,893 cases were unresolved.[31] After 1998, the number of unresolved cases and backlogs started to ease, albeit it is noted that the number of cases filed each year even during the 1990s was steadily decreasing.[32] Matters improved after 1999. The number of unresolved cases and backlogs was gradually falling as was the inflow of new cases. Nevertheless, enforcement cases and land registry were still plagued by huge backlogs.[33]

According to a 2002 report,[34] the reasons for judges' deteriorating productivity (identified as the key reason for the backlogs) were manifold. The first mentioned was the transition from the communist to a capitalist system (and thus all the accompanying legislative changes and additional legislation needed to ensure the capitalist system's functioning and legislation that was introduced to remedy all the injustices caused by the communist regime). Also mentioned were implementation of the reform of judiciary in 1994–1995 that disrupted the flow of work, negligence in monitoring the statistical data and hence the lack of any reaction to the worsening situation, the lack of experienced judges, the lack of interest in becoming a judge since lawyers had greater options after private sector jobs became more lucrative, and changes in society, which then led to more complex cases.[35]

The report also found that judges were burdened by administrative work, that the procedural legislation in civil (including enforcement procedure) and criminal matters, despite many improvements, largely remained inefficient.[36]

[28] K Zajc, 'Independence of Judiciary in Slovenia: Economic and Historic Perspective' (2014) 22 *Acta Histriae* 3, 14.

[29] Zajc (n 28).

[30] K Zajc, 'Slovensko Sodstvo med Leti 1990 in 2011' in J Prunk and T Deželan (eds), *Dvajset Let Slovenske Države* (Maribor, Ljubljana, Aristej, Fakulteta za družbene vede, Center za politološke raziskave, 2012).

[31] Zajc (n 30).

[32] Zajc (n 30).

[33] Zajc (n 30).

[34] The Supreme Court and the Ministry of Justice, *Report on the Causes and Remedies for the State of the Judiciary* (Ljubljana, Ministry of Justice, 2002).

[35] Zajc (n 28).

[36] Zajc (n 28).

The 2002 report criticised the under-regulation of judges' tasks in terms of the quantity and quality of the work required, with the same applying to the promotion of judges. The ministry then proposed that the number of personnel be increased to relieve the judges of administrative work and that the number of judges be decreased. Ministry officials stressed that the management of courts should be improved because, although the presidents of the courts held sufficient supervisory power, they were not fully executing it and that the procedural laws should be amended in order to make the procedures more efficient.

The report concluded that courts had sufficient funds to function properly and that the legal status of judges and courts should not be a cause of judges' low productivity since the legal framework guarantees them independence that the executive and legislative branches do not have, except to a small degree in the judicial administration, no influence on the judiciary.[37] Zajc also describes how even though matters improved slightly in the years following 2000, they have continued to be far from perfect and that judicial backlogs and the slow delivery of justice remain the most persistent problems in application of the rule of law in Slovenia. Further, as shown below this issue also accounts for the majority of Slovenian cases in front of the European Court of Human Rights.

However, in recent years Slovenia has successfully managed to eliminate backlogs as a systemic problem that has burdened the country's courts for two decades. The innovative, tailor-made solutions prepared within the judiciary are acknowledged on an international level. The number of unresolved cases was cut in half over five years and the length of proceedings significantly shortened, even though the number of judges has been reduced in the past decade.[38] These improvements were recognised by both the Council of Europe and the European Commission: in 2016, the Secretariat of the Council of Europe adopted a decision stating that a trial within a reasonable time was no longer a systemic problem in Slovenia. When presenting the EU's Justice Scoreboard 2018, the EC Commissioner for Justice and Consumers mentioned Slovenia as the country which had most reduced the number of unresolved cases.

Current reports show that more recently (2019–2022) the number of unsolved cases rose above 5 per cent in 2020, although the trend was reversed in 2021. The courts resolved more cases than they received and by the end of the year again reduced the number of pending cases. The number of pending cases was reduced by 4 per cent compared with 2019 and 31 per cent compared with the end of 2016, President of the Supreme Court Justice Florjančič stated in 2022 while addressing a ceremony to launch a new legal year. Yet, when speaking to reporters he noted

[37] Zajc (n 28).

[38] European Institute of Public Administration, *Improving the Quality of Justice* (Brussels, European Institute of Public Administration, 2022), available at: www.eipa.eu/epsa/improving-the-quality-of-justice-iq-justice/.

that the number of major pending cases in the previous year was up by 7 per cent compared with the pre-COVID 2019.[39]

Moreover, the European Institute of Public Administration identified two main problem areas: the quality of judicial work (skills and transfer of knowledge) on one hand and the low trust in the judiciary on the other as the biggest obstacles to the rule of law in Slovenia. Recent data on the trajectory of the clearance rate show decreasing backlogs (clearance rate in 2010: 99%; 2012: 101%, 2014: 109%; 2016: 106%; 2018: 110%) and a somewhat stationary length of proceedings in civil and commercial cases at first instance (disposition time in year by years (days): 2010 (315), 2012 (318), 2014 (270), 280 (283)).

3. European Court of Human Rights' Jurisprudence Concerning Slovenia

Between 1959 and 2021, the European Court of Human Rights delivered 373 judgments declaring violations by Slovenia of the ECHR.[40] As to a breach of specific ECHR articles, there were nine judgments on the lack of an effective investigation, 21 judgments on inhuman or degrading treatment, six on the right to liberty and security, 25 on the right to a fair trial, three on non-enforcement, one on no punishment without legal basis, 12 on the right of respect for private and family life, three on freedom of expression, three on prohibition of discrimination, eight on the protection of property, 267 on the right to an effective remedy and 263 about the length of proceedings.[41] This section offers a review of noteworthy Slovenian property law judgments decided on by the ECtHR and briefly introduces the most important rulings related to the length of proceedings.

3.1. The European Court of Human Rights and Protection of Property in Slovenia

The central judgment is the notorious *Lekić v Slovenia* case[42] adjudicated in the Grand Chamber of the ECtHR. The case concerned striking a company off the court register and the subsequent liability of its managing director for its debts. The striking off procedure was used against the applicant's company under new legislation introduced in 1999 that empowered courts to strike off dormant companies

[39] See D Florjančič, *Florjančič ob Otvoritvi Sodnega Leta Predstavil Preteklo Delo in Prihodnje Načrte* (Ljubljana, Slovenian Press Agency, 2022) available at www.sta.si/3008185/florjancic-bo-ob-otvoritvi-sodnega-leta-predstavil-preteklo-delo-in-prihodnje-nacrte.

[40] Among this 373 have been 342 judgments finding at least one violation of the ECHR and 24 judgments finding no violation and four friendly settlements.

[41] See www.echr.coe.int/Documents/Stats_violation_1959_2021_ENG.pdf.

[42] Grand Chamber Case of *Lekić v Slovenia* (2018) 36480 EHRR 07.

without first having to wind them up. The procedure led to him having to pay EUR 32,795 to one of the company's creditors, the Slovenian Railways.

The applicant complained that the failure to personally serve on him the decisions issued in the strike-off proceedings against company L.E. amounted to a violation of his right of access to a court under Art 6 § 1 of the Convention.[43] Further, relying on Article 1 of Protocol 1, he in essence complained about his personal liability for a debt of L.E.[44] In other words, he claimed that the decision to hold him personally liable for the debt of L.E., taken in the context of the enforcement proceedings pursued by Slovenian Railways against him, amounted to interference with the peaceful enjoyment of his possessions under Article 1 of Protocol 1. More specifically, it constituted a measure of control over the use of property for the purposes of the second paragraph of that article. Nevertheless, the applicant invited the Court to examine his liability as part of the wider context, notably including the 2001 decision to strike L.E. off, in the light of the general rule provided in that article.[45]

The Court reiterated that the first and most important requirement of Article 1 of Protocol 1 is that any interference by a public authority with the peaceful enjoyment of possessions should be lawful: the second sentence of the first paragraph permits the deprivation of possessions only 'subject to the conditions provided for by law' while the second paragraph recognises that States have the right to control the use of property by enforcing 'laws'.[46] It was also emphasised by the Court that the rule of law, a fundamental principle of any democratic society, is inherent to all articles of the Convention.[47]

[43] That article, in so far as it is relevant, reads as follows: 'In the determination of his civil rights and obligations ..., everyone is entitled to a fair and public hearing within a reasonable time by an independent and impartial tribunal established by law. ...'.

[44] That article provides: 'Every natural or legal person is entitled to the peaceful enjoyment of his possessions. No one shall be deprived of his possessions except in the public interest and subject to the conditions provided for by law and by the general principles of international law.

The preceding provisions shall not, however, in any way impair the right of a State to enforce such laws as it deems necessary to control the use of property in accordance with the general interest or to secure the payment of taxes or other contributions or penalties'.

[45] The impugned measure was unlawful in the applicant's opinion since the domestic law was not sufficiently precise and foreseeable. As regards the requirement of foreseeability, he submitted that when the FOCA entered into force it was unclear that he could ultimately be held personally liable for any debt of L.E. Indeed, the FOCA did not expressly provide for any such liability, but only referred to another piece of legislation: in accordance with s 27(4) of the FOCA, the members of a company struck off pursuant to the FOCA were presumed to have made a statement provided for in s 394(1) of the Companies Act 1993 which, in turn, provided that a company could be struck off on the request of its members, without any winding-up proceedings, on the condition that the members made a statement in the form of a notary deed to the effect that all of the company's obligations had been fulfilled, that any disputes with the employees had been settled and that the members assumed joint and several liability for any potential outstanding obligations of the company. As to the requirement of precision, the applicant claimed that the criteria established by the Constitutional Court in the 2002 decision were far from clear. He added that the impugned regime of personal liability for the debts of struck-off companies had undergone a number of reforms which further contributed to the overall confusion; ibid paras 79 and 80.

[46] *Lekić v Slovenia* (2018) 36480 EHRR 07, para 94.

[47] See, for instance, *Former King of Greece et al v Greece* [GC] (merits), (2000) no 25701/94, 79 ECHR 2000 XII, and *Broniowski v Poland* [GC], no 31443/96, § 147, EHRR 2004 V.

The Court also addressed the issue of the relationship between the quality of legal rules and the meaning held by of 'the rule of law' and stated that the 'principle of lawfulness also presupposes a certain quality of the applicable provisions of domestic law'.[48] In this regard, it should be pointed out that when speaking of 'law' Article 1 of Protocol 1 alludes to the very same concept as that to which the Convention refers elsewhere when using that term.[49] The Court added that it follows that the legal norms upon which the interference is based should be sufficiently accessible, precise and foreseeable in their application.[50] Any interference with the peaceful enjoyment of possessions must therefore, as explicitly acknowledged by the Court, 'be accompanied by procedural guarantees affording to the individual or entity concerned a reasonable opportunity of presenting their case to the responsible authorities for the purpose of effectively challenging the measures interfering with the rights guaranteed by that provision'.[51]

The Court considers that the regulation introduced by the Financial Operations of Companies Act 1999 (FOCA) was accessible to the applicant and that the Act's content was sufficiently clear to enable him to foresee that his company ran the risk of being deleted from the court register and that he ran the risk of being held personally liable for its debts.

In addition, the Court noted that 'any interference by a public authority with the peaceful enjoyment of possessions can only be justified if it serves a legitimate general interest'.[52]

The Court was of the opinion that the national authorities' direct knowledge of society and its needs means they are in principle better placed than an international judge to appreciate what is 'in the public interest'. Under the system of protection established by the Convention, it is hence for the national authorities to make the initial assessment regarding the existence of a problem of public concern warranting measures of the deprivation of property. Like in other fields the safeguards of the Convention extend to, here the national authorities accordingly enjoy a certain margin of appreciation.

Further, the notion of 'public interest' is in the view of the Court 'necessarily extensive'. In particular, the decision to enact laws expropriating property will typically involve a consideration of political, economic and social issues.[53]

[48] Broniowski v Poland [GC], no 31443/96, § 147, EHRR 2004 V. *Lekić v Slovenia* (2018) 36480 EHRR 07, para 95.

[49] See, for example, *Vistiņš and Perepjolkins v Latvia* [GC], no 71243/01, § 96, 25 October 2012.

[50] In particular, a norm is 'foreseeable' when it affords a measure of protection against arbitrary interferences by the public authorities; see *Centro Europa 7 S.r.1. and Di Stefano v Italy* [GC], no 38433/09, § 143, 7 June 2012. See also *Beyeler v Italy* [GC], no 33202/96, §§ 109–10, EHRR 2000-I.

[51] In ascertaining whether that condition has been satisfied, a comprehensive view must be taken of the applicable judicial and administrative procedures (see *Jokela v Finland*, no 28856/95, § 45, ECHR 2002-IV; *Capital Bank AD* v *Bulgaria*, no 49429/99, § 134, ECHR 2005-XII; and *Stolyarova v Russia*, no 15711/13, § 43, 29 January 2015); *Lekić v Slovenia*, para 95.

[52] *Lekić v Slovenia*, para 105.

[53] The Court, finding it natural that the margin of appreciation available to the legislature in implementing social and economic policies should be a wide one, will respect the legislature's judgment

In situations such as deterioration of the commercial market due to a large number of dormant and insolvent companies, there may be a paramount need for the State to step in to avoid irreparable harm to the economy and enhance the legal security and confidence of participants in the market.[54]

The Court also held that the exceptional character of the circumstances that may warrant the lifting of the corporate veil essentially comes down to the nature of the issues to be decided by the competent national court, not the frequency of such situations.[55] The Court further sees no grounds for calling into doubt the view of the Constitutional Court relied on by the government that such companies posed a threat to the market's proper functioning.[56]

Furthermore, the effect of reducing the capital below the statutory limit and eventually exhausting it completely, coupled with a prolonged failure to institute winding-up proceedings, held considerably adverse effects for the position of the company's creditor (i.e. Slovenian Railways). The latter was subjected to extended uncertainty regarding whether its debt would be repaid. Such a lengthy course of proceedings could have been avoided had L.E. applied for winding-up in due time after recognising that it was unable to re-establish sufficient basic funds to continue operating.[57]

Therefore, in this particular case the Court has no factual grounds to establish that the impugned measure, based on the statutory rule of the applicant's unlimited liability for the outstanding debts of L.E., was disproportionate.[58] The said measure did not in the specific circumstances 'entail the imposition of an individual and excessive burden on the applicant, thereby overstepping the State's wide margin of appreciation in this field'.[59]

Finally, the Court decided there had been no violation of Article 1 of Protocol 1 (protection of property).

In *Ališić et al v Bosnia and Herzegovina, Croatia, Serbia, Slovenia and 'the former Yugoslav Republic of Macedonia'*,[60] the applicants had deposited their foreign-currency savings with two banks in what is today Bosnia and Herzegovina: Ljubljanska banka Sarajevo and the Tuzla branch of Invest banka. Following the dissolution of the former Socialist Federal Republic of Yugoslavia (SFRY), they were unable to recover their deposits. This is one of a large number of cases to do with the 'old' foreign-currency savings following the break up of the former SFRY.

concerning what is 'in the public interest' unless that judgment is manifestly without reasonable foundation (see *James et al*, cited above, p. 32, § 46; *The former King of Greece et al*, cited above, § 87; *and Zvolský and Zvolská v the Czech Republic*, no 46129/99, § 67 in fine, ECHR 2002-IX). The same applies necessarily, if not a fortiori, to such radical changes as those occurring at the time of German reunification, when the system changed to a market economy;' ibid para 105.

[54] *Lekić v Slovenia*, para 106.

[55] *Lekić v Slovenia*, para 115.

[56] *Lekić v* Slovenia, para 124.

[57] *Lekić v* Slovenia, para 125.

[58] *Lekić v Slovenia*, para 127.

[59] *Lekić v Slovenia*, para 129.

[60] *Ališić et al v Bosnia and Herzegovina, Croatia, Serbia, Slovenia and the Former Yugoslav Republic of Macedonia* (2011) – 60642/08, Decision 17.10.2011 [s IV].

The main object of Article 1 of Protocol 1 is to protect a person against unjustified interference by the State in the peaceful enjoyment of their possessions. However, by virtue of Article 1 of the Convention, each Contracting Party 'shall secure to everyone within [its] jurisdiction the rights and freedoms defined in [the] Convention'. The discharge of this general duty may entail positive obligations inherent to ensuring the effective exercise of the Convention-guaranteed rights. In the context of Article 1 of Protocol 1, those positive obligations may require the State to take measures necessary to protect the right of property.[61] The Grand Chamber therefore agreed with and endorsed the Chamber's finding that sufficient grounds existed to hold Slovenia responsible for Ljubljanska Banka Ljubljana's debt to Ms Ališić and Mr Sadžak.[62] In this connection, the Court also noted the existence of certain evidence in the case indicating that most of the funds of the Sarajevo branch of Ljubljanska Banka Ljubljana ended up in Slovenia.[63] Whereas some delays may be justified in exceptional circumstances, the Court found that the present applicants had been made to wait too long.[64] The Court was therefore not satisfied that the authorities of Slovenia and Serbia, notwithstanding their wide margin of appreciation in this area, had struck a fair balance between the general interest of the community and the property rights of the applicants, who were made to bear a disproportionate burden.[65]

Finally, the Court held a violation of Article 1 of Protocol 1 by Slovenia had occurred with respect to Ms Ališić and Mr Sadžak.

In *Rola v Slovenia*,[66] a liquidator complained that he had lost his licence to act in bankruptcy proceedings after being convicted for violent behaviour. In this case too, the Court found a violation of Article 1 of Protocol 1. The applicant argued that the revocation of his licence, which was permanent in nature, constituted a form of oppression that arose from his conviction.[67] He alleged that a penalty had not been provided for by law at the time of the offence and had been retroactively imposed on him. He also argued that because his prison sentence had been suspended, it should not have entailed any legal consequences. Article 99 of the Slovenian Criminal Code applicable at the time the criminal offences were committed clearly stated that no legal consequences would apply if a convicted person was given, inter alia, a suspended prison sentence. The mentioned provision of the Criminal Code could not have been overridden by another statute.

[61] See Broniowski, cited above, § 143, with further references, and *Likvidējamā p/s. Selga and Vasiļevska v Latvia* (2013), nos 17126/02 and 24991/02, §§ 94–113, 1 October 2013.

[62] *Alisić*, para. 116.

[63] *Alisić*.

[64] *Alisić*, para. 124.

[65] *Alisić*, para. 124.

[66] Case of *Rola v Slovenia* (2019) (Applications nos 12096/14 and 39335/16). Judgment Strasbourg, 4 June 2019, Final, 04/09/2019.

[67] *Rola v Slovenia*, para 49.

This in his words meant that the punishment imposed on him held no basis in law.[68]

The applicant complained that revocation of his liquidator's licence and the bar on him reapplying for a licence was in breach of Article 1 of Protocol 1 to the Convention. In earlier cases involving professional practices, the Court had taken the view that a restriction on applicants' right to practise the profession concerned, such as a refusal to register an applicant on a professional list, significantly affected the conditions of their professional activities and reduced the scope of those activities.[69] In cases concerning the granting of licences or permits to carry out a business, the Court indicated that the revocation or withdrawal of a permit or licence did interfere with the applicant's right to the peaceful enjoyment of their possessions, including the economic interests connected with the underlying business.[70]

Turning to the present case, the Court noted that it was not disputed that the revocation of his licence had caused the applicant to be struck off the Register of Liquidators and could no longer be assigned any insolvency cases, and that he consequently lost his main income source.[71]

The Court suggested that the facts that the applicant's licence also included permission to perform certain public services and that after its revocation he could have worked in other professions were not in the Court's view sufficient to divest the licence in question of its economic nature.[72]

Further, in the Court's opinion in so far as the government referred to the legal basis for the withdrawal of the applicant's licence, this essentially related to the merits of the case. As regards the applicability, the government did not put forward any other argument calling into question the existence in the present case of an underlying professional practice of a certain worth that had the nature of a private right and thus constituted an asset.[73] The Court therefore concluded that the applicant's professional practice amounted to a possession within the meaning of the first sentence of Article 1 of Protocol 1.

Having already established that the applicant had 'possessions' within the meaning of the mentioned article, the Court then investigated whether the revocation of his licence amounted to interference with the peaceful enjoyment of his possessions.

[68] *Rola v Slovenia*, para 49.

[69] Whereas a consequence of the restrictions the applicant's income and the value of his clientele and, more generally, his business, had fallen, the Court held that there had been an interference with the right to the peaceful enjoyment of possessions; ibid, para 70. See also *Malik v the United Kingdom*, no 23780/08, § 90, 13 March 2012.

[70] *Rola v Slovenia*, para 71.

[71] *Rola v Slovenia*, para 72.

[72] The Court then found it significant in this connection that the licence allowed the applicant to carry out professional practice for which he was paid. He performed such practice for more than seven years prior to the impugned decision; *Rola v Slovenia*, para. 73.

[73] *Rola v Slovenia*, para 74.

The Court ruled that the revocation of the applicant's licence constituted a measure of control over the use of property, which must be considered under the second paragraph of Article 1 of Protocol 1.[74] The first requirement of this article is that any interference by a public authority with the peaceful enjoyment of possessions be lawful. A measure aimed at controlling the use of property can moreover only be justified if it is shown, inter alia, to be 'in accordance with the general interest'.[75]

Here, one should note that the Court observed that Article 100 of the Old Criminal Code (as well as Article 79 of the Criminal Code) set out measures which were to be regarded as the 'legal consequences of a conviction', including terminating the authorisation to perform a public function and imposing a bar on the acquisition of certain rights like the right to perform public functions and particular professions.[76]

In view of the foregoing and given that the applicant had committed the criminal offences in 2003 and 2004 when the applicable law was the Bankruptcy Act and not the Financial Operations Act on which the revocation was based, and had received a suspended sentence, the Court found that the applicant could not have reasonably foreseen that his conviction would automatically lead to the revocation of his licence.[77] The impugned measure was thereby not lawful within the meaning of Article 1 of Protocol 1. Accordingly, the Court decided there had been a violation of Article 1 of Protocol 1.

Another insightful case is *Valant v Slovenia* (ECtHR 24 Jan 2017)[78] which relates to a disputed car seized during a criminal investigation (breach of Article 1),[79] whereas *Vaskrsic v Slovenia*[80] concerns Zoran Vaskrsić, a Slovenian

[74] See, mutatis mutandis, *Tre Traktörer AB v Sweden*, 7 July 1989, § 55, Series A no 159, and *Capital Bank AD v Bulgaria*, no 49429/99, § 131, ECHR 2005 XII (extracts).

[75] An interference must also strike a 'fair balance' between the demands of the general interest of the community and the requirements of the protection of the individual's fundamental rights (see *Vékony v Hungary*, no 65681/13, § 32, 13 January 2015, and Biagioli, decision cited above, § 101; *Rola v Slovenia*, para 82). In addition, the Court noted that the Slovenian authorities in the present case relied on the provisions of the Slovenian Financial Operations Act as the basis for revoking the applicant's licence, without addressing the applicability of the relevant criminal law provisions. However, it cannot be ignored that the Slovenian Constitutional Court considered the revocation of a licence following a criminal conviction to be a 'legal consequence of conviction' and that the government itself acknowledged the pertinence of the criminal-law provisions to the present situation by submitting that the Financial Operations Act had been 'a partial implementation act within the framework of the Criminal Code or the Old Criminal Code;' ibid, para 83.

[76] Furthermore, Article 99 of the Old Criminal Code (as well as Article 78 of the Criminal Code) limited the incurrence of a 'legal consequence of conviction' to cases of a custodial sentence and explicitly provided that the measure could not be imposed if the person had been given a suspended sentence. It further provided that only the statute could prescribe 'legal consequences of conviction' and that the latter should not be applied retroactively; *Rola v Slovenia*, para 84.

[77] *Rola v Slovenia*, para 85.

[78] 23912/12 (Judgment (Merits and Just Satisfaction): Court (Fourth Section)), [2017] ECHR 90.

[79] See also *B.K.M. Lojistik Tasimacilik Ticaret Limited Sirketi v Slovenia* (2017) 42079 EHRR12.

[80] *Vaskrsić v Slovenia* (2017) 31371 EHRR 12.

national born in 1980 and living in Kresnice, Slovenia. He especially relied on Article 1 of Protocol 1 (protection of property), complaining that the sale of his home by public auction involved a disproportionate interference with his property rights. He alleged that the property was sold for 50 per cent of its market value in the course of debt enforcement proceedings arising from a principal debt of just EUR 124.

In *Kranjc v Slovenia*, relying on Art 1, Protocol 1 the applicant successfully argued that a change to the law that led to his disability allowance being halved was in breach of the Convention. The case followed many cases in the same vein. Despite reaching this positive conclusion, in its reasoning the Court relied on deeply problematic assumptions about the relationship between rights and fiscal policy and failed to interrogate harmful stereotypes of disabled persons.[81]

In the famous *Pintar et al v Slovenia*[82] (the 'subordinated bonds case'), the Court noted in this connection that it previously held that the shares of a company placed in compulsory administration for being insolvent and unable to meet its liabilities undoubtedly had an economic value and constituted possessions within the meaning of Article 1 of Protocol 1.[83]

Finally, in *Lekić v Slovenia*,[84] the Court accepted that the mere possession of a share created an interest of a proprietary nature and that the lack inter alia of assets did not remove the applicant's from the ambit of Article 1 of Protocol 1 (ibid, § 71). The Court thus found that the mentioned article did apply to the cancellation of the applicant's shares even on the assumption that the government's objection concerning their questionable economic value was valid.

In relation to the bonds, the Court observed that the bondholders in principle held a 'legitimate expectation' to have their claims met in line with the contractual clauses.[85] The Court noted the government's suggestion that due to their financial situation the banks would be unable to honour their obligations to the bondholders to any extent.[86] Yet, in the absence of any domestic judicial ruling on this point and having regard to the limited information in its possession, the Court stated that it was not in a position to conclude that the bonds in question had no economic value.[87]

The Court therefore concluded that Article 1 of Protocol 1 applied to the present case and that the cancellation of the applicant's shares or bonds amounted

[81] *Krajnc v Slovenia* (2017) 38775 EHRR 14.
[82] The case of *Pinter et al v Slovenia* (2021) 49969 EHRR 14.
[83] See also *Vefa Holding Sh.p.k. and Alimuçaj v Albania* (dec), no 24096/05, § 93, 14 June 2011.
[84] *Lekić v Slovenia* (2018) 36480 EHRR 07.
[85] See, mutatis mutandis, *Mamatas et al v. Greece*, nos 63066/14 and 2 others, § 91, 21 July 2016.
[86] *Lekić v Slovenia*, para 92.
[87] It points out that the Constitutional Court left this question open, referring those affected by the extraordinary measures to pursue their claims in the relevant proceedings. However, any such proceedings continue to be suspended to date; *Lekić v Slovenia*, para 92.

to an interference with their right guaranteed by this provision.[88] In the light of the foregoing, the Court concluded that the interference with the applicant's possessions was not accompanied by sufficient procedural guarantees against arbitrariness and was hence not lawful within the meaning of Article 1 of Protocol 1. It was thus neither necessary nor, due to the lack of relevant information, possible for the Court to ascertain whether the other requirements of that provision had been complied with. The Court accordingly refrained from expressing any opinion as to whether the extraordinary measures that led the applicant's shares and bonds to be cancelled were in the general interest and, if so, whether a fair balance had been struck between the demands of the general interest of the community and protection of the applicant's right to peaceful enjoyment of their possessions.[89] In conclusion, the Court dismissed the government's preliminary objections that were linked to the merits and found that Article 1 of Protocol 1 to the Convention had been violated.

3.2. Judicial Backlogs

The sheer number of cases dealing with the length of proceedings (263 out of all 373 judgments) may itself indicate a serious malfunction of the Slovenian judicial system and reflect the dubious quality of the Slovenian judiciary, which then also results in an eroded/suboptimal rule of law. Namely, such delayed justice is economically speaking a source of uncertainty, risk, and moral hazard that directly and indirectly reduces economic growth, productivity, cooperation, progress, and social wealth. The restrictive scope of this chapter does not permit an extensive analysis of all those cases, yet one may briefly address the most famous one.

In *Lukenda v Slovenia*,[90] the applicant suffered an injury at work and received disability benefits. In 1998, he began civil proceedings claiming an increase in his disability benefits. In 2002, the court at first instance delivered a judgment partly upholding the applicant's claim. The applicant's appeal against the judgment was allowed, with the proceedings ending in 2004 with another Higher Court judgment which increased the level of the applicant's disability benefits.[91] The total duration of the proceedings was five years and three months. Although an opinion of a medical expert was required to decide the case, the latter was neither procedurally nor factually of exceptional complexity.[92] Moreover, there was no evidence suggesting that the applicant had contributed in a significant way to the length

[88] *Lekić v Slovenia*, para. 93.
[89] *Lekić v Slovenia*, para. 93.
[90] *Lukenda v Slovenia* (2005) 23032 EHRR 02.
[91] European Court of Human Rights, Information Note on the Court's case law No 79, October 2005.
[92] ECtHR (n 91).

of the proceedings. Hence, the proceedings' overall length had been excessive, notably the more than 4-year duration of the proceedings before the first-instance court.[93] The Court unanimously found a violation of Article 13 concerning an effective remedy.

4. Discussion and Policy Recommendations: Rule of Law, Rule by Law or Rule of Judges?

Economics literature suggests that not only is law highly relevant in the development of countries, but also that particular legal systems do better than others.[94] That is, when the rule of law is missing manufacturing, trade, a peaceful social fabric, and human progress rarely flourish. In their empirical study, Castiglione et al show a positive double causality relationship exists between the rule of law and income per capita whereby as income increases, greater respect for the rule of law is acquired, and vice versa.[95] They also suggest that the rule of law (and the quality of legal institutions) has a negative relationship with pollution, confirming that the enforcement of rules is a *conditio sine qua non* to control pollution, while the reverse causality that pollution influences the rule of law does not hold.[96] Their study also offers evidence that efficient legal rules and a regulatory framework might indeed boost the sustainability (relative to the environmental sustainability) agenda and associated goals. The reinforcement of the rule of law, they argue, is

[93] As was obvious from the latest court statistics published by the Ministry of Justice of the respondent State that the length of judicial proceedings remained a major problem in Slovenia. The violation of the applicant's right to a trial within a reasonable time was not an isolated incident, but a systemic problem that resulted from inadequate legislation and inefficiency in the administration of justice. Under Art 46, a State's legal obligation is not just to pay those concerned the sums awarded by way of just satisfaction, but also to select, subject to supervision by the Committee of Ministers, the general and/or, if appropriate, individual measures to be adopted in their domestic legal order to put an end to the violation found by the Court and to redress the effects so far as is possible. In conclusion, the Court identified some of the weaknesses of the legal remedies guaranteed by the respondent State, whilst acknowledging that certain recent developments showed reassuring improvements. Hence, to prevent future violations of the right to a trial within a reasonable time it encouraged the respondent State to either amend the existing range of legal remedies or add new ones to secure effective redress for violations of this right; ECtHR (n 91).

[94] M Faure and J Smits, 'Introduction' in M Faure and J Smits (eds), *Does Law Matter? On Law and Economic Growth* (Cambridge, Intersentia, 2011). See also HR Coase, 'The Nature of the Firm' (1937) 4(1) *Economica* 386, 405; and HR Coase, 'The Problem of Social Cost' (1961) 3(1) *Journal of Law and Economics* 1, 44.

[95] C Castiglione, D Infante and J Smirnova, 'Environment and Economic Growth: Is the Rule of Law the Go-between? The Case of High Income Countries' (2015) 5(26) *Energy, Sustainability and Society* 1, 7. See also HR Coase, *The Firm, the Market and the Law* (Chicago, University of Chicago Press, 1988); HR Coase, *Essays on Economics and Economists* (Chicago, University of Chicago Press, 1994); HR Coase, 'The New Institutional Economics' (1998) 88(2) American Economic Review, Papers and Proceedings 72, 74; and RD Cooter and HB Schäfer, *Solomon's Knot: How Law can end the Poverty of Nations* (New Jersey, Princeton University Press, 2012).

[96] Castiglione (n 95).

essential for controlling environmental quality. Moreover, Castiglione et al add that in order 'to achieve the goals of economic development, it is crucial that the rules are clear, applied, and enforced'.[97]

The current legal definition of the rule of law that this chapter employs as a reference point is the United Nations' (2004, report of the Secretary General) which provides that:

> a principle of governance in which all persons, institutions and entities, public and private, including State itself, are accountable to laws that are publicly promulgated, equally enforced and independently adjudicated, and which are consistent with international human rights norms and standards. It requires, as well, measures to ensure adherence to the principles of supremacy of law, equality before the law, accountability to the law, fairness in the application of the law, separation of powers, participation in decision-making, legal certainty, avoidance of arbitrariness and procedural and legal transparency.[98]

John Rawls presents four elements of the rule of law concept, namely a law must: a) be capable of being complied with by those to whom it is addressed; b) treat equally those who are similarly situated with respect to a given legal rule; c) be public; and d) provide a means for determining the truth of any facts needed for the application of a legal rule.[99] In line with this reasoning, Judge Posner advances the thesis that all of these elements have an economic rationale and are also central to the economics concept of the law.[100]

Further, some theorists distinguish between the rule of law and what they call rule by law,[101] celebrating one and disparaging the other. The rule of law is supposed to lift law above politics. The idea is that the law should rise above every powerful person and agency in the land. Rule by law, in contrast, connotes the instrumental use of law as a tool of political power. Here, the state uses law to control the citizens but tries never to allow law to be used to control the state. Rule by law is associated with the debasement of legality by authoritarian regimes, in modern China for example.

In addition, Spač et al show that a considerably autonomous judiciary might chiefly lead to the empowerment of judicial elites.[102] This reduces the judiciary's democratic accountability, compartmentalising it from society and enabling it to promote its own interests. The authors suggest that selection processes have often been used to fill judicial benches with judges closely tied to the system.

[97] Castiglione (n 95).

[98] United Nations, *Report of the Secretary General. The Rule of Law and Transitional Justice in Conflict and Post-conflict Societies* (New York, United Nations, 2004, S/2004/616, III.6).

[99] J Rawls, *A Theory of Justice*, 2nd edn (Cambridge, Belknap Press, 1999) 237–239.

[100] Posner also suggests that the idea of the rule of law originates in Aristotle's concept of 'corrective justice,' a concept itself rich in economic significance; Posner (n 12) 337.

[101] Tamanaha (n 6) 3.

[102] Spáč, Šipulová and Urbániková (n 11).

Accountability mechanisms like promotions, disciplinary procedures or remuneration schemes have been used to reward the allies of those on the top of the hierarchy and to punish their critics. They also argue that the Slovak example reveals the danger of establishing judicial self-governance in countries where an internal ethical and institutional culture and a strong sense of judicial duty are still lacking.[103]

Finally, Lord Mance suggests that ensuring the greatest possible accountability of judges is an important part of their judicial role.[104] Lord Mance describes six focal points concerning how to inculcate the law into society and insert the rule of law into the relationships among the citizens: a) there should be an appropriately accessible and speedy appeal process; b) judgments have to address the issues, they must explain to the parties why a judge has come to the conclusions they have based on fact and law;[105] c) courts must to avoid delays – delay on any level of the court system in Lord Mance's view kills the memory and destroys the touch, it makes the ultimate task of deciding and writing judgments much more difficult; d) courts should be aware of the incentives produced by their judgments and should take them into account;[106] e) court procedures should be transparent and accessible;[107] f) judges have to attend conferences and speak publicly on legal and sometimes even other themes; and h) if judges engage in misconduct in connection to their judicial office they should expect to be disciplined.[108] In addition, Lord Mance stresses that judges should not act as primary decision-makers.[109] Justice Jacobucci states that 'in carrying out their duties, courts are not to second-guess legislatures and the executives'.[110] Moreover, the system of judicial appointments must have the confidence of society generally and provide a judiciary of appropriate quality and with an appropriate cross-section of skills.[111]

Judiciaries also develop an internal collegiality which adds to cohesive jurisprudence. However, as Lord Mance argues such collegiality should never degenerate into cliques or arrogance, or unwillingness to give effect to the judicial oath sworn by every judge.[112] In other words, although without judges there would be no

[103] Spáč, Šipulová and Urbániková (n 11).

[104] Lord Mance, 'The Role of Judges in a Representative Democracy' in G Amato, B Barbisan and C Pinelli (eds), *Rule of Law vs Majoritarian Democracy* (Oxford, Hart Publishing, 2021) 350.

[105] They must cut to the chase, focusing on the points that matter and disregard unnecessary recitation or discourse; Lord Mance (n 104) 350.

[106] Their judgment may affect third parties, society at large or the executive or legislature, their decision may constitute an important precedent or guide and hence it must be framed accordingly to be clear, understandable and usable; Lord Mance (n 104) 351.

[107] Courts should welcome visitors to court-rooms, have web-casting hearings, press releases, short oral explanations of their reasons on YouTube, have effective press office, receive members of other judiciaries, as well as school and university groups with whom Justice will frequently meet or have lunch; Lord Mance (n 104) 351.

[108] Lord Mance (n 104) 350–352.

[109] Lord Mance (n 104) 346.

[110] Lord Mance (n 104) 346.

[111] Lord Mance (n 104) 348.

[112] Lord Mance (n 104) 348.

administration of justice or rule of law at all, such a rule of law should not be turned into rule by judges.

4.1. General Policy Recommendations

The previous discussion and presented cases and data on judicial backlogs make it obvious (also the latest court statistics published by the Ministry of Justice) that the pure quality of judicial decision-making and the length of court proceedings remain the most pressing problems of the judiciary and hence for the operation of the rule of law in Slovenia.

First, the analysis of previous European Court of Human Rights' jurisprudence on the protection of property rights in Slovenia reveals shocking cases clearly demonstrating that Slovenian courts sometimes still have a vague understanding of protection of basic property rights, such as the peaceful enjoyment of an individual's property, property rights on bank deposits, shares, vehicles, occupational licences, and private houses.[113] Namely, one could argue that a sophisticated national judiciary which understands the implications of the protection of fundamental property rights should decide those cases in line with the modern western jurisprudence on the protection of property rights where such protection features as one of the key postulates of the rule of law concept. Such rudimentary property rights cases should thus never appear before the European Court of Human Rights because they should have been adequately addressed by national courts and may hence be interpreted as an indication of poor judicial quality in the administration of justice. Such vague and uncertain protection and enforcement of property rights have thus not only eroded the rule of law but may also be seen as one of the biggest sources of inefficiency, uncertainty, opportunism, and moral hazard that directly and indirectly trumps social wealth and prosperity.[114]

Second, the numerous and systematic violations of an applicant's right to a trial within a reasonable time are not isolated incidents, but, as argued, are a systemic problem that results from inadequate legislation and inefficiency (i.e. poor quality) in the administration of justice. This poor quality is also the main obstacle to the development of the rule of law. In other words, judicial backlogs and poor-quality

[113] Well-defined property rights and low transaction costs (i.e. a well-functioning legal system, enforcement of contracts and rule of law) are necessary preconditions for cooperative behaviour, allocative efficiency, social wealth and human progress. See CJ Coyne, *After War: The Political Economy of Exporting Democracy* (Stanford, Stanford University Press, 2008).

[114] See, eg D Acemoglu and JA Robinson, *Why Nations Fail: The Origins of Power, Prosperity and Poverty* (New York, Crown Business, 2012); DC North, *Institutions, Institutional Change and Economic Performance* (Cambridge, Cambridge University Press, 1990); M Olson, *The Rise and Decline of Nations: Economic Growth, Stagflation, and Social Rigidities* (New Haven, Yale University Press, 1984); and DC North and RP Thomas, *The Rise of the Western World: A New Economic History* (Cambridge, Cambridge University Press, 1973).

decisions are the greatest threat to the rule of law in the area of private law and in the relationships among citizens. Further, its transformation into rule by law or even into rule by judges might be perceived as one of the greatest shortcomings of the current Slovenian legal landscape.

Of course, the Slovenian judiciary is well aware that these problems exist and has asked the Supreme Court of Slovenia to strategically address issues regarding quality. Two large problem areas have been identified: a) the quality of judicial work (skills and transfer of knowledge), and b) the low trust in the judiciary (a consequence of the first problem). These problems have had to be addressed with limited human and financial resources, while also noting that Slovenia has no real judicial academy and there is no formal obligatory specialised training for court staff.[115] This makes the establishing of a proper, dedicated judicial academy with compulsory specialised training abroad (in the most effective and advance legal systems – e.g. in the Netherlands, Germany, Denmark, England) as well as at home an urgent priority for enhancing the rule of law in Slovenia.

Reports suggest that the activities within the IQ Justice project have been evolving organically.[116] The Supreme Court and the Ministry of Justice have committed themselves to making suitable changes in the legislation and case law. Also emphasised in reports is that in line with the living instrument approach, there is an online platform attached to every manual where judges can now comment on the content and suggest improvements.[117]

The systematic amendments made to the Courts Act have significantly strengthened judicial self-governance in Slovenia. The essential functions of judicial administration that support judicial independence (e.g. management of knowledge, the budget for courts, human resources, IT) were gradually transferred to the Supreme Court. The mentioned law also enacted the duty of a candidate for position of president of the court (including the Supreme Court) to prepare a six-year strategic programme for the Court's work, including the

[115] The goals of the project were multiple and interconnected: a) to increase the quality of judicial activity; b) to increase the competence of court staff to enable them to support judges in their work; c) the greater satisfaction of court staff and judges with working conditions within the judiciary; d) to improve communication between judges of different court instances; e) better communication with court users by providing procedural justice; f) to foster judicial self-governance; and g) to increase trust in the judiciary.

[116] More judges are trained to be mentors to new judges and thus more new judges became mentored. Similarly, judicial workshops with supervision techniques are receiving more applications, following the word-of-mouth praise of judges who took part, creating a more integrated community within the judiciary.

[117] Following the example of the manual for new judges, a special manual will be prepared for new members of court staff. The same applies, mutatis mutandis, to the procedural justice component of the IQ Justice project – the brochures and the website will be regularly updated, supplemented by new animations. The brochures were to be disseminated in all courts in the second half of 2019. To encourage even more judges and court staff to use them, more presentations would be made at training events to reach as wide a potential audience as possible. Other stakeholders would be informed including the Ombudsman, the Ministry of Justice, and the Ministry of Education, Science and Sports. Special training events were foreseen for judges and court staff across the country to familiarise them with procedural justice issues and challenges.

priority areas of its work. Current President of the Supreme Court of Slovenia Justice Damijan Florjančič defined in his six-year strategic programme the areas of quality, independence, efficiency of judicial adjudication and procedural fairness as the cornerstones of his work. In a recent remarkable interview, he also strikingly and self-critically assessed the existing problems of the Slovenian judiciary and emphasised that:

> the work of a judge is not a clerical job away from the public eye, instead our work is and must be transparent and public. A judge does not do business in a private office, and judicial independence should not be understood as inviolability in any sense. Above all, a judge must be capable of sovereign, autonomous decision-making and be able to explain his decisions concisely. Many cases from ethical judicial commission show a low level of self-criticism, which should not be characteristic of a judge's character.[118]

Another result of the pressing judicial backlogs is the procedure whereby every February the Supreme Court opens the judicial year by outlining the priorities in the area of judicial administration. For instance, at the opening of the judicial year 2015, the Slovenian judiciary committed itself to preparing a multi-annual project to improve the quality of justice. In addition, Kosar argues that the rise of judicial self-governance is not necessarily a panacea since it could lead to political contestation and the creation of new channels of politicisation of the judiciary.[119]

Finally, the presented case law analysis also shows that the rule of law in Slovenia is also expressed or realised in private law (i.e. protection of property rights). Specifically, examination of relevant judgments delivered by the ECtHR with respect to Slovenian cases of property rights and access to justice reveals that the rule of law concept is also materialised also in the domain of property law and concerns not merely the vertical relationship between the ECtHR and national states but also the horizontal inter-citizen relationships. Such horizontal effects of the protection of property rights and access to justice mitigate many of the substantive shortcomings of the Slovenian judicial decision-making process in the administration of justice, establishing horizontal certainty and predictability in the enforcement and protection of property rights and access to justice, and are thereby essential for boosting horizontal productive/cooperative behaviour and, in turn, pursuing prosperity and social wealth.

4.2. Specific Law and Economics Policy Suggestions

Law and economics literature identifies several efficient incentive mechanisms to ease the observed principal–agent problem, reduce the agency costs of the

[118] D Florjančič, 'Laže je Kazati s Prstom na Sodstvo kot mu dati v Roke Orodje za Delo' (2022b) *Delo Sobotna Priloga*, Ljubljana, 26 November 2022, 4–6.

[119] D Kosař, 'Beyond Judicial Councils: Forms, Rationales and Impact of Judicial Self-Governance in Europe' (2018) 19 *German Law Journal* 7.

career judiciary, and solve the adverse selection problem. Since Slovenian judges are self-interested, wealth-maximising, rational individuals, financial incentives (salary) might be the first appropriate mitigation mechanism. Yet, if judges (like in the continental judiciary) of the same rank are paid the same amount and given that sizeable differences in output across judges often exist, the wages then do not have a positive causative effect on their marginal product.[120] The compensation of continental judges hence does not depend on the quality of their rulings (or vice versa) and thus potential quality does not lead to any direct benefit and there is also little economic payoff for judges from their quality judging.[121] Obviously, low financial compensation will also result in the *ex ante* adverse selection problem (where the best fresh graduates are driven away) and will influence retirement decisions.[122] An increase in financial rewards for judges might accordingly be an intuitive and straightforward remedy.

However, the literature also shows that the increased financial reward incentive mechanism should be applied *ex ante* to attract better young law graduates and thus solve the adverse selection problem, albeit it loses its merit once young lawyers become judges.[123] Here, as already mentioned, the incentive effect for increasing productivity and effectiveness is lost and alternative incentive mechanisms (carrots and sticks) should be developed and applied.

The promotion prospect is a very powerful alternative to the incentive mechanism that could be offered as the first such carrot, although judges would rarely admit that a desire for promotion is a motivating factor.[124] Still, the literature provides significant empirical evidence that judges in the USA and Japan are motivated by the prospects of their promotion.[125] In a series of articles, Ramseyer and Rasmusen convincingly show that promotion prospects influence the behaviour of lower court judges in Japan – they induce them to work effectively and increase their productivity and effectiveness.[126] The desire to be promoted

[120] R Smyth, 'Do Judges Behave as Homo Economicus, and if so, can we Measure their Performance? An Antipodean Perspective on a Tournament of Judges' (2004) 32 *Florida State University Law Review* 1299.

[121] TJ Miceli and MM Cosgel, 'Reputation and Judicial Decision Making' (1994) 23 *Journal of Economic Behaviour and Organisation* 31.

[122] P Squire, 'Politics and Personal Factors in Retirement from the United States Supreme Court' (1988) 10 *Political Behaviour* 180.

[123] See K Zajc and M Kovac, 'What Do the European Judges Strive for – An Empirical Assessment' (2011) 3(2) *International Journal for Court Administration* 3, 19.

[124] The tournament theory was introduced in EP Lazear and S Rosen, 'Rank-Order Tournaments as Optimum Labour Contracts' (1981) 89 *Journal of Political Economy* 841.

[125] Cohen for example presents empirical data that the desire for a promotion influences the behaviour of district judges in the Unites States; MA Cohen, 'The Motives of Judges: Empirical Evidence from Antitrust Sentencing' (1992) 12 *International Review of Law and Economics* 13. Taha further shows that judges with higher prospects of promotion are more likely to publish their opinions; AE Taha, 'Publish or Paris? Evidence of How Judges Allocate their Time' (2004) 6 *American Law and Economics Review* 1.

[126] See MJ Ramseyer and EB Rasmusen, 'Judicial Independence in a Civil Law Regime: The Evidence from Japan' (1997) 13 *Journal of Law, Economics and Organization* 2.

is also a motivating factor in the United Kingdom, New Zealand, and even in Germany.[127]

In addition, the respect (reputation effect) of other colleagues can be seen as another incentive mechanism. Law and economics literature suggests that reputation among one's peers is a powerful non-pecuniary inducement factor for many market actors.[128] Since judges are the same as all other rational, wealth-maximising persons,[129] Miceli and Cosgel state that 'how a judge is viewed by his or her colleagues, by law professors, law students and the general public' is an incentive mechanism to perform effectively.[130] Here, Cooter adds that judges generally seek prestige among the lawyers and litigants who bring cases before them.[131]

Furthermore, there could be a special yearly prize for 'best judge of the year', a list of the top 10 per cent of judges, or a blacklist of the worst 5 per cent of judges as additional reputation-respect tools. Such awards and lists could then be made public and paid attention to by society at large (or awarded by the bar, president or prime minister, for example). Last but not least, another factor which induces judges to behave productively is the power to influence outcomes through voting and the evolution of the law (creation of precedents).[132] In other words, judges might be motivated by the prospect of leaving behind a legacy. Landes and Posner suggest that judges derive utility from imposing their policy preferences on the community at large,[133] whereas Schauer stresses that 'judges could plausibly select outcomes, or select substantive or methodological trademarks, for the purpose of maximizing their own influence'.[134]

5. Conclusions

Although since its independence in 1991 Slovenia has achieved remarkable economic and social progress and the Slovenian judiciary is on a constant trajectory of improvement, numerous challenges still lie ahead for the administration

[127] Smyth (n 120).

[128] See eg HR McAdams, 'Cooperation and Conflict: The Economics of Group Status Production and Race Discrimination' (1995) 108 *Harvard Law Review* 1003.

[129] Implying that their wealth-maximisation behaviour encompasses also their desire to perform public service and to achieve a 'higher calling'. In economic terms, this desire and motivation to perform public service represents part of their utility curve (different weight) and is included in the wealth-maximising definition.

[130] Miceli and Cosgel (n 121).

[131] RD Cooter, 'The Objectives of Private and Public Judges' (1983) 41 *Public Choice* 107.

[132] Smyth (n 120).

[133] WM Landes and RA Posner, 'Legal Precedent: A Theoretical and Empirical Analysis' (1976) 19 *Journal of Law and Economics* 249.

[134] F Schauer, 'Incentives, Reputation, and Inglorious Determinants of Judicial Behaviour' (1999) 68 *University of Cincinnati Law Review* 615.

of justice and operationalisation of the rule of law. The overriding significance of the rule of law and the commitment to by all stakeholders must be constantly nurtured and embedded in all parts of society and passed down from generation to generation. This chapter shows that ensuring as much accountability of judges as possible is a vital part of their judicial role and that there should be an appropriately accessible and speedy appeal process where judgments must address the issues and explain to the parties why the judge has come to the conclusions they have based on fact and law, and courts have to avoid delays since delay on any level of the court system kills the memory and destroys the touch, making the ultimate task of deciding and writing judgments much more difficult. Courts should also be aware of the incentives produced by their judgments and take them into account, whereas court procedures should be transparent and accessible. Judges should be required to attend conferences and speak publicly on legal and sometimes even other themes and if they engage in misconduct in connection with their judicial office, they should expect to be disciplined. Further, the system of judicial appointments must have the confidence of society generally and provide a judiciary of appropriate quality and with an appropriate cross-section of skills. Collegiality should never degenerate into cliques or arrogance, or an unwillingness to give effect to the judicial oath sworn by every judge.

Slovenian selection processes have often been used to fill judicial benches with judges bearing close ties to the system while accountability mechanisms – promotions, disciplinary procedures or remuneration schemes – are still sometimes used to reward the allies of those on top of the hierarchy and to punish their critics. The Slovenian judiciary also reveals the danger of establishing judicial self-governance in an environment where an internal ethical and institutional culture and a strong sense of judicial duty have still to mature.

Finally, the investigation shows that the rule of law in Slovenia is also both manifested in the area of property law and concerns the horizontal relationships among citizens where the ECtHR's intervention in the field of property law (as an external institutional mechanism) features as significant for enhancing the rule of law among citizens and crucial for pursuing growth, social wealth and progress (dynamic & static efficiency). The ECtHR's treatment of the length of proceedings is of the utmost importance for enhancing the rule of law both vertically and as horizontally and is of supreme importance for boosting growth, social wealth and progress. The chapter also suggests that the quality of the judiciary (i.e. judgments) is one of the most salient factors for improving the vertical and horizontal rules of law as well as pursuing the wealth of a nation where the ECtHR acts as an external institutional inducement mechanism – mitigating the shortcomings in the quality of the current Slovenian administration of justice.

Appendix

Table 1 Slovenia Macro-trends, GDP growth

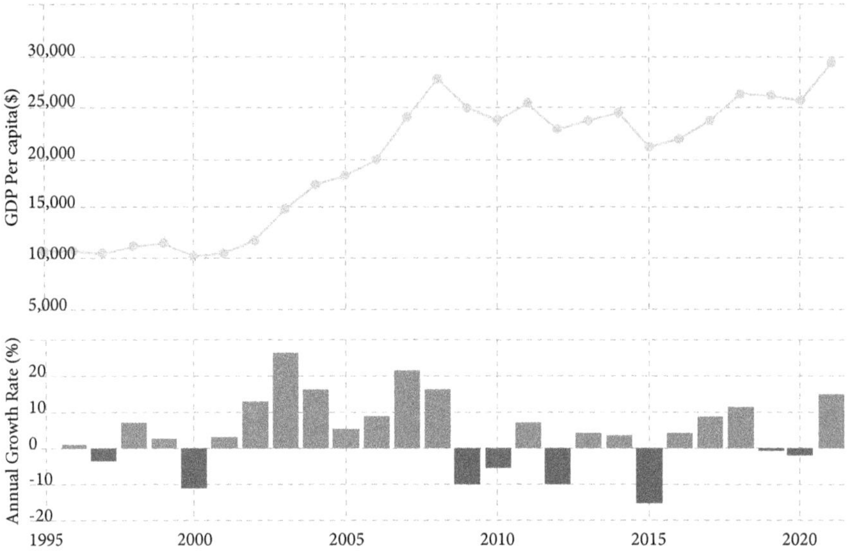

Source: World Bank 2022.

Table 2 Poverty Rate

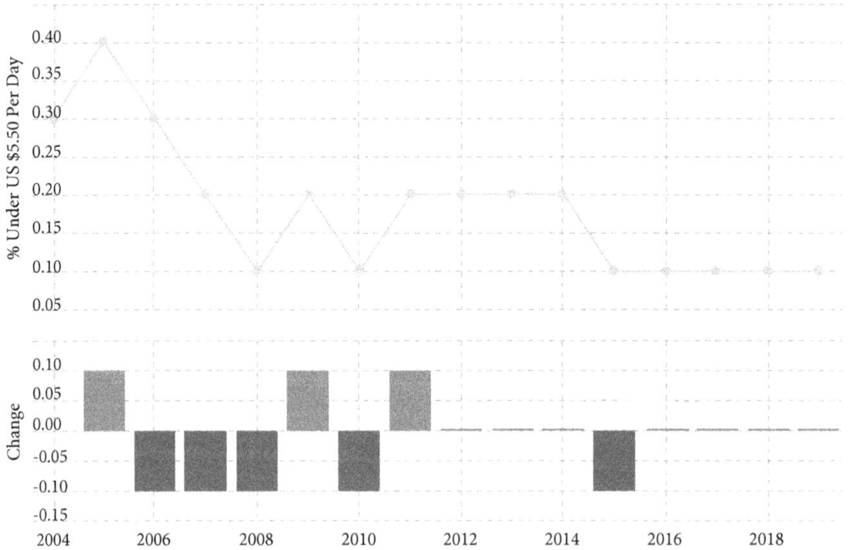

Source: World Bank 2022.

Table 3 Unemployment rate

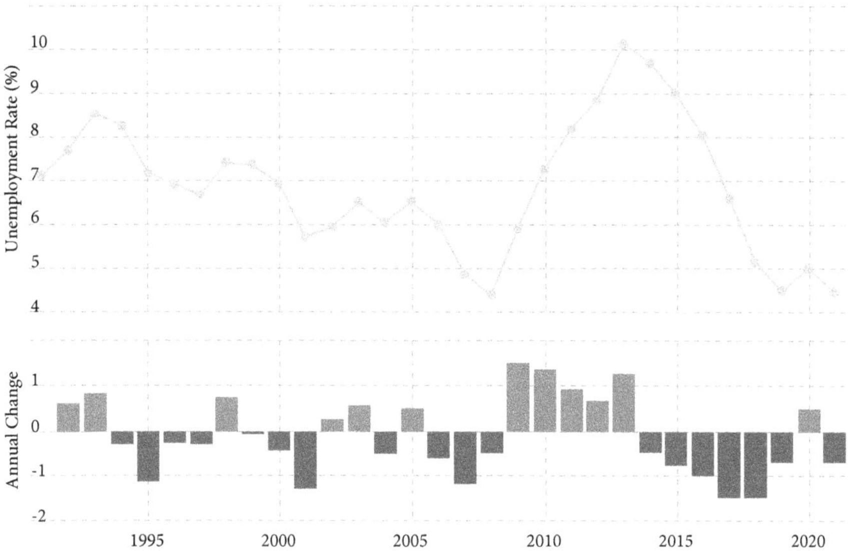

Source: World Bank 2022.

Table 4 Crime rate

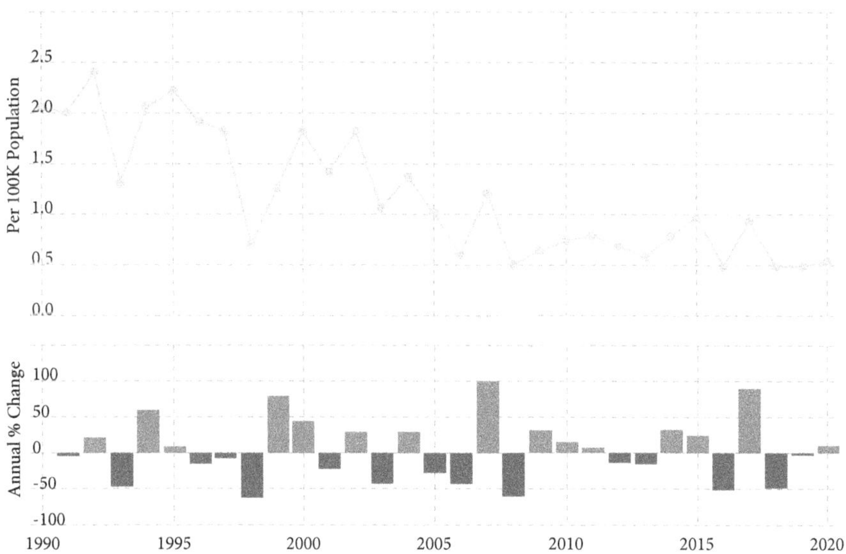

Source: World Bank 2022.

12

Private and Family Life of Same-sex Couples before the ECtHR and the CJEU. The Romanian Perspective

RALUCA BERCEA*

1. Introduction

A plurivalent, multi-layered, and therefore ambiguous concept, but also a 'concept of universal validity',[1] the rule of law has undisputedly at its core the protection of fundamental human rights. Not only has academia advanced that the rule of law can be summarised by simply referring to the guarantee of basic human rights and to the principle of equality of persons before the law,[2] but the association of the human rights and the rule of law is also enshrined in both national and international founding legal texts.

To point only to prominent examples, the continent's leading human rights organisation, the Council of Europe, presents itself as the guardian of the cardinal values of '*human rights*, democracy and the *rule of law*' (author's emphasis),[3] the achievement of which represents its essential objective. On the other hand, the Treaty on European Union stipulates in Article 2 that the Union is '*founded on the values* of respect for human dignity, freedom, democracy, equality, *the rule of law and respect for human rights, including the rights of persons belonging to minorities*' (author's emphasis). Relevantly, these values become the Unions' as they are '*common to the Member States* in a society in which pluralism, non-discrimination, tolerance, justice, solidarity and equality between women and men prevail' (author's emphasis).[4]

* This work was supported by a grant of the Romanian Ministry of Education and Research, CNCS – UEFISCDI, project number PN-III-P4-PCE-2021-0319, within PNCDI III.

[1] According to the European Commission for Democracy through Law (Venice Commission), at www.venice.coe.int/images/SITE%20IMAGES/Publications/Rule_of_Law_Check_List.pdf.

[2] P Craig, 'Formal and Substantive Conceptions of the Rule of Law: An Analytical framework' (1997) 21 *Public Law* 467, 487.

[3] General description at www.coe.int/en/web/about-us/who-we-are.

[4] Art 2, Treaty on the European Union.

Synergically, respect for human rights is a pre-condition to become a member of both the European Union and of the Council of Europe, while human rights also form the core of national member states' constitutions, often protected by so-called 'eternity clauses'. As a proof, a system of guarantees has recently been put in place at the international level to respond to the threats menacing the rule of law in various domestic legal orders. For example, under the name of 'the rule of law mechanism', a preventative tool provides a framework for an annual dialogue between the Commission, the Council, and the European Parliament together with Member States as well as national parliaments, civil society, and other stakeholders on the rule of law.[5]

It is also worth mentioning that, if, most commonly, the concept of rule of law has been described as consisting, in a nutshell, of legality, legal certainty, prohibition of arbitrariness, and access to justice before independent and impartial courts, it also repeatedly covers respect for human rights and, respectively, non-discrimination and equality before the law. After all, the rule of law would be meaningless unless granting fundamental human rights, while, equally, the protection thereof is conditioned by a strong rule of law regime.[6]

Two additional remarks are usually made concerning the rule of law issue, as understood now across Europe. On the one hand, while its basic standards must be put into practice at all levels of public power, the rule of law applies horizontally, i.e. in private law relations as well. Technically, this will translate to specific content of the States' positive obligations under the European catalogue of rights. On the other hand, the rule of law does not only mean a formal legality; therefore the mere previous authorisation of a mode of conduct by law is neither self-sufficient nor all-encompassing. As warned, 'rule by law', or 'rule by the law', or even 'law by rules' may be distorted interpretations of the rule of law.[7]

The history of Romanian constitutionalism accurately illustrates this second point. At the national level, the second half of the twentieth century saw the rise of communism, where Marxism already defined law as a simple 'superstructure' coercing the people to follow the State. Instead of the 'rule of law', Romania lived in a 'State based on the law' regime, translated in the fundamental blueprint as well, and more than a linguistic debate started over this constitutional preference for the French-inspired terminology (*état de droit*) coupled with the German ideology (*Alles Verfassungsrecht ist Staatsrecht*).[8] To date, the first article of the national

[5] More information on the setting up and functioning of this mechanism at commission.europa.eu/strategy-and-policy/policies/justice-and-fundamental-rights/upholding-rule-law/rule-law/rule-law-mechanism_en.

[6] According to the European Commission for Democracy through Law (Venice Commission), www.venice.coe.int/images/SITE%20IMAGES/Publications/Rule_of_Law_Check_List.pdf, paras 18 and 31.

[7] ibid para 14.

[8] For a detailed account on this matter see R Bercea and R Rizoiu, 'The revival of the rule of law issue. The Romanian perspective', in M Safjan (ed), *The Revival of the Rule of Law Issue* (Intersentia, Cambridge, forthcoming 2024).

Constitution, regarded as a preamble enshrining its main values, proclaims that Romania is a 'State based on the law' (*état de droit*), with the French terminology historically preferred carrying its implicit ideological load. Article 1 also mentions the supremacy of the Constitution as a basis of the legal system and the central place of legal binding rules. However, no clear definition of what a 'State based on the law' means is provided by the Constitution, which explains why national academia considers the Romanian 'rule of law' either 'an elusive concept',[9] or, even better, a standard instead of a rule, more fluid and adaptable to the context than a legal prescription[10] or again a principle in Dworkin's terms.[11] A change in this paradigm occurred after the latest revision of the Romanian Constitution in 2003, triggered by the imminent EU accession, in January 2007, with Articles 20 and 148 integrating the system of human rights treaties and the European Union binding law in the national block of constitutionality.

Against such a background, this chapter examines how the rule of law in Romania is expressed within private law. Specifically, the chapter examines the issue of same-sex relationships and its acknowledgement by the national legal system, arguing that it partakes in the rule of law not only by its close connection to the human rights constitutional core but also by the multi-levelled reactions it has recently generated. Section two describes how same-sex relationships have been perceived by the Romanian society and formalised in a correlative legal regime. Section three inquires the extent to which the specificity of the Romanian case resides in the polyphonic judicial exchanges emerging over the topic. Namely, it first describes the judicial dialogue initiated by the Romanian Constitutional Court under Article 267 TFEU, in the context of the 2018 unsuccessful popular referendum for the revision of the national Constitution regarding the redefinition of the family as 'the freely consented marriage between a man and a woman'. Second, it analyses the matter once brought before the European Court of Human Rights. Section four sums up the synergies resulting from these multi-layered perspectives while proposing a conclusion.

2. Same-sex Relations in Romania. The Social and Legal Contexts

2.1. The Social Context

As a core element to the rule of law, the principle of non-discrimination requires the prohibition of any unjustified unequal treatment under the law and/or by law.

[9] V Constantin, 'Constituția României privită din perspectiva supremației dreptului (rule of law)', in G Andreescu, M Bakk, L Bojin and V Constantin (eds), *Comentarii la Constituția României* (Polirom, Iași, 2010) 194.

[10] R Bercea and R Rizoiu (n 8).

[11] R Dworkin, *Taking Rights Seriously* (Harvard University Press, Cambridge, 1977) 22–23.

It also requests that all persons benefit of equal and effective protection against discrimination on various grounds. National legislation must therefore respect the principle of equality, by treating similar situations equally and different situations differently and by guaranteeing equality with respect to any ground of potential discrimination, including sexual orientation.

The Romanian daily reality shows, however, that in their relationship with either public or private entities, people in same-sex partnerships are far from enjoying the same treatment as that of married couples. For example, they are not recognised to have any kinship with each other in hospitals or other medical facilities, nor can they make medical decisions on behalf of their partner or have co-insured status under a partner's health insurance contract; they cannot continue the lease on their home in the event that the other partner, holder of the contract, left the premises permanently or died; similarly, if one partner died through the fault of a third party, the remaining partner cannot be compensated as would a surviving spouse; finally, same-sex couples cannot set up a family-based company, are not expressly identified by law as beneficiaries of special protection (including criminal protection) in the event of domestic violence and are not eligible to take out a loan from a bank in order to purchase a house together.

Is this de facto situation a reflection of the societal values that informally conditions or weakens a (potential) legal regime? The answer to this question is of relevance particularly for the horizontal dimension of the rule of law issue and, at first glance, it appears to be affirmative.

In 2018, based on a popular initiative to support the so-called traditional family, a referendum was held on a proposal to amend Article 48 of the Constitution in order to define the family as being founded on freely consensual marriage no longer 'between spouses', as in the current version of the text, but 'between a man and a woman'. The referendum was proposed by the Coalition for the Family[12] which went through all the stages required by the law and finally received the approval of the two Chambers of the Parliament. This enterprise was presented at the time as 'an unprecedented civic initiative in the history of Romanian democracy'.[13] However, the results of the referendum could not be validated

[12] The Family Coalition (*Coaliția pentru familie*) is an association without legal status, joined by 44 non-governmental organisations, foundations, and associations and by four Romanian federations that campaign for the promotion of conservative traditional family values. Depicted by members of the LGBTQ community and media as also expressing anti-abortion preferences and, at the extreme, as sharing an ideology of hatred (adevarul.ro/blogurile-adevarul/istoria-coalitiei-pentru-familie-1871243.html, www.observatorcultural.ro/articol/femeile-si-familia-traditionala/), the association itself justifies its mission as follows: 'We all know that the family, based on the marriage between a man and a woman, is the only inter-human relationship that provides the ideal environment for the birth, growth and education of children. In order for the family to prosper, and together with it, the Romanian society, the involvement of everyone, the entire civil society, the cults and the status institutions is needed' (coalitiapentrufamilie.ro/despre-coalitia-pentru-familie/misiune/).

[13] See www.vaticannews.va/ro/mapamond/news/2018-10/referendum-familie-romania-6-7-octombrie-2018.html.

because of a low turnout, as only 21 per cent of those entitled to vote participated in the referendum, while a 30 per cent turnout was required for it to have legal effect. The same proposed modification of the Constitution was reiterated two years later.[14] On the contrary, legislative proposals on civil partnership submitted in 2016 and 2019 have received negative opinions from the relevant national authorities (e.g. the Romanian government),[15] while similar proposals of 2010 to 2020 have been rejected.

Such a societal position appears to be in line with the European recent trend. The 2023 Report of the Secretary General of the Council of Europe on the state of democracy, human rights, and the rule of law notices in this respect a series of challenge: slow progress in adopting legislation and policies for equal rights of intersex people, legal gender recognition, same-sex marriage or partnership and for combating hate crime against LGBT+ people; also failure to adequately respond to widespread anti-LGBT+ rhetoric and a related backsliding in human rights standards. In response, capacity building of law enforcement in policing hate crime based on sexual orientation, gender identity, gender expression, and sex characteristics was carried out in various countries, including Romania, as part of European technical assistance activities to support the national authorities.[16]

However, a national survey of 2021 suggests that the Romanians' values and perception on family and marriage have slightly changed for the better as regards same-sex relations,[17] in contrast with the situation revealed by the 2019 Eurobarometer on Discrimination,[18] when statistics showed that in Romania a significant majority of people (63 per cent) had an unfavourable perception of sexual relationships between two persons of the same sex, while a similar majority (54 per cent) disagreed with the idea that gay, lesbian, and bisexual people should have the same rights as heterosexual people.

[14] Published in the Official Journal of Romania on 13 August 2020.

[15] See www.cdep.ro/pls/proiecte/upl_pck2015.proiect?idp=17751; www.cdep.ro/pls/proiecte/upl_pck2015.proiect?idp=16017.

[16] 2023 *Report of the Secretary General of the Council of Europe on the state of democracy, human rights and the rule of law, An Invitation to Recommit to the Values and Standards of the Council of Europe*, at edoc.coe.int/en/annual-activity-report/11589-state-of-democracy-human-right-and-the-rule-of-law-2023-annual-report-of-the-secretary-general-of-the-council-of-europe.html 121–123.

[17] See acceptromania.ro/wp-content/uploads/2023/05/CultMR_ACCEPT_Cercetare-familie-si-casatorie-1.pdf.

[18] 2019 Eurobarometer on Discrimination at europa.eu/eurobarometer/surveys/detail/2251. Still, an even more significant improvement is to be noted as compared to 15 years ago. The Commissioner for Human Rights of the Council of Europe conducted at that time a study examining discrimination on grounds of sexual orientation and gender identity in Europe (a second edn thereof was published in September 2011). In respect with opinions expressed on the question 'How would you personally feel about having a homosexual as a neighbour?' a 2008 report concluded that for the European Union member states 'the average European is largely comfortable with the idea of having a homosexual person as a neighbour'. However, there were important differences between countries, with respondents in Sweden (9.5), the Netherlands and Denmark (9.3) being the most comfortable with this idea on a 10-point 'comfort scale' and respondents in Romania (4.8) being the least comfortable. This conclusion was found consistent with other studies measuring attitudes and social distance that found similar patterns at that time.

By comparison, in 2021 family is considered the most important personal value by 39 per cent of the overall respondents, with faith coming in third place (9 per cent). Noteworthily, 81 per cent of the respondents declare that they do not know any homosexual people. Consistently, differences appear as to the most important reason to marry that the respondents identify when it comes to persons of different sex (69 per cent name the desire to start a family), as compared to what the general perception about same-sex couples is (only 24 per cent indicate the same aspiration to start a family as reason for marriage in this case). For heterosexual couples, marriage is justified by love in second place (63 per cent) and the necessity to be united before God in fourth place with a high score (24 per cent). By contrast, according to the general perception, same sex couples would most likely marry out of love (37 per cent). Not only do statistics show that marriage and family are not readily coupled by general opinion when it comes to relations between same-sex persons, but also, noteworthily, 25 per cent of the total sample could not mention at least one reason for which couples made of people of the same sex would want to get married. Furthermore, three important questions addressed in the survey accurately discriminate the nuances of the general perception on same-sex relations. Thus, only 26 per cent of the general population, as compared to 42 per cent of the younger one (18–34 years old) considers that same sex-couples should have the right to legally marry, as any other couples. Seventeen per cent of the general population and 14 per cent of the younger one appreciate, in addition, that same-sex couples should enjoy a form of protection, as any other couples, without however this legal regime being called 'marriage'. Still, the majority of the answers in each of the two categories (57 per cent in the general population and 44 per cent in the younger one) agrees that same sex-couples exist, but consider that they should not be legally acknowledged. The acceptance of same-sex marriages increases when the respondents have homosexual persons in their close family (63 per cent).

To positively sum up the account on the informal Romanian societal background, one must notice that a future acknowledgement by the national legislation of same-sex marriages is not rejected: 71 per cent of the general population and 74 per cent of the younger one estimates in fact that such legislative change would have no consequence on their own lives. Similarly, most of the respondents in both age categories appreciate that law should protect all families, including those made up of same-sex persons and, in any case, that it is important that all individuals – homosexuals are specifically mentioned – should be treated with due respect.

These sociological conclusions trigger legal consequences. As Section three will explain, they will be used as arguments in assessing the margin of appreciation[19] contingently allowing the national authorities to claim a pressing social need to protect the 'traditional family', thus allegedly entitling them not to efficiently protect same-sex couples.

[19] For a Council of Europe account on the margin of appreciation doctrine, see a brief explanatory paper available at www.coe.int/t/dghl/cooperation/lisbonnetwork/themis/echr/paper2_en.asp.

2.2. The Legal Context

Romania is a republic founded on a written Constitution, whose current text was enacted in 1991, after the fall of the communist regime at the end of 1989. The latest revision of the Romanian Constitution took place in 2003 and mainly aimed to fulfil the requirements of Romania's accession to the European Union. According to Article 152 of the fundamental text, certain aspects of the constitutional blueprint, such as the independence of the judiciary, political pluralism or achieved standards of human rights protection cannot be revised, the Romanian Constitutional Court being the guardian of these limits. Correlatively, the Romanian Constitution also consecrates regulatory limitations to fundamental rights' protection, by explicitly mentioning, in Article 53, the general conditions under which such rights may be legally restricted.[20] Moreover, several articles of the Romanian Constitution are relevant as far as same-sex couples are concerned, among which those enshrining the equality of rights,[21] the right to intimate, family, and private life,[22] and the one defining the family.[23]

Noteworthily, the national constitutional architecture is connected to the international legal system. Pursuant to Article 11 of the Constitution, the national legal order is a dualist one with regard to the general public international law.

By contrast, Article 20 Para (2) of the Romanian Constitution provides that, as far as human rights are concerned, international treaties can set higher standards that will have to be observed by the national system if the domestic constitutional standard is set lower.[24] The Romanian legal system is therefore a monistic one

[20] Art 53 Romanian Constitution: Restriction on the exercise of certain rights or freedoms: (1) The exercise of certain rights or freedoms may only be restricted by law, and only if necessary, as the case may be, for: the defence of national security, of public order, health, or morals, of the citizens' rights and freedoms; conducting a criminal investigation; preventing the consequences of a natural calamity, disaster, or an extremely severe catastrophe. (2) Such restrictions shall only be ordered if necessary in a democratic society. The measure shall be proportional to the situation having caused it, applied without discrimination, and without infringing on the existence of such right or freedom.

[21] Art 16 Romanian Constitution: Equality of rights – (1) Citizens are equal before the law and public authorities, without any privilege or discrimination. (2) No one is above the law. At the level of the secondary legislation, this principle is developed for example by the Government Ordinance no. 137/2000 on preventing and sanctioning all forms of discrimination, which states in Article 1 (2) that The principles [governing] equality among citizens and the exclusion of privileges and discrimination are guaranteed in particular with regard to the exercise of the following rights: … (iv) the right to marry and the right to choose a partner.

[22] Art 26 Romanian Constitution: Intimate, family and private life – (1) Public authorities shall respect and protect intimate, family and private life. (2) Any person has the right to conduct himself/herself freely, unless this breaches the rights and freedoms of others, public order or public morals.

[23] Art 48 Romanian Constitution: Family – (1) The family is founded on freely consensual marriage between spouses, their full equality, and the right and duty of parents to ensure the upbringing, education, and instruction of their children. (2) The conditions for concluding a marriage, its dissolution and annulment shall be established by law. Religious [services of] marriage may be celebrated only after civil marriage. (3) Children born out of wedlock are equal before the law with those born within wedlock.

[24] Art 20 (1) Romanian Constitution: Constitutional provisions concerning the citizens' rights and liberties shall be interpreted and enforced in conformity with the Universal Declaration of Human

regarding human rights, in that it grants precedence to the standards of protection laid down in international law in case of higher standards enshrined there. One consequence of this provision is that the Parliament, as the national legislative body, must check whether the draft legislation discussed and adopted are in line with the international treaties to which Romania is a party. Second, Article 20 Para (2) is also directly applicable by the courts that cannot rule on the constitutionality of domestic legislation but must remove them from application in the cases pending before them, *ex officio* or upon request of the parties, thus giving priority to international regulations that would grant more protection to fundamental human rights. Additionally, both the national ordinary courts and the Constitutional court itself are obliged to interpret national law in accordance with the relevant provisions of the international human rights treaties, in particular with the ECHR, as complemented by the case law of the ECtHR, equally binding for Romanian courts. Besides the provision of Article 1 ECHR itself, the system of the Convention is therefore expressly embedded in the block of internal constitutionality in a position of precedence in case of conflict of standards.

A similar integration of the national and supranational legal systems results from Romania's accession to the European Union, confirmed by Article 148 of the Romanian Constitution.[25] In a nutshell, the said article acknowledges that the provisions of the constituent treaties of the European Union, as well as the other binding EU institutional legislative acts, shall take precedence over the opposite provisions of the national legislation, in case of conflict and where EU law is relevant. The principles of primacy, direct effect, direct applicability of EU law, as well as the rule of consistent interpretation, are implicitly acknowledged by the constitutional text.

At the secondary level, the new Romanian Civil Code, in force since 1 October 2011, defines in its turn both family and marriage, preference being given to the traditional and conservative understanding of both institutions. Thus, family is 'based on the freely consensual marriage between spouses', circularly defined as 'the man and the woman united by marriage'.[26] Marriage, on the other hand, is

Rights, with the covenants and other treaties Romania is a party to. (2) Where any inconsistencies exist between the covenants and treaties on the fundamental human rights Romania is a party to, and the national laws, the international regulations shall take precedence, unless the Constitution or national laws comprise more favourable provisions.

[25] Art 148 (2) Romanian Constitution: As a result of the accession, the provisions of the constituent treaties of the European Union, as well as the other mandatory community regulations shall take precedence over the opposite provisions of the national laws, in compliance with the provisions of the accession act. (4) The Parliament, the President of Romania, the Government, and the judicial authority shall guarantee that the obligations resulting from the accession act and the provisions of paragraph (2) are implemented.

[26] Art 258 Romanian Civil Code: Family – (1) The family is based on freely consensual marriage between spouses, on their equality, and the right and duty of parents to ensure the upbringing and education of their children. (2) Family shall be protected by society and by the State. (3) The State is obliged to support, through economic and social measures, entry into marriage, as well as the development and consolidation of the family. (4) For the purposes of the instant law [the CC], the spouses are the man and woman united by marriage.

'the freely consensual union between a man and a woman, concluded in compliance with the law'.[27] Within this legislative framework, according to Article 277 of the Civil Code,[28] 'same-sex marriage is prohibited' (Para (1)), 'same-sex marriages concluded abroad between Romanian or foreign citizens are not recognised in Romania' (Para (2)), and 'registered partnerships between opposite or same-sex persons contracted by Romanian or foreign citizens are not recognised in Romania' (Para (3)). However, 'the legal provisions concerning the free movement of citizens of the European Union and the European Economic Area within the territory of Romania will remain valid' (Para (4)).

An important remark should conclude this section: given the Romanian constitutional monistic architecture, a change in the European perspective on the minimum standard of protection granted to the fundamental rights implied by same-sex relations will inherently modify the level of protection at the national level, should the international standard be higher than the national one, with, however, the margin of appreciation acknowledged to the national authorities remaining significant, in respect with the means chosen for putting into practice the minimum standard, as will be explained in Section 3.2. Moreover, the consistent interpretation requirement obliges both the constitutional court and the national ordinary courts to synergically keep in line with the developments of the European case-law even (if not in particular) when applying the national legislation not yet put in accordance with the newly emerged international minimum standards. As the second part of this chapter will argue, such constant connection to be made by a legal system that reflects the values of a rather conservative society is not without tension, hence the recently experienced need for an extended judicial dialogue that sometimes may take the form of strategic litigation.

3. Same-sex Relations in Romania as Object of the Judicial Dialogue

3.1. The Dialogue between the Romanian Constitutional Court and the Court of Justice of the European Union

A meaningful judicial dialogue between the national courts and the European ones in the matter of same-sex couples' private and family life has started on the occasion of the first and, so far, only referral made by the Romanian Constitutional

[27] Art 259 Romanian Civil Code: Marriage – (1) Marriage is the freely consensual union between a man and a woman, concluded in compliance with the law.

[28] Art 277 Romanian Civil Code: Prohibition on equating other forms of cohabitation with marriage, with the content quoted in the text.

Court to the Court of Justice of the European Union under the preliminary ruling procedure, in case C-673/16.[29]

The case concerns the relocation of a same-sex couple from the Netherlands to Romania, an EU Member State that, as pointed out in the previous section, does not recognise same sex partners as family members. One of these partners, Mr Relu Adrian Coman, is a Romanian citizen. In 2009, he took up residence in Brussels in order to work at the European Parliament as a parliamentary assistant, where, in 2010, he married Mr Hamilton, an American citizen whom he met in 2002. The two had lived together in New York from 2005 until 2009. In 2012, Mr Coman and his spouse embarked on the administrative steps with the Romanian administration in order to obtain the documents necessary for Mr Coman, with his non-EU-national spouse, to be able to work and reside lawfully in Romania for a period of more than three months. The Romanian authorities refused their request, maintaining that the extension of the right of temporary residence of a United States national on the conditions laid down in the Romanian legislation on immigration in conjunction with the other relevant legal provisions could not be granted for the purposes of family reunion. This refusal of the Romanian General Inspectorate for Immigration was contested by the two partners before the ordinary national courts.

As Mr Coman and Mr Hamilton argued that the relevant provisions of the Romanian Civil Code were unconstitutional, infringing the dispositions of the national Constitution that protected the right to personal life, family life, private life, and the principle of equality, the first instance court referred the case to the Romanian Constitutional Court. The legal issue involved, in fact, more than a problem of constitutionality, as the implicit question for the constitutional judge was whether the Romanian legislation could restrict the right of temporary residence of an US national, spouse of an EU citizen. Staying the proceedings, the Constitutional Court decided therefore to make a reference for a preliminary ruling under Article 267 TFEU, asking whether a Union citizen who had exercised free movement rights could enjoy, with his same-sex spouse, family reunification rights under EU law.

Noteworthily, the rule of law issue from the angle of fundamental rights is inherent to the interaction between the two Courts, as the Romanian Constitutional Court explicitly frames its questions within the ambit of the Charter of Fundamental Rights of the European Union. Thus, the Romanian Constitutional Courts asks as follows:

> Does the term spouse in Article 2(2)(a) of Directive 2004/38, read in the light of Articles 7, 9, 21 and 45 of the Charter of Fundamental Rights of the European Union,

[29] CJEU, C-673/16, *Relu Adrian Coman, Robert Clabourn Hamilton, Asociația Accept v Inspectoratul General pentru Imigrări, Ministerul Afacerilor Interne, intervener: Consiliul Național pentru Combaterea Discriminării*, ECLI:EU:C:2018:385. For more details, see R Bercea, 'Comment: Under article 21 EU Charter, the CJEU has, for the first time being, adopted, a rather differential model of judicial review' in F Casarosa and M Moraru (eds), *The Practice of Judicial Interaction in the Field of Fundamental Rights – The Added Value of the Charter of Fundamental Rights of the EU* (Cheltenham, Edward Elgar Publishing, 2022).

> include the same-sex spouse, from a State which is not a Member State of the European Union, of a citizen of the European Union to whom that citizen is lawfully married in accordance with the law of a Member State other than the host Member State?[30]

Equally, in this specific instance, aware of the systemic importance of its answer at the national level, the Constitutional Court proved eager to develop a caselaw that is consistent with the EU fundamental values. As it will become evident, thus lead, the judicial dialogue has not only contributed to fundamental rights enhancement, but also to making the multi-levelled system of fundamental rights one of mutual understanding.

Translated into the EU law concepts and associated to EU law grounds, the matter does not primarily concern Mr Hamilton, who cannot rely on the Directive 2004/38, as it does not establish a derived right of residence for third-country nationals who are family members of a Union citizen in the Member State of which that citizen is a national. On the contrary, being the citizen of an EU Member State, i.e. an EU citizen, Mr Coman enjoys the protection of fundamental rights granted to him by the rule of law regime characterising these interrelated legal orders. Indeed, Article 20 TFEU has been interpreted in the sense that the statute of being an EU citizen may be construed as the fundamental status of any Member State citizen, who therefore can directly invoke Article 21 TFEU and Articles 7, 9, 21, and 45 against their Member State of origin. It has become common EU law understanding that where, during the genuine residence of the Union citizen in the host Member State, pursuant to and in conformity with the conditions set out in Article 7(1) and (2) of Directive 2004/38, family life is created, the effectiveness of the rights conferred on the Union citizen by Article 21(1) TFEU requires that the citizen's family life in the host Member State may continue on returning to the Member State of which he is a national. Obviously, if no such derived right of residence were granted to the family member who is a third-country national, the Union citizen could be discouraged from leaving the Member State of which he is a national in order to exercise his right of residence under Article 21(1) TFEU in another Member State. The question becomes, in this new light, whether the term 'spouse' used in Article 2(2)(a) of Directive 2004/38, read in the light of Articles 7, 9, 21, and 45 of the Charter, applies to a third-country national of the same sex as the Union citizen to whom he or she is lawfully married in accordance with the law of a Member State other than the host State. In its relationship with the national legal context, the issue is whether the Romanian law could refuse to acknowledge the effects of a same sex marriage concluded by a Romanian citizen in another Member State without depriving of its essential content Article 21 TFEU.

[30] The Constitutional Court adds a second question: 'If the answer [to the first question] is in the affirmative, do Articles 3(1) and 7([2]) of Directive 2004/38, read in the light of Articles 7, 9, 21 and 45 of the Charter, require the host Member State to grant the right of residence in its territory or for a period of longer than three months to the same-sex spouse of a citizen of the European Union?'.

Incidentally, the same importance is conferred to the Charter (i.e. to the fundamental human rights as basic elements of the rule of law European legal order) by AG Wathelet in the Opinion that he delivers, where he notes, for instance, that:

> refusal to grant the application for entry and residence of a third-country national, of the same sex as the citizen of the European Union to whom he or she is married in accordance with the law of a Member State, may not be solely or decisively based on his or her sexual orientation, without infringing Articles 7 and 21 of the Charter.[31]

By simply referring the question to the Court of Justice, the Romanian Constitutional Court opened the national context to the European shared values – the national constitutional legal order becoming co-substantial to the European constitutional legal order. Even more, the fact that, besides the integration by the text (i.e. by Article 148 of the Romanian Constitution) this opening has been achieved by the national constitutional judge (i.e. the grantor of the constitutional fundamental values) partakes as essential element to the rule of law, both in its national and European meaning.

Less clear is whether, at the level of the European Union as a whole, this judicial interaction contributed to avoiding normative and jurisprudential conflict and, in particular, to peaceful coexistence of legal systems and judicial cultures. As one might have expected, once presented to the Court of Justice, the *Coman* case became the battlefield of the two main conflicting ideologies regarding marriage and family in Europe. Thus, several governments that have submitted observations to the Court have referred in this respect to the fundamental nature of the institution of marriage and to the intention of a number of Member States to maintain a conception of that institution as a union between a man and a woman, which is protected in some domestic legal orders by legal provisions having constitutional status. In this line of arguments, even on the assumption that a refusal, in circumstances such as those of the main proceedings, to recognise marriages between persons of the same sex concluded in another Member State constitutes a restriction of Article 21 TFEU, such a restriction would be justified on grounds of public policy and national identity, as referred to in Article 4(2) TEU.

However, in its Grand Chamber Judgement, the ECJ finds that in a situation in which a Union citizen has made use of his or her freedom of movement by moving to and taking up genuine residence, in accordance with the conditions laid down in Article 7(1) of Directive 2004/38/EC and, whilst there, has created and strengthened a family life with a third-country national of the same sex to whom he or she is joined by a marriage lawfully concluded in the host Member State, Article 21(1) TFEU must be interpreted as precluding the competent authorities of the Member State of which the Union citizen is a national from refusing to grant that third-country national a right of residence in the territory of that Member State on the ground that the law of that Member State does not recognise marriage

[31] CJEU, C-673/16, Opinion of AG Wathelet, ECLI:EU:C:2018:2, para 98.

between persons of the same sex. One must notice that while the Grand Chamber Judgement omits refererence to the Charter, choosing to mainly focus instead on Article 21 TFEU, it has also declined to grant the restriction proposed by the more conservative Member States. What, on the contrary, the Grand Chamber undoubtedly took into account was the requirement that particularly a national measure restricting Article 21 TFEU should be consistent with the fundamental rights enshrined in the Charter. By approaching the legal issue presented to it in this way, the Grand Chamber refused in fact a nationally determined meaning of the concept of 'spouse' preferring instead an autonomous one.

Even more, adding a second layer to the judicial dialogue, in the Opinion offered by AG Wathelet, reference is made to the vast jurisprudence of the European Court of Human Rights (e.g. *Tadeucci and McCall v Italy*,[32] *Oliary v Italy*,[33] *Pajič v Croatia*[34] or *Vallianatos v Greece*[35]).

As it happens, when the Romanian Constitutional Court made its reference to the CJEU in the *Coman* case, the relevant case-law of the European Court of Human Rights was already well defined. In 2013 in the case *Vallianatos v Greece* the ECtHR established that the relations between same sex persons were covered by the concepts of 'family life' and 'private life', as understood within the ambit of the Convention, a conclusion that was reiterated in 2018 when the judgment in *Orlandi et al v Italy*[36] became final. Both *Oliary v Italy* and *Orlandi et al v Italy* are also important as they establish a positive obligation of the states to acknowledge some form of legal recognition for same-sex relations. Regarding the arguments that were put forward by some governments in the *Coman* case, applying the ECtHR standards in *Tadeucci and McCall v Italy*, the AG points out that:

> based on sexual orientation, [such] a difference in treatment would be unacceptable under Directive 2004/38 and the Charter, as it must be interpreted in the light of the ECHR. In that regard, although protection of the traditional family may, in some circumstances, amount to a legitimate aim under Article 14 [of the ECHR, which prohibits discrimination], the [European] Court [of Human Rights] considers that, regarding the matter in question here – granting a residence permit for family reasons to a homosexual foreign partner – it cannot amount to a particularly convincing and weighty reason capable of justifying, in the circumstances of the present case, discrimination on grounds of sexual orientation.[37]

Consequently, the Grand Chamber notices itself that:

> it is apparent from the case-law of the European Court of Human Rights that the relationship of a homosexual couple may fall within the notion of 'private life' and that of

[32] *Tadeucci and McCall v Italy* (2016) 51362 EHRR 09.
[33] *Oliari et al v Italy* (2015) 18766, 36030 EHRR 11.
[34] *Pajič v. Croatia* (2010) 68453 EHRR 13.
[35] *Vallianatos v. Greece* (2013) 29381, 32684 EHRR 09.
[36] *Orlandi et al v Italy* (2017) 26431, 26742, 44057, 60088 EHRR 12.
[37] Opinion of AG Wathelet (n 30) para 98.

'family life' in the same way as the relationship of a heterosexual couple in the same situation.[38]

The two supra-national systems thus interconnect, while establishing the common European autonomous meaning of the central concepts of 'spouse' and 'family'.[39]

Approached at this first level (i.e. between the Romanian Constitutional Court and the Court of Justice of the European Union), the judicial dialogue triggers at least two important outcomes. First, if one is prepared to agree that *Coman* is not only a 'free movement', but also a 'human rights' case, it must be considered a landmark one as well, since it establishes that, for the purposes of EU family and reunification law, married same-sex couples must be considered as being grated the same position as married opposite-sex couples. Additionally, the obligation to facilitate the entry and residence of the national of a third State of the same sex as the citizen of the European Union to whom he or she is married has been qualified as greater, and the discretion narrower, when the Member State does not allow marriage between persons of the same sex and does not afford homosexual couples the possibility of entering into a registered partnership. The Court of Justice established that it follows from Article 8 of the ECHR, and therefore from Article 7 of the Charter, that there existed a positive obligation to offer those persons, like heterosexuals, the opportunity of having their union recognised in law and protected by the courts. Indeed, granting the spouse of a Union citizen a right of residence constitutes recognition and the minimum guarantee that can be given them. That would be deemed the very minimum standard.

In second place, but equally important, following the guidelines provided by the Court of Justice, the Romanian Constitutional Court granted a conditional constitutionality to the impugned provisions of the national Civil Code that is only if interpreted consistently with the ECJ's judgment. Specifically, as a consequence of its preliminary reference in the *Coman* case, and limited to the scope of application of EU law, in its Decision no 534 of 18 July 2018,[40] the Constitutional Court declared the provisions of Article 277 Para (2) and Para (4) of the Civil Code to be constitutional only if they afforded the right of residence in Romania to citizens of EU member States or of other States that had contracted same-sex marriages in an EU Member State.[41] On the same occasion, the Constitutional Court stated

[38] CJEU, C-673/16 (n 28) §50.

[39] Given the integratory provision of Art 52 (3) of the Charter, pursuant to which 'in so far as this Charter contains rights which correspond to rights guaranteed by the Convention for the Protection of Human Rights and Fundamental Freedoms, the meaning and scope of those rights shall be the same as those laid down by the said Convention', a common meaning should be acknowledged for the concept of 'spouse' pursuant to Art 7 CFRUE and Art 8 ECHR (and, for that matter, also a common understanding as to the minimum standard of protection against discrimination pursuant to Art 21 CFRUE and Art 14 ECHR).

[40] Published in the Official Journal of Romania no. 842/ 03.10.2018.

[41] It has also been advanced that limited to the scope of EU law, the outcome of the *Coman* case obliges the Romanian authorities to recognise the union of Mr. Coman and Mr. Hamilton as a marriage, thus going further than the ECtHR established standards (in *Orlandi* or *Vallianatos*).

that a relationship between a same-sex couple fell within the scope of the notion of family life just as much as a heterosexual relationship and triggered the protection of Article 7 of the Charter of Fundamental Rights of the European Union, Article 8 of the Convention and Article 26 of the Romanian Constitution. Equally, but again limited to the hypothesis of its decision – i.e. free movement of persons as granted by EU law – the Constitutional Court noted that in enjoying the right to private and family life, people of the same sex who formed stable couples had the right to express their personality within those relationships and to benefit from the legal and judicial recognition of the corresponding rights.

Important as they may be, the consequences of the *Coman* case are however not exorbitant. For instance, the EU Member States remain free to bar same-sex couples from marrying on their territory, which means that, except for cases of voluntary harmonisation, all purely internal situations remain regulated by the national law. Also, while the judgment applies to same-sex spouses, it does not seem to concern the registered partners. Moreover, it protects only the couples married in an EU Member State and, since Article 21 of the Charter did not function as a main element in the ECJ reasoning, it does not address discrimination on the ground of sexual orientation, being limited to the free movement of persons.

3.2. The Part of the European Court of Human Rights

On the positive side, the *Coman* case discussed in the previous section is an excellent proof of consistency, of good integration of the ECHR and of the ECtHR case law at the very heart of the interpretation that the Court of Justice provides for the very meaning of European citizenship. It is also a proof of substantial consistency at the national level, with the Constitutional Court granting that domestic law (including constitutional fundamental rights) is interpreted according to the minimum standard of the Charter, itself interpreted according to the minimum standard of the ECHR.

One can therefore only be astonished to see the European Court of Human Rights seized with an application lodged on 23 December 2020 by Relu-Adrian Coman and others,[42] whose object is the alleged discrimination of the first and second applicants, lawfully married in a Member State of the European Union, due to the impossibility for the second applicant, a third-country national, to obtain a right of residence on the territory of Romania in his capacity of spouse of a Romanian citizen. One is therefore to suppose that not only the dialogue between the Romanian Constitutional Court and the Court of Justice has been ineffective, but also that the national authorities still fail to implement the ECHR minimum standards as established by the ECtHR in the cases mentioned in the previous section, among which, in particular, *Vallianatos v Greece*. The factual summary of

[42] *Relu-Adrian Coman et al v Romania*, application no. 2663/21, communicated on 9 February 2021.

the application tells us that, indeed, following the judgment adopted by the CJEU and the correlative decision of the Constitutional Court, the applicants requested the reopening of the main proceedings before the national ordinary court that decided to refer the matter to the Constitutional Court in the first place. By a decision of 16 September 2019, this court dismissed the action as time lapsed (*perimată*), on the grounds that the applicants were at fault for not requesting the reopening of the proceedings within six months from the date of the Constitutional Court's decision. By a final decision of the Bucharest County Court of 26 June 2020, the applicants' appeal was rejected as unfounded with final effect. Therefore, relying on Article 6 § 1 of the Convention, they complained before the ECtHR in the first place of a breach of their right of access to court due to the dismissal of their action on procedural grounds without a decision on the merits, arguing that the reopening of the proceedings should have been done *ex officio*. Besides this allegation of a violation of Article 6 § 1 and an associated one concerning Article 13 of the Convention, the Court communicated to the Romanian government the following three questions:

1. Has there been a violation of the first and second applicants' right to respect for their private and family life contrary to Article 8 of the Convention, due to the inability for the second applicant to obtain the right of residence in Romania in his capacity of spouse of a Romanian citizen (see, *mutatis mutandis, Taddeucci and McCall v. Italy*, no. 51362/09, 30 June 2016)?
2. Does the first and second applicants' impossibility to obtain recognition of the status of spouses, prerequisite for obtaining the right to reside in Romania for the second applicant, amount to a breach of Article 12 of the Convention?
3. Have the first and second applicants suffered discrimination in the enjoyment of their Convention rights on the ground of their sexual orientation, contrary to Article 14 of the Convention read in conjunction with Articles 6 § 1, 8, 12 and 13 of the Convention (see *Pajić v. Croatia*, no. 68453/13, 23 February 2016)?.

The outcome of this case, that is currently still pending, is quite predictable, as, in spite the well-established positive obligation incumbent on the States Parties to the Convention to grant a legal form of recognition to the relations between same-sex partners, the Romanian reality described in the first section of this contribution shows that they currently only enjoy a de facto status. But there is even more, as the standards of *Taddeucci and McCall v Italy, Pajić v Croatia*, *Oliary v Italy, Orlandi et al v Italy*, and *Vallianatos v Greece* have already been applied by the ECtHR in cases concerning Romania. While the first one, *M.C. and A.C. v Romania*,[43] is somehow contemporary with the first cluster of cases addressed above, the second one, *Buhuceanu et al v Romania*[44] (May 2023) is presented by the ECtHR itself

[43] *M.C. and A.C. v Romania* (2016) 12060 EHRR 12.

[44] *Buhuceanu et al v Romania* (2023) 51362 EHRR 09. For a brief note on this case, see R Bercea, 'Op-Ed: On the margin: The ECtHR Judgement in the Case Buhuceanu and Others v. Romania', on the EULawLive blog, 13 July 2023, ISSN 2695-9585. Available at: https://eulawlive.com/op-ed-on-the-margin-the-ecthr-judgement-in-the-case-buhuceanu-and-others-v-romania-by-raluca-bercea/.

as an application of the principles of the new landmark case *Fedotova v Russia*,[45] adjudicated by the Grand Chamber at the very beginning of 2023. Incidentally, the justification for the inclusion of the *Fedotova* case in a new cluster of cases resides not so much in its novelty, but rather in its consolidating effect and in the fact that it comes at a moment of consolidation as well. Thus, in a context where the ECtHR previous case-law has been confirmed by what the Court sees as a clear ongoing trend in the legislation of a majority of States Parties and converging positions of various international bodies, in the absence of any form of legal recognition and protection for same-sex couples, the Court reiterates the positive obligation to provide legal framework affording such couples adequate recognition and protection and states that the public-interest grounds that might be put forward in such hypotheses cannot prevail over the applicants' interests. In fact, the States would only enjoy a reduced margin of appreciation for providing a legal framework and a more extensive one for determining the exact nature of the form of recognition and content of protection, marriage itself continuing not to be required.

As the following sections will prove, for different reasons, both *M.C. and A.C. v Romania* and *Buhuceanu et al v Romania* are highly relevant for the horizontal dimension of the rule of law issue as expressed through the fundamental rights of same-sex couples.

3.2.1. The Dynamics between the Measures to be Adopted in the Sphere of the Relations of Individuals between Themselves and the State's Positive Obligations under Article 8

In 2006, the applicants of *M.C. and A.C. v Romania* participated in the annual gay march in Bucharest, organised by ACCEPT[46] and granted police protection, during which several individuals who had actively expressed their disapproval over the gay community were stopped by the police, their pictures taken, and their identity papers checked and noted. At the end of the march, the applicants and four other participants left the area using the routes and means of transport recommended by the authorities. After boarding a metro train, they were attacked by a group of six young men and a woman who approached the victims directly and started punching them and kicking their heads and faces. They also swung from the metal bars above their heads, kicking their victims. During the attack they kept on shouting: 'You poofs go to the Netherlands!' ('*Poponarilor, duceți-vă în Olanda!*'). The attack lasted for about two minutes. While the other passengers withdrew to the opposite side of the carriage during the attack, a photographer,

[45] *Fedotova et al v Russia* (2023) 40792 EHRR (10) 30538, 43439 EHRR (14).

[46] ACCEPT is a non-governmental organisation whose goal is to provide information and to assist the LGBTI community. It usually stands itself as applicant before the ECtHR in the cases concerning the fundamental rights of this community. More details on the activity of this organisation are available at acceptromania.ro/en/home/.

who had also been at the march, took pictures of the incident and was hit by the attackers as well.[47]

The applicants complained about the state's failure to investigate adequately their criminal complaints concerning acts of violence motivated by hatred against homosexuals, and more generally about the lack of adequate legislative and other measures to combat hate crimes directed against the LGBT+ minority. They further complained that, when conducting the investigation, the authorities did not consider the fact that the offences against them were motivated by their sexual orientation. The Court communicated the applicants' complaints under Articles 3, 8, and 14 of the Convention and Article 1 of Protocol 12 to the Convention (also applicable in Romania as of 2006), to then held unanimously that there has been a violation of Articles 3 (procedural limb) and 14 of the Convention read together. The Court found that the authorities did not take reasonable steps with the aim of examining the role played by possible homophobic motives behind the attack. Pursuant to the Court's reasoning, the necessity of conducting a meaningful inquiry into the possibility of discrimination motivating the attack was indispensable given the hostility against the LGBT+ community in Romania and in the light of the applicants' submissions that hate speech, that was clearly homophobic, had been uttered by the assailants during the incident.[48]

The case provides the Court first with the opportunity to develop its caselaw on the relationship between Articles 3, 8, and 14 of the Convention and second to warn about the consequences of the state authorities' failure to fulfil their positive obligations under Articles 3 and 8 on the horizontal private law relations within the domestic legal order.

As regards the first point, the Court considers that the authorities' duty to prevent hatred-motivated violence on the part of private individuals and to investigate the existence of any possible discriminatory motive behind the act of violence can fall under the positive obligations enshrined in both Articles 3 and 8 of the Convention, but may also be seen as forming part of the authorities' positive responsibilities under Article 14 of the Convention to secure the fundamental values protected by Articles 3 and 8 without discrimination. Owing to the interplay of the above provisions, the Court appreciates that the case may be examined under one of these two provisions only, or may require simultaneous examination under several of these Articles. In the present case, in view of the applicants' allegations that the violence perpetrated against them had homophobic overtones which had been completely overlooked by the authorities in the investigation, the Court opted for a simultaneous dual examination under Articles 3 and 8 taken in conjunction with Article 14 of the Convention.[49]

As regards the second point, the Court finds that positive obligations on the part of a State are inherent in the right to effective respect for private life under

[47] *M.C. and A.C. v Romania* (n 42) paras 7–12.
[48] *M.C. and A.C. v Romania* (n 42) para 124.
[49] *M.C. and A.C. v Romania* (n 42) paras 104–106.

Article 8, involving the adoption of measures even in the sphere of the relations of individuals between themselves. While the Court concedes that the choice of the means to secure compliance with Article 8 in the sphere of protection against acts of individuals is in principle within the State's margin of appreciation, effective deterrence against serious acts, where fundamental values and essential aspects of private life are at stake, would require criminal law provisions, all the more so when vulnerable individuals are concerned. Also, the State's positive obligation under Article 8 to safeguard an individual's physical integrity may extend to questions relating to the effectiveness of a criminal investigation.[50]

3.2.2. The Wrongfulness of Claiming the Margin of Appreciation While Comforting Stereotypes

In the largest same-sex unions case before the ECtHR so far, the 42 applicants have submitted that, because their partnerships are not formally acknowledged at the national level, they are prevented from accessing social and civil rights that are provided by law for married couples. As mentioned in the sections above, this very recent case builds significantly on the *Coman* case presented before the Grand Chamber of the Court of Justice of the European Union[51] and on the *Fedotova* case adjudicated by the Grand Chamber of the European Court of Human Rights earlier in the same year (2023).[52] Different from the cooperative approach taken by the Constitutional Court within the judicial dialogue in *Coman*, and refusing to integrate the conventional standards, the Government submitted in *Buhuceanu* that the impossibility for same-sex couples to be granted legal recognition and protection at the national level was compatible with Article 8 of the Convention. Also, and despite all evidence, the Government asked the Court to note that Romanian law provided for some forms of recognition of same-sex couples and protected them (e.g. if they enter private civil law contracts).[53] The same idea was expressed in their joint dissenting Opinion by Judges Wojtyczek and Harutyunyan, who considered it to be important that the domestic law was changing, and that the Government had expressed its willingness to amend the legislation but was contested by the Civil Society Development Foundation. Supported by nine other Romanian non-governmental organisations, this intervener pointed out that the lack of legal recognition of same-sex unions in Romania was due to a lack of political will, as the legislative proposals submitted for debate in Parliament had not been supported by the Government.[54]

However, the most important issues tackled by *Buhuceanu* are the margin of appreciation to be conceded to states in the hypothesis that no form of legal

[50] *M.C. and A.C. v Romania* (n 42) paras 114–115.
[51] CJEU, C-673/16 (n 28).
[52] *Fedotova et al v Russia* (n 44).
[53] *Buhuceanu et al v Romania* (n 43) paras 49, 52.
[54] *Buhuceanu et al v Romania* (n 43) para 62.

recognition and protection for same-sex couples is granted by the domestic legal order and, correlatively, the basis on which public-interest can be grounded as to prevailing over the applicants' interests.

Regarding the first, the Romanian Government put forward the Court's unequal approach towards the margin of appreciation and alleged that, in any event, consensus was not necessarily decisive or determinative in the evaluation it makes. In particular, according to the Government:

> evolving trends and developments at the national level do not justify a Court's decision to promote consensus in areas where there were no discernible pan-European norms, on the basis of selected legislation of member States that offered a reflection of local compromises concerning current trends or developments.[55]

In respect with the second, the Government urges the Court not to disregard the existence of pressing social needs that go against the tide of the perceived majority proven by statistics indicating that in Romania a significant majority of people not only have an unfavourable perception of sexual relationships between two persons of the same sex, but also disagree that they should be granted the same rights as heterosexual people.[56] The legal weight carried by such statistics would consist in a strong indication about the existence of 'a discernible community interest amounting to a pressing social need'[57] they would justify the limitations on the right enshrined by Article 8 of the Convention in respect with same-sex couples.

Regarding this last argument, one is to notice that no substantive reason was indicated by the Government for excluding same-sex couples at the domestic level from the legal protection granted to them by Article 8, whose minimum standard was established by the Court in the first cluster of cases addressed above. Moreover, the arguments put forward by the Government comfort and encourage stereotypes, while the Grand Chamber of the Court found this to be unconventional in *Markin v Russia*,[58] where it established the States Parties' obligation to address them by modifying, if necessary, the social and cultural patterns of conduct. As the applicants rightfully point out, the public debate or even the opposition manifested at the national level could not exempt the national authorities to apply the conventional standards. Quite on the contrary:

> it was precisely when there were disagreements, opposition, and strong passions that human rights could be most under attack, and when they – and those people who were vulnerable (particularly minorities) – most needed to be defended. It was essential that Governments defended human rights by not pretending to be neutral and quiet or by perpetuating stigma.[59]

[55] *Buhuceanu et al v Romania* (n 43) para 45.
[56] *Buhuceanu et al v Romania* (n 43) para 47.
[57] *Buhuceanu et al v Romania* (n 43) para 50.
[58] *Markin v Russia* (2012) 33078 EHRR 06.
[59] *Buhuceanu et al v Romania* (n 43) para 43.

The conclusion of the Court in this context is consistent with the one reaffirmed in *Fedotova*. None of the public-interest grounds put forward by the Government, be it an allegedly hostile attitude on the part of the heterosexual majority, or the unfavourable position expressed by the national highest authorities, willing to protect traditional marriage, could prevail over the applicants' interest in having their relationships adequately recognised and protected by law at the national level. The margin of appreciation afforded to States in this respect relates only to the form of recognition to be chosen. The Court finds therefore a violation of Article 8 ECHR.

4. Synergies and Conclusions

If one agrees that fundamental rights partake to the rule of law, fundamental rights of private nature – such as the right to family and private life – to be granted to vulnerable categories of persons may be the most accurate indicator of the compliance by a European state to the rule of law standards. In this respect, Romania has come a long way, but significant room for improvement still exists. Against the background of a most conservative society and with virtually no national legislation acknowledging same-sex relationships, the system has proven its good will to integrate the European Union levels of protection. At the end of a fruitful dialogue with the Court of Justice of the European Union, the Romanian Constitutional Court stated that a relationship between a same-sex couple fell within the scope of the notion of family life just as much as a heterosexual relationship and triggered the protection of Article 7 of the Charter of Fundamental Rights of the European Union and Article 26 of the Romanian Constitution. Limited to the scope of the free movement of persons, the Constitutional Court noted that in enjoying the right to private and family life, people of the same sex who formed stable couples had the right to express their personality within those relationships and to benefit from the legal and judicial recognition of the corresponding rights. In the purely internal situations, however, none of the minimum standards of protection consolidated by the European Court of Human Rights has been respected by either the Romanian legislative, executive, or judiciary authorities. Thus, the State's behaviour seems to mirror a systemic problem needing to be addressed by also tackling homophobia within the Romanian society. After the recent condemnation in *Buhuceanu v Romania*, the defendant government might have indeed understood that such an attitude does not represent a pressing social need justifying an extended margin of appreciation that would, in its turn, allow rights restrictions.

13

Orthodoxy and Acquis Communautaire

GIOVANNI CIMBALO

Premises

The accession of new countries to the European Union, stimulated by the Ukraine crisis, will increase the component of Slavic populations and religious and cultural traditions coming from Southern Europe characterised by the important role of Orthodoxy.[1] Together, the candidate countries will bring this group of Orthodox states to about a quarter of the Union's population, i.e. more than 110 million inhabitants. The significance of this ethno-religious and cultural component will only increase if we consider the diffusion and organisation of the Orthodox diaspora in Western Europe as a result of structural economic and conflict-related migration.[2]

Overall, this represents a cultural and religious novelty, because for the first time, organised Orthodoxy will be present throughout the continent. The different relationships of the individual States with the Churches therefore deserve to be analysed not only from an institutional point of view, but also in order to understand to what extent and in what way their values will influence the *acquis communautaire*, conditioning relations between individuals and changing their contents.

[1] The candidate countries are currently North Macedonia (since 2004), Montenegro (since 2010), Serbia (since 2012) and Albania (since 2014); Ukraine and Moldova were added on 28 February 2022. Turkey has also been among the candidate countries since 1999 but its candidature is de facto suspended due to the incompatibility of its system with the EU *Acquis*, while Georgia's candidature, submitted on 3 March 2022, has been shelved for the time being. The fact that the accession procedure of the Balkan states has not been concluded, despite the long time that has elapsed, testifies to the difficulties of their legal systems in adapting to the required parameters in order to meet the requirements.

A separate topic – not addressed in this paper for reasons of space – would deserve the presence and role of the Greek Catholic Church in the area under consideration.

[2] Before the start of the war in Ukraine, the size of the Orthodox diaspora to EU countries exceeded 12 million, with the largest presence in Italy, the Iberian Peninsula, Germany, and France. To this presence, now stable and rooted in the territory, were added war refugees, mainly hosted in Poland, responding to flows conditioned by the development of the conflict. It does not seem unrealistic to estimate this presence altogether at around 15 million, distributed in communities, territorially cohesive and organised. On the consequences of the spread of Orthodoxy in the West see: T Tanase, 'Le monde orthodoxe, un objet géopolitique éconnu?,' *La revue géopolitique*, 29 December 2017. Available at: https://www.diploweb.com/Le-monde-orthodoxe-un-objet-geopolitique-meconnu.html.

1. The Acquis Communautaire as an Identity Ensemble of the European Union

The European Union, as a supranational economic structure, has transformed over time, delimiting and constructing a legal space whose characteristics have been defined in the Treaties and have progressively been nurtured through regulations, directives, decisions, recommendations, and opinions issued by the EU institutions on the basis of the powers conferred on them and within the framework of the principle of conferral, on which the limits of the Union's competences are based, enshrined in Article 5(1) of the Treaty of the European Union (TEU). It is in fact the Treaty on the Functioning of the European Union (TFEU) that specifies their extent, dividing them into three categories: exclusive (Article 3), shared (Article 4), and supporting (Article 6), whereby the EU adopts measures to support or complement the policies of the member Countries.[3] The structure of this Union of laws employs a comprehensive system of legal remedies and procedures, intended to entrust the Court of Justice of the European Union with the review of the lawfulness of the acts of the EU institutions (Article 263 TFEU), also in order to gradually build a legal system coherent in principles and cohesive over time.

This is why, unless the Treaties and procedures are amended ad hoc, the path to EU membership is a complex and articulated process that is expected to last decades. To map it out, reference must be made to Article 49, which provides the legal basis for any European country wishing to join the EU.

It is Article 2 that lists the values on which the Union is founded: respect for human dignity, freedom, democracy, equality and the rule of law, human rights, including the rights of minorities in a society characterised by pluralism and non-discrimination, tolerance, justice, and solidarity and equality between men and women.

The candidate country must also fulfil the eligibility criteria established by the Copenhagen European Council in 1993 and thus possess stable institutions guaranteeing democracy, rule of law, human rights, respect for minorities and the protection of minorities; a reliable market economy and the capacity to cope with market forces and competition within the Union; the ability to assume and implement effectively the membership obligations, including the main objectives of political, economic and monetary union. In addition, the candidate country must be able to apply Community law and ensure its transposition into national law and implement it effectively, through appropriate administrative and judicial structures (Decision of the Madrid European Council, December 1995).

[3] The areas covered by these three types of competence are clearly listed in Arts 3, 4, and 6 TFEU. In the absence of the necessary powers of action to achieve one of the objectives set out in the Treaties, the institutions may have recourse to the provisions of Art 352 TFEU and thus adopt 'appropriate provisions'. The institutions shall only use the legal instruments listed in Art 288 TFEU. The exception is the common foreign, security, and defence policies, which are managed intergovernmental. In this area, common strategies, actions, and positions are replaced by 'general guidelines' and 'decisions defining' the actions and positions to be taken by the Union, as well as the modalities for their implementation (Art 25 TEU).

As can be seen, these are difficult conditions to satisfy, which suggests that the time needed for the adaptation of the candidate countries' state systems will not be short; this might also provide a realignment of values, especially since the positive decision of all member countries is required to approve new accessions.

But if the adjustment is to move in the right direction, it is necessary to be aware of the divergences, the differences, and the difficulties, so that the process can at least be started constructively, clarifying that it is not achieved by simply adding their own values to those of the EU and then realising a melting pot, but by allowing the system the necessary balances to acquire its own internal coherence.

It is therefore necessary to examine carefully the value issues brought to the Union by the orthodox cultural-religious component to ensure that it does not have such characteristics and content as to alter the orientation and balance achieved after a gradual and laborious process of osmosis that has lasted for many decades and that has seen intense work by the community institutions, the Member States, and the European Court of Justice, which have shaped the European legal space into a pluralist, free, and laic territory.

The proposal to identify the roots of Europe in the Judaeo-Christian culture, through the formula of widening the spectrum of cultural values and contents, to Protestantism and Orthodoxy, perhaps enriched by pluralism and secularism, cannot be proposed again today, albeit in another form, because it remains a valid and comprehensive enough formula to satisfy every identity sensibility to state, as the Preamble to the 2004 European Constitution does:

> The European Union is founded on the indivisible and universal values of human dignity, freedom, equality and solidarity; it is based on the principle of democracy and the rule of law. It puts the individual at the centre of its action by establishing the citizenship of the European Union and by creating an area of freedom, security and justice.[4]

This does not mean that the Union's legal and institutional system is immutable, but that its evolution and eventual transformation takes place with the established rules and procedures involving confrontation, negotiation, debate and, on the whole, a dialogical process involving all stakeholders at different levels, such as the citizens of the Union themselves. On the other hand, the procedure of gradual and pondered accession has been designed with the intention of preventing an identity bloc from entering the Union with the purpose of implementing amendments to the founding treaties that would change its defining elements.

[4] All this unless it is to go in the direction of a reworking of geopolitical theories as does: SP Huntington, *Political Order and Social Change* (Yale, Yale University Press, 1996), G Cimbalo, 'La territorializzazione dei Diritti di libertà religiosa. Il progetto di autonomia differenziata e la ri-territorializzazione', in G D'Angelo (ed) Libertà Religiosa e Collaborazione nei processi di differenziazione regionale, (Soveria Mannelli, Rubettino, 2024) 173–218. SP Huntington., *Political Order and the Clash of Civilisations* (Bologna, Il Mulino, 2013) hypothesising a welding together of western and Orthodox civilisation, made necessary by the inevitable convergence of eastern and Pacific civilisations into a cohesive bloc. In this revisited scheme of the clash of civilisations, it would fall to Great Britain to manage the connections between North Atlantic western civilisation and a divided Europe, incapable of leadership, both its own and autonomous.

2. Rights, Values and New Member States

One of the characteristics common to the Southern European countries that have applied to join the Union is the symphonic relationship that binds the state to its church, which needs to be Orthodox and autocephalous[5] in order to support it. They are in fact 'weak states', due to their recent constitution, with sometimes uncertain borders,[6] consisting of populations with different languages and nationalities,[7] whose common trait is a shared religious affiliation[8] – the Orthodox Church – whose populations have been brought together on a common territory by recent history and political events.[9]

This scheme of relations attributes to the State exclusive competence in matters of politics and temporal activities and leaves to the Church exclusive competence in spiritual matters, through the choice and administration of worship, thereby conveying the values, intended as the set of traditions and lifestyle choices, proper to those populations.[10] Consequently, it follows that the Church does not oppose the political power of the State and the exercise of coercion to manage temporal

[5] Relations between State and Church in countries of the Orthodox tradition are regulated on the basis of the symphonic system, formulated by Justinian in the *praefatio* of the *Novellae constitutiones* no 6, of AD 535, marked by the search for cooperation between the two powers. To the State belongs the management of temporal sphere, to the Church of spiritual one. Therefore, it is the guardian of traditions, ritual, the historical memory of the people and thus of identity. The Church will support the State in ensuring efficient management of the *res publica* and activities from the 'social' point of view; the political power will constantly watch over them. MT Capozza, *Sacerdotium in Justinian's Novellae. "Consonantia" (συμφωνία) and "amplificatio" of the "res publica"* (Turin, Giappichelli, 2018). From this pattern of relations the systems of socialist democracy, having overcome the phase of militant atheism, have largely benefited to place the Churches at the service and support of the State. Once that political system entered a crisis, this allowed the Churches to represent the continuity of the institutions, supporting the neoliberal states born in Southern Europe.

[6] It is well known that as a result of World War II, the borders of Eastern European states underwent profound changes, accompanied by large population movements. As a result of these events, substantial minorities survived in many states that, while retaining their own language and traditions, found themselves forced into state structures that were not always respectful of their distinctiveness; hence the demands for recognition of their distinctive features. These situations are present in Ukraine, but especially in the Balkans where they manifested themselves tragically in the dissolution of the Federal Republic of Yugoslavia.

[7] The language problem appears particularly serious with regard to the spread of the Russian language. Russia claims sole management of Russian-speaking, which has made it one of the reasons for waging war on Ukraine.

[8] An exception in the group of states we are dealing with is Albania, which is a secular, separatist and multi-religious state, in which, however, an Autocephalous Orthodox Church operates. On religious freedom and relations between confessions and the State in Albania: G Cimbalo, *Confessional Pluralism and Religious Communities in Albania*, (Bologna, Bologna University Press, 2012).

[9] Little known, but significant, is the case of the presence of Hungarian-speaking and Hungarian-cultured minorities in both Ukraine and Romania, although their claims appear dormant for the time being.

[10] To understand what the mechanisms of identity transmission are in Southern Europe, one must take into account the coexistence on the same territory of several ethnic groups, the frequent population movements, and the political instability of states. One realises, then, that the mechanisms of cultural transmission pass through intangible culture to which religious festivities, frequently accompanied by singing, music and dance, pilgrimages, and devotional acts, contribute significantly.

affairs, while the State leaves to the Church the competence over the management of people's lives and the fundamental stages of existence, such as birth, education, marriage, and thus the formation of the basic cell of society: the family. The Church is also responsible for the end of life and the body disposition, administering through tradition and worship the terminal phase of life beyond death and up to burial.

This is why the 'socialist democratic states', once they had overcome the phase of the destruction of the temporal and financial power of religious denominations, sought and found coexistence agreements with them,[11] recognising their ability to manage the value and spiritual aspects of human relations, shrewdly using the value heritage and traditions of peoples, transmitted through ritual, to maintain and consolidate their dominion.[12] Thus, when political conditions allowed it and the State atheism that opposed religion failed in its objectives, the neo-liberal states of Southern Europe, as those of all Eastern European countries, saw an increase in interest in religion, assisted and allowed the rebirth of the Churches.[13]

[11] In all socialist democratic countries, especially after the Helsinki Conference, the status of the churches was recognised and religious denominations were able to operate in support of states regaining their role in supporting national unity.

Concerning the Orthodox Churches in the Baltic countries – which are minority Churches – see G Cimbalo 'The Latvian State imposes autocephaly by law on the Orthodox Church in Latvia' (2022) 22 *Stato, Chiese e pluralismo confessionale* 1. ID: G Cimbalo 'Orthodox Churches and States in Europe: Problems and Perspectives' *Stato, Chiese e pluralismo confessionale* 2024 forthcoming.

A separate topic should be addressed regarding Belarus where the Orthodox religion is the majority religion, G Cimbalo, 'La Bielorussia alla ricerca della propria identità e il processo di confessionalizzazione dello Stato' (2018) 39 *Stato, Chiese e pluralismo confessionale*, 1.

[12] In all the Orthodox majority countries of Southern Europe, the Orthodox Churches share a philetist orientation in that they tend to merge the spheres of action of the Church with those of the nation. Despite the fact that the Pan-Orthodox Synod of Constantinople of 10 September 1872 condemned philetism as heretical, it is in fact the dominant trend among the Orthodox Churches, especially in modern times.

[13] After the fall of the Berlin Wall, there was talk of a revival of religions, especially in Eastern European countries. In fact, the fall of restrictions on religious propaganda was accompanied by the organisation of missionary activities by many religious denominations that, by carrying out charitable activities, aimed to proselytise. However, if in an initial phase the formal opening to religious freedom led to the emergence of cult activities, including new ones, over the years the phenomenon has stabilised; traditional religions have regained predominance and the rebirth of religiosity, a crisis of ideologies has also spread throughout the West, leading to the emergence of more restrained forms of religiosity. Cf Juergen Habermans, *Rebirth of Religions and Secularism* (Marcelliana, Brescia, 2018). However, it must be said that while it is true that the communist regimes imposed secularisation from above, with the explicit aim of destroying religious traditions, and resistance manifested itself as an effect of aversion to these regimes, once the political system was liberalised, the search for God also collapsed. Despite a relative revival in the vitality of religious communities and the public role of religion, the thesis that a religious revival is taking place in Eastern European countries is not confirmed. F Molteni, 'Religious Change among Cohorts in Eastern Europe: A Longitudinal Analysis of Religious Practice and Belief in Formerly Communist Countries' (2017) 10(1) *Religion and Society and Eastern Europe* 35. Nevertheless, religious denominations remain a vehicle for the transmission of tradition and collective cultural values. See however on the revival of nationalisms and cultural heritage Valerio Castronovo, *L' Europa e la rinascita dei nazionalismi* (Bari, Laterza, 2016).

On the other hand, the Churches needed the States, because not all of them were autocephalous Churches[14] and in order to realise this condition in the Orthodox tradition, a request from the political power was necessary, addressed to the Ecumenical Patriarchate claiming competence for the concession of autocephaly,[15] so that the national Church would see its autocephaly recognised and thus be able to provide itself with the necessary recognition to be able to operate within the Orthodox ecumene as an autonomous entity. This process of reconstruction – or in some cases construction – of autocephaly has given rise to quite a few problems within the Orthodox ecumene[16] and in relation to the institutional and political

[14] The autocephaly of the Ukrainian Orthodox Church was recognised, as is known, only in 2019. On the complex and troubled events that accompanied its recognition and on the structure of religious denominations in the country see: G Cimbalo, 'L'evoluzione dei rapporti tra Stato e Chiese nella Nuova Ucraina. Alla ricerca dell'Autocefalia' (2020) 2 *Diritto e religioni* 252-; G Cimbalo, Il ruolo sottaciuto delle Chiese nel conflitto russo-ucraino (2021) 2 *Diritto e religioni* 487. G Codevilla, 'L'invasione dell'Ucraina da parte della Federazione Russa e la posizione delle Chiese' (2022) 1–2 *Il Diritto Ecclesiastico* 21.

Even more recent is the acquisition of autocephaly by the Orthodox Church of North Macedonia. On this point: G Cimbalo. 'Orthodox autocephaly and confessional pluralism in North Macedonia' (2022) 13 *Stato, Chiese e pluralismo confessionale* 1, in which it is emphasised that one of the conditions imposed by the Ecumenical Patriarchate for the granting of autocephaly is that the Eparchies established by this Church in the diaspora, as explicitly stipulated in the Tomos of Recognition, must pass under its jurisdiction, which deprives the Church of Ohrid of its main revenues.

The problem of Montenegro where the majority denomination is the Orthodox Church of Montenegro and the Littoral, Eparchy of the Serbian Orthodox Church, remains unresolved. F Vecchi, The Role of the Serbian Orthodox Church in the Transitional Dynamics and Reformist Scenarios of the Western Balkans (2015) 4 *Anuario de Derecho Canónico* 331; F Vecchi, '"Neutralist" confessional pluralism: dominant parameter of "transitional" ecclesiastical legislation in Montenegro' (2019) 8 *Anuario de Derecho Canónico* 141. F Botti, 'Religious freedom, cultural heritage and identity: the case of Montenegro' (2022) 17 *Stato, Chiese e pluralismo confessionale* 21.

[15] It is the Patriarchate of Constantinople, also known as the Ecumenical Patriarchate, the first in the hierarchy of honour of the Orthodox Patriarchates, which is believed to hold the power to recognise the autocephaly of the Churches of Southern Europe.

In order to grant the autocephaly, the Ecumenical Patriarchate lays down precise economic and power conditions that are set out in the Church's recognition Tomos: it asks for the opening of its own representation in the country, the ownership of one or more churches, a few monasteries, from which it will collect the economic proceeds, while the size of the monetary gifts bestowed by the governments of the States concerned is unknown. But what is more important is that the Ecumenical Patriarchate asks the Church receiving the autocephaly to cede the diaspora, that is, the faithful who have emigrated out of the State, to its jurisdiction, and this is because the Ecumenical Patriarchate is based in Turkey, and therefore does not have its own people of the faithful. In this way, the Ecumenical Patriarchate drains its resources from the Orthodox mainly residing in the rich dioceses of the United States, Canada, and Australia, as well as the rest of the world.

[16] A clash has broken out between the Ecumenical Patriarchate and the Patriarchate of Moscow over the pursuit and granting of autocephaly. While the former claims the right to grant it to those countries and their Churches that request it, receiving in exchange the recognition of jurisdiction over the diaspora and economic advantages, supporting the political designs of recovering the Orthodoxy of the Slavic area to the West, the latter proceeds by granting self-administration to those Churches that belong to it, first among all those belonging to the Russophonie area considering itself a universal and supranational Church. As proof of this approach, see most recently the creation of the Exarchate of North and South Africa. V Parlato, 'Recent Controversies on Territorial Jurisdiction in Orthodoxy' (2022) 12 *Stato, Chiese e pluralismo confessionale* 67.

The quarrels between the two Patriarchates that followed the granting of autocephaly to the Ukrainian Church led the Russian Orthodox Church to judge the Ecumenical Patriarchate's lifting of the excommunications on Filaret as canonically unacceptable, (*Denysenko*), Patriarch of the Ukrainian

profiles that currently shape and, in some aspects, may condition the stages and procedures for the accession of these countries to the European Union,[17] because of the necessary adaptation to the community *acquis communautaire* that accession requires.

3. Tradition and Ritual as Custodians of the Values of Orthodoxy

The essence and strength of the Orthodox religion lies in its vision of ritual: the magnificence of the temples, the splendour of the mosaics, the richness of the decorations, the sumptuousness of the sacred vestments, the 'hypnotic' role of song and music, the scansion of the ritual, the gestures of the celebrants, the magnificence and the splendour of the gold of the icons, emphasise and remind us of the greatness of God, exerting on the faithful an effect that estranges them from the contingent problems of life, bringing them closer to the kingdom of heaven.[18] The long duration of rituals has this function, as does the recurring of festivities that, by repeating themselves immutably over time, confers continuity on events and reassures the future, which will be characterised by the unchanging repetition of human history. Values and solutions are as eternal as the repeating cycles of life, supported and sustained by revelation, accompanied by the divine presence. Thus, every necessary behaviour, every problem to be faced, finds its answer in the past and in the scriptures, in the experiences of faith, in the conviction that the problems of living are immutable and can be faced through faith, and ritual that preserves memory to constitute a certain point of reference.

This conviction is so deep-rooted that not even the pandemic and the real risk of contagion was a valid reason to discontinue, even if temporarily, the use of the same spoon and the common approach to the same chalice, during the taking of the sacraments. And when some Churches adopted precautions, disinfecting the

Orthodox Church-Kiev Patriarchate and Macarius, Primate of the UAOC, arguing that it had no right to lift them, as they were pronounced and shared by all Orthodox Churches. Also recalling that in August 2018, the Patriarchate of Constantinople introduced the possibility of a second marriage for priests, he noted that this decision violated the canons of the Church. He therefore declared the Ecumenical Patriarch heretical because he proposes an 'Eastern Papism', which is impossible in Orthodoxy. It follows that for the Russians, the Patriarchate of Constantinople, by its actions, has produced a schism.

As a result, the Ecumenical Patriarch will not be mentioned in the diptychs, the faithful of the Churches belonging to the Moscow Patriarchate will not be able to legitimately attend religious services and approach the sacraments in the Churches belonging to the Ecumenical Patriarchate.

[17] G Cimbalo, 'Autocephalia vo' cercare ch'è si cara in Stato' (2020) 19 *Chiese e pluralismo confessionale* 24.

[18] It is said that having to choose which version of Christianity to convert to in AD 987 Vlodomir, Grand Duke of Kiev, sent his own emissaries to enquire about the different forms of Christianity and that they returned to his presence and reported that when they came to the Greeks, they led them there to worship God. 'And we no longer knew whether we were in heaven or on earth. There God is with men. And their liturgy surpasses all others, so that we cannot forget such beauty'. St Sophia, the splendour of its mosaics and icons, its chants, its music, had struck their imagination.

spoons or using plastic trays and paper handkerchiefs to collect the residues of the consecrated bread or wipe the lips, it was done by invoking and seeking the precedent of tradition and providing for the destruction by fire of the residual material.[19]

Although competence in the field of health and the adoption of measures to prevent contagion is acknowledged and accepted to be purely a matter for the State, there has been no lack of resistance and contestation of the measures adopted, when they affect participation in religious services or festivities and pilgrimages, giving rise to frequent disputes, nor has there been a lack of willingness on the part of States to discuss and, frequently, negotiate the measures to be adopted.[20]

While it is true that some Churches have yielded to a health policy more attentive to the needs of prophylaxis and prevention of contagion, it is also true that at the peripheral level the clergy have shown substantial adherence to the choice of maintaining ritual prescriptions concerning the performance of religious services, the participation of the faithful in rites, and the maintenance of 'community' behaviour.

Deviating from tradition and modifying the ritual would have meant ceding on identity values, on the unquestionability of dogma, renouncing the securities and certainties that tradition transmits, not relying on God's grace, on that salvation that comes from respecting his will, transmitted through the Church and its clergy, respectful of revelation, prepared to administer the sacraments as a priority objective of their mission.

4. Demographic and Gender Policies

This determination to follow the divine teachings unfolds its effects on fundamental issues such as, for example, demographic policies on which is measured the resilience of the ethical and moral message conveyed by religion. The first terrain of confrontation is conception, which must take place within the family sphere without any obstacles, giving priority to the formation of new life. Therefore, opposition to contraception in all its forms and, consequently, opposition to sex education starting with teaching in schools, a battle fought through the request for the establishment of denominational schools and through the introduction of religious instruction in public schools.[21] Accompanying the interest of the states in this area – afflicted by a strong demographic crisis – in supporting the reversal

[19] G. Cimbalo, 'Le relazioni tra Stato e confessioni religiose sotto lo stress del Covid 19' in J Mazario (ed) *El impacto del COVID-19 en la libertad de conciencia y religiosa* (Editorial Tirant lo Blanch, Valencia, 2022) 63.

[20] G Cimbalo, 'Orthodoxy. pandemic and health protection legislation in Eastern European states' (2021) 15 *Stato, Chiese e pluralismo confessionale* 19.

[21] While in Albania the secularism of the state and religious pluralism made it possible to exclude the teaching of religion in public schools, in a situation where private schooling was not widespread, after 1991 in Moldova, as in Ukraine, the presence of Christian ethics or ethics courses in public

of demographic policies through economic and legal support for the birth rate, the Churches in these countries have supported and continue to support a constant battle to ensure that State aid goes to families united in religious marriage and ask states to promote restrictive policies and repeal laws on the voluntary interruption of pregnancy, denying women's right to decide about their own bodies, even though this principle is enshrined in a well-established corpus of laws inspired by the Soviet legislation that had introduced them as one of the first measures adopted by the Russian Revolution, and then extended, after the World War II, to the states of the area considered.[22]

The widespread and growing introduction of conscientious objection in these countries has acted as a Trojan horse for the restrictive application of the legislation in force, not without adopting permissive policies on procreation and conception, when the needs of the market demanded it: this is the case of the Ukrainian legislation on surrogacy, permitted and regulated also for foreign citizens, through the stipulation of agreements that provide for a monetary consideration, which has allowed a flourishing market to develop in the sector.[23]

The current idea is that in the Orthodox Churches, second and even third marriages are sacramentally celebrated, and communion is given to remarried divorcees, in continuity and coherence with the 'mercy' practice of the Church of the first centuries. In fact, second marriages entered the practice of the Eastern

schools increased. Although there has been no development of denominational schooling in Ukraine it was only in 2019, for the first time, that the state funded private denominational schools.

Since 2001, Serbia has introduced the teaching of religion in public primary and secondary schools as optional (chosen by half a million students). Cf.: Уредба о организовању и остваривању верске наставе и наставе алтернативног предмета у основној и средњој школи [Regulations on the Organisation and Implementation of the Teaching of Religious and Alternative Subjects in Primary and Secondary Schools], 46/2001-1 There are 2,010 religious education teachers, including 1,602 Orthodox, 247 Islamic, 131 from the Roman Catholic Church and 30 from the Reform Churches.

Religious instruction has had a mixed and complex path in North Macedonia, a country where Art 26 of the Закон за основното образование, [Law on Primary Education] *Сл. Весник на Р. Македонија бр.103/08 од 19.08.2008 година*, introduced it as optional. The Constitutional Court intervened on the issue with a ruling У.Број: 202 / 2008-0-1 ruling that Art 26 of the Primary Education Act was unconstitutional. The result is that a student may choose an optional religious instruction after the age of nine, when he or she is deemed to have matured his or her own ability to choose.

In Montenegro, Title IV of the Law *Zakon o slobodi vjeroispovijesti ili uvjerenja i pravnom položaju vjerskih zajednica*, [Law on Freedom of Religion or Belief and the Legal Status of Religious Communities], *Official Gazette of Montenegro*, no 74/2019 is dedicated to religious schools: the pivotal provision of this title is Art 54, which states 'A religious community may establish religious schools at all levels of education, with the exception of primary school, as well as dormitories for the accommodation of persons attending these institutions'. This is because, as Art 51 states, 'The participation of a child in religious education requires the consent of the parent or guardian, as well as the consent of the child if he or she is over 12 years old'. This means that religious schooling can be opted for after primary school under the conditions of Art 51, similar to the situation in North Macedonia.

[22] G Cimbalo, 'Sovereignist strategies and family politics in Eastern Europe' (2018) 2 *Quaderni di Diritto e Politica Ecclesiastica* 3. G Cimbalo, *Population policies in Albania and Kosovo. Matteo Mandalà dhe albanologjia sot*, (Fast print, Tiranë, 2018) 119.

[23] The Family Code of Ukraine [Сімейний Кодекс України, *Відомості Верховної Ради України (ВВР), 2002, № 21–22, cm.135*] provides on the matter of artificial insemination with the help of modern reproductive technologies not protecting the interests of the biological mother, but giving

Churches at a late date, towards the end of the first millennium, as a result of the influence exercised by civil legislation, of which the Church was the executor. In any case, second and third marriages have never been considered a sacrament but are permitted in different forms and with quite a few differences between the Churches of these countries and the Russian Orthodox Church. The dissolution of first marriages is almost always, for these Churches, the simple transcription of a divorce decree issued by the civil authority.[24]

While the positions on indissolubility are notable for their openness to the demands of civil society and compatibility with the *acquis communautaire*, the Orthodox Churches of Southern Europe are moving in a completely different direction, as is the civil legislation regarding the problems of the end of life and therapeutic treatment.[25]

While openness is recorded in both spheres – civil and religious – in limiting and circumscribing support for life at all costs, supporting the terminally ill with palliative care, and a certain willingness is recorded on the opposition to futile treatment, the closure towards the legalisation of euthanasia procedures is total, as is also the case in the Catholic sphere.

On this point there is a radical disagreement with the secular components of society in relation to the very concept of quality of life that underlies all legislation that provides for an openness towards the needs of subjects for whom the quality of life has become such that they feel the quality of an acceptable life lived with dignity has disappeared, and therefore consider it permissible to ask for an end to their suffering.

5. Opening to the Market and the Issue of Ethnic and Denominational Cemeteries

However, the interest of denominations and believers is also projected on what happens after death and therefore on the rituals and funeral rites that accompany the deceased to his final resting place. In particular, the choice of the religious structure that will celebrate the funeral rite is as much a matter of contention between the different churches as the choice of burial place. The death of a member of the community impoverishes it, but his or her burial place can still perform a useful

priority to the agreement concluded between the surrogate mother and the spouses. Further provisions are contained in Ch 2, Art 139 of the Civil Code of Ukraine and in Resolution of the Ministry of Health of Ukraine No 787 [Про затвердження Порядку застосування допоміжних репродуктивних технологій в Україні, Наказ, 09.09.2013 № 787.

[24] See in this regard the essay on marriage and divorce in the Orthodox Church by the Slovak Archbishop Cyril Vasil; C Vasil 'Separation, Divorce, Dissolution of the Bond, and Remarriage: Theological and Practical Approaches of the Orthodox Churches' in R Dodaro (ed) *Permanere nella verità di Cristo. Matrimony and Communion in the Catholic Church*, (Cantagalli, Siena, 2014).

[25] М Ярема. *Orthodox bioethics. The history and particularities* (Rome, Pontifical Athenaeum Regina Apostolorum, 2016).

function in remembering the belongingness of that land to an ethnic group, to a population, and it is for this reason that the administration of cemetery facilities is entrusted to local authorities, which, in turn, increasingly entrust their management to private companies, through tenders and agreements.[26]

In response to a situation that is far from defined in the correspondence between the sphere of state jurisdiction, the ethnic composition of the population, affiliation to a nation, and the ethnic distribution over the territory, attempts are underway to rearrange identities and the tendency to recover a correspondence between the state structure and the actual consistency of the nation. If this contradiction reaches its apex in the Balkans, the dissolution of the Yugoslav federal entity was accompanied in many areas by 'ethnic cleansing' in an attempt to extinguish the presence of ethnic and religious minorities, in other areas of Southern Europe the situation is affected by the shifting political borders of states and the incorporation into them of substantial ethnic and linguistic minorities against whom legislative measures are being implemented with the aim of assimilation.[27]

This phenomenon becomes a further destabilising factor for state structures that are in search of a balance between the different components of the populations, and in any case produces a strong ideational uncertainty that pushes these countries to seek a homogeneous ethnic-religious and linguistic physiognomy and structure, trying to mask the undeniable tensions that arise in the relationship with the principles of protection of minorities that characterise the Treaties and the *acquis communautaire*. It must be remembered that the European Union cannot be seen only as an economic space useful for development but is identified with the search for a common home within which nationalisms, ethnic and religious differences are overcome.

It is for these complex reasons that accession (or persistence) in the Union today takes place even when sovereignist policies prevail in the country; and it is in this cultural and political context that Eastern European countries refuse to accept even minimal quotas of migrants, fearing that their presence would end up calling into question the homogeneous and identity-based composition sought at the price of a harsh confrontation between the different components of society, which in some cases has resulted in armed clashes.

[26] In Ukraine, the Institute of Ukraine, in order to strengthen national identity, has adopted initiatives aimed at the knowledge and appreciation of the cemeteries of Ukraine. See: Кладовища України – Пантеони історії, http://ukrainica.org.ua/ukr/projects/cvintari. For an analytical review of cemetery legislation in Eastern European countries see: G Cimbalo. 'In search of lost identities: the growing demand for private and religiously managed cemeteries in Eastern European countries' (2018) *Ecclesiastical Law* 703.

[27] Whereas in Romania, the problems of the Hungarian minority populations *deiszékelyek* (in Hungarian) or *secui* (in Romanian), find protection within the Romanian legal system, conditioned by what the Community Acquis provides for the protection of minorities, there are currently no prospects for the Magyar populations of (sub)Carpathian Ruthenia, crushed by Kiyv's assimilationist policies that impose the exclusive use of the Ukrainian language not only on the Russian-speaking component of the country, but on all minorities, to the point of having closed down even the schools of the Romanian minority.

This is a deep-rooted feeling of which the reasons and causes must be understood in order to initiate a policy of overcoming fear and dread, since there is no doubt that the changes taking place in the distribution of the population on a planetary level must be faced with a very different strategy, in the consciousness that in history this is not the first time that Europe has found itself the object of migration from other geographical areas: this happens punctually when there are better living conditions in an area of the planet, moreover in demographic decline, than in poorer and less developed areas plagued by hunger and famine.

This does not mean that in this process of osmosis the indigenous populations do not try in every way to practise identity politics. It is the danger of succumbing, a fear more often perceived than real, certainly magnified, that drives the bearers of an identity that has become weak and insecure, to rediscover its roots, to do everything possible to reaffirm them, to claim them and make them manifest, through behaviour, including all the traditional practices that are rediscovered and renewed, when not created, and that range from the appreciation of food, to the choice of architectural models and the use of the landscape, to lifestyle habits, religious affiliation and burial practices.

The latter in particular are used to mark the territory, to demonstrate its secular belonging to a given community, ethnic group, religious group, as a means of strengthening the claim of possession that legitimises the exclusive administration of that territory, as proof of the secular rootedness that would legitimise the exclusive availability of the disputed areas, as the original and perennial place of residence of those traditions, customs and habits that are functional to affirming identity and that constitute its essential component.

In this task, the Orthodox faith aids and assists, which provides specific rites for burials, both in the execution phase of the funeral and in the activities of burial and burial services.

In this context, the evolution of legislation on burials and burial administration assumes importance, revisited in the light of the Union's legislative and regulatory activity that has broken the monopoly of state management of burial grounds, placing related services within the sphere of economic and business activities.[28]

This has led to the creation and rediscovery of private and ethnic cemeteries as sought-after burial places, to bear witness to one's ethnic or religious affiliation (sometimes political or category-related, as is the case with military cemeteries) supported by a business activity and placed in thc orbit of the activities of the religious denominations that manage the funeral phase, when not the cemetery facilities themselves.[29] It should be noted that for the sector, membership of the Union and the sharing of EU legislation is extremely functional in meeting these needs.

[28] See Dir. 12-12-2006 no 2006/123/EC, Directive of the European Parliament and of the Council on services in the internal market, published in the O.J.E.U. 27 December 2006, no L 376.

[29] G. Cimbalo (n 26).

6. Towards Possible Solutions

At the level of the freedoms and values of coexistence, Europe must measure itself against new challenges ranging from the crisis of marriage and the family to same-sex relationships, gender, contraception, responsible motherhood and pregnancy termination, therapeutic measures and the end of life, orderly demographic growth and regulated emigration, and the notion of quality of life. Nor is it enough to remain within the enclosure of morals and values because, as the Catholic Church has intuited, there are issues such as the salvation of the planet, the climate, the exhaustibility of resources, to which an answer must be given.

Instead, the perspective in which the Ecumenical Patriarchate is moving is to bring Orthodoxy into Europe as one of the constituent components of the unitary humus, transferring, decanting, the baggage of values of which the more traditional Orthodoxy is the bearer into the community space. The conditions are thus created for a no-holds-barred clash in which orthodoxy wants to play a conditioning role, on the strength of the relations it is building on an institutional and political level, in fact aiming at a convergence with those similar tendencies within the Union; a convergence that all secular and progressive forces can only oppose.[30]

To oppose this aggression, the countries that wanted and established the EU have only one road to take: that of addressing the rising 'Orthodox question', delaying the accession of the countries of Southern Europe over decades, conditioning them to a verified and effective sharing of the *acquis communautaire* and in the meantime, intervening on an institutional level, recognising an autonomous role of representation of religious interests to the religious formations of the diaspora,[31] State by State, attributing to them civil legal personality, recognising them as autonomous Churches. This would break the Ecumenical Patriarchate's claimed monopoly of representation in favour of the Churches with a national dimension, opposing to its schemes the bilateralism of relations with the social formations actually present on the territory, giving religious confessions that role that is theirs to contribute, together with lay associations and non-denominational philosophical associations to develop that social dialogue, that harmony of

[30] The convergence with Polish and Hungarian positions on personal and civil rights and freedoms would only increase the dangers for the EU *Acquis*.

[31] There is no doubt that with changing lifestyles and the growth of relative affluence in Eastern European countries, secularisation is bound to increase, yet there is a long way to go from assuming that society will inevitably evolve towards an inclination to secularisation. We must be aware that history does not always move in the direction of progress, but that society, customs, and social relations can regress towards assets that seemed outdated. The symphonic relationship between State and Church, typical of Orthodoxy, conditions and favours the role of preserving values performed by the Orthodox Churches, which see themselves as the primary custodians of immutable traditions and principles and, with the strength and power of faith, re-propose them, supported by the State's power, which in these cases is similar to the role played by the ethical State on the one hand and theocratic systems on the other. G Cimbalo, 'The Orthodox Churches and States in Europe: Problems and Prospects' (2023) 10 *Stato, Chiese e pluralismo confessionale* 1.

relations that is proper to an open and united society, which values equality between diversities, under the banner of pluralism, gender equality, respect for free affective unions and a life worth living, of growing social justice, as indeed Article 17 of the TFEU sanctions.

Only a balanced and well-considered contribution of all the continent's cultural, religious and ethnic components to redefine and strengthen common values, reinforcing the *acquis communautaire* without distorting it, but rather reorienting it towards more egalitarian and social justice contents, can make it possible to find the way back to an orderly development of the continent.

INDEX

www.ingramcontent.com/pod-product-compliance
Ingram Content Group UK Ltd.
Pitfield, Milton Keynes, MK11 3LW, UK
UKHW020259051026
15470UKWH00021B/1550

9 781509 958085